I Go to America

I Go to America

Swedish American Women and the Life of Mina Anderson

Joy K. Lintelman

Minnesota Historical Society Press

www.mhspress.org
The Minnesota Historical Society Press is a member
of the Association of American University Presses.
Manufactured in the United States of America
10 9 8 7 6 5 4 3 2 1
∞ The paper used in this publication meets the minimum requirements
of the American National Standard for Information Sciences—
Permanence for Printed Library Materials, ANSI Z39. 48–1984.

International Standard Book Number
ISBN 13: 978-0-87351-835-2 (paper)

Library of Congress Cataloging-in-Publication Data
Lintelman, Joy K.
I go to America : Swedish American women and the life of Mina Anderson /
Joy K. Lintelman.
p. cm.
Includes bibliographical references and index.
ISBN 978-0-87351-835-2 (cloth : alk. paper)
1. Swedish American women—Social conditions—19th century. 2. Swedish American women—Social conditions—20th century. 3. Swedish American women—Biography. 4. Women immigrants—United States—Biography. 5. Halgren, Minnie, 1867–1955. 6. Swedish American women—Middle West—Biography. 7. Women immigrants—Middle West—Biography. 8. Women pioneers—Middle West—Biography. 9. Sweden—Emigration and immigration—Social aspects—History. 10. United States—Emigration and immigration—Social aspects—History. I. Title.
E184.S23L525 2009
305.893'97073—dc22

2008035193

Cover and text design: Wendy Holdman
Maps: CartoGraphics, Inc.

To Clarice Mae Barke Lintelman, another strong woman who, like Mina, left a rich legacy for her descendants

The publication of this book was supported, in part, through generous grants from the June D. Holmquist Publications and Research Fund, the Ken and Nina Rothchild Endowed Fund for Women's History, and the Minnesota Humanities Center.

Acknowledgments

This project began one day in the summer of 1993 with a phone call to my husband from the kitchen of Fru T's café in Växjö, Sweden. Barely able to contain my excitement, I shared with him how I had happened upon a fascinating memoir about a single Swedish immigrant woman named Mina Anderson. Her life story illustrated so many of the experiences of Swedish immigrant women I had discovered in my years of study. Wouldn't it be great, I mused, if I could write a book based on Mina's life to tell the story of Swedish immigrant women's experiences. Fifteen years later, those musings have finally become a reality, but not without the help of a very long list of people and institutions. Those debts are also recorded in my notes, but I would like to offer special recognition to a number of institutions and individuals, spanning two continents, that were especially supportive and helpful in making this book possible.

Across the Atlantic, the archivists and research staff at the Swedish Emigrant Institute in Växjö, where Mina's memoir is located, provided valuable assistance for my work during several research trips there and via email and the Internet. Thanks especially to Christina Persson, archivist, and Yngve Turesson, librarian, and to the Emigrant Institute's fellowship program, which helped fund some of the research I conducted there. Several of the historical images of Sweden were generously provided by Ulla Hallbäck of Västergötland's Museum, Gunilla Sjökvist of Föreningen Krafttaget, and Bo Andersson of Dalsland, Sweden.

Matti Gustafsson of Åmål, Sweden, shared with me his time, his curiosity and enthusiasm, his car, his home, and even his family, making my visit to Dalsland in search of Mina's childhood an unforgettable experience. Thanks also to Bo Johanson, who kindly led me through a forest to Mina's birthplace. Olof Ljung and Annelli Andersson of Mellerud Museum and Genealogy Archive helped broaden my knowledge and understanding of life in Dalsland in the nineteenth century. And a former student, Anna Peterson, was also very generous, helpful, and hospitable on a trip I took to eastern Norway to investigate Mina's servant work there.

Back in the United States, Mina's descendants, especially Merrill Halgren and Beverly Siedow, were remarkably accepting of the total stranger who appeared asking questions about their grandmother. They generously shared pictures, documents, and memories and patiently answered my numerous questions. Anne-Charlotte Hanes Harvey was also instrumental at this project's inception, generously providing me with taped translations of Mina's memoir. Elisabeth Thorsell, editor of the *Swedish American Genealogist*, provided copies of parish records.

The Minnesota Historical Society not only provided collections that contributed to this study but also made available research funding for the book in its early stages. Special thanks to Debbie Miller for her assistance in finding useful collections and for allowing me to use facilities in a research suite at the Minnesota Historical Society, and to Sally Rubenstein for encouraging the project even as it took so long to complete. Grants from the Minnesota Humanities Center and from Concordia College, Moorhead, also supported the research and writing of Mina's story.

Because I teach at a small liberal arts college in northwestern Minnesota, interlibrary loan is essential for my research. Lola Quam and then Leah Anderson were especially important in helping me obtain primary and secondary source materials for this study, from nineteenth-century Swedish American publications to the most recent studies in immigration and women's history.

Several friends and colleagues also read and commented on the manuscript as it progressed. Carroll Engelhardt, Colette Hyman, and Marita Karlisch all provided very helpful comments and critiques. Marita supplied help with tricky translation questions as well. However, I alone am responsible for any omissions or errors of fact or interpretation in this work.

Jo Engelhardt and Judith Sinclair, assisted by a long line of Concordia College history department work-study students, supported this project by retrieving library books, making photocopies, and assisting with data entry and computer formatting.

Debts of gratitude are also owed to Emma, Hannah, and Noah, who during most of their growing-up years put up with their mother's fascination with Mina. Last and most significant, I offer thanks to my husband, Rick Chapman. From a Fulbright year in graduate school when he followed along to Sweden and served as *dagpappa* for Emma, to his continued probing questions, sharp critiques, and editorial expertise, his support and assistance have made this a much better book than it would have been otherwise.

Contents

I Go to America

Introduction

"Go only if you will have things better."[1] Mina Anderson's family gave her this advice in 1890 when she told them she planned to leave Sweden and emigrate to America. Mina was one of nearly a quarter-million young single women who left their Swedish homeland for the United States between 1881 and 1920.[2] Perhaps recalling that early advice, she reflected in a memoir nearly six decades later, "I have never regretted that I came here! I have had it better here."[3] Mina elaborated on why it was better in America in an unpublished memoir entitled "Livets skola" (The school of life), which she wrote to provide "a brief, realistic portrayal of my childhood and youth in Sweden, my journey here, and my experiences as an immigrant."[4]

Swedish immigrant women have left few written records. Mina (pronounced MEE-na) explained why: "It is people who have been educated and can write, who write most of what is published. Those who actually have lived the pioneer life do not write. They are uneducated and have never during their hard working life had time to write, even if they had been able to do so."[5]

In spite of her own strenuous working life, Mina Anderson made time to write not only a memoir but poetry, short stories, and letters to Swedish American newspapers as well. She did this usually under the pseudonym Cecilia—and variants Cicelia, Cicilia, and Cecelia. Her words form the core of this book and provide an unusually detailed, highly personal, and remarkably intimate vehicle for understanding the lives and experiences of Swedish women who immigrated to the United States in the late nineteenth and early twentieth centuries.

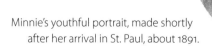

Minnie's youthful portrait, made shortly after her arrival in St. Paul, about 1891.

The quantity and quality of Mina's writing is unusual, but the toils, troubles, and triumphs her words reveal are not. Mina's experiences are echoed by those of other Swedish immigrant women who tell of their lives in letters, autobiographies, and other primary sources. Although this book is, first, Mina's story, it also tells the history of many "Minas" whose lives complement her own.

Mina Anderson was born in the western Swedish province of Dalsland in 1867. Self-supporting by age sixteen, she worked as a domestic servant first in her home province and later across the border in Norway. When an uncle in Wisconsin offered her a ticket to America in 1890, Mina gladly accepted. She entered the United States at New York City, traveled to Wausau, Wisconsin, where she worked as a servant long enough to learn English, then moved to St. Paul, Minnesota, in search of higher wages. There, Minnie Anderson, as Mina became known in the United States, met Jacob Halgren, a Swedish immigrant tailor whom she married in 1892. In keeping with Mina's own experience, in this book I will refer to her as Mina Anderson when describing her life in Sweden and as Minnie Anderson or Minnie Halgren when telling of her life in America.

When the economic downturn of the 1890s hit St. Paul, along with a wave of illness, Minnie and Jacob decided to take their one-year-old son, Henry, and move out of the city. In the summer of 1894 they purchased 120 acres of cutover timberland in Mille Lacs County and built a log cabin home in Bogus Brook Township near Milaca, Minnesota. Jacob continued his trade as a tailor, living and working in larger cities such as St. Paul and St. Cloud for six to eight months of the year. His absences left Minnie to operate the homestead and care for their family, which grew to include seven children. Minnie and Jacob also later raised two grandchildren. After Jacob died in 1945 Minnie remained on the farm, though she periodically traveled, seeing other parts of the country and visiting family and friends. She died on April 5, 1955, at the age of eighty-eight.

Mina and Kristina

For many Swedes and Swedish Americans, the phrase "Swedish immigrant woman" brings to mind the image of Kristina Nilsson, the central female character of Swedish author Vilhelm Moberg's immigrant tetralogy. In Moberg's novels, Kristina is strongly opposed to emigrating; only the death of her four-year-old daughter from hunger and her deference to her husband cause her to consent. But even after her harrowing ocean journey is over and the family has arrived safely in Minnesota, Kristina's unrelenting longing for Sweden shapes her worldview and her immigrant experience. A counterpoint to her husband's optimism, accomplishments, and confidence, she never masters English and lives a lonely and isolated life on the Minnesota frontier. Her homesickness is conquered only in death.[6] So strong is this image that it has even been set in stone. In the Swedish harbor city of Karlshamn and in the Minnesota town of Lindstrom are statues of Moberg's two main characters, Karl Oskar and Kristina. In both places, Karl Oskar stands tall and proud, bravely facing ahead toward the new land with stolid determination. Kristina provides a stark contrast. She looks not forward but back over her shoulder to her beloved Swedish homeland.[7]

Vilhelm Moberg was a gifted, prolific, and at times controversial author. His immigrant novels, *The Emigrants, Unto a Good Land, The Settlers,* and *The Last Letter Home*, describe in richly detailed prose the experiences and attitudes of Kristina and Karl Oskar Nilsson and a small group of immigrants from the Swedish province of Småland who immigrated to Minnesota Territory in the middle of the nineteenth century. Originally published in the late 1940s and early 1950s and republished in 1995, the books have had a steady audience even into the twenty-first century.[8] Two films based on the novels were made in the 1970s and nominated for Academy Awards. A highly acclaimed Swedish musical, *Kristina från Duvemåla*, was written and performed in the 1990s.[9]

A central reason Moberg's immigrant novels remain so popular is his thoroughly researched and richly detailed writing. Moberg spent years in the United States investigating Swedish immigration. His work brought him to archives and museums, small towns and farmsteads. He read books, memoirs, and diaries and corresponded with and spoke to elderly Swedish Americans, including his own relatives who had immigrated. So strong was his desire to be precise in his descriptions that when he wanted to have Kristina plant a flower bed he investigated what types of flower seeds a settler might plant in 1850s Minnesota.[10]

His painstaking research is also illustrated by the shelves of books and archival boxes found in the Vilhelm Moberg Collection in Växjö, Sweden. Located at the Emigrant Institute, an archive focused on Swedish emigration and immigration, this collection contains the documentary materials Moberg gathered in his background research for the immigrant novels. Among these materials are Mina Anderson's two lined tablets containing her memoir "Livets skola."

In researching his novels, Vihelm Moberg wanted to hear firsthand about the Swedish immigrant experience. In a 1960 newspaper article, he wrote:

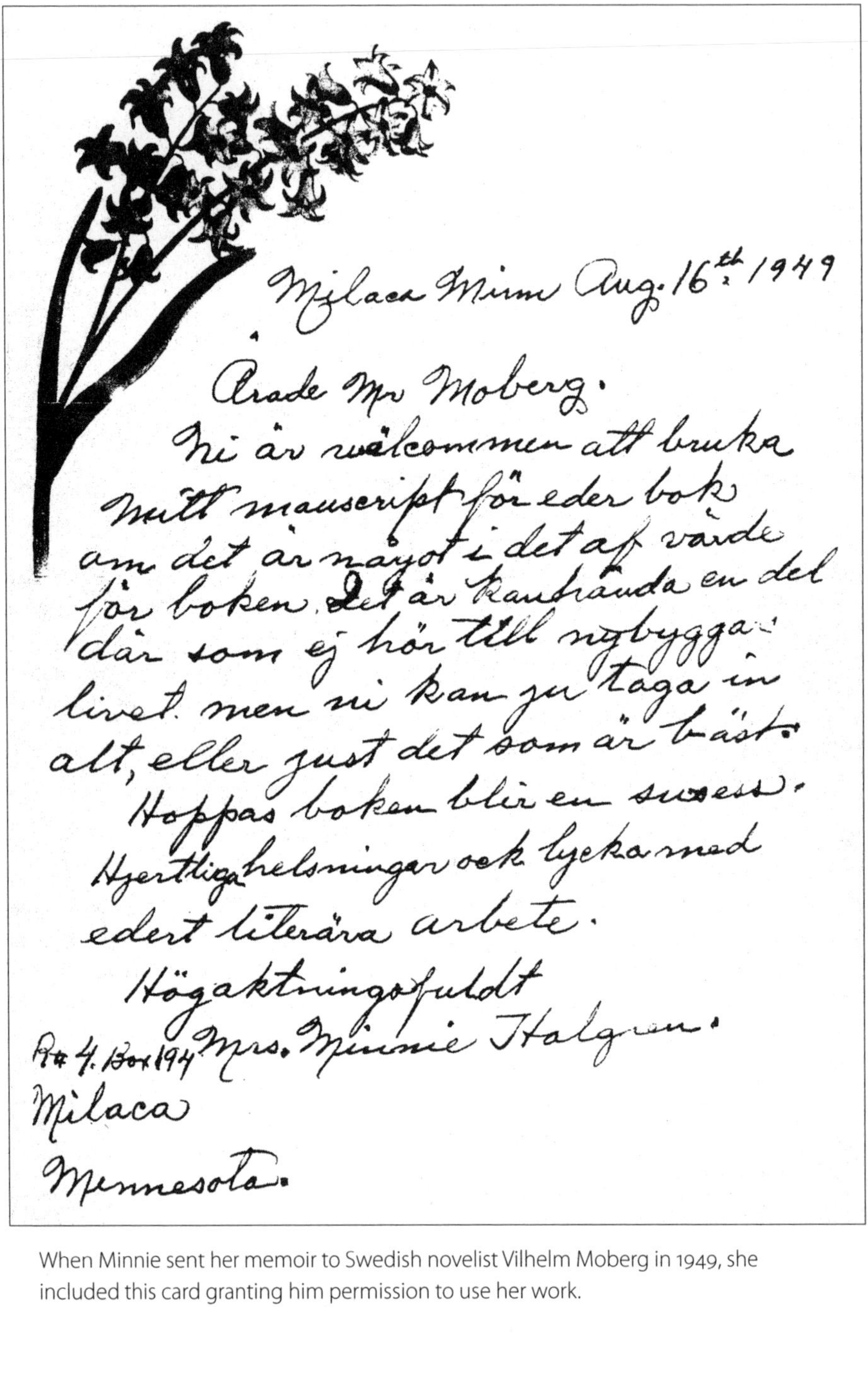

Milaca Minn Aug. 16th 1949

Ärade Mr Moberg:

Ni är wälcommen att bruka
mitt manuscript för eder bok
om det är något i det af värde
för boken. Det är kanhända en del
där som ej hör till nybygga-
livet. men ni kan ju taga in
alt, eller just det som är bäst.
Hoppas boken blir en sucess.
Hjertliga helsningar ock lycka med
edert literära arbete.

Högaktningsfuldt
R# 4. Box 194 Mrs. Minnie Halgren.
Milaca
Minnesota.

When Minnie sent her memoir to Swedish novelist Vilhelm Moberg in 1949, she included this card granting him permission to use her work.

"Already during my first American visit in 1948 I sought immigrants' own surviving documents, their own words, expressions and sayings—the source itself."[11] Mina Anderson was one of these sources, though it is unclear whether she and Vilhelm Moberg ever met face-to-face. What can be documented about their relationship is the existence of the memoir and a note on flowered stationery, which must have accompanied the memoir, dated August 16, 1949, and penned with the following lines: "Honored Mr. Moberg, You are welcome to use my manuscript for your book if any of it is of value for the book. . . . You can of course use it all, or just that which is best. I hope the book will be a success. Heartfelt greetings and luck with your literary work. Yours truly, Mrs. Minnie Halgren."[12] This letter does not reveal if the two ever met, but Vilhelm Moberg did use experiences related by Mina in her memoir to write his immigrant novels.

There is evidence of Moberg's fascination with Mina's life on the pages of her memoir. In sharp contrast to her careful and consistently uniform longhand are underlining and scribbled, barely legible annotations. A note scrawled on one page reads: "Kristina and the children eat raspberries [Kristina och barnen äter hallon]."[13] These annotations and markings were made by Moberg, who at one time even considered using Mina's immigration as a model for Kristina, writing in his notes, "Kristina comes alone to America = Cecilia."[14] Mina's memoir is also listed in the bibliography of sources Moberg included at the outset of each of the immigrant novels, though he retitled Mina's memoir "A Pioneer Housewife's Memories."[15]

Careful comparison of the novels with the memoir reveals other examples of material drawn from Mina's words. A line from *The Settlers* reads: "They talked of the land they never again would see."[16] The same line is scrawled across the top of a page of "Livets skola," where Mina described herself and other immigrant pioneers, noting: "None of us saw Sweden again."[17] Mina also wrote of her happiness upon hearing the distant sound of a new neighbor's hammering and pounding: "I used to walk across the forest in the direction where I heard that they were building and introduce myself. I said that I was happy we would be neighbors and bid them welcome."[18] In this instance, however, Moberg used Mina's ideas and experiences but attributed her actions to his central male character, Karl Oskar, who in the novel hears the sounds and strides through the forest to investigate and greet the newcomer. (Moberg did indicate Kristina's happiness at having neighbors, but in his novel it was Karl Oskar rather than Kristina who went to greet the new neighbor and wish him well—and to make sure his land claim was not threatened.)[19]

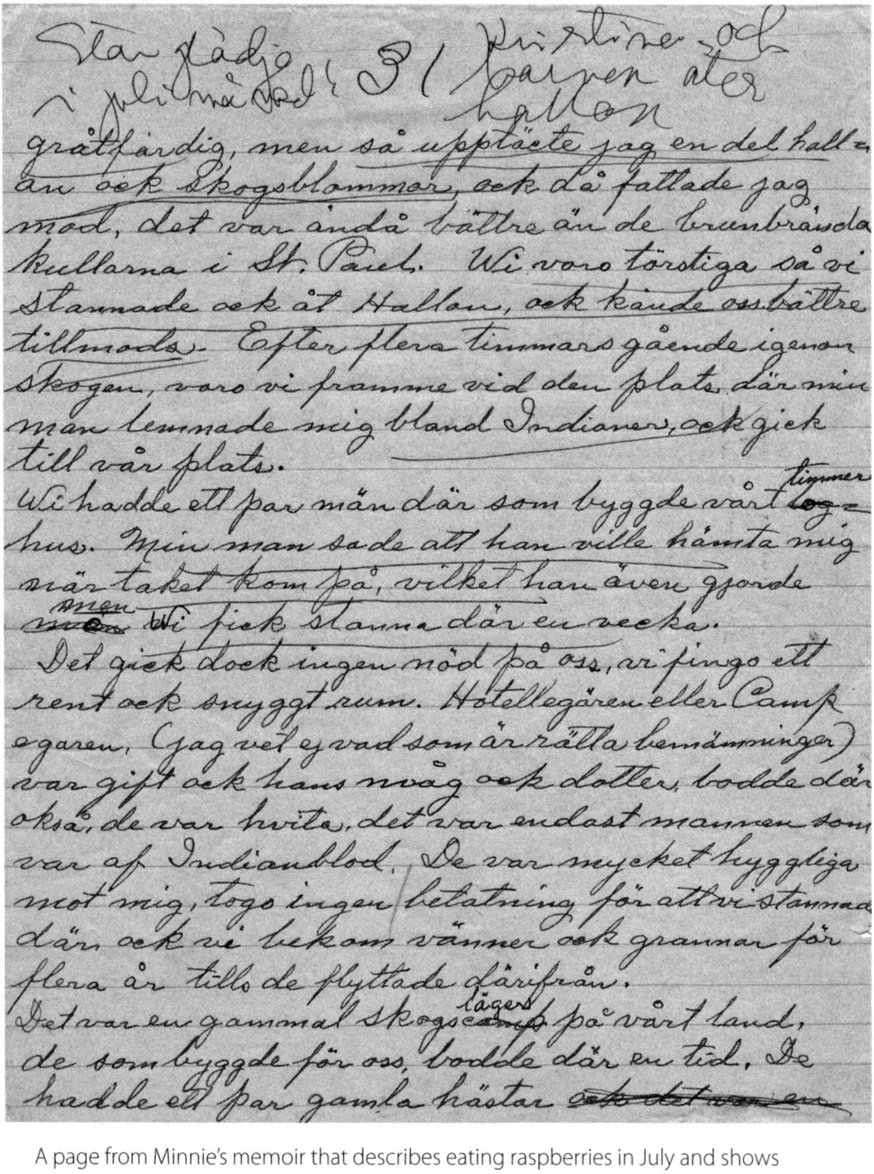
[illegible] i juli [illegible] 31 Kristina och barnen äter hallon

gråtfärdig, men så upptäcte jag en del hall-
ån ock Skogsblommar, ock då fattade jag
mod, det var ändå bättre än de brunbrända
kullarna i St. Paul. Wi voro törstiga så vi
stannade ock åt Hallon, ock kände oss bättre
tillmods. Efter flera timmars gående igenom
skogen, voro vi framme vid den plats där min
man lemnade mig bland Indianer, ock gick
till vår plats.
Wi hadde ett par män där som byggde vårt ~~log~~ timmerhus. Min man sade att han ville hämta mig
när taket kom på, vilket han även gjorde
~~men~~ men Wi fick stanna där en vecka.
Det gick dock ingen nöd på oss, vi fingo ett
rent ock snyggt rum. Hotellegären eller Camp
egaren, (Jag vet ej vad som är rätta benämningen)
var gift ock hans [illegible] ock dotter, bodde där
också, de var hvita, det var endast mannen som
var af Indianblod. De var mycket hyggliga
mot mig, togo ingen betalning för att vi stannade
där, ock vi bekom vänner ock grannar för
flera år tills de flyttade därifrån.
Det var en gammal Skogs~~camp~~ lägers på vårt land,
de som byggde för oss, bodde där en tid. De
hadde ett par gamla hästar ~~ock det var en~~

A page from Minnie's memoir that describes eating raspberries in July and shows Moberg's underlining and notes about "Kristina," the heroine of his novels.

But there are significant differences between the life of Mina Anderson as a Swedish immigrant woman and the lives of Swedish immigrant women as imagined by Vilhelm Moberg. Both Mina and Kristina are strong, faithful, and caring women, but Kristina's character emphasizes her isolation, loneliness, and a continued longing for her homeland. Mina's memoir and other writings reveal a continued fondness for Sweden but not the all-encompassing and life-consuming longing that Kristina felt. Though some immigrant women, like Kristina, certainly emigrated out of a sense of duty or obligation to their husbands and families and regretted leaving their homelands, this "Kristina archetype" ignores the majority of Swedish immigrant women, like Mina, who made their own decisions to leave, achieved many of the goals they had set for themselves in immigrating, and did not feel continuing anxiety for the choices they had made. Although Mina and other Swedish immigrant women experienced some ambivalence about accepting certain elements of modern American society, given the opportunity, many of these women would probably have written, as did Mina: "I have never regretted leaving Sweden. I got a better life here from the start."[20]

Fiction and Reality

Moberg was a novelist, not a historian. Writers of historical fiction often bend and shape factual historical material to make a good story. Moberg's interest in writing was not in historical accuracy, as such, but in making his story believable to the reader and in providing an "illusion of reality."[21] But serious distortions can emerge when literary imagination blends made-up events with history. The result is spurious collective memory. Tourists stop in Chisago County towns, the settlement location for Moberg's fictional characters, seeking directions to Karl Oskar's farm and Kristina's grave. The perception of Moberg's work as reality has also been reinforced by the creation of tourist sites such as the Karl Oskar House in Lindstrom, Minnesota. It is not surprising that when the topic of Swedish immigrant women arises, it is the image of the isolated pioneer farmwife that comes to mind.

Historian Joseph Amato writes the following about historical fiction: "The popular mind tends to see the world as writers have cast it. . . . And once [a popular work] . . . becomes an idol of the marketplace, it impedes competition for alternative views. The literature that yesterday taught us to imagine the past prohibits us from exploring and explaining it today."[22] To overcome this prohibition, the stories of Mina and others like her need to be explored and explained. Their stories merit our attention, both on their own terms and because they alter, fundamentally, conceptions of Swedish immigrant women framed by literary figures and lodged in popular thinking. Telling Mina Anderson's story puts the lives of Swedish immigrant women on a more ample stage and allows a much richer understanding of them as historical actors.

Methods

In this book, I assume that gender, along with social class, race, time of migration, and marital status, worked to shape Swedish immigrant women's experiences. I also consider women as historical actors in their own right—not, as suggested in Vilhelm Moberg's writing, as largely shaped by the males in their lives. I use Mina Anderson's words and experiences as a central narrative through which to understand what it meant to be a Swedish immigrant woman in America. Her life experiences connect to many of the prominent themes of immigration, as well as to women's and American social history: the constellation of economic, social, and personal motivations for migration; the challenges of a journey to a new land; finding employment; Americanization and acculturation; marriage and family; the ethnic community; and the immigrants' growing old. Each chapter begins with Mina's own writing. I juxtapose her words with interpretation that deepens her commentary and places her experiences within a broader historical frame.

Following the pattern of Mina's own life, the book begins with chapters on Mina's childhood and youth, describing the social and economic conditions for women in nineteenth- and early twentieth-century Sweden and why and how young women like Mina decided to emigrate. The book then describes the journey of Mina and other young Swedish women as they traveled to America and their patterns of settlement once they arrived. An examination of employment experiences, focusing especially on domestic service, the most common occupational choice for single Swedish immigrant women, follows, along with a chapter about Mina's life as a pioneer farm woman and the roles that Swedish immigrant women played as wives, mothers, farmers, and contributors to the family economy. Participation of Mina and other Swedish immigrant women in social worlds outside the home and the meaning of ethnicity in their lives are also addressed. The book concludes with reflections on what Mina's life reveals about the female Swedish immigrant experience.

Mina Anderson's voice in these pages is strong, but it does not stand entirely alone. To gain a fuller understanding of Swedish immigrant women's experiences requires examination of other immigrant women's lives, using interviews, letters, and personal narratives, the Swedish American press, and their published writings. Swedish and American government studies and statistics, census and land records, religious records, and contemporary scholarly studies provide additional documentation, as do photographic images and material culture.

In 1946 a Swedish researcher placed a notice in *Svenska Amerikaneren Tribunen*, published in Chicago, asking for pioneer stories. Mina Anderson (Minnie Halgren) responded, sending in a brief essay about her life as a pioneer woman. She introduced her contribution with the line: "Perhaps among all of the weeds in this writing you can pluck out some grains that can be of use."[23] Were Mina able to read this study of Swedish immigrant women that is based upon her writing, I hope she would be pleased with the rich harvest her words have produced.

A rural Swedish man with his wife, who knits as they walk, 1901.
(Photo by Karl Fredrik Andersson)

CHAPTER I

"I Grew Up on Simple Fare"

The School of Life, by Cicelia

Chapter 1

In the forest, by a beautiful lake, lay the so-called castle. That was not its proper name, but it was called so since it was larger than the other crofter cottages. It was actually a place where old workers lived after they had worn themselves out working for the company and there was no room for them anywhere else.[1]

Many different families lived here during the course of the years. There were over six families there. Each had only one large room. For the most part it was old people, but young families with children also lived there. Sons of some of the old parents, if they married, were sometimes allowed to stay there if there was no space for them at the ironworks or any cottage available. Here lived Glaad [meaning glad] who was appropriately named, and his angry wife.[2] *Rolig [meaning funny], who also deserved his name, could tell stories that could make the worst sourpuss laugh. In the upper rooms lived a couple of widows, who often came to blows with each other. An old torpare [crofter] couple with their daughter also lived there—they were decent and kind folk. Another family also lived there; the father was unable to work. They had many children and the mother was often away working. They were very poor and since the mother never had time to be home, the children were both dirty and ragged, and most of the time, hungry.*

All who lived there were poor, but they helped each other. In illness and poverty they helped each other. If someone was ill they shared their meager supply of food with that person. If one family was without, there were always some of the others who shared what they had. The women sat up until late at night and spun or knitted for their better-situated neighbors. To keep themselves awake they used to walk together. They sang songs, told stories, and boiled coffee if they had any. There was always much to do before Christmas, with stockings and mittens for Christmas presents.

There were many [residents] who died and a few of the younger [occupants] were lucky enough to be given space at the ironworks or to be given a cottage. [When a resident moved out of the castle] there was always somebody ready to move in again. There were never any empty rooms.

It was a diverse group of people who lived there. Some of them were quarrelsome; others accepted everything with patience. Some swore so that you could smell sulfur far away [Satan's smell]; others were God-fearing, read their morning and evening prayers, and sought to live an orderly life. Nobody drank strong drink; they were too poor for that. They worked with anything, the younger ones working for the company; one made baskets, another cobbled shoes or played the violin for dances for a few öre's pay [the smallest denomination of Swedish coin]. Thus, although they lived in the castle, it was not so royal.

Chapter 2

In this environment, I first saw the light of day. My father had moved to the castle with his parents. When he married, there was no housing at the foundry where he worked, so he and his family were allowed to live on at the castle for many years. I grew up on simple fare and became a strong and cheerful girl. Of course it wasn't the best environment for an impressionable and gifted child to grow up in. And there were many edges that were formed that later had to be ground down in the hard school of life.

My father was quiet, and like other workers at the time he was, after a ten- or twelve-hour workday and three-kilometer walk, so tired that he went to bed immediately after supper. My mother was a witty and cheerful person who did not so easily lose her courage. My cheerful disposition is an inheritance from my mother; my good health is an inheritance from both father and mother. Mother taught me early on to work; she also taught me to read so that I could read fluently before I began school. And she taught me also to be, above all, honest and always to tell the truth. She was strict but fair, at all times happy and merry. And she always relied on God's providence. Those were the teachings from her I took with me out into life. God bless her memory. Our home was so poor that it didn't teach me much of what was demanded of a female servant; that I had to learn bit by bit after I had come out into the world.

There were several other children who grew up in the castle, so there was no lack of playmates and we had fun. We fished and swam in the nearby lake in the summertime. In the winter we skated and skied. We sledded in the steep hills around the lake and sometimes came home with our faces cut and bloody when the sled upturned and spilled us nose-first into the sharp-edged snow crust.[3] *Another delight was to take our sleds and walk across the lake to gather wood. We cut the wood in the forest, threw it down the steep hillside onto the lake, and pulled it home on the sled. It was hard work, of course, but it was fun. We had no boat, but my father made a raft that we rowed with [in the summer] on the lake.*

The forests were full of berries. Though we had to walk all over the mountain to find cloudberries and wild strawberries, the raspberries, blueberries, and lingonberries grew everywhere. We often walked in the forest all day. Sometimes we had a bit of bread with us, but we lived on the berries. We picked a lot of berries to sell and got some money for it, but the money was not spent for sweets or amusements. It became material for a skirt or a pair of pants or a pair of shoes. We were all so proud and happy when we could earn something ourselves. The only bought toy I had in my childhood was a cheap porcelain doll that my father gave me.

I was fond of everything in nature. The trees in the dark forest, the flowers in the meadow, the clear lake, and the bubbling brook where my father helped me build dams and made a water wheel and hammer that beat against a piece of iron. But the hammer made such a noise that it scared the neighbor's sheep, so I had to give up that amusement. All this made me early on think of our Creator, and I was happy that I had been given the gift of life and could enjoy everything. When one of my friends my same age died, I remember that I thought: poor Tilda who had to die and leave the beautiful world and didn't get to live and see the beautiful spring and summer. She died just when the trees were beginning to bud.

I loved school and learned things easily. I went to school at Bäckefors, and my teacher's name was A. F. Skogsberg. He was a good and kind teacher. . . . [Omitted here is a short poem that Minnie wrote about her schoolteacher and the sadness she felt upon leaving school.] I was not quite twelve years old when I received my final grades from the folksskolan [primary school]. Many were the tears I then shed as I walked home from

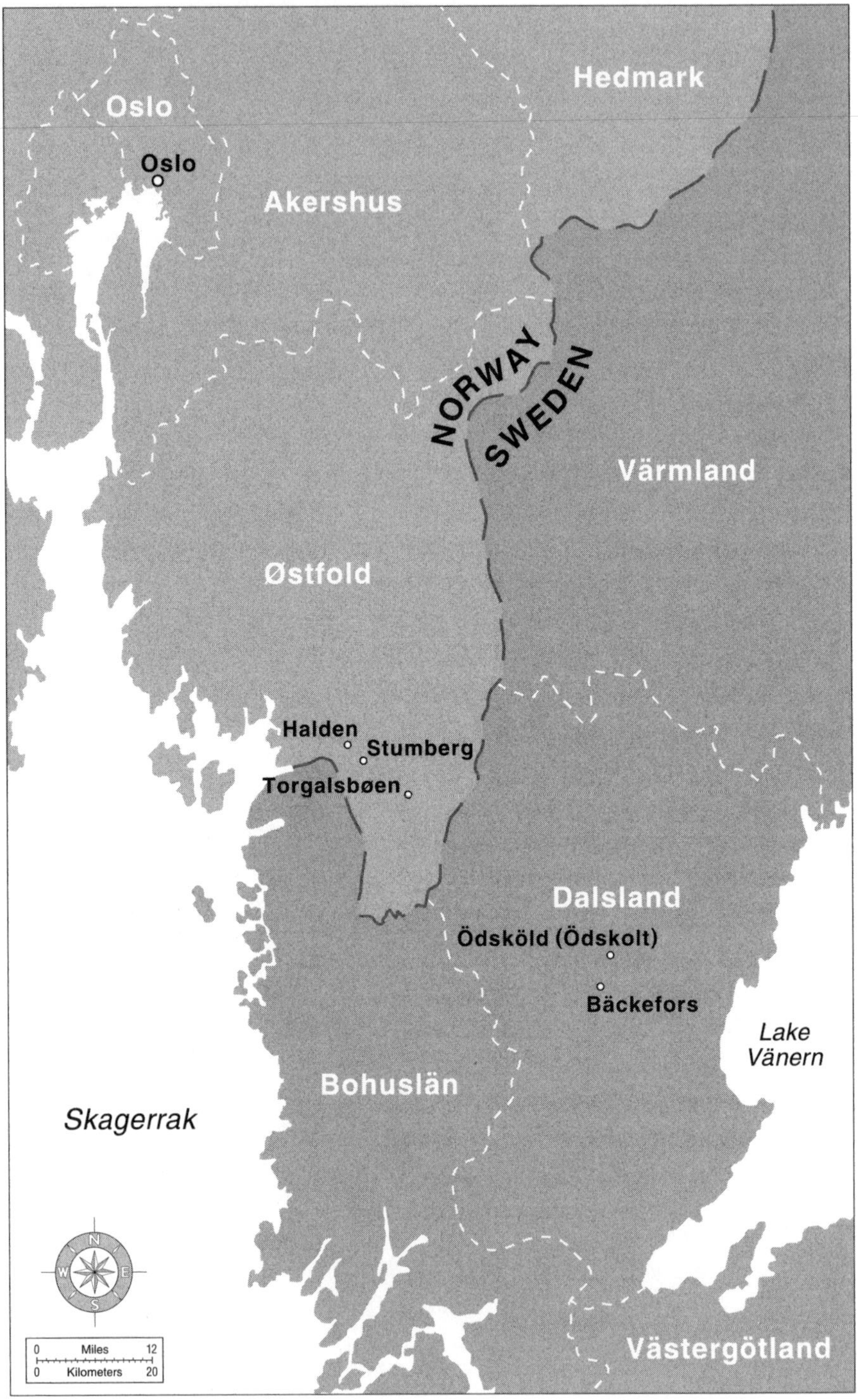

Area of Sweden and Norway where Mina lived and worked before emigrating to the United States in 1890. (See region map at right.)

school that last time. If I had only been allowed to continue school and the studies that I loved so dearly. But we were poor, so that was not to be considered at the time, seventy years ago. I was too young to study to be confirmed, so I stayed at home until I was [old enough to be] confirmed. I helped out by working for others sometimes. Then came confirmation. I was ready to go out into life. I was then fifteen years old.[4]

MINA ANDERSON BEGAN HER MEMOIR MUCH LIKE A FAIRY TALE—"in the forest, by a beautiful lake, lay the so-called castle." Her castle, however, was occupied not by royalty but by fellow down-and-out Dalbon—people living in the province, or *landskap*, of Dalsland in west-central Sweden. Like Mina, many Dalbon eventually immigrated to the United States. In fact, Mina's home area of Dalsland had one of the highest

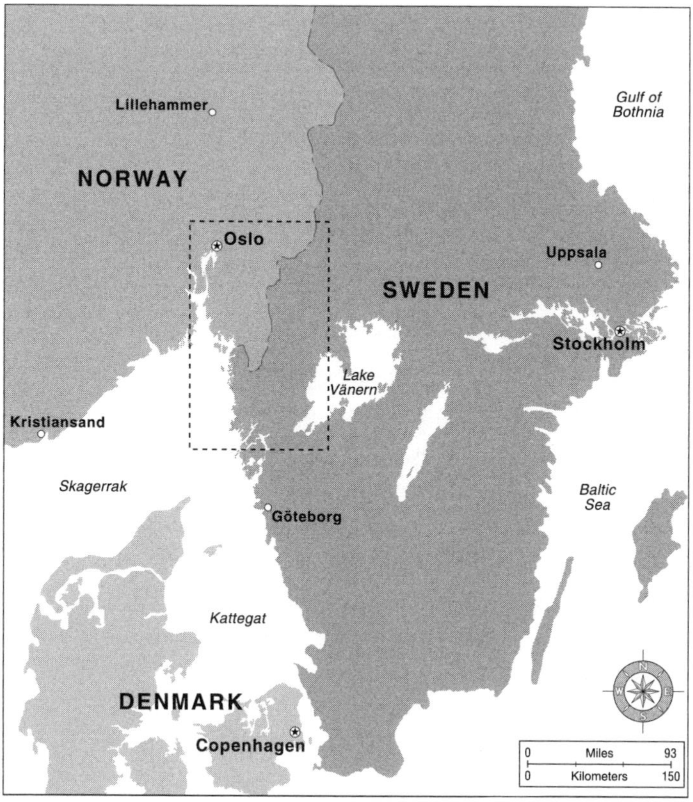

rates of immigration to America during the late nineteenth and early twentieth centuries.[5] Emigration from Sweden to the United States began with a trickle in the 1840s and grew to a stream in the late 1860s when the nation experienced crop failures and famine, a stream that ebbed and flowed for the next sixty years. Dalsland's first major out-migration to the United States occurred during the 1860s famine era, helping to establish a tradition of migration in the region, but the flow of Swedish single females emigrating from Dalsland in particular and Sweden in general was strongest during the decades from 1880 through 1920. Mina's emigration in 1890 was part of this broader female migration trend, and her girlhood has much in common with the experiences of many women growing up in late nineteenth- and early twentieth-century Sweden who would one day choose to journey to the United States. Most of these migrating women had, like Mina, grown up on the lower end of the socioeconomic scale.[6] In the first two sections of her memoir, Mina provides a brief but illuminating glimpse of the physical, social, and economic milieu of her childhood, which suggests what it was like to grow up poor and female in nineteenth-century Swedish society.

The Homeland: "I Was Fond of Everything in Nature"

In physical size as well as population, Mina's native Dalsland is one of Sweden's smallest provinces, nestled between Norway on the west and Lake Vänern on the east and the provinces of Värmland on the north and Bohuslän and Västergötland on the south. In spite of its small area, it is geographically diverse, with large regions of forest as well as meadows, hills, mountains, lakes, and streams. The two parishes where Mina spent most of her youth, Bäcke and Ödsköld, were, at the turn of the twentieth century, still about three-quarters forested.[7] In these surroundings, Mina's love of nature was nurtured, already evident in the early sections of her memoir. There she writes of her fondness for forest, flower, lake, and brook and expresses sorrow at a friend's death just before the advent of spring. Winters are long and dark, even in central Sweden, and Mina cherished spring, marked by the return of migratory birds, the blossoming of spring flowers, and the increasing hours of daylight. Her everyday living was shaped in part by the shifting seasons of the year. Simple daily chores such as gathering wood or fetching water for the family's needs brought her out-of-doors daily. Many of the foods her mother prepared for the family were drawn from what was grown and harvested locally. In her native Dalsland, Mina likely noted spring's arrival when she saw the first blossoms of the snowdrops and crocuses push through the snow or the blooming cowslips and hepatica as she gathered wood for fuel in the forests of pine, spruce, and birch.[8] As spring shifted to summer, Mina gathered blueberries, lingonberries, and raspberries in the forests, perhaps passing elk and roe deer as she picked. Growing up in this rich natural world, the girl understandably developed a deep and intense appreciation of nature, a trait shared by many Swedes (and Swedish Americans) past and present.

In describing her childhood, Mina mentioned only one Swedish community, Bäckefors, as the place where she attended school. She must have meant Bäckefors *bruk* (ironworks), because other writings and the location of her childhood home indicate she attended school at Bäckefors bruk, not in the village of Bäckefors.[9] Bäckefors bruk was a settlement that had developed around iron production, located a couple of kilometers from the village of Bäckefors, in the former administrative district (*härad*) of Vedbo and the parish (*socken*) of Bäcke. Mina walked the three kilometers between the castle and her classroom at Bäckefors bruk each school day, morning and afternoon. The ironworks was also her father's place of employment. Established in 1767, Bäckefors bruk was one of the largest early ironworks in Sweden, and, in 1829, it became the first ironworks in the country to use the Lancashire method for refining iron ore, a new process that used coal-fired welding to produce a high-quality bar iron.[10] This innovation was very successful, and Bäckefors bruk was, in the second quarter of the nineteenth century, one of the principal iron foundries in Sweden. During this period of economic boom, the number of employees increased significantly—from 77 in 1824 to 367 in 1855. Mina's great-grandfather Nils Pihl and her father, Anders Jansson, were among these workers.[11]

But by the time Mina was born, in 1867, profits for the company were decreasing, due in part to competition from other foundries that could produce larger quantities of iron using a roller production method. The owners of the ironworks struggled to make up for losses by developing new production. In the 1870s they imported equipment for horseshoe manufacture from the United States but had little long-term success. Bought and sold several times in the late nineteenth and early twentieth centuries, Bäckefors bruk ceased producing metal goods in 1920. A small hydroelectric power station was built there in 1948, and from 1950 to 1977 metal goods were again produced—this time by a company manufacturing bolts and nails. In the 1980s the Bäckefors Hembygdsföreningen (local history society) purchased Bäckefors bruk to restore it and establish a museum, giving visitors a glimpse of the early industrial and agricultural milieu in which young Swedes like Mina grew up.[12]

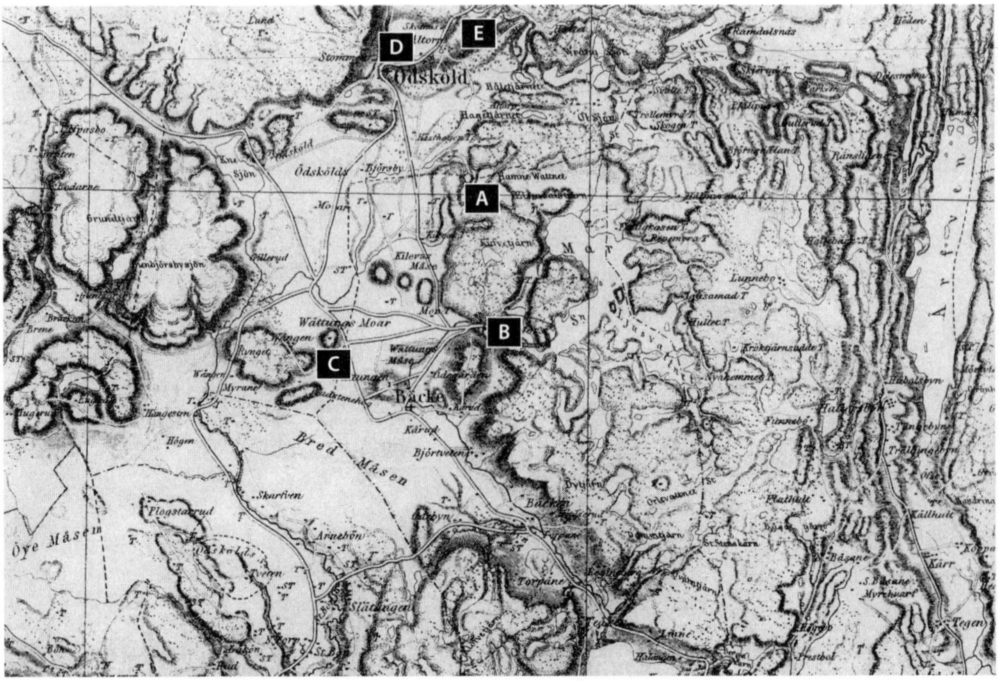

Bäckefors area, Dalsland, Sweden.
A Hamnevattnet, Mina's birthplace and childhood home
B Bäckefors, the village where Mina was baptized, located about 1.5 miles from the ironworks where Mina's father worked.
C Wättungen (or Vättungen), the estate established by the owner of the ironworks in the eighteenth century; Hamnevattnet was located on the estate.
D Ödsköld (now Ödskolt), the village where Mina attended confirmation
E Altorp (now Alltorp), the location of the local courthouse and service buildings where Mina obtained her first full-time servant position

Developing around early Swedish industrial manufacturing, a Swedish bruk shares some of the qualities of American nineteenth-century "factory towns," with the manufacturer owning the production facilities as well as the workers' housing, a school, and a store where employees could purchase foodstuffs and other goods.[13] But, in bruk communities, the production facilities were located in the rural countryside, and the company owned the land surrounding the factory, where many workers lived as tenant farmers, producing food for themselves and the community. These bruk communities operated in many ways as small, self-sufficient societies. In Mina's home area, the estate called Wättungen (or Vättungen) was established by the initial owner of the Bäckefors bruk, Leonhard Uggla, in the second half of the eighteenth century. It was a large estate cultivated in part by tenant farmers.[14]

Tenant farming was an increasingly widespread practice in nineteenth-century Sweden and included several different types of tenancy representing varying degrees of economic security. *Torpare* (crofters, tenant farmers) and *backstugusittare* (cottars, farm laborers who occupy cottages and sometimes a small holding of land, usually in return for services) were the most common. These classes of nonlandowning farmers had developed beginning in the eighteenth century due in part to the movements for consolidation of landholdings (laws promoting these changes were passed in 1749, 1772, 1807, and 1827), as well as the removal of restrictions on subdividing and renting out small portions of holdings. Landowners reorganized their farms, combining their various holdings to improve management and then subdividing and cropping them using new systems of tenant farming. A nineteenth-century torpare or crofter owned no land of his own but rented and farmed a small piece of land, often the landowner's least productive. The torpare had a small home on the land and paid rent to the estate owner, not in cash but with physical labor (though by the twentieth century, payments were most commonly made in cash). The system allowed landowners to maintain a good supply of cheap agricultural labor, because a crofter usually found it difficult to accumulate enough money to purchase land of his own.

In the case of the Bäckefors bruk, industrial labor was part of the mix. Ironworks employees usually received wages in both cash and kind, with in-kind benefits such as a torp or smaller piece of land, feed for a dairy cow, or the right to hunt or fish on company land. Tenant contracts also were inheritable, so the system allowed tenants some degree of economic security. Backstugusittare were similar to torpare in that they also rented land and paid for it with their labor, but the amount of land they rented was much smaller than that of torpare. Their rental contracts lacked the security of the crofters' contracts; during difficult times they might have to seek day labor wherever they could find it. Even worse off were the people referred to as *inhyseshjon*, or "live-in laborers." As the name implies, these people had no permanent homes of their own and typically lived in the homes of landowners or *torparna*, providing labor in return for room and board. Their level of security was even less than that of farmhands or servants—regular servants had labor contracts and usually some form of cash wages, but these live-in laborers could be turned out with little or no warning.[15]

Mina's father, Anders Jansson, was the grandson of a *mästersven* (helper to a master blacksmith) at Bäckefors bruk, Nils Pihl, and Anders probably obtained his position as *smältare i gjuteriet* (blast furnace man) in part owing to the employment there of this maternal grandfather. Pihl worked at the ironworks in the late eighteenth and early nineteenth centuries.[16] Anders's father, Jan Bryngelsson, did not work at the bruk but was a torpare on the Wättungen estate, on a torp called Hamnen. Anders, born in 1829, grew up on this torp, and by 1851 it was Anders rather than his father who was listed as torpare at Hamnen. The family clearly met with hardship sometime after that, because in 1856 Bryngelsson, his wife, and their four children (including Anders) moved to housing that had been established by the ironworks for torpare and backstugusittare who were unable to support themselves—Bryngelsson is listed in Hamnevattnet records as *krympling* (cripple). Anders lived with his family there and continued his employment at the ironworks. He married in 1864, and he and his wife, Maja Jansdotter, born in 1840, stayed on at this residence.[17]

Mina was born to Anders and Maja on February 15, 1867. Breast-feeding was one source of the good health Mina described inheriting from her parents, and Mina was probably, like most Swedish children, breast-fed for one to three years.[18] As an infant Mina would have been wrapped tightly in swaddling clothes until she could walk. Swaddling was thought to provide protection against evil spirits, and it also protected infants from cold wood or dirt floors and kept them away from open fires. Once able to walk, both boys and girls wore dresses for several years. Clothing was differentiated by gender sometime between the ages of three and seven, with boys wearing trousers and girls wearing long dresses.[19] In the only childhood image of Mina I have been able to locate, of Mina with her father, she is wearing one of the dresses common for young children.

The *slott*, or so-called castle, where Mina was born was named Hamnevattnet. A Bäckefors local history describes Hamnevattnet as a *fattigstuga* (poorhouse)—a place where a community's poor or infirm could live when they had nowhere else to go.[20] Swedish law had mandated since the eighteenth century that every parish provide a home for parishioners who did not have the means to support themselves.[21] Mina's description of Hamnevattnet suggests that it was somewhat more than a typical poorhouse. Owned by the ironworks rather than the parish, Hamnevattnet not only housed former ironworkers physically

Young Mina with her father, Anders Jansson, standing on the outskirts of the village of Bäckefors, about 1870. The candid photograph suggests a playful relationship between father and daughter.

unable to continue working at the forge, a role typical for a poorhouse, but also provided shelter to families of able-bodied workers who, like Mina's father, could not find living accommodations on other company property.

Hamnevattnet included a two-story dwelling, measuring about thirty-three by twenty-six feet (which provided housing for six families). If that space was divided evenly, each family occupied a room approximately thirteen feet by eleven feet. The property was about four acres in size and during the nineteenth century included a provision shed with root cellar as well as a garden where the residents of Hamnevattnet could grow food for their own use.[22] When I went searching for Hamnevattnet on a visit to Sweden in the spring of 2005, I walked for twenty minutes through a forest from the nearest road to the site, guided by the local forester. I was disappointed, though not surprised, given the passage of time, to find the dwelling itself gone. I discovered later that it had been dismantled and used to construct a house in the village of Bäckefors. All that remains now of the home where Mina was born are remnants of its stone foundation, faint outlines of the exterior walls that are gradually being overtaken by forest. In the area surrounding the home are a stone pile and vestiges of a stone wall. Though the structures at Hamnevattnet have nearly disappeared, one element remains intact—the picturesque setting. As I stood on the hilltop on one of Hamnevattnet's foundation stones, I found myself in the forest by a beautiful lake (called Hamntjärn), just as Mina had described.

Most residents of Bäcke parish, where Mina grew up, were both rural and industrial workers, with male family members usually employed at the ironworks but living with their families in the countryside and supporting themselves in part with their own crops, livestock, and gardens. Though the Bäckefors ironworks represented early Swedish industrialization, it was located in one of Sweden's most rural provinces and coexisted with the farms surrounding it. More than three-quarters of Sweden's population was rural in 1900, and Mina's childhood in rural Dalsland was typical of the setting in which many Swedish girls in the nineteenth and early twentieth centuries found themselves, particularly those growing up in the increasing numbers of nonlandowning families. (Even many of the Swedish females listed in official records as emigrating from cities had actually grown up in rural areas and migrated to an urban area before deciding to journey to the United States.)[23]

Most young Swedish girls did not live in the type of communal housing that Mina experienced at Hamnevattnet but rather grew up in single homes. Swedish rural dwellings ranged from two-story landowners' houses (two bedrooms upstairs, kitchen and living room below), to torpare cottages (a kitchen and a combination living room/bedroom), to tiny one-room backstugusittare homes. *Backstugusittare* translates literally to "cottage that sits in a hill," and some of these homes were indeed simple dugouts. The term also refers more broadly to the housing of those who due to their insecure economic status moved frequently in search of work and could afford few furnishings. Only those at the lower socioeconomic levels would occupy this type of housing. With only one room per family at Hamnevattnet, Mina's home was similar to torpare and backstugusittare homes.

Mina noted that Hamnevattnet drew a diverse group of tenants, and it would have been difficult for residents to avoid knowing each other's business, with six households living in the castle at any given time, each with only one room to occupy. It is not surprising that Mina, even after half a century had passed, was able to recall many of the more colorful residents, including two

A thatch-and-moss-roof Swedish cottar's home, or *backstuga*, 1895. (Photo by Karl Fredrik Andersson)

quarrelling widows, a jovial man with an angry wife, and a struggling family in which the father was unable to work. In spite of the mother's labor outside the home, the children suffered from hunger and need.

The lack of empty rooms at Hamnevattnet during Mina's childhood reflected the increasing economic struggles the Dalbon faced as the nineteenth century progressed. In addition to the 1860s downturn of the iron industry, in the 1880s the market for oats, one of the central cash crops for southern Dalsland farmers, plummeted as competition from world markets increased.[24] The population in Dalsland and in Sweden as a whole had also increased rapidly in the eighteenth and much of the nineteenth century, as death rates dropped. Contributing to decreasing mortality rates and longer life spans were agricultural reform and consolidation of landholdings, which resulted in increased agricultural production, the introduction of new crops, and the decrease in the virulence of illnesses.[25] As the population grew, more and more Swedish families lived on the margins. In good years they could get by, but when economic crises occurred, many families faced extreme adversity, and young people had little hope for advancement. Emigration from Sweden came to be seen as a possible solution.

Alarmed by the number of its citizens emigrating (most to the United States), in the early twentieth century the Swedish government conducted a detailed and lengthy study of "the immigration problem." The study's findings were printed in twenty-one thick volumes, entitled *Emigrationsutredningen* (the Emigration Investigation), published from 1907 to 1914. One section of the investigation includes local case studies (*bygdeundersökningar*) and contains an examination of the very administrative region (*härad*), Vedbo, where Mina grew up. The study highlights the extent to which the economic, social, and demographic developments of the nineteenth century wrought significant changes in the lives of Swedes in general and the Dalbon in particular. In 1907, seventeen years after Mina's departure, investigator Ernst Lundholm spent most of the summer in Vedbo, speaking with local government officials as well as pastors, schoolteachers, and residents in each parish to gain a better understanding of why so many Dalsland Swedes were emigrating and what the government might do to reduce those numbers. His findings reveal the economic and social conditions that helped Mina decide to emigrate.[26]

Early in his study, Lundholm described the Vedbo conditions in the 1860s and 1870s, the era during which Mina was born and living at Hamnevattnet and when the first significant emigration from Vedbo took place. Food supplies became so limited then that women were at times forced to bake "bark bread" or "famine bread" for their families. In preparing this food, the layer of bark just under a tree's rough surface was scraped and cut, hung up to dry, and eventually ground and mixed with flour for bread.[27] It was neither tasty nor nutritious but could help satisfy hunger and stave off starvation. Lundholm noted that "suffering was extremely high among the numerous torpare and backstugusittare in Vedbo, and it was widely reported how the roads were overflowing with beggars who offered their labor in exchange for meals."[28] Although he did not interview any residents who had firsthand experience of conditions in the 1860s and 1870s, he noted that the statistical record clearly indicated how economic need forced many people at that time to find new means of supporting themselves. Land use and population growth statistics for Mina's home district from 1805 to 1880 reveal significant increases in population, especially between 1805 and 1865, when the number of residents in Mina's parishes of Bäcke and later Ödsköld (the former where she attended school, the latter where she was confirmed and found her first full-time employment) more than doubled. The amount of arable land in both parishes was only about 11 percent, and Bäckefors bruk was, as noted, a struggling economic venture from the 1860s on. Lundholm also found that in 1865 there was still only limited use of the region's forest resources, which would later become an important sector for economic development, with the manufacture of paper and wood products. (See Appendix, Table 1.)

Although Mina's fellow Bäcke parish residents relied in part on the ironworks for their livelihood, agriculture remained an important economic activity both there and elsewhere in Vedbo. Lundholm's report highlights how the relationships between the people and the land changed over time. Most significant was the steady increase in torpare and backstugusittare.[29] In addition to his statistical evidence on these social groups, Lundholm noted physical evidence of their increase and of their emigration from Dalsland. He was surprised at the number of abandoned torpare and backstugusittare dwellings he observed while traveling through Vedbo: "On trips through forest districts one is astonished at the large number of crofter and cottar cottages, now [in 1907] mostly abandoned and decaying." (Lundholm also noted that marginally arable forest land cleared as the population grew was, by the early twentieth century, being reclaimed by the forest.)[30]

If Mina's family was ever among the beggars overflowing the roads of Dalsland, she did not mention it in her memoir. Her father's employment at the ironworks and the communal arrangement of the family's housing likely helped them avoid such desperate measures while Mina was young. The physical proximity and shared penury of living at Hamnevattnet built among its tenants mutual caring and solidarity. As Mina noted, food was often shared between households: "If one family was without, there were always some of the others who shared what they had."[31]

Family: "My Good Health Is an Inheritance from Both Father and Mother"

Historian Margareta Matovic found close family relationships in her study of nineteenth-century Dalsland, which Mina's family possessed as well, although the situation for nineteenth-century families elsewhere in Sweden is less clear.[32] Some scholars have characterized Swedish family relations as strict and unfeeling; others have called them close and understanding.[33] Mina's family structure was, like that of most families in nineteenth-century Sweden, patriarchal. The relationship of wife as subordinate to husband was spelled out clearly in the traditional Swedish wedding vows: "God has established marriage / and set forth the man as the woman's head / that he will be her guide / lead her in the fear of God / to love her as Christ loved His people. . . . Likewise shall the woman obey the man / love him / keep him as her guide / keeping in mind / that she is created for man's sake. . . . The woman shall always remember / that she is to obey the man."[34]

Nineteenth-century family ideals were also influenced by the guidelines set forth in the *Hustavla* (house table), a set of biblical quotations included in Martin Luther's Small Catechism about the relationships within and between Luther's three social orders: church, state, and household. These guidelines were both patriarchal and hierarchical, placing women and children in subordinate positions. Just as wives were expected to obey their husbands, so were children expected to respect and obey their parents, especially their fathers.[35]

In spite of a patriarchal family structure, evidence about Mina's family suggests close and caring relationships between family members. Though descriptions of Mina's relationship with her father are limited, probably because his labor at the ironworks was demanding and tiring, leaving little time for father and daughter to spend together, other details hint at a close relationship between the two. Mina's father made time to build dams and a water wheel in a nearby brook with her. He purchased the only "bought toy" Mina ever received, a doll, and in a later section of her memoir Mina mentions a playhouse her father helped her build. Father and daughter must have enjoyed each other's company and been able to spend time together, at least occasionally.

It is, however, Mina's bond with her mother, Maja, that emerges in her writing as an especially cherished relationship. In a community based upon iron manufacture, a male-dominated industry, and in a time and place where women's activities revolved around the household and home, this strong mother-daughter relationship is not surprising. Mina certainly spent more time at Hamnevattnet with her mother than with her father. And although she acknowledged positive traits she had inherited from both parents, she credited her mother with teaching her important life values such as honesty and religious faith. It was her mother who taught her to read fluently before she attended school. In 1900, the year after her father died, and ten years after her own immigration, Mina brought her mother over from Sweden to live on the Halgren family farm in rural Minnesota. Earlier, Mina had helped her sister and her brother to immigrate, again underscoring strong family ties and a clear sense of personal responsibility for the welfare of immediate relatives.

Close and loving family relationships might seem surprising considering the crowded living conditions at Hamnevattnet. Mina grew up in one room with her parents and eventually her siblings. Mina's sister Kristina was born in 1876, and a

Mina's parents, about 1864.

brother, Wilhelm, was born in 1879. Another sister, Anna, was born and died in 1882. Her family size was slightly smaller than typical. In 1880 Swedish families averaged six children, though family size declined thereafter, reaching an average of two children per family in 1930.[36] For most Swedish families in the nineteenth century, crowded conditions were the norm rather than the exception. When Mina's family was finally able to move from the room at Hamnevattnet to possibly more spacious company housing in Bäckefors bruk in 1889, Mina had already left the household to seek employment.

Children's Work: "I Knit My First Pair of Socks"

Mina wrote: "Mother taught me early on to work."[37] In nineteenth-century Sweden, children by the age of seven were expected to share in the labors of supporting the household and family. A child's labor within the family and household varied to some degree according to gender. Swedish girls were expected to assist with household domestic tasks (cleaning, preparing food, and producing textiles or other handcrafts) and to care for younger siblings. In a letter to the Swedish American newspaper *Svenska Amerikanska Posten*, published in Minneapolis, Mina recalled the pride she had felt as a girl in learning how to perform some of these tasks: "I will never forget how happy and proud I was, when I knit my first pair of socks and spun my first spool of yarn."[38]

Swedish boys would assist their fathers with the care of livestock and crops. Both girls and boys herded livestock at pasture (common in the southern, less-forested region of Dalsland), fetched water, cut and gathered wood for fuel, and picked berries for consumption or sale.[39] Mina does not mention tending livestock (the family may have been too poor to own any), though she did have younger siblings to look after, and she gathered wood and picked berries as a child. Selling berries provided her with some cash, but she was expected to use this money for necessities such as clothing and shoes.

Mina's description of her work as a child does not convey resentment at the labor required of her, though some recollections by women growing up in Sweden at that time did offer more negative assessments of such work. Swedish immigrant Hilda Linder related in her autobiography how overburdened she felt by the duties expected of her as the oldest of nine siblings in her household. Born in Västergötland, a province adjacent to Dalsland, in 1896, she complained, "For as long as I can remember, it was my responsibility to look after the children. I never got to learn to play, only to work."[40] Likewise, Emma Persson, born in southern Sweden in 1879, was required to "work out" already at age nine, when she spent the summer helping to care for the children and performing other household tasks at a nearby farm. Emma's wages for that summer's work were in kind—a dress. In the following years, she received as pay a pair of shoes, wool to make stockings, and a half-kilo of potatoes to be planted on the farm. Just as Mina's berry-picking money was used to purchase necessities, Emma's in-kind wages provided goods that contributed to her own support (shoes and clothing) and to her family's general welfare (potatoes).[41] As long as a Swedish child, girl or boy, was still considered a child rather than an adult (confirmation, usually at the age of fifteen, was the rite of passage marking this shift), the results of his or her labor at home or elsewhere were seen as contributions to the family economy.

Women's Work: "She Had to Go to Pasture and Forest and Field"

In Dalsland (and in Sweden more generally) women's work involved food preparation and textile production in the home, as well as duties such as washing clothes and taking charge of dairy production.[42] Although field work traditionally fell within the male domain, women were expected to assist when needed, such as with the planting and harvesting of crops (work performed in addition to domestic responsibilities).[43]

For her mother's ninetieth birthday Mina wrote a poem that she later published in a Swedish American newspaper. Her words illustrate the strong affection and admiration she felt for her mother but also reveal the variety of duties and roles that Swedish girls and women were expected to fulfill.[44]

"Mother"

She had to go to pasture and forest and field
long before she was big and strong
and mind the goats, sheep and cows,
separated from father and mother,
and blow the horn in major and minor keys
when wolves lay in wait.

She never lived in wealth,
for the purse was most often empty,
She received no inheritance from mother and father,
but owned what was even better,
good health and a spirit
that stood her through all changes.

Every day father went to the foundry,
but meager was the wage he received,
and mother worked and smiled
and hauled wood and food by toboggan;
when the snow went away she just as securely
took the burden upon her back.

She wove, spun, and knitted,
until she nodded from fatigue;
she treadled her spinning wheel long evenings
and taught us our lessons at the same time
because mother, she could spin
at the same time she was a teacher.

When we moved down to the village,
she found no more time to spin,
but sold coffee, baked
and cooked and washed
and carried in wood and water
and looked after cow and cat.

And she also helped others,
they only had to call for Maja,
she allowed herself little rest
and could never say no,
and even if she was upset herself
she always helped others.[45]

Mina Anderson

Women in Swedish households—mothers, daughters, and female servants—often worked together at household tasks. Mina's memoir evokes the female networks within and beyond the household when she recalls her mother and other women of Hamnevattnet struggling to stay awake late at night to complete handwork to sell. The women shared conversation, coffee, and song, and sometimes walked together to keep awake as they toiled at their spinning and knitting. Conditions at Hamnevattnet likely encouraged its residents to think of the building as one large household where female labor was often a communal activity. But even women in physically separate households came together periodically for cooperative work. In Dalsland, neighborhood women came together to work, typically meeting twice a year for washing days in spring and fall and for baking *knäckebröd* in May and November. The women also worked collectively to slaughter livestock or make cheese.[46] Mina's comments about the Hamnevattnet women struggling to stay awake to complete their work also suggests that Swedish women typically worked longer hours managing household and family than did Swedish men in farm or foundry, echoing the familiar adage that women's work is never done.

Women in Sweden supplemented family income or at times wholly supported families by sewing or taking in laundry. Nineteenth-century Swedish attitudes concerning gender roles discouraged married women's wage labor outside the home, but such labor occurred, especially among widows or women whose husbands were unable to work or whose wages were not adequate to support the family.[47] Mina described one such woman who lived at Hamnevattnet ("Another family also lived there; the father was unable to work. They had many children and the mother was often away working"[48]). Mothers working outside the home faced numerous challenges. The children of working mothers were often left at home to fend for themselves. Fathers did not usually assist with the care of children or household domestic tasks.[49] Mina's associated description of the family with the unemployed father illustrates both the gender expectations for women and the possible negative consequences for children in families where mothers had to seek employment outside the home: "They were very poor and since the mother never had time to be home, the children were both dirty and ragged, and most of the time, hungry."

School: "He Shook His Head. Too Expensive"

Despite growing up in difficult economic circumstances, Mina expressed regret about only one area of her childhood, her lack of education: "If I had only

The main, and only, street in Mina's village, Bäckefors bruk, about 1900. At left are the mine foreman's building and (behind trees) the mine owner's home. (Photo by Arne Waern)

been allowed to continue school and the studies that I loved so dearly." Mina's intelligence and aptitude for learning are evident in her memoir and other writings. Conscious of her own abilities, she referred to herself as "gifted" when she recollected the sometimes-inappropriate atmosphere of Hamnevattnet when housemates exhibited unusual or untoward behavior. Her abilities are apparent also in the fact that she was able to read before beginning school. Swedish law required public primary schools in 1842, and in 1878 and 1882 mandated a full six years of public education. Mina was born in 1867 and probably began school in 1874 at age seven. Since she completed her required education in only four years, she may have just missed falling under the law extending public education to six years or parish authorities may have been lax in implementing and enforcing the legislation. Working-class parents in nineteenth-century Sweden often had to balance their own need for a child's labor with his or her education. It is unclear whether Mina's departure from school was due to her having mastered all that was offered there or whether the family's need for her earnings was deemed more important than continuing her education (or both). Yet even if her writing reveals her sadness at her schooling's end ("many were the tears I then shed"), she does not blame her parents, instead accepting the social and economic conditions that prevented her from continuing her formal education in Dalsland.[50]

Though unable to continue her education beyond *folkskola* (primary school), Mina at age eleven was too young to begin the next step toward adulthood, her confirmation instruction. She instead continued to live mostly at home, probably looking after her siblings, assisting her mother with household tasks, and, as she noted, "working for others sometimes,"[51] including watching children, herding livestock, and assisting with elements of household production, as had Emma Persson, who helped out at a nearby farm.[52] In nineteenth- and early twentieth-century Sweden, discontinuing a child's schooling so that he or she could help support self and family was a widespread practice.[53]

Many young Swedish women struggled when the desire for continued education and intellectual capacities conflicted with hard economic realities. Attitudes toward gender also limited a girl's access to higher education. Even families with sufficient money to support further education for their children considered it more appropriate to provide boys with formal instruction than girls. To pay for the education of a girl who, it was expected, would sooner or later leave the paid workforce to marry and raise a family was considered a poor investment. For example, Ingeborg Frankmar wanted desperately to attend a high school in southern Sweden in Skåne in 1901. She recalled that when she showed her father an advertisement for the school she hoped to attend, "he shook his head. Too expensive." Since Ingeborg was one of nine children, such thinking seems understandable from a class perspective. Yet Ingeborg's father was willing to support her brother's education at a high school in spite of the large family and limited finances.[54] Social class, as well as gender, shaped the direction and course of Swedish girls' lives.

Mina grew up in a poorhouse, had her education cut short, and contributed to the family's support at a young age, yet she could still be considered more fortunate than some other nineteenth-century Swedish children, who had lost one or both parents or whose mothers had never married and could not support them. For such children a system called *utackordering* provided an ostensible safety net. Once a year in front of the local church building, parishes auctioned off these children to families who were willing to accept the least compensation from the local authorities for providing them room and board. The parish would pay the foster family in kind (usually with grain) or in cash. As members of these lowest-bidding households, the children would be expected to contribute their labor to support the household. Hilda Hammar's mother died when Hilda was a young girl, leaving her father to struggle with the care of eight children. He was unable to support them all, so at age six Hilda was auctioned out to a large farm and required to work very hard. Sometimes these arrangements provided suitable foster homes; other times exploitation and abuse resulted.[55]

Play: "We Had So Much Fun That We Forgot the Pigs"

Nineteenth-century Swedish girlhood was not focused only on work. Mina describes the dam and water wheel that she built with her father and the doll that he gave her. But Mina's play stretched beyond activities by herself or with a parent. Her memoir suggests that playmates were not difficult for Mina to find, especially given the number of families occupying Hamnevattnet. Like so many other Swedish children then and now, Mina recalled a variety of outdoor activities she shared with friends, including swimming, skiing, and sledding. Mina drew a particularly vivid image of one winter activity with her description of landing face-first in icy snow while sledding and arriving home with face "cut and bloody."

The recollections of Olga Pettersson, born in 1891 in Småland, provide other examples of Swedish childhood play. The daughter of a soldier, Olga grew up on a torp that the government provided to support soldiers' families (their cottage had a vestibule, kitchen, and bedroom). Interviewed for a Swedish television program in the 1970s, Olga reported spending much of her time at home caring for her young siblings—she was the fourth of twelve children. But she had opportunities for play as well as work. Like Mina, she lacked store-bought toys but was able to make her own playthings. She and her siblings carved wooden whistles. They created miniature farms with animals made of pinecones and sticks. Olga made clothes for a doll she constructed from a doll's head, found on a trash heap, into which she had pushed a stick for the body. She recalled an unsuccessful attempt at boating on a nearby pond, using as her watercraft the large wooden tray in which her mother kneaded dough. She and her siblings also constructed small huts in the nearby forest.[56]

Olga's and Mina's memories of childhood pastimes illustrate the way in which the lines between work and play were often blurred. Olga recalled a time when she, at age ten, and her brother, at age twelve, were left by her parents to care for their younger siblings and the family's pigs. As Olga reported: "We played with them [their siblings] and had so much fun that we completely forgot the pigs," resulting in the premature demise of one of the pigs.[57] Similarly, Mina's descriptions of fishing, gathering wood, and picking berries reveal activities that she and her friends clearly enjoyed but that also contributed to the physical or economic support of the household.

Confirmation: "I Worked for a Farmer to Be Near the Church"

Like other Swedish adolescents, Mina prepared for confirmation as she approached her fifteenth birthday. Religious tradition and practice considered her old enough then to take confirmation instruction, commonly referred to as "reading for the pastor" (*att läsa för prästen*), an important rite of passage in Swedish society, after which time the young man or woman was considered an adult. Confirmation training meant attending classes at the local parish church, usually over a period of several weeks to months. In Dalsland the training lasted eight months.[58] If a daily walk to the parish church was too difficult, young Swedes might have to do what Nellie Baskette did: take service at a farm near the church in order to attend confirmation. Nellie grew up in a fishing village in the province of Blekinge and in later life recalled her confirmation training: "One . . . thing that still grips me, when I think back, was how I had to work during the time we went to the church and read for the pastor. I worked for a farmer to be near the church. I was only thirteen years old. I had to get up while it was dark, milk ten to twelve cows, carry out all goods to the wagon and drive it out to the fields and meadows, crawl in the rows and pick potatoes, drive loads of potatoes with two pairs of oxen in to the farm and empty it, and then back again. If there were some minutes I had to myself to rest, then I could knit stockings and other things. That was my youth."[59]

As Nellie's words attest, in nineteenth- and early twentieth-century Sweden, confirmation in the state Lutheran church marked an important ritual considered worth making sacrifices to accomplish.[60] Formalized by the church in the early nineteenth century, confirmation served several functions that sup-

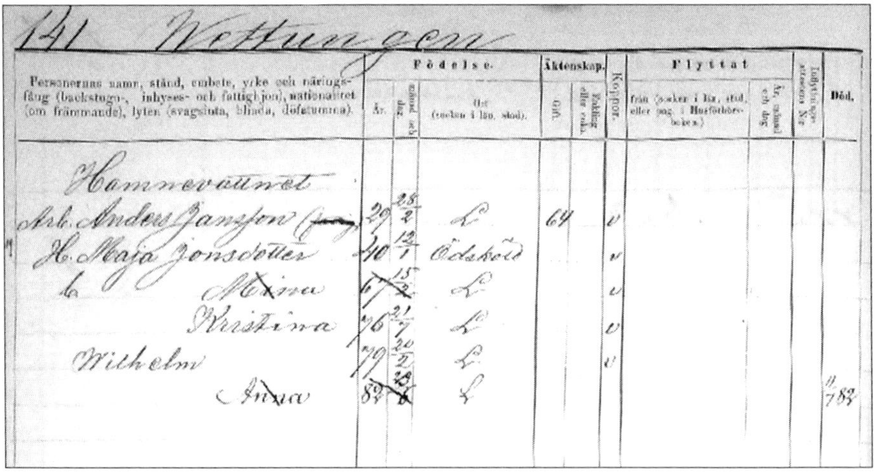
141 Wettungen

Personernas namn, stånd, embete, yrke och näringsfång (backstugu-, inhyses- och fattighjon), nationalitet (om främmande), lyten (svagsinta, blinda, döfstumma).	Födelse: År	månad och dag	Ort (socken i län, stad).	Äktenskap: Gift	Enkling eller enka	Koppor	Flyttat: från (socken i län, stad, eller pag. i Husförhörsboken.)	År, månad och dag	Inflyttnings attestens №	Död.
Hamnevattnet										
Arb. Anders Jansson	29	28/2	L	64		v				
H. Maja Jonsdotter	40	12/7	Ödsköld			v				
d. Mina	67	15/2	L			v				
Kristina	76	21/7	L			v				
Wilhelm	79	20/2	L			v				
Anna	83	23/8	L							11/7 83

The parish record for Wättungen estate, where Mina lived with her parents, Maja Jonsdotter (Jansdotter) and Anders Jansson. The line through Mina's name indicates her move in 1883 to work as a servant in the neighboring parish of Ödsköld.

ported both church and state. Along with teaching the history and practice of the Lutheran faith, confirmation instruction served to reinforce student literacy and encouraged the development of character traits such as respect for authority. As membership in non-Lutheran denominations increased in the nineteenth century, the government, in 1878, made confirmation voluntary. Most young Swedes still chose to be confirmed, due in part to the fact that proof of the Lutheran state confirmation was required for entrance into some occupations and educational institutions.[61]

A strong knowledge and understanding of Luther's catechism, as well as the ability to read the catechism and Bible, was also expected of all Swedish citizens. Until the late nineteenth century, members in every Swedish household were regularly given oral and reading examinations in these subjects by local parish authorities. Careful examination records were kept, called *husförhörslängder* (household examination records). Some records contain evaluative grades for examination performance and other personal notes, but Mina's record shows only that she passed her examinations.[62] The household examination records also indicate dates when communion was taken. Mina was confirmed in 1882 at the age of fifteen.

The state emphasis on religious knowledge and recordkeeping helped maintain Sweden as a literate population and today also provides an important historical and genealogical resource. The records list entire households, not just family members. In addition to examination notations, dates of taking communion, and accounts of vaccinations, the records provide other details about every individual: name, gender, birth date and birthplace, relationship to head of household, marital status, and occupation. For example, these records reveal that Mina was vaccinated against smallpox. A small section for comments sometimes also contains parish officials' remarks about an individual's health, character, or economic status. In the records for Bäcke parish, 1891–95, the notation *hör tidtals litet* (literally, hears little at times) is given for Mina's brother, Wilhelm.[63]

Household examination records also indicate when individuals left a parish and the destination of their move. Since the examinations were required yearly, the records provide a resource for tracking movements of individuals and households. The household examination records for Bäcke parish reveal that on November 15, 1883, Mina moved from Hamnevattnet to the neighboring parish of Ödsköld. Mina had completed the rite of passage to adulthood that confirmation represented, and she, like other young men and women of her social class, was expected to leave her home and family and become self-supporting.

* * *

The childhoods of Swedish women were shaped in part by their own distinct characters and the individual choices they made. Mina's memoir reveals her traits of optimism, intelligence, and creativity. That she worked hard at the tasks and responsibilities placed before her is evident from her descriptions of her childhood. She enjoyed and appreciated the natural environment around her and had affection and respect for her parents. She completed her confirmation instruction and believed in a Creator. But Mina's choices were made within and shaped by the broader framework of the society in which she lived.

Socioeconomic status determined options for Swedish girls. Most contributed to the family economy at a young age, but the balance of time spent between work and play could shift significantly depending on the family's economic position. Household skills learned growing up in a one-room home or a poorhouse were of a different degree and nature than those learned in a landowner's home with servants or a multiroom torpare cottage. These skills shaped employment options for young women, as well as their ability in the future to maintain a household or support a family with work outside the home. Whether a girl completed primary school or obtained further education or training also depended in part on her family's socioeconomic status. In spite of her family's relatively low socioeconomic status, Mina experienced a childhood that included a healthy mix of work and play. However, growing up in a poorhouse constrained her ability to learn marketable household skills. She wrote: "Our home was so poor that it didn't teach me much of what was demanded of a female servant; that I had to learn bit by bit after I had come out into the world."[64] Mina's words convey an intense sense of disappointment and regret that her education was cut short after only four years.

Social attitudes and practices regarding gender norms also represented part of the framework shaping Swedish girls' lives. Gender influenced such fundamental elements of individual experience as appearance—with girls (including Mina) wearing dresses and having long hair. Within the family, girls were primarily taught skills deemed appropriate for the female sex—for Mina, learning to knit, spin, and weave. And just as being poor contributed to the limited formal education for girls like Mina, so did being female. In a patriarchal society where women were considered subordinate and girls were expected to marry and raise children, education for females was not often considered a practical investment of time and money. Mina's childhood was relatively happy, but upon reaching adulthood she found herself in a Swedish society that offered her few choices and limited hopes for the future.

CHAPTER 2

"So Tired of Hard Work and Disappointment"

On My Own

Now it was time for me, as for many others, to go out and earn my bread myself. I applied for a position as a nursemaid, but it was already taken. I then took a position as a farmer's maid. I was of course only fifteen years old; it was hard work and I hadn't learned so much of such work.[1] *I was ignorant about most of it but it didn't take so long to learn. I had to get up at 5 o'clock in the morning and was rarely finished before ten o'clock at night. My hands cracked—I wasn't used to alternating cold and water so I suffered much from that. But I learned to take care of my hands better and then they healed. I received twenty-five kronor, two pairs of shoes, and a few other small things for a whole year's work. It was my good health and cheerful disposition that enabled me to endure it, young as I was. I didn't know anything better and was satisfied.*

After I had been there for a year, I traveled far from my own region and took service on a larger farm in Norway. I was one of several servants there. I worked with this family for several years, first at the parents' home, later at the daughter's. The work was hard, but better than at my first position. This was in the 1880s and things were different then than now. My master and mistress were young and cheerful. Sometimes the master took his violin and played in the evenings and we all took a turn [dancing] in the large kitchen after we had finished work. There were a lot of young people on the large farms and there was a group of us who always gathered Saturday and Sunday evenings and then there would always be dancing. I once read a poem by Karlfeldt about summer dancing, which sounds like this:

I danced one summer,
it was a beautiful summer
and never has there been
dancing here
like there was then.

People played in the evenings
from farms and other places.
We walked so far
marching two by two.

In the clearing in the forest
on the hay loft dance floor
I danced on all of them
when I was nineteen years.[2]

These lines could in every way be applied to us. We all knew each other, and we behaved properly. I have often wondered about the youth of our time with their many opportunities for more sophisticated amusements—their automobiles, clubs, and parties—do they have as good a time as we did?

We servants of course had to keep to ourselves. The class distinction meant that we were never together with the young sons and daughters of the big farms. I once by accident happened to be at one of their dances. A boy who didn't know who I was danced with me several times, until some-

A Swedish woman domestic servant, or *piga*, milking a cow, about 1912. Employers expected farm servants to milk cows, along with performing regular duties in house and farmyard, and to do field work during planting and harvest seasons. (Photo courtesy Walter Andersson)

one who knew me took him aside and told him that I was only a servant girl. To his credit I must say that he did not care about that.

When I think of how important those [people] were who owned a piece of land at that time, it often makes me feel good to see here [in America] farmers' sons walk side by side in hard labor with people from all nations, and the farmers' sons have not been considered better than others. It is most often those who are used to hard labor, and to doing without, who manage best here.

The First Love

I met my first love here [at the farm in Norway]. He was a young fellow servant. We were both so young and inexperienced. We didn't think so much about anything, it was just so much fun to be together. We played like a couple of children; wrestled to see who was the strongest, raced out in the meadows, turned each other upside down in the haystacks, played "Svarta Peter [Black Peter]" and sooted each other so that we looked like negroes. [Black Peter is a card game similar to Old Maid, but in this case the person who loses is rubbed with soot.] Young and inexperienced as we were, nothing was ever said, and we parted. We met several years later; we lived far from each other but corresponded for a long time. But he became wild and wasn't worth a girl's love.

Meanwhile I learned to know and care about someone else. We were both young and poor, and then misfortune struck. He got blood poisoning in a leg, was in the hospital for a long time, and came back a cripple. There was no future for one so unfortunate, since he did not have any training for anything other than hard labor. I have, however, to my joy, heard in later years that he has a small country store and is doing well. . . . I was now so tired of hard work and disappointment that I gladly accepted the offer of a relative who wrote that he would send me a ticket if I wanted to go to America.[3]

By the time Mina's uncle offered a ship's ticket in 1890, Mina had been supporting herself for seven years. She had changed employers several times but had met with little success in improving her social and economic status. Her brief formal education and the limited domestic training her mother and a few employers had been able to give provided her with few employment options. Marriage might have afforded her an opportunity for greater economic security or less arduous labor, but she had by age twenty-three not yet found a suitable mate. What Mina had discovered was that her chances of improving (or even maintaining) her social and economic position in her homeland, whether through employment or marriage, were very meager indeed. Thus Mina came to view emigration to the United States as her best chance for a better future, a promising alternative to the weariness and disillusionment of life in Sweden. In the nineteenth and early twentieth centuries, single Swedish women like Mina experienced limited employment opportunities, a diminishing supply of eligible marriage partners, and a rigid class society. Books, newspapers, letters, photographs, and visits home of Swedish Americans conveyed images of America as a land of opportunity for women—and when the chance to obtain a ship's ticket came up, many young Swedish females decided to emigrate.

Legal and economic equality for Swedish women improved over the course of the nineteenth and early twentieth centuries. Women were granted rights of inheritance equal to those of men in 1845. In 1846 the state ruled that women were entitled to practice certain trades and handicrafts independently (though this was due more to an increase in illegitimate births and increasing pressure on local welfare resources than to a shift in thinking about women's abilities).[4] In the 1850s women gained the right to teach in elementary schools and to become legally independent at age twenty-five. Teacher training schools for women were established in the 1860s, and by 1862 women were permitted to vote in local elections. In 1864 a law was passed allowing single women to establish their own small businesses such as millinery or other handicraft shops. Some limited government funding was made available for establishing private secondary schools for girls in the 1870s, and women could take exams for university admission beginning in 1870.[5]

But middle-class and upper-class women were best positioned to take advantage of advances in Swedish women's political and economic rights. Equal inheritance had limited significance when there was little if anything to inherit. Practicing trades and handicrafts usually required training, and starting a small business required capital that would be difficult for women like Mina to accumulate. The Swedish teacher training colleges established for women were too expensive for landless rural families, as were the privately owned girls' academies for secondary education—not until 1927 were girls allowed to attend publicly funded secondary schools.[6] As was the case for Mina, daughters in households of the lower social classes had limited funds for higher education, had scarce chance of sizeable inheritance, and lacked both the training and capital necessary to enter trades or sell handicrafts.[7]

Domestic Service in Sweden: "Laborious and Joyless and Heavy"

Most Swedish youth in poor households became self-supporting very soon after confirmation.[8] Records indicate, however, that although Mina was confirmed at age fifteen in 1882, she did not obtain a full-time servant employment contract until 1883. She most likely continued to work temporarily at neighboring farms and to help out at home, as she had done prior to confirmation. The birth and death of her youngest sibling, Anna, in 1882 may have meant that Mina was needed at home.

When Mina sought a full-time position in 1883, at age sixteen, she hoped to work as a *barnpiga*, a household servant or nursemaid whose primary responsibility was child care and assisting with household work. Instead she took a job as a common *piga* (domestic servant) on a large farm called Altorp a few kilometers from her home. Swedish parish records, which include records of births and baptisms, marriages and deaths, movements in and out of a parish, and household examinations, make possible the tracking of the moves of individuals within Sweden and the identification of the time of emigration from

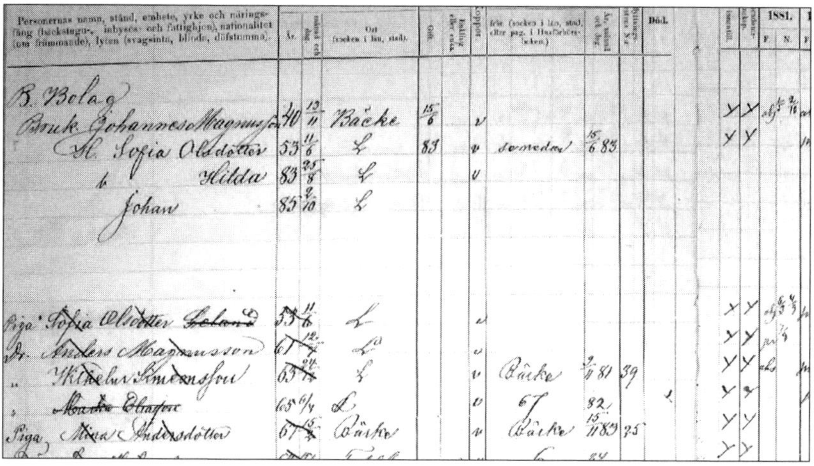

This 1885 parish record from Altorp (Alltorp) reports that Mina (at bottom) worked as a common servant, or piga; an adjoining page shows the reason for the line through her name, her move to Norway for work in 1884. (Mina's surname is written as "Andersdotter" here, reflecting Sweden's traditional patronymic naming tradition, which was eliminated in 1901 because it resulted in many duplicate names.)

Sweden. Because Sweden had a state church, local pastors also acted as government officials, and these officials kept track of the moves of their parishioners. This was fueled in part by the need to make sure that a parish would not have to provide support for in-migrants unable to support themselves. Those moving to a different parish needed to get a migration certificate (*flyttningsbetyg*) and also had to inform the pastor of the parish to which they were moving. The household examination records document Mina's move from Hamnevattnet to Altorp in Ödsköld parish in November 1883 and from Altorp to Ids parish in Norway in October 1884. Once Mina moved to Norway, her precise employment record is unclear because, although Norway was still at that time under Swedish rule, the Swedish government did not require the Norwegians to maintain the same kinds of detailed records. Mina noted in other records, however, her employment at two farms in Norway, Stumberg and Torgalsbøen, as well as in the Norwegian city of Halden (formerly Fredrikshald).

In her first contracted position as a piga, Mina was one of seven servants on an estate, three female (*pigor*) and four male (*drängar*). Her duties included milking cows, caring for livestock, assisting with the harvest, and helping with household chores such as food preparation, laundry, and textile production. When girls left the family home after confirmation, employment as a piga often represented the only available work.[9] Even sons and daughters of landowners served in other households, though they tended to leave home much later and work for shorter periods of time before marriage than those in the landless classes. Some landowners' children sought positions because of economic need, but service might also help a young man or woman learn useful and necessary farming skills—serving as a kind of apprenticeship—or might provide improved marriage options. Most positions as pigor were found in the countryside. When Mina began working as a full-time piga in 1883, over 80 percent of the Swedish population lived in rural areas. Even by 1920 only about 30 percent of the population lived in urban areas.[10]

For young Swedish women like Mina, marriage and family were presumed to be their goals. Thus, females were seen as temporary workers and were expected to enter only feminine occupations—in keeping with their roles as future wives and mothers. For the lower social classes, work as a piga was considered ideal. By working as servants young women could both earn their keep and practice their domestic skills as they waited to find a husband and marry. These attitudes also shaped middle- and upper-class women's opportunities. The first types of skilled work open to women in nineteenth-century Sweden were in the areas of health care, education, and social welfare—occupations considered extensions of women's work as mothers and caregivers within the home.

From her childhood at Hamnevattnet, Mina was already familiar with some of the physical labor required to maintain a rural household, including indoor domestic work such as spinning and weaving and outdoor tasks such as gathering wood and clearing rocks from cropland. Even so, she soon discovered that employment as a full-time domestic worker held new challenges ("It was hard work and I hadn't learned so much of such work.")[11] As the oldest daughter in a landless household, Mina had probably spent more time minding her younger siblings while her parents worked than learning the skills of a rural domestic. And at Hamnevattnet she had lived with her family in a single room. Altorp, in contrast, was the site of the local courthouse (*tingshus*) and included several residences, a building where court was held, and a barn. Typically she rose at 5:00 A.M. and was not finished with her assigned tasks until 10:00 P.M.—a seventeen-hour workday. She complained about developing painful cracks in her hands, probably from scrubbing wood floors and washing clothes by hand in the cold winter months.

Domestic service in Sweden varied slightly from region to region and from rural to urban households, yet most Swedish maids had similar working conditions and length of service, shaped in part by the Swedish state. The government in 1833 had passed regulations for domestic service that clearly favored employers of domestics rather than the domestics themselves. This legislation, the Household Servant Law (*tjänstehjonstadga*) required domestics to accept one-year contracts. For much of the nineteenth century, October 24 was set as the day to change contracts, likely chosen because harvest work would be completed by that time. Servants would have several days following this day free from employment, providing them a few days off as well as time to move to the new employer's household. (Stockholm was an exception to this rule—domestics there had two moving days, one in April and another in October.) Moving to a different job between the contract-changing dates was forbidden. The Household Servant Law also required servants to perform whatever tasks their employers assigned them or face serious punishment. Until the middle of the nineteenth century, employers had the right to flog their domestic employees. In 1858 the right to flog adults was abolished, but the employer could still use corporal punishment for males under age eighteen and females under age sixteen. Indigent women could be forced to enter domestic service. Until 1885, the Swedish Vagrancy Law (*försvarslöshetsstadgan*) required that adult women with no means of economic support (either

The workers' residence at Altorp, the local court center where Mina obtained her first servant employment at age sixteen.

through their own labor or through the assistance of others) who were physically able to work had to take a year's service.[12] The Swedish government and the Household Servant Law left only limited opportunities for domestic employees to negotiate for better employment terms.[13]

Swedish maids were poorly paid. For her first year of full-time domestic service, Mina's wages were "twenty-five kronor, two pairs of shoes, and a few other small things." Her cash wage was below the average wage of about sixty-eight kronor per year for female farm servants in the 1880s. And female servants typically earned half the wage of a male farmhand. Sometimes younger domestics received no cash wages at all, their employers claiming that room and board was payment enough. For example, although Hilda Linder received no cash wages for her first year of work as a rural domestic at the age of thirteen in 1909, she was given material for a black dress when she left the job in 1910. In her next position she received seventy-five kronor, half of the going rate for domestics at that time, justified by her employer on account of her youth.[14] (See Appendix, Table 2.)

As Mina's payment of money, shoes, and "small things" suggests, wages often took the form of goods as well as cash. The servant contract for Kattrine Andersdotter, who worked as a domestic for Johan Andersson in 1872, provides an example of a typical servant's payment agreement. For one year of employment, Kattrine received thirteen kronor, along with the following goods: one pair of boots, one shift, one kerchief, one apron, one half-peck of flaxseed sown, some potatoes planted, half a kronor's worth of flaxtow, and five marks' wool. (Flaxtow is made of coarse fibers of flax to be used in spinning, and a mark is a measure of weight, 340 grams.)[15] The boots and clothing could be put to immediate use. The wool, flaxseed, and flaxtow suggest either that Kattrine was also expected to spin, weave, and sew some of her own clothing or that she was allowed to contribute to her family's maintenance by sharing with them some of her in-kind payment.

Many Swedish servants echoed Mina's assessment of domestic service as hard work. It was physically demanding, and for rural domestics, it included long hours of both household labor and field work. As one farm servant pointed out to a government investigator, during hay harvesting she worked alongside the field hands but still had to take care of the livestock and do the milking upon her return from the fields.[16] Such "double duty" was common. According to a study of domestic servants in Dalsland in the early twentieth century:

> while the man in a farming community, small farmer as well as hired hand, worked at lumbering or farming during the day and, "after a well performed task," rested, slept, or sat completely unoccupied at day's end, the women continued to work in the household.
>
> When the hired girl was done with the day's activities, when she had finished milking, washed all the milk pails and the separator, fed the animals and cooked, served and cleaned up after the evening meal, then, if there was any time to relax before the fire went out and the lamp was blown out, she could not sit without something in her hands. She carded or scrubbed wool, knitted, or wound linen thread onto the shuttle. But it was the gray knitting for household use that dominated.[17]

A position could be even more difficult if the food was unsatisfactory or meager. An investigation of working conditions for young women in southern Sweden sponsored by a woman's organization in 1889 found complaints about substandard food. One woman stated: "A domestic here gets no more than 30–40 kronor for a whole year and bad food, a bit of cornbread and herring tail."[18] Another study of servants in nineteenth-century southern Sweden found that farm employers who provided "good and plentiful food" were able to recruit and maintain servants much more easily than employers who provided inadequate or poor-quality food.[19]

Poor housing conditions were another common grievance of Swedish domestics, though Mina did not mention having poor accommodations as part of her experience. Sleeping arrangements could be less than commodious. A young woman from southern Sweden reported waking at 5:00 A.M. to milk eight cows, but she was rarely able to go to bed before 11:00 P M. because she slept in the kitchen and could not go to bed until everyone else in the household had retired.[20] Another young woman from the southern province of Halland slept in her employer's kitchen with another female farm servant and three of the employer's children. She complained bitterly to a government investigator about the demands of her position, where she was not even allowed enough free time to perform such tasks as mending her clothes. She reported that her employer felt that he was entitled to her services twenty-four hours a day and that servants doing work for themselves constituted stealing from him.[21]

The demands employers made upon servants' time varied, and young women took into account the amount of free time an employer allowed them when they were seeking new positions. In addition to the "free week" that all servants received in late October, some employers allowed servants to attend Sunday church services. Others, like Mina's employers in Norway, permitted their servants time off on Saturday evenings or Sundays to socialize, visit family, or do work for themselves, but time off was more difficult in smaller farm households with fewer servants (the cows needed milking, even on weekends). Servants might also find time for socializing as they carried out their duties, such as when maids were sent to market at nearby villages or towns to buy or sell goods for the household. Servants might also be allowed to participate in public festivals and feasts such as Midsommar—a national Swedish holiday that celebrates the summer solstice and is even today celebrated with a maypole, dancing, food, family, and friends—though probably watching the employer's children all the while.

In addition to long hours, cramped housing, unsatisfactory food, and physically demanding work, domestics also complained of loneliness and lack of intellectual stimulation. Looking back on her domestic work years later, Hilda Linder remembered her limited access to reading material and the dearth of stimulating conversation: "I could feel how I went down intellectually. . . . I felt subservient and uncertain."[22] The physical and social environment of the rural domestic was also aptly described in a book by Swedish journalist Ester Blenda Nordström entitled *En piga bland pigor* (A maid among maids).

Curious about rural domestics and their lives, as well as the difficulty farmers were having in obtaining domestics, Nordström worked as a farm servant for a month in the 1910s. In words paralleling Mina's expression of hard work and disappointment, Nordström lamented rural domestic service as "laborious and joyless and heavy."[23]

After her year of service at Altorp, Mina took a job on a large farm in Norway, where she found that "the work was hard, but better than at my first position." Young Swedish women dissatisfied with their domestic positions might try their luck in a different rural area of Sweden (or Norway—in the 1880s still under Swedish rule). A study of nineteenth-century servant migration from southern Sweden found that a servant's decision to move was based on "a rational decision comparing costs and benefits."[24] A servant girl might change employers in pursuit of better food and lodging, higher wages, more free hours, or a better selection of potential marriage partners. In his study of emigration from southern Dalsland in the second half of the nineteenth century, Paul Noreen found servants migrating to Norway because of higher wages available there.[25] A domestic might also leave a position where she did not get along with her coworkers or where she felt there was sexual harassment or an inappropriate relationship. An informal local network existed among servants, by which they could exchange information about the conditions of service at households in the area.[26]

Migration did not always result in improved conditions. A twenty-two-year-old woman who had grown up in the northern Swedish district of Västernorrland moved to central Sweden, to Värmland, around 1906 in search of higher wages. There she found that although her wages had increased the work was very heavy and the cost of living high. Clothing was especially costly. She reported that a domestic might easily spend all her wages on clothing, "if she wanted to be clean and neat."[27] Even if a domestic worker found a position where the work was tolerable, wages adequate, and employers amiable, she could not count on continuing her service indefinitely. Employment as a domestic held little security for the employee beyond the one-year contract. The needs of employers varied as family size and structure changed, as suggested by Mina's first working for one family in Norway and then obtaining a position with the family's married daughter. A farm family with very young children might hire a domestic to help with household work, child care, and the tending of livestock, but when the children were old enough to perform household and farmyard tasks, or when economic pressures on a family increased, domestics might be regarded as unnecessary luxuries.

In addition to seeking better servant positions in other rural areas of Sweden (or, like Mina, across the border in Norway), some servant girls attempted to improve their situations by finding employment in Swedish towns and cities. Sweden was slow to urbanize, but as city populations grew women migrated to serve in middle-class and upper-class urban households. The number of urban domestics doubled between 1870 and 1900, and Stockholm, the largest city in Sweden, drew the highest numbers.[28] Urban domestics could obtain higher wages and avoid field work, but young women unaccustomed to high costs of living in cities might find that the wages that had sounded so attractive in a rural setting were in reality barely adequate for survival in an urban environment. And, like their rural counterparts, urban domestics found working conditions poor and complained of limited free time, heavy work, and low status.[29]

It was difficult for rural domestics, many of whom worked alone or with one other servant on isolated farmsteads, to come together as a group to discuss mutual problems and pose solutions. Urban domestics had the advantage of geographic proximity and organized for a time in several Swedish cities (though not until after Mina had emigrated). Servants associations were part of a broader movement for social equality in Sweden that developed during the late nineteenth century, which also included the trade union movement among the working class and the establishment of the Social Democratic Workers' Party, as well as efforts by women to obtain higher education, entrance into the professions, and suffrage.[30] Stockholm domestics established the *Stockholms Tjänarinneförening* (Stockholm Maidservant's Association) in January 1904 and began publishing a newspaper entitled *Tjänarinnebladet* (the Maidservant's Paper) in May 1905. According to the first issue of its newspaper, the organization sought to obtain set work schedules and time off, improve the system of contracting and termination of employment, offer educational opportunities, and establish a servant-run employment bureau. The newspaper also contained references to similar organizations working to "raise the members' social position" in the cities of Malmö in southern Sweden and Karlstad in central Sweden.[31]

At first, the Stockholm organization included both domestics and employers, and the two groups were able to work together on a number of issues. But the housewives generally saw matters more conservatively—for example, the organization tried to propose servant contracts that would clearly state working hours and time off but the housewives thwarted these attempts. When the maids eventually became too demanding for the employers, the housewives created their own servants organization.[32] In fact, these differing and often conflicting class interests that made it impossible for the maids to continue working alongside employers in the Stockholms Tjänarinneförening were reflected in the broader women's movement in Sweden as well. Although middle-class women complained of the shortage of good servants and lobbied for domestic training schools, working-class social democratic women called for improved working conditions and unionization.[33]

Tjänarinnebladet served a variety of functions for its readers. It kept members informed of the organization's activities; attempted to recruit new members; reported on the progress of other servants organizations in Sweden and elsewhere; and suggested ways to improve the lives of Stockholm domestic servants. Many of its features were hard-hitting attempts to convince servants to join the association and to choose domestic service over factory work, reflecting the interests of maids as well as employers. A serialized novel published in several 1906 and 1907 issues of the paper entitled "Ur verkligheten: Stockholms bild" (From reality: A picture of Stockholm) is a good example. The story tells the experience of two young Stockholm women—Anna and her sister Hilda. Both are dissatisfied with domestic work, but they choose different strategies to improve their lives. Hilda leaves domestic work and obtains a factory job but eventually dies from lung inflammation caused by her working conditions. Anna joins a servants organization, which enables her to find a better domestic position. At the story's close, Anna marries and cares for her own home—happy because the money she earned as a domestic helped to purchase the home and because the skills she learned as a domestic she could now apply to her own household.[34]

Other issues of *Tjänarinnebladet* encouraged domestics' self-improvement as well as changes in employer practices. Servants were advised to read during their free time and to "seek knowledge. . . . Because knowledge is power and power gives freedom, there is no freedom without knowledge."[35] A 1907 article addressed issues of employer respect for employees, suggesting that servants should not be addressed by their first names. The writer noted that if employers expected servants to act like adults, they should treat them as such. Employers were also advised to allow their employees time off to attend schools and classes to further their training.[36]

Largely ignored by servants organizations was the plight of domestics who became pregnant outside of marriage; sometimes a man from the family where she was employed was the father.[37] Conception outside of marriage was not uncommon in Sweden in the nineteenth and early twentieth centuries, and to have a child born before nine months of marriage had passed was not usually stigmatized. However, for a young servant to be pregnant with no prospect of marriage and to give birth outside of wedlock was a bleak situation. Because a servant's moral behavior reflected on her employer (heads of household were considered responsible for all members of the household), a "fallen" woman was typically dismissed from her position and might find it difficult to obtain a new one. Her new position might be below that of the other household domestics and might involve more outdoor work and heavier physical tasks.[38] If the mother was unable to support her child and had no friends or relatives to assist her, the child could be turned over to the parish and auctioned out to foster families.

Emigration became an alternative for some of these women, though it is difficult to determine precise numbers. Some documentary evidence exists, such as descriptions of women coming to the United States and leaving illegitimate children with family or friends back in Sweden or women emigrating with their illegitimate child (or children) in tow. In one local parish study, of the 629 women who emigrated between 1868 and 1893, 274 were unaccompanied women and 25 were unaccompanied women with children. Of the latter group, 16 were listed as domestic servants with illegitimate children (*oäkta barn*).[39]

Servants and servants organizations were not alone in recognizing problems with domestic employment. The Swedish Social Democratic Workers' Party in 1892 published a lecture by Norwegian women's doctor Oscar Nissen, "On Our Servant Girls' Position," which described the problems associated with household employment and made recommendations for improving domestic servants' conditions. Nissen called for shorter hours with regular time off for the domestic's own use, higher wages, and better living conditions. Swedish anarchist Gustav Henriksson-Holmberg published a study of Sweden's urban domestic servants in 1907, in which he also drew attention to the long working hours, noting that most servants worked fifteen or sixteen hours a day, with little or no free time. Like rural domestics, servants in urban households had difficulty finding time even to clean and repair their clothing. Many used their hard-earned wages to hire a seamstress to do their mending. Henriksson-Holmberg tried to correct what he felt were commonly held assumptions that domestic work required little physical or mental ability by discussing the difficulty and complexity of many domestic tasks and the skills required to perform them.[40]

Swedish Women's Industrial Labor: "Altogether Too Low Wages"

Mina Anderson spent her Swedish working life as a domestic servant, and aside from hoping to become a *barnpiga* (child care servant), she never expressed interest in other Swedish employment options. Domestic service was the most accessible to young single Swedish women, but it was not always the only alternative. Particularly as the nineteenth century drew to a close, the number of positions available for women in Swedish industry increased (though the bulk of industrial expansion was in heavy industry, which employed primarily male workers).[41]

But industrial work did not offer significant advantages over work as a Swedish domestic servant. Joseph Linck studied female industrial laborers in the 1870s in the tobacco, textile, match, paper processing, and glassworks industries. He discovered that women's wages in these fields were consistently lower than men's and did not provide a living wage.[42] The situation for female industrial workers outside the factory was also poor. Seamstresses in late nineteenth-century Stockholm usually worked twelve-hour days in cramped and close rooms called *systugor* (sewing workshops) with four or five other girls. Seamstresses received no wages until they had learned their trade, and even then did not usually earn even a subsistence wage.[43]

This situation did not improve significantly even as the nation's industrialization progressed. Journalist Gerda Meyerson studied early twentieth-century female industrial workers' employment, housing conditions, and recreation and found that most industrial labor was centered in Stockholm and involved large numbers of workers earning "altogether too low wages to be able to have living conditions worthy of a human being."[44] Good, low-cost housing was difficult to procure, and Meyerson found housing conditions for many women workers dismal. Some women roomed or boarded with families in order to get by. Meyerson visited an eighteen-year-old textile worker in 1898 who lived with a tinsmith's family in Stockholm. The family of six had two other boarders, all living in one large room plus a kitchen with a "low ceiling and much decay." Other women chose to live with other single females. Meyerson described the situation of two female factory workers who had rented a room in an attic: "The room was so little that the beds, which were pulled out during my visit, filled nearly the whole room and if one wanted to go out or in through the door, one had to walk over them."[45] For most female industrial workers, meeting basic expenses could mean sacrificing leisure activities, forestalling purchase of clothing, or scrimping on food. Illness or injury that prevented employment could be devastating. To put away any savings under these conditions was extremely difficult.

If Mina had been able to obtain further formal education or training, she might have moved to Gothenburg or Karlstad, the two largest cities near her home province, to work in the gradually expanding Swedish service sector.

But employment as a clerk, secretary, or salesgirl would not have offered her much brighter options than did domestic labor. An investigative survey of Stockholm's female office and shop workers conducted in 1900 found the wages so low that most women lived with or received assistance from their parents to survive. For this reason, most of these workers were Stockholm-born rather than migrants from rural areas. Survey respondents indicated that they typically worked overtime but rarely received extra pay for such work and also complained of having to spend most of their incomes on clothing, because dressing well was a job requirement for many of these positions.[46] Thus, neither industrial employment nor work in the service sector represented better options than employment in domestic service.

Social Activities: "There Would Always Be Dancing"

Describing her move from her native province of Dalsland to Norway, Mina wrote: "The work was hard, but better than at my first position."[47] But as she continued, she did not tell of differences in work tasks or wages but instead described some of the social activities in which she participated. Apparently, Norway was better in part because it allowed Mina more time away from work for social activities. In spite of the many challenges of employment in domestic service in late nineteenth- and early twentieth-century Scandinavia, most servants still had some opportunity for leisure and recreation.

Dancing was one of Mina's favorite pastimes. She fondly recalled dancing in her employer's kitchen when he would play his fiddle some evenings after the work was finished. The polska (a simple Swedish dance in three-quarter time), waltz, and schottische were some of the dances Mina probably performed with her coworkers as well as when she danced elsewhere with her friends. That "a lot of young people . . . always gathered Saturday and Sunday evenings and . . . there would always be dancing" indicates that her own and other Norwegian employers gave their servants regular time off on the weekends.[48]

Mina's description of her teen romance suggests other common social activities for Swedish girls and young women. Mina and her "first love" found great pleasure in being outdoors, wrestling, racing in meadows, and jumping in haystacks. Playing cards was another pastime, probably resorted to when the weather kept them indoors. In searching for domestic positions, Mina may have intentionally avoided the households of Norwegian or Swedish pietists, where dancing and playing cards would have been strictly forbidden and viewed as sinful.[49]

Mina danced and played cards, but she saw moral behavior as an important issue. She was careful to point out in her memoir that she and her dancing partners "behaved properly" at all times. Also indicative of the importance to her of good morals was her consideration of potential spouses. Mina wrote that when her first love "became wild," he "wasn't worth a girl's love."[50] She does not elaborate on her definition of "wild." She may have felt that he could not be trusted to maintain a monogamous relationship, or she may have found the young man emotionally unsupportive.

Economic calculation as well as morality influenced Swedish girls' courtship and marriage decisions. Mina developed a serious relationship with another young man during her time working in Norway. When he became ill with blood poisoning and was eventually permanently disabled, she wrote: "There was no future for one so unfortunate."[51] His work had been manual labor, which he was no longer able to perform, and Mina surely recognized the difficulty they would have had in supporting a family. That her decision to break off the relationship was difficult is also evident in her memoir—she expresses her joy at hearing that her former beau had found success later in life.

The Importance of Social Class: "We Servants Had to Keep to Ourselves"

Mina's writing reveals ways in which class shaped the experiences of young women in Sweden. Her socioeconomic status influenced her activities by determining with whom she could socialize. In describing her dancing, she notes, "We servants of course had to keep to ourselves. The class distinction meant that we were never together with the young sons and daughters of the big farms." And when circumstances unexpectedly placed Mina at a dance with her social superiors—the daughters and sons of landed farmers—others warned her dancing partner that she was "only a servant girl."[52]

The rigid class structure in Sweden influenced young women's marriage options. The potential pool for finding a husband and starting a family decreased as the nineteenth century drew to a close. At the same time that emigration diminished the supply of marriageable males, class divisions further limited young women's marriage options. According to historian Sten Carlsson, young Swedish women could choose to participate in one of two major marriage markets. Those who remained in rural areas usually had a good chance of marrying, but only if they were willing to marry into a lower social class. The remaining young rural males may have been those too poor to emigrate, while the wealthier rural men often chose to migrate to cities or to America. Young women who moved to urban areas were less likely to find a marriage partner. A wife was less essential in an urban setting than in the rural areas, where women assisted in the productive work on the farm, so men felt less urgency to marry. Those few urban women who were able to find partners often married into a higher social class.[53]

Images of America: "You Could Scrape Gold from the Streets"

Mina wrote: "America was the promised land, where everyone who was able should go."[54] Immigration was for Mina the way out of a life that seemed to hold few prospects for the future. Young Swedish women in the late nineteenth and early twentieth centuries had from childhood been exposed to images and detailed information about the United States from a wide variety of sources. Mina's personal documents include little detail about the image of America she had developed prior to her immigration, but the ample evidence contained in documents of other Swedish women illustrates the ideas Mina most likely held about a possible future in the United States.

Ingeborg Frankmar described her decision to emigrate to America as follows: "You thought you could scrape gold [from the streets] with carving knives out there. You heard so much about the wonderful land from those who had been 'over there' and been successful."[55] Even before the era of mass emigration, Swedish journalists and writers had written about the United States in the popular press.[56] After emigration from Sweden to America began in the 1840s and 1850s, publication of travel experiences as well as immigrant letters became more and more common. By the 1880s, when Mina was already longing to go to America and the number of single female emigrants was rapidly increasing, a great deal of information about the United States was available. The images conveyed to Mina and other young women in Sweden were enticing, not only of the economic opportunities but in regard to personal freedoms, social status, marriage opportunities, and even wardrobe.

Books and Newspapers

Articles about the United States, with particular attention to the conditions there for women, appeared in Swedish newspapers of the late nineteenth and early twentieth centuries. *Uppsala Nya Tidning* in the 1890s encouraged the migration of Swedish servant girls, referring to America as "the promised land for domestics."[57] *Östgöten*, a newspaper from east-central Sweden, presented its subscribers with a booklet about America as a premium in 1893. The newspaper's editor, Isidor Kjellberg, had visited the United States in 1890, and in the booklet he shared his impressions. A section entitled "How Servant Girls Have It" provided specific information about working conditions and benefits of domestic service in America. He wrote:

> An average Swedish maid, one who has a basic knowledge of things, but not much experience . . . can have up in the Northwest [the northwestern United States] 2 dollars (about 7 kronor) a week in the beginning. . . . Her wages rise to 2½ dollars as she becomes more familiar with the order of things, and if she can cook, up to 3 dollars a week (over 10 kronor). A really capable and efficient servant—one who is both able and willing to cook, clean rooms, wash and iron, perhaps scrub some floors—gets wages up to 5 dollars (around 18 kronor) a week. Her workday is from 6 A.M. to 7 P.M. (the evening meal is taken here [in America] at 6 P.M.). Every Sunday and Thursday afternoon she is free from all work in service, and she can go out wherever she desires. Christmas presents from one's employer can be expected. Service is not taken for a year or half year, but for a week at a time.[58]

How different from working as a piga in Sweden! Household service in the United States as portrayed here represented significant improvements in wages, hours of work, benefits, length of service, and ability to change positions. Other published brochures and books included similarly sanguine discussions of American domestic work. Oscar Nilsson had traveled for several years in the United States, and, in 1881, in a city not far from Mina's hometown, he published a booklet about Minnesota. In it he counseled: "Young Swedish women who are clever at household tasks have a good future [in Minnesota] and earn two to three dollars a week and free room and board."[59] Similarly, in 1890, Axel E. Lindvall described domestic service in a way that, although somewhat exaggerated with regard to the role of the mistress, made emigration to America sound very appealing for Swedish pigor:

> Among our emigrants the Swedish servant girls are very sought after. As soon as they come to their new place, the young girl is instructed as to how everything should be done, at which point she then manages the house on her own. The lady of the house does not enter the

> kitchen for months, but gives orders from her rocking chair. Servants' tasks are . . . according to what I found in many households, as a rule these: Every Monday washing, Tuesday ironing, Wednesday general scrubbing, Thursday afternoon free, Friday sweeping the house from cellar to attic. . . . The work becomes easy . . . and they [servants] are considered nearly as a member of the family.[60]

Ernst Beckman, in an 1883 publication, singled out Swedish domestics as particularly appropriate candidates for emigration to America: "Servants are perhaps comparatively the best situated of all the waves of emigrants which are carried over the Atlantic."[61] America as depicted in fictionalized accounts of female immigration also contributed to the image of a promised land. A novel entitled *Guld med täljknivar: Roman om svenskamerikaner* (Gold with carving knives: Novel about Swedish Americans) recounted numerous success stories of immigrant Swedes, including one of a servant girl who became an American actress and another who married and settled down happily in the United States.[62]

But some negative depictions also circulated. In 1907, a group of Swedes who saw emigration as a loss of important human resources from the homeland established Nationalföreningen mot Emigrationen (the National Society against Emigration), although most of this organization's efforts were focused on preventing the departure of young men. The lack of concern over the loss of women probably stemmed from a number of factors. Given the role and status of women, especially single women, in Swedish society in the late nineteenth and early twentieth centuries, the loss of women as laborers was not as threatening to industry and business as the loss of male workers. And the number of male migrants typically outnumbered that of female migrants, and women outnumbered men in Sweden. And to argue that immigration did not constitute a significant improvement in these young women's lives would have been a very hard sell.

Still, a few attempts were made to stem the flow of female emigrants.[63] In 1908 the National Society against Emigration published a story entitled *När Maja-Lisa kom hem från Amerika* (When Maja-Lisa came home from America). The story went as follows: Lured by favorable and enticing descriptions of life in the United States in letters from friends, seventeen-year-old Maja-Lisa emigrates to America. She finds employment but is unable to achieve the level of earnings she had expected. In spite of her economic struggles in the United States, in her letters home to Sweden she is careful to give an impression of great success. She plans a visit back home. Hoping to impress her friends and relatives, she spends her hard-earned money on cheap imitations of the latest fashions. Once back in Sweden, she performs admirably: "Naturally the whole village was down at the station when Maja-Lisa Jönsdotter stepped off the train, 'genteel,' a little . . . thinner than before, nose in the air and in every movement a certain something that said, 'It is me to whom the world belongs and I want you to know that.' "[64]

Maja-Lisa returns to America after a two-month visit home, but now she does not even have enough money to claim her luggage. Meanwhile, her influence on the home parish is felt as many young people from the area decide to emigrate. The story closes with the following words of advice: "It is the Maja-Lisas and Anna-Stinas who bring about so much pain, and if one could force them to the truth, maybe the Huldas, Gretas, and Brittas would be convinced that old Sweden, when all is considered, is a pretty good place for them to live—if they only took advantage of the occasions and possibilities that had been offered them."[65]

Other organizations expressed concern for young female emigrants as well. In 1904, the Swedish Society for Temperance and Education (Svenska Sällskapet för Nykterhet och Folkuppfostran) published a pamphlet entitled "Do You Love Your Fatherland?"(Älskar du ditt fosterlandet?). The author had visited the United States, and she related some of her conversations with Swedish Americans, emphasizing the struggles of Swedish immigrants in the United States, their longing for Sweden, and their regrets about emigrating.[66]

These publications may have deterred a few young women from emigrating, but most published works repeated hopeful themes backed up with particulars covering employment opportunities, wages, and work tasks. Detailed information about the United States lay as close as a newspaper vendor, library, or bookstore. But the most influential sources encouraging women to emigrate were more personal—letters, photographs, visits, and purchases.

Letters and Photographs

Immigrant letters represented firsthand accounts of life in America from reliable sources—relatives and friends. Mina evidently maintained correspondence with some relatives in the United States, since she reported that her uncle wrote and offered her a ticket. Like published sources, immigrant letters overflowed with information about the United States, most of it positive where young women were concerned.

Already in the 1850s, a time when traveling to the United States involved an arduous journey of many weeks and only a few thousand Swedes had done so, the image of America for single women was optimistic and hopeful. Female writers focused on their employment and on their views of American society. Maria Janson wrote to her family in 1855: "My employers are excellent and kind people." Several months later she reflected on her immigration: "I have not worked outside a single day; it is not common for women to work out here in this country. . . . Here [there] are absolute equal rights for all and no difference of respect for other persons. After having absorbed the free atmosphere of life in America, I believe I would not be happy in Sweden."[67]

Similarly, a young Swedish immigrant woman in 1850s Chicago wrote home describing her situation in glowing terms. Employed as a domestic, she made a higher wage than she had in Sweden and did not have to perform any outdoor work. According to a pastor in Sweden who read her letter: "She could not wish for anything better, does not miss Sweden, will never regret her going, and only wishes she could get her spinning wheel sent over." She found her rewards in America to be far superior to what they had been at home in Sweden, where she had "worked for twelve *riksdaler* [the Swedish currency until 1873, when the Swedish *krona* was adopted], ate oatmeal bread, and had to sleep in a bunk with a few rags on it."[68]

As Swedish immigration became a mass movement and many more single women joined the immigrant stream, descriptions of America in letters home remained largely favorable. Josefina Larsson wrote to her friend Augusta Nilsson in 1898, urging her to emigrate and writing that domestics in America were respected like everyone else and not debased as they were in Sweden.[69] Less glowing but still encouraging were the remarks of domestic Anna Nygren to her family in 1908: "Work here [in Flatbush, NY] is nearly the same as in Borgholm [Sweden] but I need not work so hard here as I had to there. . . . To come to America is not so dangerous."[70] Women writing home commonly compared their opportunities in America with those back in Sweden. Employment concerns were primary, as evident in the letter Elisabet Olson wrote to her family in January 1913: "I long to go home to Sweden but to be there and work (to go and work as a domestic, I mean), that I certainly won't do because I have it as good here as I can have it. I could not have such a good place in Sweden, with such good pay and nice people to work for and everything."[71] In their letters, Swedish American women responded to questions from relatives back home about the opportunities available in the United States. Olga Johnsson wrote to her father in 1896: "Anders Ols asked if I thought it was profitable for

Ingrid to come here. I said definitely, that for all girls who want to work to get ahead they should come to America."[72]

Just as Mina received a letter from her uncle asking if she would like to emigrate, so did other young Swedish women receive letters encouraging them to leave the homeland. A letter to Anna Israelsdotter read: "Anna, I hear that you are thinking of coming to America. . . . For one who will . . . go and work for others, here is much better than in Sweden."[73] Another young woman wrote to her brother in 1907: "I saw in [cousin] Alma's letter that she will go to Hedrud's and serve. . . . I wrote to her asking if she wanted to come here. . . . She would have it much better here than she can get in Sweden."[74] When Alma did not emigrate, the writer was persistent. A letter in 1909 to her cousin Alma read: "Alma, you never say if you will come here or not. You would have it very good if you came here. Much better than in Sweden."[75] Another nineteen-year-old woman reported that her brother had written many times telling her to emigrate. When an aunt finally sent her a ticket, she felt she could not refuse.[76] A twenty-five-year-old woman from Västernorrland told an interviewer in the early twentieth century that she had asked her friends in the United States many times if conditions were really better there. She told them that she could wait for things to improve in Sweden. The friends responded with assurances of good conditions and the advice that "you will never regret it if you come." Contemplating the hard work she was performing in Sweden and her inability to save any money, in 1907 she finally decided to emigrate.[77]

Some writers may have exaggerated their good fortune in letters home to friends and family, but most conveyed their situations realistically. As more and more young Swedish women immigrated to the United States, writers knew that the information they conveyed could be verified in the letters and visits of other immigrants or from other published sources (newspapers and immigrant guidebooks). Claims of opportunities available and offers of assistance to the potential immigrant—tickets, housing, or help in finding employment—were usually honest and heartfelt.

The photographs that Swedish immigrant women sent home with their letters provided additional evidence that powerfully communicated the benefits of emigration. Often after only a few months in the United States, immigrant women went to studios and had their portraits taken to send home to friends and relatives. To viewers back home, these young women must have appeared utterly transformed. They had seen sisters, friends, and neighbors leave the home village simply dressed, hatless, and in homespun. The images sent home showed the same women in store-bought dresses and wearing fancy hats. It

This image of a single immigrant woman in Pennsylvania was sent back to Sweden, where it inspired another young woman to emigrate. She wrote on the photograph's back that the image had "lured me to America. I thought then that she had such a fine hat and stood in a field of flowers, that I would have it as good."

was not just the clothing that appealed to young Swedish women but also the personal freedom and economic means that the clothing and studio portraits represented. Hats, in particular, were a symbol of social class. In Sweden, only upper-class women were permitted to wear hats. Swedish American women intentionally wore hats for their portraits in order to convey a message of social advancement. Acquisition of a fashionable wardrobe may also have been seen by these women as necessary to attract male suitors.[78]

A Swedish pastor reporting to the government about his parish in 1908 also noted the influence that pictures and other American goods sent to Sweden could have on emigration:

> America is viewed as not such a faraway and unknown land, and it is actually not surprising . . . [that] with modern communications . . . correspondence is very easy. People's parlors are filled up with portraits of friends and relatives from America. American postcards in postcard albums, portraits of American song clubs,

> portraits of workers, portraits of homes in America hang on the walls, American calendars sometimes. In a word, the whole air in the home is filled with "American" and it cannot be anything so strange that the young, who want to earn money . . . go there.[79]

Visits and Purchases

As suggested in *När Maja-Lisa kom hem från Amerika*, the arrival of Swedish Americans returning to Sweden for a visit could also make strong impressions on women's desires to leave the homeland. One woman wrote: "Nearly every Sunday one saw women who had come from America. Their fine hats, suits, high-buttoned shining leather shoes, silk stockings and gloves made an impression on growing-up youth."[80] Another young Swedish woman saw "with clear eyes how good her aunts [visiting from Chicago] had it. They were dressed in the most beautiful hats and clothes, just like fine ladies." When one aunt offered her a loan to purchase a ticket she "did not hesitate a moment to go."[81]

And the economic success of Swedish women in America hit the mark in still other ways. May Vontver emigrated at age seventeen, and by age twenty-one her earnings enabled her to buy a house for her mother in Sweden.[82] Adina Eriksson knew of two sisters from her parish who had emigrated to the United States and earned enough money working as domestics to purchase a home for their parents in Sweden. So impressed was Adina that when one of the sisters came home for a visit, Adina followed her back to the United States.[83] Deciding to emigrate when Swedish Americans visited was not unusual. Many visiting Swedish Americans returned to the United States with one or more new immigrants in tow. Hulda Neslund emigrated to Chicago in the early twentieth century when distant relatives came to visit their hometown area and invited her to return with them.[84] Another young woman reported to a government investigator that she was emigrating with her sister-in-law and brother when they returned after a visit to Sweden.[85] A woman from Blekinge recalled that it was common for young women of her area to leave in the company of friends or relatives who had been home on a visit.[86]

As the amount of information available about Swedish women's experiences in the United States increased, emigration came to be included among the array of possibilities young women considered when they sought better employment. In fact, for Hilda Linder, moving to the United States seemed less daunting than moving to an urban area in Sweden: "I was afraid to travel to the city and seek a servant job because I was too naive. So I thought America was the only way out. There I would learn everything new."[87] She may have feared being perceived as an unsophisticated and uncultured girl from the countryside in a Swedish urban area, but in the United States Linder could enter the economic playing field on equal status with thousands of other young Swedish women who would need to learn a new language, a new culture, and new work routines.

Goals: "Confidence That I Would Improve My Economic Position"

Mina's references to "hard work and disappointment" suggest that she hoped to find in the United States employment that was less physically demanding and more remunerative and that provided adequate free time and a degree of respect. Eva Nydahl, who left Småland in 1907, stated that her primary reason for leaving was to "earn a better living." She knew that job opportunities for young women in America promised real advancement, especially with regard to occupations as domestic servants or seamstresses.[88] C. W. Olson reminisced about her emigration as follows: "I was fifteen years [old] when I left Sweden with confidence that I would improve my economic position."[89]

A section of *Emigrationsutredningen* focusing on female emigrants underscores the primacy of economic concerns as a motivation for emigration. A housing inspector from Stockholm, Kerstin Hesselgren, interviewed numerous female emigrants. Her work resulted in forty-six interview summaries that are included in volume seven of *Emigrationsutredningen*. Many of the interviewees described the difficulty of their work in Sweden and their hopes of improving their lot in America. An eighteen-year-old woman told Hesselgren that she had learned to sew and expected to make a considerable sum of money in America. Another stated that she preferred going to America to serving as a domestic in Sweden. The interviewer also reported on a nineteen-year-old who "left to earn a little more [money] and get something of her own." Another young woman stated: "We girls travel to America because our working time is so horribly long and our wages so small in relation to what everything costs, and we get no respect—a servant is worth nothing [in Sweden]."[90] The prospect of being treated respectfully—in spite of performing relatively low-prestige work—helped draw young Swedish women to the United States. Mina noted that farmers' sons in America were not considered better than others, revealing that the less rigid class hierarchy and mutual respect she found in America were important to her as well.

As immigrant letters home revealed, immigration also represented the opportunity to gain more freedom as well as better pay. Moli Nilsson wrote home about her life as a domestic in the United States, praising the fact that domestics there had "more freedom here than home; when one is finished with work in the evenings one can go and do what one wants."[91] Swedish immigrant domestics in America also had more freedom to search for new positions or move to different regions, because they were not bound by one-year contracts as they had been in the homeland. For some, a desire for adventure and excitement played a role. Hesselgren's interview summaries contain a number of statements that illuminate these desires. She described a twenty-four-year-old as "eager and interested to see a little of the world." Another "had a desire to travel and learn things," and still another had a "desire to look around."[92]

Opportunities to marry well also influenced the decisions of some women to emigrate, and Mina's reference to "disappointment" may in part reflect her desire to find a suitable spouse. Emigration to the United States gradually emerged as a marriage market alternative to rural and urban Sweden as the number of young Swedish men departing from the homeland increased. Oscar Nilsson noted that many young Swedish women who came to America poor were "now fine ladies in the cities or well-off housewives in the country, which is one gift resulting from the preponderant male population's immigration; women have it quite easy in this way to win an independent position and a good home."[93] With the exception of a few years in the 1890s, single men outnumbered single women in the migration stream from Sweden to the United States.[94]

Good marriage prospects in America are also exemplified in the story of a young Swedish woman named Anna. Born in 1880, Anna had grown up in a town in south-central Sweden in a prosperous household where she was not required to perform heavy work or to learn a trade. But this comfortable upbringing limited her options as an adult. She considered domestic work below her status and lacked the skills or higher education that might have enabled her to become self-supporting. Eligible bachelors of her social position were difficult to find in her home region, so her parents decided she should seek a husband in America. At age seventeen she was dispatched to an uncle in Minnesota. Before long she was married to a Swedish American landowner and living on his farm near St. Paul. (It is unknown whether Anna helped with the farmwork in Minnesota, but records indicate that in 1898 she and her husband moved to Alaska in search of gold, where they died in an avalanche.)[95]

An escape from personal problems might also be the goal of emigration. Single women who became pregnant sometimes chose, or were forced, to emigrate to avoid disgrace, ostracism, an unwanted marriage, or other difficult consequences at home. When a young woman named Emma became pregnant and the child's father was deemed "unsuitable," she was sent to America, where she gave birth and eventually married a more "appropriate" man.[96] Another young woman, Alida, emigrated to North America from the district of Gävleborg because she was pregnant. A farmer who needed a wife was willing to pay her ticket and marry her in spite of the pregnancy.[97] Another woman emigrated to Iowa in the 1880s to live with her sister because she was pregnant and was not in love with the child's father.[98]

It is impossible to ascertain the goals behind every individual woman's emigration from Sweden to America, but some of the most common are apparent: to increase economic and social status as well as personal freedom, to experience adventure and excitement, to find a husband, or to escape difficult personal situations. There certainly were other motivations for migration, but these were less prevalent in Mina's experience and in the personal documents examined for this book. Religion motivated some women to emigrate, especially with the earlier migrations, such as in the case of the followers of Eric Jansson in the 1840s, who settled in the community of Bishop Hill, Illinois. A number of women also migrated to the United States in the nineteenth century after joining the Mormon church.[99]

Thus Mina, like thousands of other young Swedish women of her time, decided to emigrate to America. Given women's social and economic status in nineteenth- and early twentieth-century Sweden, the decision made by these women is not difficult to understand. An eighteen-year-old Swedish woman in 1907 succinctly summed up the feelings of quite a few young Swedish women when she told an interviewer she was emigrating because there "was no future and that was why she wanted out."[100] It was in America that many Swedish women saw the opportunity for a better future. As one Swedish doctor observed in 1909, the United States attracted female immigrants when they heard they could "have more time off, have nice clothes, [and] be respected and noticed."[101] When the opportunity to obtain passage to America presented itself, Mina and many others like her embraced it as an offer they could not refuse.

CHAPTER 3

"I Go to America"

Like so many others in the 1880s and 1890s when the immigrant stream to America was at its peak, I had long wished that I would be able to go but could never save enough of my small wages for a ticket. At that time it was hard for poor people in Sweden, and everyone who could possibly scrape together [enough money], or receive a ticket from anyone, went. America was the promised land, where everyone who was able to should go. . . . Sure, it wasn't so much fun to leave those I had worked for who had always been good to me, although I had had to work hard. The last thing I did there [at my employer's] was to set up a weave that was striped. I have often wondered if there were many wrong stripes in that weave, it was hard to keep my thoughts collected.[1]

I came to my home where I stayed a couple of months before I left [for America]. My parents had moved to an estate where my father worked. I had gone to school there, and [I] met many of my school friends and spent a pleasant time in my home. I left Sweden in the month of May and everything was in full bloom. It was so beautiful on the estate and in the area surrounding it. Nothing could be more beautiful than a Nordic spring. It was not fun to leave all that I loved: father, mother, siblings, friends, and land of my forefathers. I walked around in the forest to all the places I had visited as a child. I walked to my childhood home and saw the playhouse my father had helped me to build. An apple tree and a couple of gooseberry bushes that I had planted that had grown and bore fruit—all I had to see and bid farewell to. I became so sad that if I had stayed longer, I think I would have never been able to leave. Thus the day arrived when I tearfully said farewell to all that had been the joy of my childhood and youth.[2]

The Journey to America

When the train rolled out from the station, and father, mother, and siblings were waving good-bye, I burst into unstoppable tears. But youthful courage asserted itself. I wiped away my tears. I was fully determined to forget the old and begin anew. I would go first, clear the way, then bring my siblings here [to America], a promise I later fulfilled. My siblings came, and when my father died, my mother came, too.

We stopped in Gothenburg for three days. I had never been in a Swedish city, since I had stayed for many years in Norway. A few other immigrants and I did sightseeing in Gothenburg. We traveled by trolley, which at that time was pulled by horses. We saw Haga Park, the Garden Association, and other places. I still remember an episode from the hotel. A girl who worked in Gothenburg came to the hotel to say good-bye to some acquaintances. She brought an accordion with her and somebody asked her to play and sing. She had a beautiful singing voice and sang Tegnér's poem from Frithiof's saga.[3] *"Hail to you, you high north. I'm not allowed to stay upon your soil. I am proud to count you as my ancestor. Now nurse of heroes, farewell, farewell." She sang and played the entire song. When she was finished, there were not many dry eyes in the entire flock of emigrants. She was from Småland and the Smålanningar [people from Småland] felt proud of her. She was also good-looking. One Smålanning said, "Such girls they have in Småland!"*

I traveled alone without any companions that I knew. We went by an old ship called Romeo *to Hull in England. We had a severe storm in the North Sea. When we had come out into the Skagerrak [the strait in the North Sea between Norway and Denmark], the waves started to break over the small ship, and some of us who had stayed on deck were told to go down belowdecks so that tarps could be spread over the hatch. It turned out to be a stormy night. We were all seasick and cried Ullrik [euphemism for vomiting] all night. Some idiot had opened one of the portholes so that the water was streaming in. Somebody had enough sense to close it, but we ended up with a couple inches of water on the floor. All the single women were sharing one large room. I remember an older woman who had packed some fine [china] cups in her bag. It stood on the floor, and when the boat tossed and turned, it floated from one side of the room to the other. Of course the cups were crushed to pieces and lay there rattling. She was too seasick to get up and take care of them and she just lay there and moaned about her fine cups. The whole thing looked quite funny.*

We could not eat anything—they gave us coarse bread with butter, but we were not given coffee. It was storming too hard so they could not

This English "feeder" ship carried emigrants from Sweden to England, for transfer to transatlantic steamers. Shown here departing Gothenburg in 1881, the *Romeo* held almost 800 passengers in steerage class. When Mina, traveling in steerage, left Gothenburg, the ship's deck would have been crowded with immigrants waving hands and handkerchiefs to friends and relatives.

prepare it. When, after much rolling and seasickness, we finally arrived at Hull and the ship stopped, we got well in a hurry. I remember that they served pea soup, and the cook said that it was thin because seawater had sloshed into the pot. That was a joke of course; perhaps he thought that we were stupid enough to believe it.

We traveled by train from Hull to Liverpool. I still remember how England was both beautiful and ugly. The countryside was beautiful with its green fields, with hawthorn hedges instead of fences. We also traveled through the mining district with its soot and its many tunnels. We stayed in Liverpool for three days and waited for the transatlantic steamer. We were in the White Star Line Hotel, and there was a hall where we danced each evening until late at night. I danced myself out then. I have not danced like that since I came here [to America].

The last day we were there, the agent who was taking care of us woke us at three o'clock in the morning. We sat out-of-doors, on a fence next to the sidewalk, and waited for the agent who was going to bring us to the train that took us to Alexandria Dock. I sat and nodded and slept. Then the agent came and poked me in the side and said with a smile, "You should not have danced so much yesterday evening, then you would have been able to keep yourself awake now." He was a young man from Stockholm and he often came in and danced with the emigrants. The boat was ready to depart and after a couple hours' train travel we arrived at Alexandria Dock, bade farewell to the Old World, and stepped toward the great unknown. We were over 400 Scandinavian immigrants on board the ship. There were over a thousand emigrants on that ship from all countries of Europe. There was dancing on board the ship also. But a few others and I suffered from seasickness so we kept quiet. The wind blew hard for the most part so it was not a pleasant voyage.

We landed in New York on June 14, and it was very hot. We had to stand in line for four hours at Castle Garden[4] *before our papers were looked through, and then we were sent out by different railroads to our destinations. We traveled by so-called immigrant trains to Chicago, all who were going to the Northwest. There were only hard wooden benches to sit and lie on. In Chicago we were sent here and there, then we were able to travel by ordinary passenger compartments. I ended up the only immigrant in a small station in northern Wisconsin in the middle of the night. I was going to change trains there to go to Wausau, which was my destination. There was, I think, a boardinghouse there where I would have been able to stay. The agent probably tried to tell me that but I did not understand him. I sat in the waiting room until eight in the morning. I had a bit of dry bread left in my knapsack. I ate a little of it and then I went behind the station and shook the rest of the crumbs from my bag. I understood from my ticket that the next stop was my destination. I was very thirsty and there was no water at the station. I saw the agent come with a bucket of water and take it into the ticket office. Resolutely I followed him and helped myself. The agent looked at me and smiled.*

Journey's End

After a couple of hours of travel I had arrived at my destination. There was no one I knew there to meet me. My relative who had sent me a ticket lived twelve miles from town, but he had spoken to a family whom he knew in town and asked them to take care of me when I came. I arrived just at the dinner hour. The husband in the family was working at a lumberyard quite close to the station, and when he saw them unload my Swedish chest he came to meet me and showed me the way to his home. I had to stay there until Sunday when they had time to bring me to where I was going. Then they rented a horse and carriage and drove me there.[5]

MINA FOUND IT DIFFICULT TO CONCENTRATE ON HER WEAVING work as she began to plan for her emigration to America. Her memoir suggests the mix of emotions that filled her mind. She felt excitement and optimism that her long-held dream of emigration to the "promised land" of America would be fulfilled. But she understood that realizing that dream also meant leaving friends, family, and homeland. After she spent several weeks revisiting the people and places of her childhood home, the ensuing melancholy made her departure both challenging and painful.

Yet Mina overcame her sadness about leaving and joined the thousands of young Swedes emigrating to America in the late nineteenth and early twentieth centuries. Her recollections, along with details from the experiences of other young women like her, show how single women's emigration fits into the broader patterns of Swedish migration, what issues and concerns young Swedish women who chose to emigrate faced, and what they experienced on their journeys to their American destinations.

Patterns of Swedish Female Emigration: "Like So Many Others in the 1880s and 1890s"

Mina's emigration in 1890 followed shortly after peak emigration years in 1881–82 and 1887–88, when agricultural crises in Sweden and high demands for labor in the United States caused many to journey to America.[6] Mina left Sweden during what historians have identified as the third of five phases of Swedish mass migration. The phases are distinguishable not only by periodic increases and decreases in the number of migrants but also by the motivations for migration and the demographic characteristics of the emigrants.[7]

About 15,000 emigrants left Sweden in the first phase, which lasted from approximately 1845 to 1855. Primarily a family migration, it included many landed farmers who saw in the American Midwest the opportunity to improve their economic status while continuing to make their living from the land.

Many migrants in this phase were also members of religious sects who left in part because of ostracism by the Swedish government and the Lutheran state church. The followers of Eric Jansson, who established the colony of Bishop Hill, Illinois, in 1846, are one example of this early religious and agricultural migration. To travel in groups of families from a specific region to a particular destination in America, as did the waves of Janssonists, was common in this era.[8] The provinces from which most of these early emigrants were drawn included Östergötland, Småland, and Blekinge, areas where the agricultural economy was especially poor, as well as parts of Hälsingland, Dalarna, and Uppland, centers of religious conflict.

Female emigrants during this phase were primarily wives and daughters of landed farmers. (Married couples and children made up 60 percent and single women 12.5 percent of the Swedish emigrants in the 1850s.)[9] As with Vilhelm Moberg's Kristina, these wives and daughters were not the primary decision makers regarding the family's emigration and often emigrated not because of their own desire but by virtue of their obligation to obey their husbands or fathers. The circumstances faced by early female emigrants could be challenging and at times traumatic, illustrated in the situation that confronted several families of early migrants from Jönköping County in the early 1850s. When this group arrived at Gothenburg, their port of departure, they discovered they had only enough money to pay for the passage of the adult males in the group. The women and children remained in Gothenburg, subsisting by begging or eating the refuse they found in the fishing harbor, until their male relatives sent them tickets to America. The tickets the women and children had been sent took them only to Philadelphia, and upon arrival there the destitute travelers, which included a woman with a newborn child, found themselves alone in rainy weather with no roof over their heads. Sympathetic strangers took pity on them and provided shelter. After three days a local Swedish American collected funds to pay for their journey on to Chicago, where the men were staying. Once sufficient funds were gathered, the group finally arrived at their original destination—a forest region in Michigan. Throughout the era of mass emigration, but especially in the earlier phases, it was common for a husband and father to travel to America first to obtain land or employment, earn some money, and eventually send tickets to Sweden to allow the family to reunite. Women who were left behind to struggle to support themselves, and often a number of children as well, were referred to as "America widows."[10]

The second phase of Swedish mass migration, occurring from 1868 to 1873, included over 100,000 emigrants and was set off by crop failures in Sweden in 1867 and 1868. Information networks established with migrants of the earlier phase increased knowledge about agricultural opportunities in the United States, and the Homestead Act of 1862 tempted many rural Swedes with offers of free land. Like the first phase, this second phase still included considerable family migration, but the emigrants' social and economic backgrounds differed from those of the first phase. Now not only landowners but also members of the growing landless classes emigrated to America, including farmhands and rural domestic servants. No longer limited to very specific regions in Sweden, the migration spread over the entire country. It was during this second phase of mass migration that Swedes from Mina's home province of Dalsland began to emigrate in significant numbers, with about 700 Dalbon traveling to the United States in 1869 following the crop failures and famine of 1868 (another 400 migrated to Norway).[11]

The years 1879 to 1893 marked the third phase of Swedish mass migration. Close to half a million (493,000) Swedes emigrated to the United States over these fifteen years. Mina Anderson was one of nearly 16,000 who emigrated from Dalsland at this time. Economic difficulties in Sweden continued to be a primary motivation for leaving the homeland, but although Swedes in the earlier phases mostly sought to acquire land and to farm in the United States, many in this third phase responded to the needs of America's urban industrial labor market and sought employment as industrial workers or as servants in urban households. This phase also marked a significant shift in the composition of migration, which now contained mostly single adults. An economic downturn in the American economy in the 1890s brought this phase to an end.[12]

Entering the United States in New York, young Swedish women frequently traveled inland by train, often to relatives or friends waiting in the Midwest. These two Swedish girls on their way to Wisconsin in 1902 wear the headscarves and traditional clothing that indicate their very recent arrival. (*The World's Work*, October 1902)

The fourth phase of Swedish mass migration lasted from 1900 to the beginning of World War I. Although the number of Swedish immigrants entering the United States during these years was lower than in the third phase (approximately 289,000 as opposed to 493,000), the characteristics of this fourth migration phase were very similar to those of phase three, with large numbers of single labor migrants making up the bulk of this emigrant stream. During these years about 8,500 young men and women emigrated from Dalsland to America.

During the fifth and final phase of Swedish mass migration, the 1920s, over 100,000 Swedes entered the United States. The tendency for single laborers to migrate found in phases three and four continued, but this fifth phase included significantly more male than female migrants (with a ratio at times of three males for every female). The decrease in the proportion of female migrants in this phase resulted from increasing economic opportunities for women in Sweden after World War I and decreasing opportunities for them in the United States. (For example, a 1923 Swedish civil service reform opened up upper-level state jobs for women, adding to the growing numbers of women already in public sector positions.)[13] Emigration from Dalsland did not make up a significant proportion of this phase.

According to Swedish emigration records, women were more likely than men to leave the homeland from an urban area. But many of these women leaving Swedish towns and cities had been born and raised in rural Sweden. Just as Mina had migrated to Norway in search of better employment, so did other young Swedish women migrate to urban areas to improve their economic status. When, after a number of months or years, they experienced little advancement and had the economic means to emigrate, many decided to try their luck in the United States.[14] (See Appendix, Table 3, which shows the proportion of single adult women emigrating primarily to the United States between 1861 and 1930.)

As the statistics reveal, single adult male migrants usually outnumbered single adult female migrants. The number of single women emigrating did, however, increase significantly from the 1860s through the next three decades, and their numbers exceeded those of single males for a few years in the 1890s. The overall dominance of males among Swedish emigrants has several explanations. Historian Hans Norman points out that women were less likely to migrate during the early phases because emigration at that time was a "hazardous, physically daring enterprise."[15] However, while knowledge of the difficulty of the journey probably discouraged some women from emigrating, even in the early phases of mass migration a combination of factors influenced their decisions. The economic and legal status of women in Sweden, information about the migration process, and family reactions all shaped women's choices regarding emigration throughout the decades of Swedish mass migration to America. The differences in migration between the sexes stemmed from how these factors interacted in individual Swedish women's lives and how their situations compared to that of Swedish men.

Financing Female Emigration: "My Uncle in America"

Mina had hoped to emigrate long before she had the means to do so. Those characteristics of life in Sweden that made young women want to leave were often the same characteristics that made it difficult for them to do so. It was hard for single women like Mina to save enough money to purchase tickets to America. This point is well illustrated in an analysis of female emigrants' ticket financing. In a study of the forty-six women interviewed in 1907 as part of *Emigrationsutredningen,* Ann-Sofie Kälvemark found that the tickets of twenty-five of the women were paid for by relatives in the United States, and two were paid for by relatives in Sweden. A former employer who had emigrated had purchased one woman's ticket to America, and Swedish American girlfriends of another woman had pooled their earnings as domestics in the United States to pay for her passage. Only five of the women interviewed paid for their ticket themselves, and one of these had been able to purchase a ticket only after receiving an inheritance. (Twelve interviewees did not provide information about payment of their tickets.)[16]

According to a collection of immigrant questionnaires gathered by Swedish ethnologist Albin Widén in the 1940s (including one completed by Mina), most women had relied on the assistance of others to purchase passage to America. When asked, "How did you obtain the money for your ticket?," fourteen of the nineteen female respondents indicated they had obtained their tickets with the help of relatives. Mina's answer: "From my uncle in America." Another three women wrote of obtaining loans to finance their tickets, including Sylvia Malmberg Brown, who had "borrowed from [a] bank." Only two of the nineteen women had financed their tickets entirely with their own money. The first, Alfrida Nilson, had saved up her wages and tips for the ticket; the second, Svea Erikson, wrote simply that she had "saved it myself."[17] Anna Håkansson emigrated in 1893, and she borrowed from relatives and friends as follows: thirty kronor from a brother, twenty kronor from another brother, fifty kronor from her father, forty kronor from her sister, and thirty kronor from her traveling companion.[18]

The fifty-nine Swedish immigrant men responding to the ticket-financing question were better able to purchase tickets on their own. Although slightly less than half of the men had financed their tickets through a relative, nearly one-third were able to pay for their tickets with their own money. One of these, Axel Renberg, responded that he had "saved [for] my own ticket." Jack Pearson wrote that he had financed the ticket "[through my] own economy." Seven men indicated borrowing money from a nonrelated individual or a bank in order to finance their journey, and there was one instance of contract labor.[19] Though Swedish women almost certainly had as strong a desire to emigrate as Swedish men, they had greater economic difficulty in acting upon that desire.

Preparing for the Journey: "I Had with Me a Little Blue Wooden Chest"

Guidebooks to assist Swedes in transit to the United States had been published even by the first phase of migration, and many others became widely available by the late nineteenth century. Agents of steamship and railroad lines frequently distributed them, as did immigration representatives from states in America wanting to encourage immigration. The guidebook *Vägledning för svenska utvandrare till Amerika* (A guide for Swedish emigrants to America), distributed by several steamship lines in 1890, was typical. It answered questions such as "Who should emigrate?" and "How should one be equipped to travel to America?" and described "The journey over the Atlantic Ocean." Readers received instructions on what items to pack for the journey; for example, the guidebook stated that a third-class (steerage) passenger should bring for use on board a plate, cup, water container, silverware, mattress, and sheets. The schedule for the journey was described in detail, as were the different passenger ships owned by the steam lines. The guidebook concluded with "advice for those who wish to obtain land in America" and a word and phrase list with Swedish-English translations and pronunciations.[20] Guidebooks also contained information geared toward female emigrants. *Vägledning*, for example, included in its phrase list questions such as "Are you in need of a servant-girl?" and "Can you sew with a sewing machine?"[21] Mina did not write about consulting guidebooks, but she might well have done so as part of her preparations.

Before departing for America, Mina traveled from Norway back to her native Dalsland. Her memoir intimates that she wanted to put things in or-

36

Svenska.	Engelska.	Uttalen.
Jag betalar mitt arbetsfolk, efter hvad de uträttar.	I pay my labourers according to the work the do.	Ej pä mej läbörers, äckårding to the oåark the do.
Hvad är Ert yrke?	What are you by trade?	Watt ahr ju bej trähd?
Jag är Skräddaregesäll (Skomakaregesäll, Snickaregesäll).	I am a tailor, (shoemaker, joiner).	Ej äm ä tähler, (Shoumäker, djöiner).
Har Ni arbetat här i staden?	Have you been working in this town?	Hävv ju binn vårking in dhis taun?
Jag har arbetat på flera verkstäder.	I have been employed in several workshops.	Ej hävv binn vårking in sevorell oårkschapps.
Behöfver Ni någon tjenstepiga?	Are you in need of a servant-girl (maid-servant?).	Ahr ju in nihd öv ä sörventgörl (mähdsörvänt?).
Kan Ni stryka?	Can you iron?	Kän ju ejren?
Kan Ni laga mat?	Can you cook?	Kän ju kauck?
Kan Ni sy med symaskin?	Can oyu sew with the sewing-machine?	Kän ju si hit dhe såingmäskin?
Hur länge har Ni varit här i landet?	How long have you been in this country?	Hau lång hävv ju binn din dhisköntri?
Ett år; ett halft år; tre månader.	A year; half a year; three months.	Ä jihr; häff ä jihr; tri månts.
Kan Ni tala Engelska?	Can you speak English?	Ka ju spik inglisch?
Ja litet, min Fru.	Yes, madam, a little.	Jess, mäddäm, ä littel.

Shipping lines distributed emigrant guidebooks containing travel information and useful phrases for adjusting to life in the United States. The first column on this page lists a phrase in Swedish, the second column its counterpart in English, and the third column a phonetic pronunciation of the English phrase for a Swedish speaker. (Joachim Prahl, *Vägledning för svenska utvandrare till Amerika*, Helsingborg, 1890)

der for her journey and to bid farewell to the places of her Swedish childhood rather than to seek her family's blessing or financial assistance for her emigration. Young women like Mina who had been on their own since their mid-teens had made their own decisions in the few areas where single Swedish females could exercise some agency—changing employers or moving about geographically in search of better positions. The families of young Swedish women perhaps felt concern for their welfare and safety regarding emigration and did not want them to travel so far away, but there was little to prevent a daughter or sister from emigrating if she had the means to do so. Though a legal dependent living at home required parental permission to seek employment outside the family home, after once obtaining permission to move outside the parental household, young workers could move about without a parent's consent.[22] When Anna J. Olson's parents refused to help her finance her emigration because they did not want her to leave Sweden, she borrowed money from an uncle to make the trip.[23] Alfrida Nilson, when asked about her family's response to the idea of her emigration, replied, "*Det var mitt eget beslut*" (it was my own decision). Acknowledgment of young women's independence is also suggested in the response Mina's family had offered when she announced her decision to emigrate: "*Res bara om du får det bättre*" (go only if you will have things better).

Swedish daughters who remained at home had less freedom to choose their destinies. From 1858 to 1883 single women over twenty-five could achieve legal majority status only if they made an official request to authorities. The opportunity for independent decisions improved when in 1884 new legislation gave single women majority status at age twenty-one.[24] Family financial support was also a more significant issue for landed daughters. There was greater concern about "marrying well" for these young women when inheritance and transfer of property were involved. As the propertyless classes in Sweden grew, class divisions increased and these landed daughters were less likely to seek domestic employment than their landless counterparts (not wanting to be mistaken for one of them). They were thus less independent—socially as well as financially—than daughters in landless families and may have looked to their families to purchase their tickets as well as offer their consent.[25] The extent of such cases is unknown, but certainly not all young Swedish women who desired to emigrate were allowed to do so. Pernilla Ingvarsdotter wanted to join several of her siblings who had emigrated to the United States, but her father would not allow it because he needed her help to operate the family farm. (Her desire to emigrate remained with her over the years, however, even after she had married and raised children. She finally was able to fulfill her desire at the age of eighty-nine, when she joined her ten children already in America. She died at age ninety-five and was laid to rest in Galesburg, Illinois, fulfilling her long-held desire to be buried in America.)[26]

The emigration decisions of Swedish women were usually contingent upon financial or familial situations, but Swedish men faced some additional legal restrictions. The government was concerned about the loss of men and the financial support they might provide (not surprising given the nature of Sweden's patriarchal society in the nineteenth century). As one 1903 article pointed out, a petition against emigration had been presented in the Swedish parliament that talked about the loss of Sweden's sons, "but of the nation's daughters not a word was said."[27] By the 1860s, statutes barred Swedish men from emigrating if it meant leaving a family behind that relied on local poor relief or if they had unpaid debts. As the number of single male emigrants increased, the government, in the 1880s, also strengthened regulations forbidding young men who had not performed their obligatory military service to emigrate until their service was completed. A number of males emigrated illegally, perhaps motivated by a desire to avoid military service.[28]

In preparing for her journey, Mina would have packed her most precious and useful belongings, as well as some clothing and food supplies, in a sturdy wooden trunk or chest. Her "America chest" has not survived to the present day, but a grandchild recalled its having been stored in the rural Minnesota home where she lived most of her days—a wooden trunk with metal bands, latch, and trim.[29] Mina did not write about her trunk's contents, but she probably packed items similar to those described by a woman emigrating in 1904: "I had with me a little blue wooden chest and on the cover stood painted in gold letters my name and the address of my sister. In the chest was found favorite undergarments and a lot of food that my dear mother sent with me, it was knäckebröd and herring among other things, that should be eaten on the trip. As clothes I had a dark blue dress with frills, leather boots, a coat with wide arms and a big wide collar and a cap on my head."[30]

Chain Migration: "I Think That I Untied a Knot"

Though Mina found it difficult to leave her homeland, she calmed herself by setting a clear goal: "I would go first, clear the way, then bring my siblings here [to America], a promise I later fulfilled. My siblings came, and when my father died, my mother came, too."[31] Her goals included "having things better" for herself and for her family members as well. Mina's migration, made possible through her uncle, and the eventual migration of much of Mina's family, were an example of what immigration authorities at the time and scholars since have termed "chain migration," patterns of migration in which family, community, or other related groups move from one geographic location to another over time, such as from Sweden to America. In chain migration, personal connections—between friends, relatives, neighbors, or coworkers—influence both the decision to emigrate and the emigrant's destination. Mina's participation in chain migration fits one of the most common types. One family member emigrated, settled, found employment (or operated a farm or business), and saved money to support the emigration of other family members. Some of these migration chains centered on Swedish emigrant women. Soon after her own immigration to America at age fourteen in 1884, Maria Elfström began to save money to help the rest of her family join her. By early 1895 she had assisted four of her siblings (three sisters and a brother) to emigrate, and she purchased tickets for her mother and two remaining siblings later that year.[32] Tilda Northen immigrated to Sioux City, Iowa, in 1885 and then brought over one sister in 1887 and another in 1891.[33]

Often occurring simultaneously with family-based chain migration was community- or neighborhood-based chain migration. Robert Ostergren studied geographically based chain migration from the Rättvik region of Sweden to Isanti County, Minnesota.[34] Like family-based chain migration, geographically based chain migrations were motivated by the desire to maintain relationships with family, friends, and neighbors who had already emigrated. Young Swedish immigrant women were savvy about the operation of chain migration. Elisabet Olson wrote to her family in 1913 about the number of young people leaving her home area. She speculated that her own migration had influenced others: "I think that I untied a knot."[35] Ida Petersson's words illustrate the other side of this connection. She wrote of her emigration in 1909: "One after the other of my comrades and best friends left their homes and went away to the great land in the west. I missed them a lot and so I began to brood and wonder how I ever could get there."[36] Although young women's emigration was rarely motivated solely by a desire to maintain close relationships with family or friends, it certainly encouraged their departures.[37]

The Voyage: "We Had All Left Our Loved Ones Behind Us"

Ticket, documents, and baggage in hand, Mina began her voyage at the local railroad station, where she bade farewell to her parents and siblings. Though she made no mention in her documents of receiving parting gifts, it was customary to give flowers to a departing loved one, and leave-taking descriptions and pictures of emigrant women at train stations often included flowers.[38]

Mina's leave-taking was tearful, yet even amid her sadness as the train pulled out of the station, she looked to the future. As she recalled: "I was fully determined to forget the old and begin anew." The journey diary of another young woman who emigrated in 1891 reveals a similar mix of emotions: "Tuesday the 5th of May I left my home to begin my long journey to the land in the west. My family came with me to the city and stayed until the train departed. I felt melancholy when they disappeared from my view. It was wonderful, too, to be on a train. It was the first time I had been on a train. I thought it was so fun to go, and I saw so much beauty during the trip to Gothenburg."[39]

Waiting for her ship to depart, Mina spent a few days in Gothenburg. This interlude before boarding ship was typical, and some of the time was spent completing official papers or medical exams. Emigrants had to show a *flyttningsbetyg* as well as a ticket and medical form to the police office in their port of departure in order to leave the country. If it was an emigrant's first visit to a large city, as it was for Mina, the time gave the opportunity to sightsee and explore. Mina and some new acquaintances passed the hours visiting several of Gothenburg's outdoor attractions, especially beautiful during the Swedish springtime. Although sightseeing might keep emigrants' minds occupied with things other than homesickness for a time, during this waiting period they often also experienced waves of both nationalism and nostalgia. When Mina recalled a young woman visiting her hotel and performing a traditional song, she noted, "There were not many dry eyes in the entire flock of emigrants."[40]

Not all of the songs the emigrants sang rang with nostalgia. As the era of Swedish mass migration progressed, so did the number of emigrant songs. Some warned of the dangers of emigration; others celebrated the act of emigration with lyrics painting a rosy image of the United States.[41] One popular song of the latter sort was entitled "Amerikalekan."

"Amerikalekan"

Roligt roligt ska vi ha, att resa till Amerika, till den stora, gyllne stad söka där vår lycka.	Jolly, jolly shall it be to travel to America to the great golden city where we seek our luck.
Staden är av bara guld gatorna av socker staden är av flickor full dejeliga dockor.	The city is of pure gold the streets are of sugar the city is full of girls lovely dolls.

According to May Vontver, who ventured to the United States at age seventeen in 1908, young Swedish children, especially little girls, sang this song as a rhyming song similar to "Ring Around the Rosie."[42] Singing such songs may have planted the idea of emigration in the minds of Swedish girls at an early age. Another immigrant woman, Nina Svärd, recalled singing similar verses as she left on her journey to the United States in 1904.[43]

The mode of transportation used and the particular routes traveled by young women from Sweden to America varied across the different phases of mass migration. In the first phase, before 1860, women, usually in family groups, journeyed on clipper ships that traveled directly from a Swedish to an American port. It was an arduous trip; the immigrants might be at sea from ten to twelve weeks depending on the wind and weather. Conditions were usually poor on these ships. Passenger holds were crowded and had poor ventilation and limited supplies of food and water. Many people did not survive such a voyage.[44]

Mina left Sweden via a steamship departing from Gothenburg. When steamships came into use in the second, third, and fourth phases of Swedish migration (from the 1860s through World War I), the journey was significantly shorter, usually lasting from ten to fourteen days, even though it was split into two segments, Sweden to England and England to New York. Most emigrants during these years followed a path similar to Mina's, boarding ships in Swedish ports that took them across the North Sea to Hull on the eastern coast of England. The prevailing winds and currents usually made for rough waters during this passage.[45] Many emigrant women's accounts of the North Sea voyage are filled with descriptions of, as Mina did, becoming seasick and spending much of the two-day journey crying "Ullrik."[46] From Hull, a train transported the emigrants to Liverpool, where the steamships bound for America lay in port. In addition to Gothenburg on the western coast, common ports of departure for Swedish emigrant women included Christiania (Oslo), Norway, in the west; Malmö, Sweden, and Copenhagen in the south; and Stockholm in the east. (A smaller number of emigrants, mostly from southern Sweden, traveled to Germany and then sailed from Hamburg or Bremen to America.)[47] By the fifth phase of migration, steamship passenger lines had been developed that transported emigrants directly from Gothenburg to New York. The Swedish American Line transported immigrants beginning in 1914.[48]

Mina traveled to Hull on the steamship *Romeo,* leaving Gothenburg on May 30, 1890. As a young woman traveling alone, she shared a room on board with several other single women. Though she referred to it as an "old ship," *Romeo* was at the time of her emigration only nine years old. It had been built by the Wilson Line, one of the major English "feeder ship" companies operating out of England, in 1881. Feeder ships transported emigrants from their homelands to England, "feeding" them into the transatlantic steamer lines. Clearly designed for the task of transporting emigrants, *Romeo* had passenger space for 38 in first-class accommodations, 18 in second-class, and 780 in steerage. *Romeo* may have appeared old to Mina because of the heavy use it had received during the 1880s.[49]

Though Mina writes that she "traveled alone without any companions," hers was not a lonely or isolated sojourn.[50] Twenty-three years old when she emigrated, Mina boarded ship with many other Swedish women about her age. Between the years 1861 and 1915, women from twenty to twenty-four years of age made up the largest proportion of female Swedish emigrants, ranging from 19 percent of the female Swedish emigrants in the 1860s to about 25 percent in the remaining decades. Women ages fifteen to nineteen and twenty-five to twenty-nine also made up a significant proportion of emigrating Swedish females; the bulk of the male emigration from Sweden was also in the age group fifteen to thirty.[51]

The journey from Liverpool to America could range from sustained misery to pleasant ease. Misery meant seasickness, which had plagued Mina and others already on the North Sea passage, and which for some, including Mina, continued, making the transatlantic voyage grueling. In spite of the availability of potential partners, there was no dancing for Mina on board ship. Seasickness could last the entire voyage, as it did for Anna J. Olson in 1903, making the misery interminable. She wrote: "The boat I took to New York was named *New York*. We were seven in the cabin. The trip took nine days. I was seasick the whole time both day and night. I didn't eat any food on the whole trip." Another woman recalled of her voyage that "we were all so sick we didn't care about anything, we vomited over everything."[52]

The quality of Swedish emigrant women's accommodations and food, as well as the sociability of roommates, also shaped the way in which young women experienced the journey. Most Swedish emigrants traveled in steerage class, but steerage conditions could vary greatly. Nina Svärd was one of the fewer numbers of Swedish emigrant women traveling to America via a transatlantic voyage from Hamburg, Germany, in 1904. She boarded the *Moltke* and was assigned a room with twelve bunks and no bedding (she had thought that bedding was included in the passage price). Social interaction was difficult because her roommates were German and Polish. She found the dining arrangements especially disagreeable: "We got the same food every day; it was in a big pot with food placed on the floor; there was no dining area. It was sauerkraut and green cabbage and red cabbage. It was awful. We got dry sourdough bread, no butter, no coffee. There was no milk, either."[53] Swedish emigrant women traveling from Liverpool were more likely to be able to communicate with their fellow passengers. On Mina's transatlantic voyage, of over 1,000 emigrants on board, about 400 of them were Scandinavian.

Some Swedish women found the journey quite agreeable. Hilma Svenson enjoyed her voyage from Jönköping to Chicago in 1901. She wrote in her diary that her room on board ship was scrubbed every day and kept "clean and neat." She and her roommates "cooked coffee in our coffeepot two times a day. When it was cooked we got good cakes from the baker on the boat. All the crew were so polite to us. We got good food and service the whole time. . . . Slept well all nights."[54]

Others especially appreciated the music and dancing on deck. Opportunities for recreation and socializing on board could lift spirits. One woman, traveling with seventeen other young men and women from her village, wrote: "We had all left our loved ones behind us, our hearts were heavy, but just then one of the boys got up with an accordion and it got lively on deck, then dancing began and we all got to know one another."[55]

Arrival in America: "I Thought I Was in Heaven"

On June 14, 1890, Mina Anderson landed in New York harbor. After gathering her belongings, she joined the other steerage passengers and was led to the Barge Office, the central U.S. port of entry for immigrants from April 1890, when Castle Garden (where immigrants entering New York City had been processed since 1855) was closed, until January 1892, when Ellis Island opened. Like the ocean passage, the process of officially entering the United States could be good, bad, or, as it was for Mina, indifferent. Following her long, seasick journey, Mina stood in line in hot weather for four hours to complete the process of officially entering the United States. For women who had experienced an especially difficult ocean voyage, immigrant processing could represent welcome safety and shelter. Nina Svärd, who had complained bitterly about her journey from Sweden via Germany, remembered Ellis Island in 1904 as "warm and good. . . . It was a long row of beds, with warm blankets where we lay down all together. I can remember we all got a big mug and a

Castle Garden, located on Manhattan Island's southern tip, served as an immigrant landing depot from August 1855 through April 1890. Many Swedish immigrants entered the United States through Castle Garden, shown here in 1884. (*Harper's Magazine*, June 1884)

big roll, and it was good; I thought I was in heaven; I had not eaten any food for sixteen days."[56]

Arriving immigrants were required to pass a customs inspection and then face a series of questions and examinations to determine their "fitness" to remain in America. The primary job of officials was to prevent individuals who were likely to become a public charge due to physical or mental disabilities from entering the United States and to admit those likely to be productive members of the industrial labor force. But biased determinations by officials regarding morality or political views also influenced whether or not a particular immigrant was allowed to enter.[57] The Ellis Island experience of a Swedish immigrant named Selma (her surname is unknown) in 1892 provides an example of a relatively smooth entrance process:

> At 7 o'clock on Sunday morning we were able to debark; our trunks were now opened. . . . For me the customs inspection was soon in order; he only looked in a corner and I was able to close it [her trunk]. . . . Now we were taken with our things to an island. . . . One had to go through 5 different areas, [where] we were questioned about our origin, where we were going, how much money we had, etc., one at a time. I answered that I had what I needed, was asked how much, 20 dollars I said though I didn't have more than 12. Then I was able to go. We left New York at 8 o'clock Sunday evening.[58]

Thus "fitness" included having some cash on hand (or having a sponsor who was willing to provide it). The amounts varied over time and were minimal, but they provided some assurance that the immigrant would not immediately become a public charge. The amount of cash on hand also determined the quality of food one could buy, the level of comfort for a journey to an inland destination one could afford, the standard of board and room in the first weeks, and the degree of urgency felt in seeking out paid employment. And just as more male than female emigrants had the money to pay for their own tickets, men were able to bring with them to America larger sums of money than were women. When asked on a survey how much cash they brought with them to the United States, some Swedish immigrants listed amounts in kronor, others in dollars. In whatever currency, males on average brought to the United States considerably more cash than did females. Average in-hand cash amounts for the women were 62 kronor and 25 dollars, while averages for the men were 266 kronor and 318 dollars. Mina brought with her the tidy, and tiny, sum of 10 kronor in cash.[59]

Some women believed immigration officials treated them impersonally, more like animals than humans. One woman recalled her interrogation at Ellis Island in 1916. After asking her a barrage of questions, officials "pin[ned] a paper ticket on me, like they do at a horse show."[60] Other immigrant women remembered being placed in "cages," a reference to the system of gates and enclosures used to sort immigrants into different groups at Ellis Island.[61] Certainly, many found the arrival experience humiliating. Adina Eriksson had traveled on board ship with a friend who had already been in the United States, and after passing through Ellis Island, Adina was left to watch the baggage while her companion made travel arrangements. Her friend told her to say "New York" to anyone who spoke to her. She followed her instructions carefully, but her "New York" was met with mixed responses, including nods as well as laughter. By the time her friend returned, Adina felt ready to turn around and go back to Sweden. She overcame her embarrassment and remained in the United States for many years.[62]

For all immigrants arriving in America, the possibility remained that they might be turned away and sent back to the homeland. Immigrants who appeared to be mentally or physically ill or suffering from contagious diseases could be denied entrance, but such determinations were often subjective.[63] Immigration restriction guidelines also reflected a concern for morality, denying entry to persons who had been sentenced for dishonorable crimes—especially prostitution (prostitutes were restricted already in 1875 under the Page Act). Female immigrants traveling alone were vulnerable to investigation and potential denial of entrance, because entrance officials assumed they were likely to become public charges if they did not have a male present to provide material support.[64]

Even if entrance into the United States went smoothly, Swedish immigrant women still faced danger and risk, especially those who traveled alone and whose immigration did not take place within a network of previously immigrated family or friends. An article by Swedish women's rights activist Gertrud Adelborg in 1904 underscored possible hazards. She described an advertisement that was placed in a Stockholm newspaper stating that female gymnasts could find gainful employment in the United States and listing a contact in Stockholm for further information. Women who pursued the opportunity received an address in New York City as their immigration destination. One prospective emigrant decided to check out the New York address and discovered that the building in question was located in a disreputable neighborhood. The Fredrika Bremer Förbundet, a woman's rights organization (founded in 1884 and still active in the twenty-first century) followed up by sending inquiries to New York officials. Their investigation resulted in the closure of what was discovered to be a brothel. Adelborg's article continued with a discussion of connections between immigration and white slavery and a plea for stronger Swedish governmental control of immigrant agents and advertisements.[65]

Immigrants, like Mina, who were not planning to reside in New York City continued their journey, usually via train, to their final destination. By the late nineteenth century, when an emigrant purchased a ticket to America transportation to the final destination was nearly always included. Because many immigrants chose to settle in Chicago and because Chicago served as a gateway to the transportation lines heading west, travel companies were able to fill entire trains with immigrants traveling from New York City to Chicago. Mina traveled to Chicago on one of these immigrant trains. As her description of the wooden benches implies, the immigrant trains typically operated with goals of profit and efficiency, not of comfort. Only when Mina continued her journey from Chicago to Wausau, the Wisconsin town near her uncle's home, did she travel in more pleasant passenger compartments. She probably would have preferred familiar company to comfort, however, given the lonely night she passed in the Wisconsin train station.

The challenges Mina faced as she was completing the journey to her uncle were typical. That letters might take weeks to travel across the ocean or might become lost, coupled with the mobility of Swedish Americans, meant that miscommunication could occur and that young Swedish women might find themselves alone at their final destinations. Charlotta Jansdotter left Sweden in 1888 at the request (and expense) of Per Johan (Pete) Bergsten, a former resident of her hometown in Dalarna, who hoped to marry her. She expected him to be waiting when she arrived in Schuyler, Nebraska. But, according to a letter she wrote home, the only thing she found in Schuyler was "the confusion of Babylon" (*Babylons förbistring*). She found neither Per nor anyone who spoke Swedish. After twenty-four hours in the train station, she finally found a Dane who could understand her a bit and who helped her find a place to stay. After a few days and with the help of another Dane, she was able to ascertain that Pete had moved to Ogden, Iowa, to open a blacksmith and carpentry business. A telegram and train ride later she finally met up with her future husband—over a week later than expected. Pete had contacted the agent for Charlotta's shipping line to change her ticket, but the task was somehow never completed. The two eventually married and raised four children, ultimately settling in Dunnell, Minnesota. Similarly, Swedish immigrant Ellen Seagren expected to meet her father in an Indiana city, but no one was there to greet or assist her when she arrived.[66]

As Mina's memoir suggests, when a Swedish immigrant woman traveled alone, it was not easy to know whom to trust. One woman recalled suffering much anxiety because her brother-in-law had purchased her ticket during a railway rate war in 1885. The ticket required her to travel from Malmö, Sweden, to Minneapolis via Canada rather than the more common route through Chicago. The Canadian train left her one evening at a small rail station in north Minneapolis, which she described as "only a shack." Alone and unable to speak a word of English, she finally had to trust a Swedish-speaking man who, after striking up a conversation with her, said he lived near her sister. Though the woman had been warned by her father prior to emigration "never to believe any man in America," she felt she had no other choice but to walk with the man from north to south Minneapolis. She recalled her trepidation:

> Every time we came near trees, I got frightened, fearing the man might drag me into the woods. At last we stopped before a large brick building. Half a dozen men were sitting outside. I thought this can certainly not be where my sister lives. This must be a wicked place! So I said to him, 'No, I will not go with you here,' but the man went in. When he opened the door, there stood my brother-in-law and my sister. . . . The men who were sitting outside my sister's home were boarders.[67]

Many Swedish immigrant women journeyed to regions where friends and family had already settled. Swedish immigrants were concentrated heavily in the Midwest because during the earlier phases of immigration, when Swedes were seeking farmland, most of the available land was located there. Many Swedes received 160 acres of land through the Homestead Act of 1862, and midwestern towns and cities developed as settlement and railroad transportation moved westward. Swedish settlements were established, attracting Swedes who were arriving in later phases. Chain migration encouraged this tendency, but even when immigrants lacked friends, relatives, or former neighbors in the United States, going to areas where Swedish Americans lived helped ease the adjustment process of settling in a new land. Arriving in a Swedish American community, a young Swedish woman could seek advice from others who spoke her language, participate in familiar institutions such as Swedish American churches or associations, and enjoy some cultural and leisure activities similar to those in the homeland.

Determining exactly how many Swedish immigrant women traveled to specific Swedish American settlements is difficult. The U.S. Census Bureau only rarely distinguished male and female immigrants in its reports of the censuses of 1860 through 1920 and did not usually differentiate between single and married immigrants. Moreover, Swedish immigrant women like Mina often moved from place to place in search of the best combination of wages, work tasks, and social life they could find, just as they had done in Sweden. Single women in the later phases of Swedish immigration settled not only in numerous towns and cities and in the large urban areas of the Midwest, including Chicago, Minneapolis, and Duluth, but also in large cities on the East and West Coasts such as New York, Boston, Worcester, and Seattle.[68]

Census data do, however, reveal that Swedish women more often settled in towns and cities than did Swedish men. In 1910 the two cities with the largest Swedish populations were Chicago (63,065) and New York City (34,952), and Swedish women outnumbered Swedish men in both of these urban centers. Among first-generation Swedish Americans, the ratio was 96.8 males to 100 females in Chicago and 83.7 males to 100 females in New York City.[69] Swedish women outnumbered Swedish men in a study of Swedish immigrants up to 1920 in New York City, Chicago, Detroit, Milwaukee, Boston, and the state of Rhode Island.[70] In the rural areas studied, however, Swedish men outnumbered women.[71] Swedish women were drawn to urban areas because they promised the best opportunities for women to work as domestics, in the textile industry, or in other service industries such as hotels and laundries.

Swedish immigrant women numbered among the earliest waves of Swedes to settle in the United States as they accompanied their husbands and fathers to the new land in the west. As the emigrant stream grew, single women made up an increasing proportion of the female migrants, with their numbers highest in the last two decades of the nineteenth and the first decade of the twentieth century. Given their social and economic position in the Swedish homeland, and considering the positive image of the United States prevalent in Sweden during this time period, women's desire to emigrate is not difficult to understand. Their ability to carry out this desire, however, was rarely easy or straightforward. To a greater extent than their male counterparts, single Swedish women like Mina had to rely on assistance from friends and relatives in order to pay for a ticket for the transatlantic voyage. Daughters in property-owning families and women lacking majority status might also find it difficult to emigrate without family approval and support.

Swedish emigration, male and female alike, often took place within the context of chain migration, with previously emigrated friends and relatives providing not only ship's tickets but also important advice and guidance as preparations for the emigrant journey began. Although Swedish emigrant women might find leaving friends and family emotionally difficult, the opportunity to experience new places, coupled with hope for a better future—and the thought of possible reunification of family and friendship networks—could make the journey to America an adventure. Seasickness and poor conditions on board ship might make the ocean voyage unpleasant, but the passage could also provide opportunities to meet new people and enjoy social activities. Swedish immigrants who met admission requirements and passed a series of examinations were granted entrance to the United States, although women who, like Mina, had traveled alone might find themselves subject to sharper scrutiny by authorities than immigrant men.

For most Swedish women, the journey to their American destination did not end with successfully navigating through the bureaucracies of Castle Garden, Ellis Island, or another port of entry but continued with other transportation to a final destination farther west. Some women had good fortune and the company of fellow travelers on these last legs of their journey and found familiar faces waiting for them. Others struggled to make their way alone, attempting to negotiate in a foreign language and foreign culture. Most, like Mina, ultimately made their way to their destination successfully, usually a town or city with a Swedish American community. Mina wrote provocatively and memorably of a "promised land, where everyone who was able to should go."[72] Understanding the validity of her claim, compounded of myth, hope, and experience, requires a close examination of her fortunes and that of other Swedish immigrant women during the months and years following their arrivals.

CHAPTER 4

"A Good Position"

My relative was an older man who had never been married. He had worked in the forests in Norrland and saved a small amount, large enough for a ticket to America and to buy 40 acres of land near town. If he'd had sense enough to remain on that place he would with time have become a rich man, if he had been allowed to live. The area later became a part of the town [Wausau, Wisconsin], and when I visited the town many years later there was a city park there.

He sold this land for a low price and bought land twelve miles from town. He bought it for the sake of the forest. It was an area that had never been touched by saw or ax and there were trees several feet in diameter. It is obvious that this land was almost impossible to clear for farming; he had only managed to clear a few acres and build a log house. He used to work in the forest in the wintertime, but when I arrived he was sickly and did not have the strength to work. He died a year later. Since I could not be alone in the forest with a sick man, he gave the land to a German family who lived in the vicinity in exchange for their taking care of him.

I am glad that by the time of his death, I had managed to pay him for my ticket. He needed that money for the doctor and medicine. Now I was quite alone, without relatives or friends. I was lucky enough to have good health, and my cheerful disposition never failed me.

One time, however, I did lose my courage. Uncle had thought that I would stay with him, but since he did not own anything more than the land and the log cabin, I soon realized it was impossible. I could not feel at home there. I remember that I went out and sat down behind the cabin and wept for a long while. I did not really want to tell him that I didn't want to stay, for I knew that it hurt him. I was young, only twenty-three years old and I realized it would have been no future for me if I had stayed there. I told him that I wanted to go to town and get work. I packed my clothes in a knapsack and walked twelve miles to town one hot day in July, carrying the knapsack, on foot. I stayed with the family who had received me when I arrived, until I found work. He was Swedish and she was Danish, and they were always so nice to me. I worked for Swedes for a month, and then I quit there. I wanted to have an English place so that I could learn the language. So I looked and found a place with a Scotsman. The man in the family that had met me at the station had taught me to ask in English if they wished to have a maid, and I did understand of course if they said no or yes. But I did not understand when the missus said that I should come on Saturday. I didn't know which day that was. So I walked all the way home and just repeated "Saturday, Saturday" to myself so as not to forget it before I met somebody who could tell me which day that meant.

I was lucky enough to get a good place. The missus taught me to read in the cookbook, and it didn't take so long until I understood what they said. There were two girls there, and they had a nursery maid who was German, but born here, so there was nobody who could speak anything but English so I learned fast.[1] *It was a good position with only four members in the family. Things were good for me there. They had a little boy who was four years old; he would rather be in the kitchen and help me bake than be with the nursery maid. I learned so much English from him; he was such a sweet and kind boy. When I left he wept, and the missus tried to comfort him and said that I would come again, and he said, "No, she won't because she's taking her trunk along."*

It was a good position, but the most they paid in that little town was a couple of dollars a week at that time. I got one dollar fifty at first, later two dollars. I stayed there for six months. Then I decided to go to a bigger city where I could get more pay, and I left for the Twin Cities, Minneapolis and St. Paul.

Now I knew the language so I could manage wherever, and I received fourteen or fifteen dollars a month. . . . I have never regretted that I came here! I have had it better here.[2]

SWEDISH AMERICANS IN THEIR WRITTEN AND ORAL ACCOUNTS HAVE sometimes referred to their first years in the United States as *hundår* (dog years). Defined in Swedish-English dictionaries as "years of struggle," for immigrants *hundår* identified the time when they found adjusting to life in

America demanding and difficult, especially in economic and social terms.[3] When Mina (or Minnie Anderson, as she was now known) was asked in a survey, "How long do you consider your 'dog years' to have lasted?" she responded: "I had no dog years."[4] A number of other women answered similarly, and among all respondents the males noted more (and lengthier) *hundår* than the females. How did these young Swedish immigrant women, like Minnie, succeed in limiting or avoiding the "years of struggle"? The existence of ethnic communities into which Swedish immigrant women were welcomed, the particular advantages of domestic service as an occupation, and the personal freedom accorded to Swedish servants and other wage-earning single Swedish immigrant women in the United States—all of these contributed to the relative ease with which these women adjusted to life in the United States.

Most single Swedish immigrant women found employment soon after their arrival in America. Many, like Minnie, found it relatively easy to obtain "a good position" as a domestic servant that paid higher wages, included better food and housing, offered more comfortable accommodations, allowed more personal time, and demanded less arduous physical labor than had been their experience as domestics in Sweden. These comparisons help explain why domestic service was the most popular employment choice of single Swedish immigrant women. As these women became accustomed to their new environment and developed social networks that provided information about the labor market, they became even more discriminating in their job choices. Frequently changing employers and geographic location, they chose positions in domestic service as well as other occupations that offered them the best combination of wages, working conditions, and time off. Minnie's writing about this period of her life illustrates these trends, though her comments are brief. Swedish immigrant women's personal documents (letters, diaries, memoirs, autobiographies), government documents, and social investigations echo and expand upon her experiences, and these provide ample evidence that most single Swedish immigrant women found things better as a result of their immigration to the United States—and comparatively easier than for male migrants from Sweden.

The Importance of Ethnic Networks: "I Will Teach You What I Can"

Minnie Anderson walked the twelve miles to town unaccompanied, but once she arrived in Wausau she exchanged isolation for an ethnic network to which her uncle had already connected her. Until she found her first job as a domestic, Minnie stayed with the Swedish/Danish family in Wausau who had originally received her and about whom she wrote that "they were always so nice."[5] That Minnie's first employer was Swedish also indicates her reliance on ethnic networks in her first weeks in America. Friends and relatives or countrymen and countrywomen supported the single immigrant woman newly arrived from Sweden as she became accustomed to the new language and culture, often in the form of temporary room and board while she looked for work and assistance in locating employment. After arriving in Illinois with three hometown friends (sisters Helda and Elvira and another young woman, Augusta) in 1882, Lina Ericksson spent her first days in the company of Helda and Elvira's family. Meanwhile, the girls' father found domestic positions for both Elvira and Lina in the nearby city of Moline. Lina commented on his assistance in a letter home to her family, writing that her friends' father "would be as much of a father to me as he is to Helda and Elvira, if I get sick or don't like the place [where I am working], I can come there when I want; he rents a little farm."[6] Swedish immigrant Hilma Andreen wrote assuringly to her niece in 1902 about her impending immigration: "I will teach you what I can and help you on your way."[7] The existence of support networks like these eased the adjustment period for women like Minnie, Lina, and Hilma.

Swedish immigrant women might even have jobs waiting for them upon arrival, arranged by previously immigrated relatives and friends. In her initial position, Maja Johansson, who immigrated in 1903 at age twenty-two, labored as a domestic alongside her sister, who had already lived in the United States for five years.[8] Maria Sorensson's sister gave up her own job to Maria when she arrived, quickly locating another position for herself.[9] Brothers, fathers, and other male friends and relatives helped female Swedish immigrants as well. Minnie's uncle had connected her to a family in Wausau, and Lina Eriksson was assisted by the father of her friends. Swedish immigrant Carl Karlgren's 1889 letter to his sister Hulda included a ticket to America, detailed travel instructions, and a promise of a job.[10] Likewise, Anna J. Olson's brother helped her find employment close to his home after her arrival in 1903.[11]

Not all Swedish immigrant women had networks of friends and family upon which to rely, and some Swedish communities established facilities to meet these young women's needs. Boston's Swedish Home of Peace (Fridhem) was established in 1903 "for servant girls who are out of employment or temporarily in need of rest and for girls from the Scandinavian Countries coming to Boston in search of employment and for girls who through sickness and other misfortunes have become destitute and are in need of temporary care and shelter."[12] Similar institutions serving the needs of young Swedish and Scandinavian immigrant women cropped up in Chicago, Denver, and New York.[13]

Employment bureaus, or intelligence offices, as they were often called, found in many urban areas in the late nineteenth century represented another source of support Swedish immigrant women used to obtain employment, though arrangements at employment and intelligence offices varied. In some instances, employers registered their employment needs, paid a fee, and waited for potential employees to come to their home for an interview. Interviews might also take place at the employment agency. At other offices, servants looking for work would register their interests and pay a fee. If there were not places immediately available that they chose to accept, they could sit in intelligence office waiting rooms until suitable employment was secured. After moving from Wausau to the Twin Cities, Minnie may have used the services of someone like Swedish-born Johanna Stromquist, the operator of an employment agency in Minneapolis. In cities with a sizable Swedish immigrant population, intelligence offices were operated specifically for Swedes. Othelia Myhrman began managing the Swedish Free Employment Bureau in Chicago in the 1890s, and Annie C. Anderson operated the Swedish Employment Parlors in Worcester, Massachusetts, in the early twentieth century.[14]

Some women found employment through more informal ethnic networks. Hilda Linder obtained a job just after her arrival in Proctor, Vermont, when the Swedish cook at the local hospital—who had heard about the arrival of a new Swedish girl in town—came asking if she needed work.[15] Alexandra Johnson entered a shop in Woodbridge, New Jersey, after seeing the Scandinavian name Peterson on a shop window. Discovering that the shop owner and his wife were Danish (and could therefore understand Swedish) she asked if they knew of anyone who needed servant help. The wife knew of a potential employer and accompanied Alexandra to the family's home to serve as interpreter, and Alexandra began her position as a domestic servant there the following day.[16] Over time, domestics themselves developed extensive networks to convey information about available positions, as did Elisabet Olson, who told her family about changing employers in 1915 when she heard of an opening from a friend. She wrote: "It is never hard for me to get places [as a domestic], it seems; I need not go and ask after any at all."[17]

Hilda Linder described in her autobiography how, becoming dissatisfied with her work as a hospital cook, she found a job in private household service

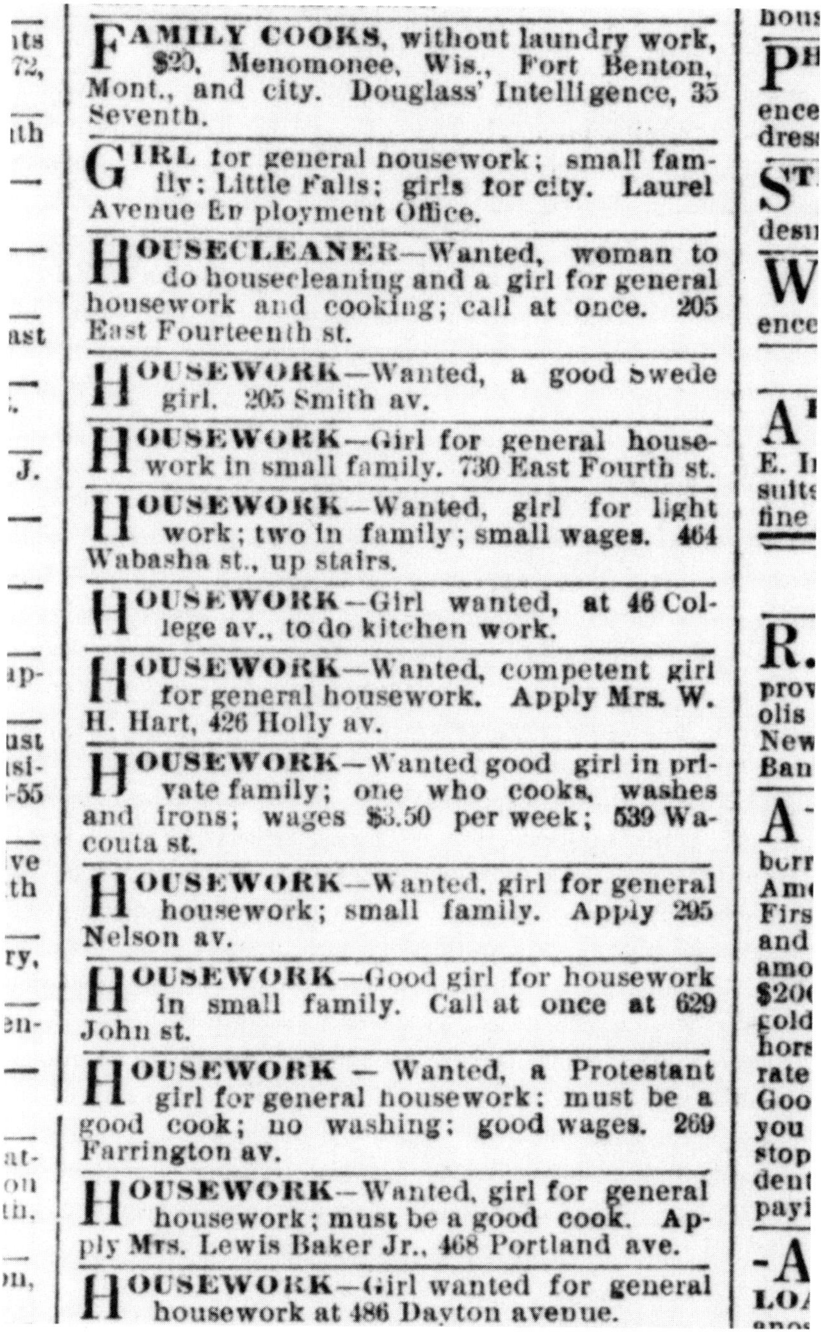

FAMILY COOKS, without laundry work, $20, Menomonee, Wis., Fort Benton, Mont., and city. Douglass' Intelligence, 35 Seventh.

GIRL for general housework; small family; Little Falls; girls for city. Laurel Avenue Employment Office.

HOUSECLEANER—Wanted, woman to do housecleaning and a girl for general housework and cooking; call at once. 205 East Fourteenth st.

HOUSEWORK—Wanted, a good Swede girl. 205 Smith av.

HOUSEWORK—Girl for general housework in small family. 730 East Fourth st.

HOUSEWORK—Wanted, girl for light work; two in family; small wages. 464 Wabasha st., up stairs.

HOUSEWORK—Girl wanted, at 46 College av., to do kitchen work.

HOUSEWORK—Wanted, competent girl for general housework. Apply Mrs. W. H. Hart, 426 Holly av.

HOUSEWORK—Wanted good girl in private family; one who cooks, washes and irons; wages $3.50 per week; 539 Wacouta st.

HOUSEWORK—Wanted, girl for general housework; small family. Apply 295 Nelson av.

HOUSEWORK—Good girl for housework in small family. Call at once at 629 John st.

HOUSEWORK — Wanted, a Protestant girl for general housework; must be a good cook; no washing; good wages. 269 Farrington av.

HOUSEWORK—Wanted, girl for general housework; must be a good cook. Apply Mrs. Lewis Baker Jr., 468 Portland ave.

HOUSEWORK—Girl wanted for general housework at 486 Dayton avenue.

Swedish immigrant women, accustomed to working as servants in their homeland, frequently sought employment as domestics in the United States. Employers appreciated their experience, as well as their strong work ethic, and often advertised specifically for good Swedish girls to do housework. (*St. Paul Daily Globe*, May 2, 1897)

through the local newspaper: "I saw in the newspaper that a servant was wanted. Not much experience needed. (One learned to read the advertisements for help wanted first.)"[18] Many newspapers included advertisements from households seeking domestic servants. Some even specified ethnic preferences.

Another Swedish immigrant woman took a slightly different approach. Hilda Hammar successfully located a domestic position by placing her own advertisement—"a green Swedish girl for household work"—in a newspaper. The term "green" was used to indicate that she had only recently arrived from Sweden and would thus be unfamiliar with some aspects of American domestic service.[19]

That some advertisements indicated a Swedish preference attests to Swedish domestics' good reputation among employers (such preferences may also have represented a way for employers to make their racial biases clear). Edith Svensson Edgren, who emigrated just after World War I, recalled: "It was easy to get jobs doing housework because the families all wanted Swedish girls. I guess they thought the Swedish girls were used to more work."[20] Another woman recalled: "The Swedish girls had a very good reputation. One could now and then see in the ads, that a Swede was wanted."[21] The Swedish American press was quick to take note of American praise for their countrywomen. An 1892 *New York Herald* article entitled "Swedish Women Make Excellent Domestic Servants" was proudly described in an Omaha, Nebraska, Swedish-language newspaper. Written by a woman who had employed servants of many nationalities, the author found Swedish servants to be the best, listing favorable qualities such as their good knowledge of household work and their academic education from their required schooling in Sweden; their religiosity and good morals; and their traits of honesty, reliability, and sobriety.[22]

Evidence drawn from outside the Swedish American press not surprisingly provides a more diverse assessment of Swedish domestics. In 1887–88, the Minnesota Bureau of Labor conducted a study of women wage earners, including domestic servants, undertaken by interviewing the women themselves, employment agents, and employers. Although one employment agent praised Swedish domestics for their versatility, another said that Swedes were not as clean and therefore less preferred than other nationalities. Yet another agent noted that when Swedish (and Norwegian) girls arrived in the United States they were willing to work for low wages because they wanted to learn English. She complained, however, that "after they have the language learned they are inclined to consider themselves better workers than girls of other nationalities and keep constantly changing from one place to another." Swedes were also included in one employer's list of domestics of the "foreign element" that she deemed "hard to manage."[23]

In a 1902 Minneapolis newspaper, the operator of an employment bureau sang the praises of domestic servants from Scandinavia (the majority of whom were Swedish). She noted that even though language could be a problem with newly arrived immigrant domestics, "they have only to be shown" what to do. She added: "Most new comers have to [be] 'broken in' to American housekeeping; there are some[, however,] . . . who have worked in first class families in Stockholm, Christian[i]a, Copenhagen, and other large cities, and who can often give our American women points on etiquette and cookery."[24]

Domestic Service and Learning the Language: "It Is Better to Be with a Swedish Family in the Beginning"

Minnie's decision to take her first domestic job with a Swedish American family cushioned her transition to America by allowing her to adjust without having to struggle at the same time with a new language. She learned some of the basics of an American-style kitchen and gained familiarity with American foods and patterns of household work. Other Swedish immigrant women used this approach, as well, including Hilda Pärson, who wrote to her family in 1879: "I serve with a Swedish family. It is better to be with a Swedish family in the beginning until one becomes more accustomed to the country." A few months later, when she had obtained employment with "Yankees" (her way of referring to white nonimmigrants), Pärson wrote, "It is not so difficult [working for Yankees] when one has worked for Swedes because one knows how one should work and gets to learn a little such as names and counting and things."[25]

Minnie exhibited the same aptitude for learning in her first domestic position that had been evident in her Swedish schooling. After only four weeks she had gleaned what she needed from the job and gave it up because she "wanted to have an English place." Her need to repeat the word "Saturday" over and over again so she would know when to begin her position suggests the value of having at least a rudimentary knowledge of English when searching for employment.[26] It also illustrates the difficulty of learning a foreign language and the degree of concentration and effort language acquisition required. A Minneapolis employment bureau operator's comment on the increasing numbers of Scandinavian immigrant women coming to Minneapolis underscores the value they placed on having facility with English: "Many . . . [Scandinavian girls] have gone first to relatives on farms. But in order to support themselves and to get a knowledge of English, the girls have come very quickly into town, within a few weeks, maybe, from the time they landed at New York."[27] Swedish immigrant Ingeborg Johansson refused a position as a kitchen maid for railroad magnate James J. Hill when she discovered that the head cook was Swedish—she was afraid that she would never learn English adequately in such a position.[28]

Inability to speak and understand English created workplace challenges. Added to the physical labor required of domestic service was the mental effort of acquiring facility in another language. One young woman wrote to her sister in 1887 about learning English: "I am now happy because I think that the worst time is over. I can soon understand all that they [her employers] say; it is the hardest time the first half year as long as one cannot manage with the language."[29] A poor understanding of English could cause conflict between employer and employee. Swedish immigrant Else Larsson angered her employer by ruining a brunch when, because of her limited English skills and unfamiliarity with American foods, she boiled grapefruit instead of broiling it.[30] Limited ability to communicate might also mean being taken advantage of by coworkers. In the process of immigrating to the United States, Olga Johnsson worked for a few months in and near Quebec, Canada, before gaining entry to America. During this time she knew very little English and absolutely no French. She wrote to her father about her language difficulties and the negative consequences with a fellow servant that resulted from her inability to communicate. The fellow servant was "nice enough in one way but I cannot defend myself with the mistress properly yet so I suffer wrongly many times and work more than my share."[31]

Poor English-language facility could increase potential dangers facing the newly arrived Swedish immigrant woman, especially if she had traveled to the United States on her own, with no relatives or friends to meet her. In 1880 Eliza Engstrom endured three months of abuse from a Swedish tailor in New York City who had hired her as a seamstress and housekeeper directly upon her arrival at Castle Garden. A newspaper report of her case noted that she was "perfectly helpless, because she could speak no English, and it was only through the good offices of a countrywoman who keeps an employment agency that she was finally able to get away."[32] Unfortunately, a shared nationality was no guarantee of safety or honor. The case of Annie Jansen was probably also exacerbated by language difficulties. In a newspaper report with the byline "A Swedish Girl Disappears," it was noted that Jansen was "18 years of age and unable to speak English."[33]

Fortunately, most young Swedish women working as domestic servants caught on to English quickly. Immersing themselves in an English-only environment facilitated the process. As Minnie states regarding her second domestic position, "there was nobody who could speak anything but English so I learned fast." Her "missus" taught her how to read a cookbook. Her employer might have done so by using a copy of the *Swedish-American Book of Cookery and Adviser for Swedish Servants in America*, first published in 1882. Designed for "the newly-arrived Swedish servant girl," it contained advice, menus, and recipes in double-columned pages with Swedish on the left and English on the right. Between 1882 and 1923 the book was published in seven editions, attesting to its utility and to the continuing stream of young Swedish women seeking employment as domestics.[34] English might also be learned through attending night school, though most employers of domestics were unlikely to allow their workers so much time off. The "English school" Charlotta Andersson attended in 1901 met four nights a week from 7 to 9 P.M.[35]

The presence of children in an employer's household could speed language acquisition. Minnie recalled learning "so much English"[36] from the company of her employer's four-year-old son. When asked on a survey how much time it took for her to learn to speak English, she responded that she could "speak and understand so that I managed well in six months."[37] Similarly, in her first domestic position after her arrival, Ellen Seagren shared schoolbooks with her employer's young son: "I right away took those books and read them and studied them, and studied all I could. In fact, I had a good education in Sweden so it was a little bit easy for me."[38]

Benefits of American Domestic Employment: "I Have a Little Closet to Hang My Clothes In"

Minnie described her employment with a Scottish family in Wausau as "a good position," and her writings include positive assessments of American-style domestic labor. Employed as a servant in a variety of American households and cities from shortly after her arrival in 1890 until her marriage in March 1892, she consciously chose domestic service. In this she was not alone. Swedish immigrant women seeking wage work favored this occupation. In 1900 over half of all Swedish immigrant women wageworkers were domestic servants (a higher percentage than in any other immigrant group at that time).[39] Though nonimmigrants often disdained employment as household servants, for young, recently arrived Swedish women, it was an attractive, worthwhile, respectable

mangnidet. Omrör alltsammans i en panna och låt det koka. Servera med sellerisås och stufvade krusbär. Garnera med stekta ostron. Välj en kalkon, som väger åtta a tio pounds. Om kalkonen under stekningen blir för brun, så lägg hvitt papper bestruket med smör öfver den.

dish. Serve with celery-sauce and stewed gooseberries or cranberries. Garnish with fried oysters. Select a turkey of eight to ten pounds. If in roasting it is likely to brown to much, cover with a white paper, buttered.

Stekt kalkon på amerikanskt sätt. Roast Turkey, in American way.

Stekt kalkon på amerikanskt sätt.

Bered kalkonen på vanligt sätt; gnid den både på in- och utsidan med salt och peppar, hvarefter den bör ombindas med snöre. Låt kalkonen koka i två timmar eller tills den börjar blifva mör. Under tiden bör locket som oftast lyftas och kalkonen lätt stänkas med salt.

Roast turkey in American way.

Dress and rub the turkey well, inside and out, with salt and pepper; truss or twine it; put in a steamer and steam two hours, or until it begins to grow tender, lifting the cover occasionally and sprinkling lightly with salt; then take out, loosen the legs, and rub the

Like other young Swedish women, Minnie learned to read English from a cookbook. Cooking instructions were also helpful as Swedish women adjusted to American kitchens and American cuisine. (*Fullständigaste Svensk-Americansk Kok-bok*, 1897)

occupational choice.[40] After all, many of them had worked as servants in the homeland. Although Minnie left behind few details of her own experience as a domestic servant, a variety of personal documents from other Swedish immigrant women have survived to provide information about the occupation's nature and benefits.

Swedish immigrant women described daily and weekly work tasks and work patterns in their correspondence, often in response to questions from family and friends in Sweden. A typical example is a letter from Elisabet Olson to her family in 1912 describing her weekly schedule and work tasks in a house with three stories and twenty rooms:

> It is not a little to clean and keep neat but I can divide it so I don't need to do it all at once. . . . Sunday. Change beds and put new cloths on the table. Collect dirty clothes and lay them in the water. Dinner ready 1:30 or 2:00 P.M. and when I have done the dishes I am free. . . . Monday. Wash clothes. Tuesday. Iron. Wednesday. Organize the bookcases and wash pictures and mirrors and if needed wash carpets and bedding. Thursday. One week mop and clean upstairs and the next downstairs. The bathrooms are upstairs and are done every week. Friday. Clean the kitchen and pantry and veranda. Saturday. Clean and prepare a little food for Sunday.[41]

Letters also revealed details about housing conditions. Thilda Janson wrote to her mother in 1882: "I have a nice room. My furniture is a bed, a table, a commode and two chairs and I have a little closet to hang my clothes in."[42] Elisabet Olson was especially pleased that she had a mirror: "I even have a bureau with a big mirror in my room so I can see my whole self. I have my room highest up. A fine room, I have a rocker, too, and there I can be altogether alone and I sit there now and write."[43] That Olson noted that her room was a place where she could be "altogether alone" also implies a positive comparison with domestic service in Sweden, where maids did not usually have their own rooms, and in fact might be expected to sleep in the kitchen.[44]

Many Swedish immigrant women's writings contain implicit and explicit comparisons of their work in American households with their experiences in Sweden. Hilda Pärson noted how in Sweden her sister Tilda had "worked for farmers and slaved and got nothing except perhaps a little food and clothes when the year was over." But after a year in the United States, Tilda possessed "fine clothes and paid off her ticket."[45] In an 1890 letter, Moli Nilsson wrote home from Omaha that she "avoid[ed] going out and slaving like the poor girls in Sweden. . . . I do not want to go back to Sweden because they work too hard."[46] Similarly, Anna Nygren in 1908 described her work in Flatbush, New York, as "nearly the same as in Borgholm [Sweden] but I need not work so hard here as I had to there."[47] Echoing Minnie's own comment about America prior to departing, one young Swedish immigrant male rhapsodized to his sister in 1910, "America is the woman's promised land."[48]

Swedish immigrant women working as domestics found wages significantly higher than they had been able to earn in the homeland. Even the wage that Minnie thought unsatisfactory in Wausau, two dollars a week, surpassed servant wages in Sweden. The average yearly wage for female farm servants in Sweden in the 1890s was 94.9 kronor. Minnie's two dollars a week converted to 7.46 kronor, or 387 kronor per year, about four times the Swedish average. And the fifteen dollars a month she was able to earn in St. Paul equaled 671.4 kronor per year.[49]

Employment as an American domestic servant appealed to Swedish immigrant women in part because it usually meant working in a town or city rather than on a farm. Women who had, like Minnie, been employed as pigor on farms in Sweden were pleased to discover that domestic employment in American urban areas was truly household employment. Women who first worked as domestics in the rural United States were also attracted by urban domestic service. Kristina Eriksson wrote to her family from the town of Pennock, Minnesota, in 1906: "It is my first place in a city. On the farm there is much more work and less pay."[50] However, for young Swedish immigrant women, even working on an American farm could be an improvement over such employment in Sweden, because rural female servants in America were, unlike in Sweden, not expected to milk cows. One Stockholm newspaper in 1902 published an article discouraging young Swedish men from emigrating, noting in particular that male farmworkers in the United States were expected to milk the cows.[51]

The degree to which young Swedish immigrant women found opportunities and prospects in America more attractive than in Sweden is also evident in their remigration rates. Research by Lars-Göran Tedebrand revealed a strong male dominance in remigration from America to Sweden.[52] Evidence about remigration was included in a letter from Hilma Andreen about three girlfriends from Småland who had intended to return to Sweden: "They had earned well and decided to stay home with their parents but they returned here in the fall; they said there was nothing in Sweden for them. They had two newcomers with them."[53] In the summer of 1900 the *Minneapolis Journal* included an article attributing the shortage of servant girls to the visits they were making to their homelands. Readers were assured that the shortage would soon be remedied, however, because "girls who once came to America and are able to return for a visit are seldom if ever content with their native country, according to the stories they tell the managers of the employment bureaus." The article went on to explain that immigrant women were "independent to a degree" and "able to secure wages that enable them to start bank accounts." One young woman was quoted: "I do not believe any girl will be contented in Scandinavia after she has been in America once."[54]

Within a year, Minnie had gained a working knowledge of English and familiarized herself with the duties of domestic servants in her new homeland. Noting that "the most they paid in that little town was a couple of dollars a week" and recognizing that her experience enabled her to "manage wherever," Minnie moved to the Twin Cities in search of higher-paying domestic employment.[55] A St. Paul city directory for 1891–92 listed two Minnie Andersons, one a widowed woman working as a seamstress, the other a domestic at 347 East Magnolia, the residence of Mr. and Mrs. Frank W. Noyes. It appears from account books the family left behind that Minnie worked for the Noyes family from April through July 1891 at a wage of twelve dollars and then fifteen dollars a month.[56]

Minnie was the only domestic in a household of five that included Frank and Lillian Noyes and their boys Albert ("Bert," born in 1882), Arthur (born in 1888), and Clarence (born in 1890). According to a recollection by Bert, due to his mother's poor health the family "had a hired girl for awhile."[57] Minnie likely slept in a heated attic room accessible by a pull-down stairway and trapdoor. Since she was the only domestic in the home, her tasks were varied and probably included cooking as well as cleaning and laundry duties. Though it appeared Minnie stayed in this position for only a few months, even her starting wage of twelve dollars a month was significantly higher than the eight dollars per month possible in Wausau. Minnie's move to the Twin Cities and brief employment with the Noyes family also illustrates the employment agent's complaint that Swedish domestics changed positions frequently once they had learned to speak and understand English.

The demand for domestic workers also contributed to the appeal of this occupation for Swedish immigrant women. Using the popular press as an indicator, it appears that rarely in the later decades of the nineteenth and the early decades of the twentieth century was the number of women seeking domestic

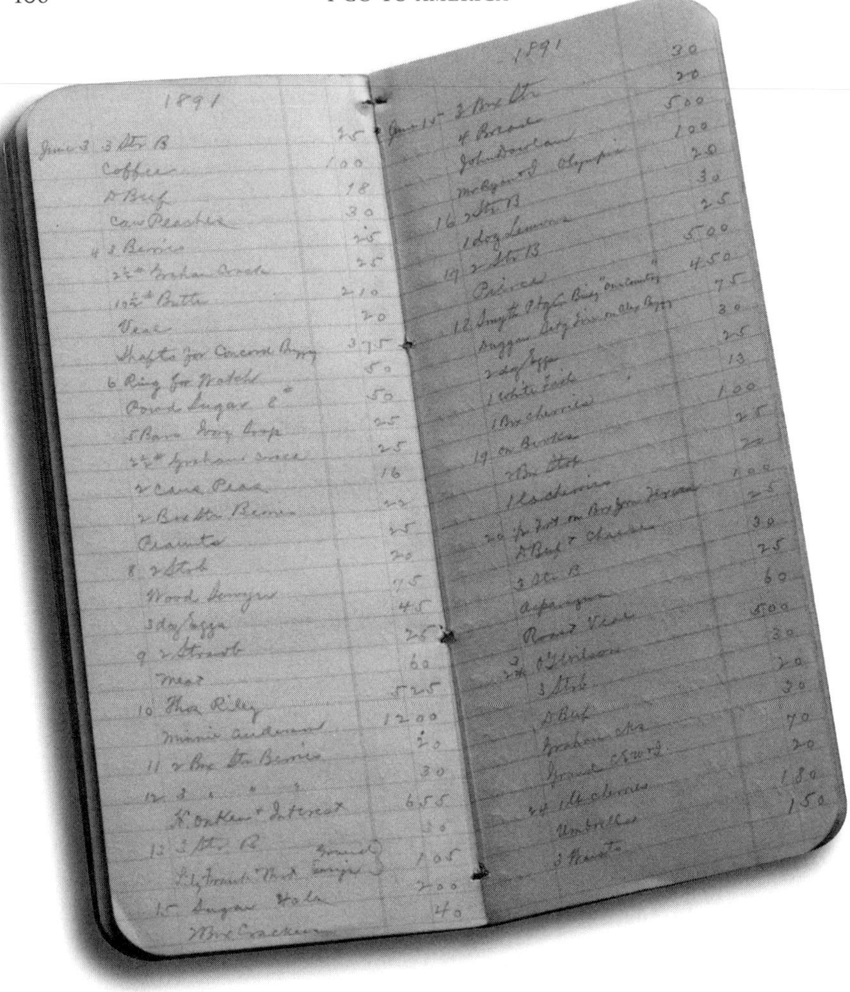

Minnie worked for the Noyes family from April through July 1891 at a monthly wage of $12, later $15. She also received room and board in the household. Minnie's name appears eight lines from the bottom of the left-hand page.

service adequate for the demand. The need was so high in turn-of-the-century Minneapolis that some women waited to meet immigrant trains at Union Depot to try to convince potential domestics to work for them. A newspaper article about this trend noted: "In several instances young women have been taken out of the depot by Minneapolis ladies after consultation with their parents through an interpreter, to be taught the mysteries of domestic service and to receive more money per week for learning it than they could have earned per month in their own countries by exercising every faculty they possess."[58]

Domestic jobs were plentiful enough that Swedish immigrant women did not hesitate to leave positions where the daily duties, wages, or accommodations were deemed inadequate. Signe Nygren wrote to her family about leaving her current position because "the work was too hard . . . and I get no food except by stealing little bits so it is a bother."[59] The job market gave them a degree of power within the employer/employee relationship. If a Swedish domestic had a job where her employers were happy with her work, the domestic might obtain wage increases or increased time off by threatening to leave. Thilda Janson told a friend in 1887, "My employers will move in May. I don't know yet where I am going, but if I promise to come to them in the fall when they get their new house in Omaha finished then they will pay me half my week's pay wherever I go in the summer."[60] Thilda accepted her employer's offer and visited Sweden during the summer while collecting her half-salary. As Swedish immigrant women gained familiarity with American household work, learned to prepare American foods in American kitchens, and developed their language abilities, their value to their employers increased. It took time and effort for mistresses to train household employees, and they might choose to increase an employee's wages rather than hire a new "green" servant. Employers with a high turnover of domestic servants might also earn a bad reputation among potential employees. All of these factors gave Swedish immigrant domestics more leverage in the employer-employee relationship than they would have experienced in the homeland.

Elisabet Olson discussed in a letter to her family how she thought domestics should behave toward their employers. She wrote that she "read out the old woman [her employer] sometimes . . . if she says something that is not right. . . . It is the way to handle them [the employers]. They think more of the girl also, if they get to see that they can't handle her however they like. One should let them see that one has a little understanding, and show spirit even though one is only a worker girl."[61] Olson's comments suggest that Swedish immigrant women showed less deference to employers than would have been tolerated in Sweden. Though most domestics were not as outspoken as Olson, their actions, in leaving positions where they did not feel they were treated with appropriate respect, spoke louder than their words.

Some Swedish domestics told of the opportunity to obtain high-quality clothing from their employer's castoffs, though others found such "gifts" insulting. A few lines included in a midwestern Swedish American newspaper addressed these issues in a humorous fashion in a notice entitled "Our Servants":

"Do you know that lady over there?"

"My fur coat, our daughter's parasol, my sister-in-law's hat, and clearly our cook's face."[62]

The reference to "lady" in the first line reveals that when young Swedish women socialized outside of their workplaces, they often dressed and carried themselves in ways that made their class status difficult to distinguish. This was likely also part of what drew Swedish immigrant women to domestic service—they were able to dress and behave in ways that were impossible for women of their social class in the homeland. Though the second line of the joke suggests a sense of superiority and class-consciousness on the part of the employer that was certainly felt by the domestic when she was working, her experience outside her employer's household could be one of social status and respect.

Swedish American domestics in their letters and personal documents might have been reticent to tell of the negative aspects of their work. Especially if a woman's migration had required significant effort to accomplish in either financial or emotional terms, she would probably downplay misadventures and failures. But most likely these cases are limited. The steady, continuous stream of Swedish women seeking employment in America during the period of mass emigration is revealing. The families of Swedish American domestics were probably concerned about the safety and happiness of their daughters and siblings, but most of the women studied had, like Minnie, worked and lived away from their homes for several years prior to emigration, and it is doubtful that these women, many of whom had already proven their capabilities as independent laborers in the homeland, felt very much of a need to assure their families of their well-being.[63]

As Minnie's decision to "go to a bigger city where I could get more pay" shows, Swedish immigrant women knew the wage market and made carefully reasoned employment and migration decisions.[64] Wage information traveled by word of mouth and by letters between relatives and friends and was found in Swedish American and American newspapers in the form of help-wanted advertisements as well. For example, Elisabet Olson informed her family in 1916, "I have decided that I will not work for less than 30 or 35 [dollars] a month, because I hear that so many of my friends (Swedish girls) get that."[65] Her comment also reveals the sense of power she felt within the employer-employee relationship.

The abundance of domestic service jobs also allowed Swedish immigrant women a significant degree of geographic mobility. For example, Hilda Pärson

En barndomsbekant, mycket förändrad.

"A childhood acquaintance, greatly changed," a commentary on the ways in which Swedish women transformed themselves in America. (*Jan Olsons Äfventyr*, 1892)

wrote her family in 1880 that she was thinking of moving from Woodhull to Chicago, because "there they pay the most wages."[66] Another woman wrote in 1897 about moving to a position she considered "the best I have had in America, good pay and not much to do."[67] After Hilda Linder worked for several months in two Vermont towns, she heard from a friend in Worcester, Massachusetts, about higher wages and decided to seek employment there. Linder's changing of employers was not, however, always tied to higher wages. Two years after moving to Worcester, she decided to head west, her curiosity and desire for adventure piqued by reading books about the Wild West (probably dime novels) given to her by her employer. After working for a time in the small town of Columbia, South Dakota, she moved to Minneapolis, where she found employment as a domestic until her marriage in 1920.[68] A 1901 Minnesota survey study reported that "one-fourth of the correspondents have been in their places less than three months; some girls have changed [employers] ten or twenty times; and many can't remember at how many houses they had worked."[69]

Locating a domestic job in a household close to friends and relatives was one of the factors women considered as they looked for a "good position." When Minnie wrote of being in Wausau "without relatives or friends," she expressed feelings of loneliness and homesickness. Heavyhearted after leaving her only relative in America sick and alone in the forest, she probably missed her friends and family very much. Though Swedish immigrant women's loneliness did not appear as a constant theme in their personal documents, sometimes it was poignantly revealed, contributing to a "dog year" for some. Anna Nilsson wrote to her parents in 1908 that "not a night has passed that I haven't dreamed I was home. . . . I am of course so lonely."[70] Elisabet Olson, who immigrated to Portland, Oregon, in 1912, had an aunt and cousins, as well as friends, close by, whom she visited whenever she had time off from work. She wrote home to her family: "Think if I had not had anyone here. Then it would all be quite difficult and gloomy."[71] When Elisabet Lindström took a domestic position outside of New York City, where her brother Wille lived, she wrote, "I feel very lonesome in this big land because I am many miles from Wille."[72] Similarly, Charlotta Andersson wrote to her brother about a mutual friend named Albertina: "She lives only a few houses from me and she is as a sister to me."[73]

Initially Minnie lacked a close-knit support system in America, and, like most Swedish immigrant women, she probably realized that the first months would be difficult but that life would improve with the passage of time. Olga

Johnsson found it particularly difficult to be away from home for her eighteenth birthday, which took place about seven months after her arrival in America in 1895. In a letter she thanked her father for the birthday card he had sent but bemoaned the fact that "it will probably be the only one I get because here there is no one who knows that it is my birthday." She continued: "Now I will complete my letter and it is on my birthday. I have cried a few times when I think of it."[74] She summed up what was likely a common attitude when she wrote home: "Next Tuesday it will be a whole year since I came here. I know a lot that I didn't know then, but I am glad the time is past."[75] In contrast to Minnie's experience, Johnsson, as her comment suggests, may have experienced her first year in the United States as a "dog year."

Homesickness and loneliness might be remedied with an active social life, and clearly another element making up a "good position" was the ability to pursue social interaction, entertainment, and personal leisure. Elisabet Olson worked for several years for a family in Portland, Oregon, and wrote to her family frequently about her employment. The amount of free time allowed her figured high on Olson's list of the benefits of a "good position." She wrote of a favored position as follows: "From 7 P.M. I am free always and can go where I want, and be out as long as I want, which is so nice, and then I can go to church when I want."[76] It was only when her employer came upon difficult economic circumstances and could no longer afford to pay her that Elisabet sought another position, and she worked for brief periods in several different households before finding one that suited her. She wrote to her family: "I have a new place again, you can believe that I change around a bit, but that is the way it is in America, to find something one likes, [and] not work oneself at a bad place. . . . There are so many others one can try."[77]

Household employers usually permitted domestic servants some time each day to see to personal needs, as well as one afternoon and one evening per week (often some combination of Thursday and Sunday afternoon or evening). Like Elisabet Olson, some women chose to spend their free time attending religious services and church-sponsored activities. Ellen Seagren, who worked in Minneapolis in the 1910s, asked for and received permission to attend certain church events on weeknights.[78] In an early twentieth-century study of Swedes in Chicago, E. H. Thörnberg found that "above all the Swedish American servants take a noticeable place with [church] societies, Lutheran as well as Reformed." He also noted that Chicago Swedish church congregations were mostly women.[79]

Formerly impoverished girls sent photos of themselves wearing their finest clothing to Sweden to suggest their improved social standing; photo 1890. A fashionable American wardrobe was an outward expression of the increased self-respect and confidence many women gained through their immigration.

Young Swedish women could choose from a wide variety of other activities to occupy their free time, although church membership in some denominations limited women's choices for social activities—for example, Swedish Baptists disapproved of dancing. Women who, like Minnie, worked in cities and towns where sizable Swedish American ethnic communities existed could take advantage of businesses and social events sponsored by their ethnic group. By the time Minnie had moved from Wisconsin to Minnesota, both St. Paul and Minneapolis contained Swedish American neighborhoods that offered shops, restaurants, bars, and theaters where she could spend her time off.[80] Else Olsson's experience, though taking place many years after Minnie's domestic employment, illustrates the importance of the ethnic community as a place for Swedish immigrant women to find social interaction, entertainment, and recreational activities. Else and her sister Nancy worked for a wealthy Minneapolis family during the 1930s. They spent their time off "with other Swedish immigrants in Lodge activities and special celebrations—Midsommar, Svenskarnas Dag, Lucia and Jul celebrations, and during summers at Vasa Park and Birch Bluff." The two locations had special appeal, because they both contained "large open-air dance pavilions where Swedish immigrants by the scores would dance polkas, waltzes, and the schottische under strings of multi-colored lights with the breezes off the lake [Minnetonka] blowing through the birch trees high on the bluff."[81] Along these same lines, Stina Johansson moved from the small town of LaCenter, Oregon, to Portland in 1913 because she wanted to participate in the Swedish American community activities available there.[82]

But all of this could make it difficult for Swedish immigrant women to save money. Charlotta Andersson moved from New Britain to Meriden, Connecticut, where "not so many Swedish entertainments" existed in 1901 in order to save money for a trip to Sweden. She wrote to her parents: "I think I will definitely save money here. It is certainly quiet and dreary compared to New Britain."[83] Activities during free time did not always have to be costly. Eva Wallström recalled her first months in Chicago, when, because she was still paying back the cost of her ship's ticket, she had little extra money for recreation and leisure: "To begin with it was exciting enough to go on afternoons off to the city center and look at everything that was new and exciting. Marshall Field's big department store was a worthy sight to see. . . . It was the meeting place above all others. . . . Around the loop were skyscrapers with theaters, restaurants, and bars."[84]

Olga Johnsson's letters to her parents related her usual Sunday afternoon activity, when she went to visit a Swedish woman where "all the Swedish girls meet and have a good time."[85] She also found other times during the week to socialize. A good friend was employed in a home nearby so they could "meet every day and talk about everything."[86] And she was able to meet and develop relationships with young men through a variety of social activities, although her American social life was apparently lively enough to provoke the concern of her family—one of her letters home contained the following assurance: "You write in your letter that I should put my free time to good use. I do, dear father. I am not so dizzy and wild that you need to be worried about me but I accept your warning with thanks."[87] Perhaps she had attended a party like the one Selma Carlson described for her family in 1886: "It was very fun; we were over 30 there; it was 6 o'clock [presumably in the morning!] before I came home. . . . We had it better than at a wedding in Sweden."[88] Employed in multiethnic towns and cities where anonymity and independence could be found, many young Swedish women attained in immigration a degree of social freedom and experimentation that would have been unimaginable under the eyes of employers, family, and parish officials back in Sweden.

Domestic Service and Social Advancement: "Not Debased Like in Sweden"

As Minnie finishes the section of her memoir recounting her experiences as a single immigrant woman, she notes how she never regretted that she came to America and that she "had it better here."[89] Her attitude reflects that of many women who experienced immigration from Sweden to America as a positive step and employment as a domestic servant as social advancement. Better working conditions and higher wages compared to those in the homeland represented one type of social advancement. Many women had, like Minnie, been unable to earn enough money in the homeland to adequately support themselves, let alone purchase a ship's ticket to America. Yet once immigrated and employed as a domestic in the United States, Minnie and others like her were not only able to support themselves but able to pay for the immigration of their relatives, save money for the future, and send money back home. Pleasure and pride in these accomplishments are clear in Maja Johansson's recollection of how good it made her feel to "get one's wages and send money home and still have enough for oneself."[90] Swedish immigrant women's letters frequently included references to money they were sending to family back home. Lina Eriksson mentioned in her letters sending money for gifts, for medicine, and even on one occasion for chewing tobacco for her grandmother (*snuspengar*; money for snus).[91] In a study of Chicago Swedes, Swedish scholar E. H. Thörnberg observes that, of the money being sent to the homeland, "the lion's share . . . [was] sent by Swedish-born servants."[92]

A 1901 Minnesota Department of Labor study also illustrates why young women might choose domestic service employment. In an effort to address the "domestic problem" (that is, the shortage of domestic servants) the department surveyed both employers and employees. A newspaper report of some of the findings stated that when servant girls were asked about their choice of employment, they indicated "that domestic service is preferable to working as a clerk in a store or a 'hand' in a factory, because the servant enjoys more of a home life, and because she can usually save money." The article also noted that among the servant respondents 70 percent were treated courteously by their employers, 75 percent had warm sleeping rooms, and 80 percent were allowed to entertain visitors.[93]

Swedish immigrant domestics also experienced social advancement through the respect they were given, both in the workplace and within their central social network, the ethnic community. When Josefina Larsson wrote encouraging a friend back home to come to America, among the benefits of immigration she noted was the higher respect given domestics, who were "not debased like in Sweden."[94] Similarly, among the statements included in the Swedish government study of immigration, *Emigrationsutredningen*, is praise for American domestic service, where, according to one woman, a servant was (unlike in Sweden) "treated like a human being."[95]

That so many Swedish immigrant domestics worked in large urban areas probably also contributed to their improved social status within the ethnic community. Domestics who worked in urban households in Sweden—and these were a minority of positions available during most of the period of mass immigration due to slower rates of urbanization in Sweden than in the United States—gained social status in Sweden as they adopted urban practices, manners of speaking, and habits.[96] Swedish domestic servants also maintained their own sense of hierarchy, based on both the type of work performed—a cook would have a higher status than a general maid—as well as on the wealth and status of the employer. This hierarchy was most likely based in part upon wage differences among the different positions.[97]

The Swedish American ethnic community's respect for and support of their countrywomen's employment as domestic servants is also evident through the institutional support provided—the employment bureaus and women's homes—as well as through positive representations in Swedish American literature and the Swedish American press. For example, in a 1912 book about Swedish America, Johan Person wrote: "We could not be other than proud of our serving sisters." He also stressed the "honor that these Swedish domestics bring to Swedes in America."[98] A 1905 editorial in a Chicago Swedish-language newspaper emphasized the excellent reputation held by Swedish maids in America, as well as their having received awards in an exhibition for cooking and for length of service.[99]

Domestic service employment also offered Swedish immigrant women opportunities for social advancement by contributing to the ease with which they could acculturate. Swedish American domestics' employment offered them a firsthand view of the habits, behavior, and accoutrements of middle- and upper-class Americans and a wage that allowed them to adopt and adapt some of what they saw to their own lives. Alma E. Swanson spoke positively of her employment in the household of wealthy Americans: "It is a wonderful thing for any girl if she knew enough to go into a place like that because you learn more in a place like that than you do by sitting at a desk or in an office."[100] Observers frequently commented on the transformation that Swedish immigrant women underwent through immigration—often represented by their fondness for purchasing fancy hats and having themselves photographed wearing them, a practice considered strictly within the domain of the upper class in the homeland. On a visit to Minneapolis in the 1890s, newspaperman Isidor Kjellberg noted how Swedish domestics dressed "just like American women" and that soon after their arrival Swedish servants became "unrecognizable."[101]

Some of the clothing and hats may have been a wealthy employer's castoffs, but Swedish immigrant domestics also spent their earnings on fashionable new American clothing. According to Margareta Matovic, Chicago Swedish domestics usually spent from 110 to 160 dollars per year on "clothes for balls and parties."[102] Their purchases may also represent an attempt to create their own sense of "ladyhood style" to counter the sense of lower status accorded their employment by the broader nonimmigrant society, an attitude noted by Nan Enstad among New York City working-class women.[103]

The transformation of Swedish immigrant women involved more than a wardrobe shift. It also revealed a change in the self-consciousness of these young Swedish women. For many, emigration to the United States resulted in a greater sense of self-worth. One newspaper article noted a change in "their manner and the way they carry themselves."[104] Swedish author Inge Lund, who worked for a time as a domestic in America and returned to Sweden to publish a book about her experiences, also described this metamorphosis. She wrote that after about a year in American domestic service, young Swedish women could "carry themselves with a confidence and independence that in no way resembled [that] of the formerly poor, clumsy farm girl."[105]

Minnie comments in a positive way about American domestic service, and the letters and biographies of other women present a largely favorable image of the occupation as well. Yet Swedish immigrant domestics certainly encountered problems in their work, and some women found that America was not always a "promised land." Complaints about wages or workloads and frequent changes of employment to remedy these issues suggest the type of problems encountered. Other dangers and risks faced by domestics might not be so easily remedied and could contribute to a Swedish immigrant woman experiencing "dog years."

The cost of living and the prices of consumer goods represented an area of complaint that some Swedish immigrant domestics included in their letters home. Anna Pettersson wrote complaining about her expenses, especially those for her dental care. Her mother wanted her to come to Sweden to visit, but Anna said she did not have enough money saved for the trip. She wrote: "It costs so much money for my teeth. I have had them filled with gold again . . . so now I have laid out $62.00 for my teeth and I have bought a sewing machine and paid $55.00 and it is always something one must lay out money for."[106] Other women found it difficult to acculturate to American society and looked forward to returning to Sweden, though, as already noted, women were a minority of Swedish immigrants returning permanently to the homeland.[107]

Some difficulties never found their way into letters to relatives and friends. A serious problem in domestic service, the extent of which it is impossible to determine from surviving sources, was sexual exploitation. Romantically misled by her employer's brother, Swedish immigrant domestic Martha Johnson became pregnant while working in Lawrence, Kansas, in the 1870s. A forced marriage occurred, whereupon the husband disappeared. Martha gave birth to her child in a woman's home.[108] In a similar vein, a 1923 novel entitled *Lummox* told the sad story of a domestic servant (the author made her ethnicity unclear, though suggested she was Swedish) who became pregnant after being seduced by her employer's son.[109] Although Swedish immigrant women did not usually write home about problems with male employers, two women interviewed for this study indicated that it was an issue. Each of the women had left at least one domestic position because of sexual advances on the part of employers.[110]

Historians have depicted American-born domestics as desiring to leave household service for other kinds of employment at the first possible opportunity, primarily because of the low social status associated with domestic work.[111] But Swedish immigrant women were not so eager to leave domestic service. In spite of some problems and difficulties associated with domestic service, the letters, biographies, and autobiographies written by Swedish domestics indicate that they found their work attractive and rewarding. Of the domestics investigated for this study, many worked in this occupation for one to three years, up to the time they married, and some worked as long as ten to twenty years. Matilda Johnson won a prize at the 1902 Minnesota State Fair for her long term of domestic service. She had been working for the same St. Paul family for over twenty years.[112] Swedish American domestic servants were able to support themselves, as well as contribute to the support of their families in Sweden. Rather than feeling ashamed of employment in household labor, they felt proud of their economic independence and respected within their primary social networks. Some even delayed marriage, not quite ready to give up their independence or desiring to build an economic reserve before establishing their own households. For example, Elisabet Olson was already thinking about marriage when she wrote to her family about a new domestic position in 1920, but she clearly found it difficult to end her employment. She described her employer as "the nicest woman I have worked for yet. So I think I will put the thoughts of marriage aside for awhile, and stay with them over winter, and save a little money, so we will have it that much better." Wages were especially high at this time because World War I and a changing economic landscape in Sweden had

Twin Cities Swedish-language newspapers published ads for Swedish American female professionals, including these ads for midwife (*barnmorska*) services. (*Minneapolis Veckobladet*, January 11, 1893)

MRS. I. HALL,
Exminerad Barnmorska.
254 Cedar Ave., Minneapolis, Minn.

MRS. CH. SODERLING,
SVENSK BARNMORSKA.
2505 12th Ave. South, Minneapolis, Minn.

Mrs. M. Lindblom
Exam. Svensk Barnmorska.
1917 Wash. Ave. N., Minneapolis, Minn.

MRS HEL. MAGNUSON,
I Sverige utexaminerad Barnmorska.
2417 10th Ave. S., MINNEAPOLIS, MINN

MISS C. E. HAGSTRÖM
EXAMINERAD BARNMORSKA
tillhandahåller
Kuriko o. Oleodlinnement.
1011 Washington Ave. S., Mpls.

Dr. West's Nerve and Brain Food.
KURERAR alla nervsjukdomar, såson försvagad hjernkraft, dåligt minne, sömnlöshet, hufvudvärk, nattliga sädesutgjutelser, nedtryckt sinnesstämning, förlorad mandom, elaka drömmar, försagdhet, nervsvaghet, brist på sjelfförtro-

decreased the stream of immigrating Swedish domestics. Elisabet was making sixty dollars a month at her new position. When she finally married in 1921, she was twenty-eight years old and her husband was thirty, and they likely began their marriage on an excellent financial footing.[113]

Swedish Immigrant Women in Nondomestic Wage Work: "A Lot of Work Available"

When Minnie wrote about having "a good position," she was clearly referring to employment in domestic service. Yet Swedish immigrant women could find "a good position" in other forms of employment as well. Although most Swedish immigrant women seeking wage work were employed as domestics, Swedish immigrant women also filled the ranks of the American labor market as textile workers, factory operatives, laundresses, midwives, and nurses, to name some of the most typical nondomestic occupations.

Much like their "sisters in service," nondomestic wage earners aimed to improve their material and social conditions and found opportunities that would not have been accessible or remunerative enough in the homeland. When nondomestic jobs opened up in the United States and could help single Swedish immigrant women reach the goals they had set for themselves, some chose to enter these occupations. Like their serving sisters, they exhibited practicality, determination, and independence in their occupational decisions as they worked toward their dreams in America and were not afraid to change occupations when their working conditions or wages were unsatisfactory or when better opportunities came along. Though they certainly met obstacles along the way, the qualities they brought to their lives and work in the United States assured that many of these women, like Minnie, had things better in America than what they had left behind.

The typical single Swedish woman who entered the United States felt concern about employment options even before arrival on American shores. Even if servant work was the best-known and most readily available employment, the newly immigrated woman could still cast about for other alternatives. Eva Wallström, relating her experiences as a single immigrant in 1907, noted that for young Swedish immigrant girls in the United States "there was a lot of work available. Sewing shops employed large numbers of seamstresses, and well-off families often had as many as six to eight domestics."[114] Similarly, Thörnberg noted the range of employment opportunities in Chicago in the 1910s: "Many single women among the Swedish immigrants here in Chicago are employed in families as chambermaids, waitresses, cooks, and cook's helpers, and in some cases a sort of middle position between servant and companion. Among those emigrating women we have further seamstresses, laundresses, cleaning women, factory workers, [and] waitresses in restaurants."[115]

Finding detailed statistical data on the numbers of Swedish immigrant women who chose nondomestic employment is difficult. Most census data on female employment, if they include ethnic categories at all, do not distinguish between Swedish and other Scandinavian immigrant women. Another difficulty is that women moved between domestic service and nondomestic jobs to suit their needs at particular times. Census reports and governmental studies provide only a snapshot of their careers, capturing them at only one moment in their employment history and hiding the frequency with which they moved in and out of different sectors of the workforce. The qualitative sources examined for this study sometimes offered more detailed work histories. For example, the letters of a single Swedish immigrant, Ida Rasmusson, from 1902 to 1907 revealed her movement between jobs as a domestic worker, a laborer in a watch factory, and a seamstress.[116] Reports of the U.S. Immigration Commission (Dillingham Commission) reveal the general outline of Swedish immigrant women's work histories. (See Appendix, Table 4, which lists the occupations in which most Swedish immigrant women supported themselves at the turn of the century.)

Language also shaped occupational choice. Most women arrived with little or no knowledge of English. Therefore, being a "greenhorn" meant that they would not be hired for occupations requiring fluency in English. The small number of first-generation Swedish immigrant women holding such jobs as saleswoman, clerk, or stenographer (under 3 percent in 1900) likely had been in the country for several years and had attended English-language classes and even technical school before obtaining these positions. Yet, even within these constraints of gender role and language, single Swedish immigrant women chose occupations from a range of alternatives.

Reasons for choosing employment outside domestic service varied. Some women's first experience in domestic service was unsavory, and rather than try their luck at another household job, they chose to leave service altogether. For example, Maria Elfström immigrated to the United States in 1884 at age fourteen. During her first several months in America, she worked as a domestic for her aunt. For reasons that she did not detail in her letters, the experience was unpleasant, and as soon as she was able she sought other employment. Maria obtained work as a seamstress in a coat shop, where she remained for eight years.

She then found a job at a ready-made clothing store, supervising the alterations department. She wrote in 1895 that she had "a very responsible position and I have fifteen dollars a week, which is approximately fifty kronor a week."[117] Other Swedish immigrant women came to the United States with occupational skills that they hoped to use. Olga Johnsson had received instruction as a seamstress in Sweden prior to emigration. When she switched from domestic service to sewing, she wrote home that she was "glad my training can be put to good use."[118]

This was certainly also the case for Swedish women immigrating to the United States with professional training or degrees. A newspaper clipping collection drawn from Swedish and Swedish American newspapers in the late nineteenth and early twentieth centuries revealed a handful of such women, including Hanna Kindbom, who had received training as a barber-surgeon in Sweden but was too young, at age eighteen, to take the Swedish qualifying examination for her profession. She left for the United States instead and obtained permission from authorities in Campello, Massachusetts, to open and operate a practice. She later became professor of hygiene and care at the University of Texas.[119] Nellie Gustafson, a midwife, graduated from Lund University in Sweden before practicing her profession in Lindström, Minnesota.[120] Similarly, a Swedish American newspaper from the western United States advertised the services of Karin Klint, a midwife, indicating her experience as director of the Southern Maternity Hospital in Stockholm.[121] In these and other cases, women's training and employment experience had a direct bearing on occupational choices in the United States.

Most Swedish immigrant women, however, viewed occupations not as careers but, instead, as a means to an end. Wage work allowed women to support themselves and to accumulate savings for the future. Some earned money to send home. Others saved money for specific purposes such as education or marriage. Still others hoped to earn enough to return to Sweden and prosper. Although constrained by gender and language, single Swedish immigrant women chose among available occupations those in which they found the most tolerable working conditions and which would best help them meet their particular needs and goals. For many women this meant frequent changes in location as well as in type of employment. Perhaps the best way of understanding the options available to single Swedish immigrant women, the relationship between their domestic and nondomestic employment, and the determination, independence, and practicality they exhibited is to examine closely the experiences of one woman who, though she had worked as a domestic in American homes, preferred other forms of wage work.

Evelina Månsson: "My Own Little Nest in a Big Noisy City"

Evelina Månsson was born in Frillesås, in the province of Halland, Sweden, in 1880. She came to the United States in 1901, visited Sweden in 1904, and returned to the United States again that year, where she remained until her remigration in 1907. In Sweden, she opened a business and eventually also worked as a journalist.[122] In 1930, the Swedish Folk Society published a memoir by Månsson covering the time she had spent as a Swedish immigrant woman in Minnesota. Though relatively brief, this account provides fascinating detail about the occupational choices, work experiences, and way of life of Evelina and other Swedish immigrant women working outside of domestic service.[123]

Evelina's story has several parallels to Minnie's—assistance from a relative to migrate to the United States, the importance of ethnic networks in obtaining employment, and movement from a small town to a large urban area with a Swedish American ethnic community. When twenty-one-year-old Evelina traveled to the United States in 1901, she stayed in her uncle's home near Hector, a small town about seventy-five miles west of Minneapolis, for a time. This uncle had lent her the money for her ship's ticket and had promised to help her find a domestic job in Hector. She was eager to find work to pay off her passage and begin to save money for her dream of returning to Sweden with enough capital to start a business.[124]

Evelina's uncle fulfilled his promise and found her a job with a Swedish American family in Hector, and she told her employers she would stay as long as they would have her. However, she wrote in her memoir that her intent was otherwise. Like Minnie, Evelina had her own goals in mind: "I decided to stay . . . until I learned the language and habits well enough that I could find something better." She realized that for the time being, other types of employment were difficult for a newcomer to find in a small town. Determined to accumulate "America savings," yet cognizant of the options and alternatives available to her, Evelina chose a practical and expedient way of beginning to work toward that goal.

Evelina's memoir expresses some of her feelings during these first months in the United States, including isolation, language difficulties, and loneliness. Although her employers were Swedish American, they made little effort to make Evelina feel at home, particularly with regard to language. They spoke Swedish only when absolutely necessary and subscribed to English-language newspapers. Evelina eventually borrowed a Swedish American newspaper from a friend to keep up with news. And she countered her loneliness by visiting a Swedish family named Lindberg in her free time. There she felt comfortable and at home.

After four months at this job, Evelina was ready for a change. Though she could not yet speak English fluently, she felt dissatisfied enough with her job in Hector to try her luck elsewhere. She wrote to several Swedish girlfriends in Minneapolis, who invited her to come and promised to help her find a job. As had Minnie, Evelina recognized that large urban areas were more likely to offer broader occupational choices and higher wages: "Perhaps in a large city . . . I could find some other type of work."

Her friends were all employed in a laundry and lived together in Minneapolis. When Evelina visited them, she was immediately impressed with their way of life. They had a nice apartment they had furnished and decorated, and they prepared all their meals at home. Evelina disliked extravagance and saw cooking at home as a sensible alternative to taking meals in restaurants, as many working girls did: "These girls had only been in the country a few years' time and already had things so well. I was filled with happy expectations for the future." Unfortunately, the laundry where her friends worked had no job openings when Evelina arrived. She instead contacted a woman — probably Swedish, since her name was Mrs. Lindqvist — who ran an employment bureau in Minneapolis. Lindqvist immediately located a job for Evelina as a kitchen maid in a boardinghouse. After looking over the building and meeting the other staff, Evelina borrowed an apron and began work on the spot.

But Evelina had little tolerance for what she considered unpleasant work tasks or working conditions. By the evening of her first day's work in the boardinghouse she had decided the job was too physically demanding. She gave notice and left. Though she had little knowledge of the city and spoke very limited English, she managed to locate the home where her aunt (who had accompanied her to Minneapolis) was visiting. She purchased an evening paper and examined the "help-wanted" section, where she found listed "hundreds of positions of all possible types." Among them, Evelina noticed an advertisement for a family seeking a Swedish girl for a three-person household. The home was close to where she was staying, so she walked over to check things out. The job seemed attractive — domestic servant for an elderly Swedish couple and their thirty-two-year-old son — and she began work the following morning. Finally, Evelina seemed to have found a comfortable situation, describing herself as "satisfied and contented" and noting that she had more free time and more pay than in the Hector position. Work tasks she also found more pleasant. She particularly enjoyed shopping for the household in the neighborhood Swedish stores. But her job satisfaction evaporated at the end of three weeks when the mistress accused Evelina of having a romantic interest in her son. Deeply insulted at being falsely accused, she gave her notice and moved out within a week of the incident.

Evelina then moved in with a friend while she searched for another job. Given her recent bad luck, she was reluctant to take another job without careful consideration. But her comments reveal that a broad range of occupational choices were available to her and other young immigrant women like her. She noted the many service-oriented jobs: "single-maid [meaning one maid for a whole household] for worker-families, [positions] with shopkeepers and innkeepers, and many others, but they did not tempt me." Nor did she consider restaurant work appealing. She contemplated domestic service, but reflecting perhaps on her past negative experience as a single-maid, she showed interest only in the very large and wealthy households that employed many maids per family. But being "green" and lacking language and employment experience in such households ruled out these positions. Jobs were also available with a number of Swedish businesses, but even these required more English proficiency than she had yet acquired.[125]

After several weeks, Evelina decided to try her luck at textile work and obtained a position at the Carlson Manufacturing Company in Minneapolis. On her first morning at the company, she was ushered to an electric sewing machine, given a package of cut-out shirts, and warned against "sewing her fingers." She had no idea how to operate her machine or carry out her work tasks. Though she eventually located an instructor, the person was too busy to help her. She spent her morning doing nothing. At noon, when the factory girls left for lunch, so did Evelina. Unlike the others, she never returned. Evelina next tried employment in a laundry, where she was expected to operate a washing machine, but her machine broke down. The laundry owner had to call in her husband to help, and when he arrived, he "glared angrily and spoke loudly." Though she could not understand what he was saying, it is likely that she was accused of having caused the problem, and while the angry couple was busy at the repair, she slipped out the door.

Evelina's unwillingness to settle for a job where she was not happy eventually paid off. She wrote in her memoir that she was not afraid of hard work, but what she dreaded was "constraint, confinement, and lack of understanding." And of course the job needed to pay well enough for her to be able to accumulate savings. After trying five different jobs and considering many others, Evelina at

Many Swedish women, including Evelina Månsson, supported themselves by working in factories such as Minneapolis's North Star Woolen Mill; photo about 1905.

last found a position that satisfied her. With the help of a Swedish immigrant girlfriend from her home area in Sweden, Evelina obtained employment as a cleaning woman at the Guaranty Loan Building in downtown Minneapolis. Her job was to clean the offices located on one floor of the building. Beginning at 5 A.M., she dusted and aired out the offices, making certain that she was finished before the businessmen arrived to begin their day's work. She reported back again in the evening, when she mopped and washed the floors. She used a mop and wringer system, which she described as a "nice way to clean floors." She earned one dollar a day, a five-dollar Christmas bonus, and gifts from some of the businessmen whose offices she cleaned. Evelina also found pleasure in the fact that most of the cleaning staff were Swedish. She created a "fringe benefit" at her job as well, illustrating her ability to grasp any opportunity for advancement that presented itself. One of the offices that she cleaned housed a business school. She had always wanted to learn typing, so she decided to come to work an hour early each day to practice on the typewriters there. To comply with a building rule that permitted no electric light use before 5 A.M., she learned to type by candlelight.

Evelina gradually settled into a life in Minneapolis. At first she roomed with another female employee of Guaranty Loan. But by the end of her first year in the United States she had paid off her passage ticket, rented a place of her own, and furnished it herself. Evelina's furnishings, for which she spent only about thirty dollars, included furniture, a sewing machine (which she must have taught herself how to use), bedding, kitchen utensils, and even a cookstove. Evelina's pleasure and pride at having her own home was evident in her memoir: "To think, my own little nest in a big noisy city in a foreign land! And so free and independent now!" Though her primary goal was to accumulate savings, she valued her autonomy and privacy as well.

Evelina expressed pleasure that her work schedule allowed her considerable free time. Because she worked early mornings and evenings, she could spend many daytime hours at one of her favorite pastimes—walking in the parks of Minneapolis, particularly Elliot Park (informally known as "Swede Park"). Her memoir included a chapter describing this and other recreational activities, indicating the social opportunities generally available for young Swedish immigrant women. She described the events found in the Swedish neighborhoods of Minneapolis—"dances, masquerade balls, and similar activities," which took place at the meeting halls and organizations such as "Swedish Brothers, Dania, Norrmanna, and others"[126]—but Evelina chose not to take part in these gala events. Finances were certainly one issue she considered when choosing how to spend her leisure time. She noted how many young women unwisely spent money trying to "out-dress" one another at the dances and balls. But her sense of morality and proper decorum was probably also a consideration. She mentioned attending musical events sponsored by Swedish churches as well as illustrated lectures, which she probably considered more acceptable than the dances and balls. And as Byron Nordstrom has noted in his discussion of social events in the Minneapolis Scandinavian neighborhood of Cedar-Riverside in this time period, some of the entertainments were "rather sordid . . . [and] good girls simply did not go there."[127]

Evelina could choose not to attend social events she felt were inappropriate, but she could not altogether avoid exposure to some of Minneapolis's negative elements. In fact, her memoir includes a chapter entitled "Various Experiences," which describes some of these unfavorable episodes. For example, her employment as a cleaning woman required her arrival at the workplace before daylight. Though she usually walked to work with some female coworkers, on some mornings she walked alone. On one such morning, a man followed her. She varied her route to "lose" him, but he continued to follow. When she noticed another man walking in front of her, she was relieved, thinking that she could get protection from this person if necessary. Her relief was temporary, though, because she realized the walker ahead was black, and she "abhorred negroes." Just when she thought all was lost, the man following her approached and spoke in Swedish. He informed her that he had been following her out of concern for her safety.[128]

Evelina related other examples of her exposure to the "underside" of Minneapolis: "Often upon my arrival home in the morning I read that a murder had taken place, once even that a person had shot him/herself at about the same time that I had passed their house on my walk home. One time I went both evening and morning past a house where six persons lay dead—murdered." She also recalled in her memoir witnessing a streetcar run over a young boy, a horse and buggy run over an old man, and a young man fall from a high ladder to his death. She was herself the victim of misfortune when someone broke into her apartment. Though Evelina was not home at the time, the thief made off with a watch that had significant sentimental and monetary value.

In spite of the ugly realities that young urban workers like Evelina faced in turn-of-the-century urban America, they continued to encourage other young women to follow in their footsteps. Evelina's satisfaction with her experience is reflected in her decision to bring her sister over to the United States. One and a half years after her own arrival, Evelina and her just-arrived sister moved into a south Minneapolis apartment together. Evelina found a position at Guaranty Loan for her sister similar to her own. Both sisters worked in Minneapolis until 1904, three and a half years after Evelina's arrival. By then Evelina had saved up what she thought was enough money for her business venture in Sweden, so they boarded a ship and left for home. To Evelina's dismay, she discovered that her savings of a thousand kronor were inadequate for her plans. And not only were her capital assets limited, but there was no space available in her home area to rent shop facilities. Unable to carry out her plans and frustrated with the lack of educational and recreational opportunities at home, Evelina returned to Minneapolis.

Evelina had learned English and gained much from her earlier experiences in the United States, and she had no difficulty obtaining satisfactory employment this time around. Upon her second arrival in Minneapolis, she took a job at the Sterling Manufacturing Company. Though she quite quickly managed to sew through her fingernail, she endured and remained on the job. After three weeks of employment, she was earning over seven dollars a week (nearly twenty-seven kronor, according to her own calculations).[129]

While working at Sterling, Evelina was offered a cleaning position at the Fenix Building in Minneapolis. She remembered her positive experiences at Guaranty Loan and for a time tried to work both jobs but found it too strenuous. After her Fenix employer convinced her that the pay for textile work was unstable, she quit the sewing job. However, when she later discovered that one of her roommates was making more per week than she was, she left the Fenix and started working at Weum Watt (another clothing manufacturer). She occasionally earned extra income by filling in at the Fenix job in emergencies. Evidently satisfied with her pay, work schedule, and working environment, Evelina remained at Weum until her marriage and remigration to Sweden in 1907.

With an unusual richness of detail, Evelina's memoir illustrates several important features in the lives of Swedish immigrant women in nondomestic employment. It is evident that many job opportunities outside domestic service were available for these women, and, judging from Evelina's experiences, these jobs paid fairly well. Without major compromises in living accommodations, clothing and personal purchases, and recreation, Evelina was able to accumulate considerable savings (over three hundred dollars in three and one half years). The experience of Maria Elfström, the domestic-turned-seamstress, also supports this assertion. Over the course of ten years, Maria purchased tickets for four of her siblings' emigration to the United States and intended to bring over her mother and the two siblings remaining in Sweden as well. In addition to providing passage money, she shared her household with her siblings after their arrival and supported them while they became accustomed to their new environment. For example, she provided housing and economic support for her sister Ingeborg (who emigrated at age thirteen) while Ingeborg completed high school and the training to become a teacher.[130]

One might think that such devotion to her family's welfare caused Maria to make great sacrifices. But her comments suggest otherwise. She remarked in a letter to her brother that he might think it odd that she was not yet married (Maria was twenty-five years old at this time). But she indicated that she was not certain that she even wanted to marry, because she could earn so much money herself. She wrote, "When I am alone I can always be elegant. [Who knows] what can happen, I might not get an outfit once a year if I were married." Maria's employment as a seamstress provided her an income substantial enough to support family commitments as well as the luxury of dressing in an "elegant" manner. Her immigration had resulted in an economic security that allowed her to make her own choice as to whether to remain self-supporting or to marry.

The experiences of Evelina and Maria also highlight another important factor in the Swedish immigrant woman's life—that women did not consider all jobs equally satisfactory. Just as domestic workers like Minnie frequently changed employment so they could find the best combination of wages, working conditions, time off, and access to friends, for similar reasons women like Evelina and Maria changed jobs frequently, moving both within the nondomestic employment sector and between domestic and nondomestic employment. Though many of the themes in Evelina's memoir were positive, her writing also revealed negative aspects of life as a nondomestic laborer in America. During her first attempt at textile work, there was no organized job training offered, and she certainly must have been at risk for injury. Similarly, she was not trained at the laundry shop yet was expected to be responsible for the washing machine's proper functioning. Evelina's Fenix employer warned her about the instability of factory worker wages. In an era when labor unions were relatively weak (especially women's) and women filled mostly low-paying positions in the industrial sector, females were among the first laid off when hard times fell. Evelina's problems were not unusual but were problems many other Swedish immigrant women workers faced. Swedish immigrant Olga Johnsson described one such instance in a letter to her parents in 1896: "Times are bad here in America. Thousands are out of work here in Boston. It sounds unbelievable, but three thousand were let off from a clock factory at one time. They were mostly girls."[131]

Industrial workers also faced arbitrary wage decreases. At her textile job at Weum's, Evelina did piecework. She was paid eighteen cents for every dozen shirts she completed and wrote that she frequently earned over two dollars a day.[132] But one day when she went to turn her work in to the manager, he told her that the rate for the shirts was set too high and would have to be lowered. The explanation he offered reflected commonly held attitudes toward women workers in the late nineteenth and early twentieth centuries. He explained that she was earning as much as most men, many of whom had families to support. Employers assumed that women had fewer financial responsibilities than men and that for a woman to be making as much money as a man or more was to take away (if not in terms of cash, at least in terms of dignity) from men's earnings. For women who worked more slowly than average, earning a living through piecework was difficult. Adina Eriksson and her girlfriend Alice took employment applying pearl embroidery to silk blouses and dresses, but they did not work quickly enough to suit the employer's tastes. They looked for another job when they realized they could never support themselves doing that type of work.[133]

Poor working environments and lack of safety precautions in the workplace were also problems. Having given up on pearl embroidery, Adina Ericksson and her friend sought work in a munitions factory. They stood in a long line of girls, waiting to apply for positions. But, as Adina later wrote, when they were close enough "to see how dark and dirty the factory was we turned around and went home." Though these two women avoided what appeared to be a dangerous and unpleasant working environment, other young Swedish immigrant women found themselves in jobs that damaged their physical and mental health. According to the findings of a U.S. government study published in 1910, laundry work could have deleterious physical effects on women workers. The report described several single Swedish women who complained of pains in the back and side from standing for hours, as well as foot ailments resulting from running a treadle-operated ironing machine. One thirty-five-year-old Swedish woman who had been in the United States for four years complained of "foul air and moisture in the laundry where she works and [the] bad condition of water-closets." She also reported instances of sexual harassment on the job. In her place of work there was only one bathroom, which was unisex, and it was located in the basement. The report explained that she blamed her hemorrhoids on the fact that "many times men would call after her and chase her until she would not go [to the bathroom], but would wait until she got home."

Faced with difficulties in nondomestic occupations, women sometimes turned to labor unions to try to improve their wages and working conditions, although, unlike their Irish-born counterparts, Swedish immigrant women are not well known for labor union participation.[134] But they no doubt made up a part of the rank and file in industrial labor unions. Union meeting notices in Swedish American newspapers suggest both the desire of unions to encourage Swedish women's participation as well as some interest on their part. The *Svenska Amerikanska Posten* included the following notice in a 1900 issue: "The city's seamstresses and dressmakers union held a meeting last Tuesday afternoon. Questions concerning a nine-hour workday were discussed, but a decision will not be made before the committee from the Trades and Labor Council has presented its report. The organization has increased with 35 new members."[135]

The relatively limited union activism of single Swedish immigrant women may be due to their numbers in domestic service, a type of employment that has been, as David Katzman has noted, because of its "isolation and atomization" typically very difficult to unionize.[136] The fact that the conditions of domestic service work were generally much better in the United States than they had been in Sweden likely also served as a deterrent to Swedish immigrant domestics' labor activism. Evidence of labor activism among Swedish immigrant and other domestics does, however, exist. Swedish immigrant Hilda Linder participated in an attempt to unionize domestics in Minneapolis and St. Paul in 1919.[137] And a union for Scandinavian domestics existed in Seattle, Washington, in 1917.[138]

Another exception to limited labor union participation by Swedish immigrant women can be found in Mary Anderson, who eventually became director of the Women's Bureau of the U.S. Department of Labor. In 1889, at the age of sixteen, Anderson immigrated to the United States with an older sister. She initially took a dishwashing job at a lumber camp in Ludington, Michigan, where she earned two dollars a week. Bright and self-motivated, during her free time she studied newspapers and magazines to learn English. After a few years in domestic service, she moved to Chicago and worked in a shoe factory. During her time in factory work, she became aware of the problems that workers faced, and, convinced that positive changes could be made if workers banded together, Anderson became actively involved with the union in her industry. She eventually served as her local union's president and devoted increasing amounts of her free time to union activities. Anderson gradually gained a reputation as an expert on women's industrial labor and was the first woman to serve on the executive board of the National Boot and Shoe Worker's Union.[139]

During World War I, Anderson was selected to be part of the women's division in the War Department's Ordnance Department, which led to work in the Woman-in-Industry section of the Department of Labor. When in 1920 Congress established a Women's Bureau in the Department of Labor, Mary Anderson was appointed as its head. The bureau's task was to investigate the conditions of wage-earning women and to suggest legislation to address the woman worker's specific needs. Among the many issues that Anderson helped study were equal pay for women, gender-based hiring discrimination, and the equal rights amendment. Certainly some of her ideas and concerns stem from her early years in the United States as a female immigrant worker.[140]

Like Minnie Anderson, Evelina Månsson, and Mary Anderson, most Swedish immigrant wage earners found themselves doing household service or industrial work. But a small percentage of Swedish women entered less common vocations. Though details of women's participation in these positions are difficult to find, archival material and brief biographical information from newspaper articles and obituaries can outline some of the occupational patterns these women followed.

A few single Swedish immigrant women chose to become farmers. Because of the capital necessary to begin such an enterprise, these women typically worked first at other jobs while they accumulated money to purchase land and equipment, a plan followed by Emma Persson, who left Sweden in 1906 to become a farmer. She journeyed to LaMoure, North Dakota, where she worked at both rural and urban domestic jobs until she had paid off her ticket and saved up some money. After several years she was able to settle on 160 acres of North Dakota prairie. She received help from neighbors and friends to build a shelter, but she lived alone on her homestead and worked the land herself. Apparently successful in her first year of farming, she paid off her land within fourteen months of settling on it.[141]

Some Swedish immigrant women were drawn to business and management. A Swedish American newspaper in 1952 described the experiences of one woman who had success in business at the turn of the twentieth century. At age sixteen, Erika Näslund emigrated alone to the United States. She began as a minor hotel employee, but over the next fifteen years she managed to pur-

Fortunate Swedish American women, such as these young nurses in the classes of 1901 and 1902, trained at the Swedish Hospital School of Nursing in Minneapolis.

chase a hotel in Butte, Montana. Though a specific chronology of Näslund's business progress is not included in the article, it indicated that she eventually became the owner of three successful hotel companies.[142]

The field of nursing attracted other single Swedish immigrant women. Many received their training from one of several Swedish American hospitals, which had been established in the United States by the turn of the century. For example, the *Svenska Tribunen Nyheter*, published in Chicago, announced the graduation of thirty-four Swedish American nurses in May and June of

1909. They had received training at the Swedish Englewood Hospital and the Swedish Augustana Hospital in Chicago.[143] Leaders in the Minneapolis and St. Paul Swedish immigrant community established the Swedish Hospital in Minneapolis in 1898 and the following year instituted a nurse's training school. In existence for nearly three-quarters of a century, the program drew primarily young Swedish American women as students.[144]

A desire to minister to fellow immigrants led some single Swedish immigrant women into church and missionary work.[145] Sigrid Hansen came to America at age twenty-two. She attended a Salvation Army school in Chicago and spent the next decade working among Swedes and other immigrants along the Pacific Coast.[146] Esther Scherling, who immigrated to the United States in 1903, became a missionary for the Swedish Baptist church, serving in Denver and Salt Lake City. She eventually became the matron of the Scandinavian American Women's Christian Home in Denver.[147] Maria Rabenius was trained as a handicraft teacher in Sweden before her emigration to the United States. After teaching for a time in the Swedish community of Lindsborg, Kansas, she began a children's and young people's home in Avon, Massachusetts, which she managed and operated for over three decades.[148]

Whether single Swedish immigrant women worked as domestics, seamstresses, farmers, or teachers or in other occupations in the United States, all took advantage of opportunities available to them. Like Minnie, they came to America determined to improve their material and social conditions. Willing to begin at the bottom of the occupational hierarchy, they still maintained standards for wages, working conditions, and personal freedom. Just as Minnie had, most Swedish immigrant women changed employment frequently. Though always keeping in mind their particular hopes and dreams, they continually sought to improve the situations in which they worked toward their goals. And while it may have seemed to native-born Americans that these women worked in the least favorable jobs, for many these jobs were an improvement in economic and social terms from those they had left behind. Most found, like Minnie, that "things were good" and that, compared to the opportunities available to them at the time in Sweden, life in the United States meant that they "had it better here."

CHAPTER 5

"A Nice Little Nest"

I was saving money to pay for a ticket and send for my sister. When she came I had just married, so I had a home in which to receive her. I had, after some time, met an orderly and kind man whom I learned to love and who gave me a home and his love. We were both alone, strangers in a strange land. . . . My husband was a tailor. First we lived in town and had a good life, but then came the difficult years in the 1890s. There was little work. We had saved a little so we decided to buy land. There were many who went out from the cities and bought land in northern Minnesota. . . . We moved out into the country in July. The summer had been very dry and hot. We had a little boy a year and a half old who had been ill and we decided to go out into the country as soon as possible for his sake. It was so warm and unhealthy in town and many children were sick. Our log house where we were going to live was not finished, so I and my son had to stay at a place where there was a kind of hotel for people who drove supplies to the logging camps, where they could stay overnight. This was owned by a half-blood Indian who owned a sawmill in the vicinity and cut lumber in the forest. . . .

Our nearest town was five miles from our land. It wasn't so far, but there was no road. The city had a large sawmill, the only industry there. Tree stumps and rocks were in the middle of the streets between the few houses and I remember wading in large piles of sawdust when we walked out of the town. My husband had been there before, so he knew the way, but there was no road. We followed a small river through brush and morass. My husband carried our son; I carried a cat in a basket. The baby screamed and the cat mewed, kicked, and wanted out of the basket. I complained and said that we'd come so far from civilization that we would never see people anymore. I have always been a friend of nature but that time it was almost at the point of becoming too much nature. I was almost ready to cry. But then I discovered some wild raspberries and also some forest flowers. And then I plucked up my courage. It was still better than the brown singed hills of St. Paul. We were thirsty, so we stopped and ate some raspberries and our spirits were lifted. After several hours walking through the forest we arrived at the place where my husband left me with the Indians, and he walked on to our land.

We had a couple of men there who were building our log cabin. My husband said he would come and fetch me when the roof was put on, which he did, but we had to stay at the Indian camp for a week. . . . There was an old forest camp on our land. Those who built for us lived there for a time. They had a couple of old horses, and there was a logging road through the forest. They drove our furniture and furnishings there. We had a nice little nest. Most of our furniture had to stay in the attic for many years until we could build a better and bigger house. Some of it we traded away or exchanged for our first horse.

We were the first who built in this area, and our home became a place where other settlers could stay until they had their own houses finished. We had four men here that first winter while they were building their own houses. They had to sleep in the top and bottom bunk in the kitchen. One time we had two others and they had to lay on the floor. We had the other room to ourselves. Our home looked like a forest camp. We almost always had somebody staying with us those first years. . . . We paid for our land and paid those who built for us but then our savings were gone. We borrowed money for our first cow from a German colleague of my husband.

Nobody could make a living from the land until it was cleared. Most went into the forest and cut lumber in the wintertime and in the summers they worked at the sawmill. But my husband of course had a profession. He walked to the big cities and worked in spring and fall season, so I was alone a great deal. It was such hard times then and there was little work, but he knew a profession and made more than a laborer and also found it easier to get work than they, when times were hard. There were not so many ready-made clothes at that time as now. Actually, we did not suffer. It was worse for many others. . . .

We had moved here to the country and lived here for a couple of months when the fire came. It burnt here on the same day as in Hinckley although Hinckley is nearly seventy-five miles from here. The summer of 1894 had been unusually hot and dry. Everything was dry as tinder. They had been cutting lumber around here and left all the twigs and the tops of the trees lying on the ground. There were fires in several places in the forests that were lying there, and smoldered now and then, when suddenly the entire area was in smoke and flames. A strong wind had blown up as it always does when there is a fire. We saw the fire approaching but luckily the wind was blowing away from us, toward the fire. If the wind had been from the other direction we would have been lost.

My husband had left a few days earlier to work in St. Paul, but I was not alone. Two men who had built our house were still there waiting until their own house was ready [although one man had set off for Milaca when the fire started]. . . . The fire approached our house more and more closely. The man who was going to help me said we should carry water and have it ready in case of a fire on the roof. But I said, "If the fire comes that close, we are lost." There was a big pile of dry sticks only a few feet from the house that they had chipped off the logs when they were building. I said, "If the fire catches them, then the house, too, will go. We must set a backfire." In spite of his protests I took a gunny sack, a bucket of water and matches and set fire to the dry grass and extinguished the fire near the house with the wet gunny sack and then let the fire go in order to meet the other fire. Since it was burning in the direction the wind was blowing, it soon picked up full speed. When the two fires met, the flames were at least 50 feet in the air. It crashed and thundered and sounded like rifle shots. It is a spectacle I will not forget. This saved our house. Towards evening it got calmer and the fire died down. However, it took two weeks before there was any rain. If there was any spot that did not burn that first day, it caught fire again here and there, and burned. The smoke was so thick in the mornings that I had to tie a woolen cloth around my mouth if I went out. Windows and doors had to be closed not to let in the smoke. In the daytime when the wind picked up it was better. Every tree stump was burning and in the evening one could see the area looking like a large city with all lights lit.

The fire had, however, done a good job of clearing. Without the fire, it would have taken much longer to get the forestland arable. There were not many green trees left—only an oasis here and there that the fire had passed by. For long stretches there was not a green leaf. It took a year before anything green started to grow shoots. . . .

Some of the settlers were lucky enough to have a horse, but many among us had none in the beginning. But neighbors who owned horses were kind and brought home what we needed, and it did not take long before we bought a horse. Neither my husband nor I had ever put a harness on a horse. My husband had worked in his profession as a tailor and had lived in town but we soon learned. As my husband was out working so much those first years, I had to learn how to drive. And soon I could drive any horse at all. . . . My husband usually came home from his work in town late on Christmas Eve. What a hurry I had, to get everything in order. Sometimes before our sons were grown up enough to help, I myself had to drive into town to meet him at the train that arrived late in the evening. The children were quite wild because papa was coming home and there was always a happy Christmas Eve although it was always late and sometimes I was very tired before we were ready to go to bed.

He used to stay home until March when the spring season began. Then I was alone until the Fourth of July when he came home and stayed at home until September when they started to sew winter clothes. I was alone so much. We lived near a small stream that always overflows its banks when it rains a lot or when they open the dam in the Rum River and the stream is then 8 or 10 feet deep, with a strong current . . . . When the children were small there was always the danger that they would drown in the stream when the water was high. I used to scare them by telling them about "Näcken" [a water sprite in Swedish folklore, who will pull you under the water and take you away if you are not careful], and they had respect for him until they were big enough to watch out for themselves.

I never dared leave the children alone when they were small. I used to have them with me in a cart wherever I went. When I walked to get the horse in the meadow, they always came to meet me. I then put them up on the horse's back, as many as would fit. We had five sons so there were plenty of little riders, but of course we got more horses with time, too. The children thought it was fun and so did I. . . . I was glad to live in the country with the children, it is better for them in the country than in town. They have their freedom and can live a natural life out in God's free nature and not be so much in touch with bad company. . . . First when we came here we planted some shade trees and fruit trees around the house. I especially remember one time when my husband and I stood in the window on the second floor in spring when the fruit trees were in bloom, how beautiful we thought it was and how happy we were. It was ours; we had built it with the labor of our own hands. We felt proud and happy. . . .

Times were still hard. There was no work to be had, so the land was taken up. After ten years there was almost no land worth buying for sale around here. Settlers came in everywhere. No one bought large pieces of land. Forty or eighty acres—it was so hard to clear the land, so that was enough. But those who settled in the forested area had the advantage of having wood and logs for their log houses. Nobody who could chop wood needed to freeze, even if the house was not so warm. I myself have taken mud and put it in the cracks where the plaster had fallen out. I used to go over the house that way every fall before it froze up, before we lined the house with boards on the outside. . . .

When we had lived here for two years our third son was to be born. My husband stopped his work [early] to be home so that I no longer was alone. When he had been home for a few days he took ill with typhoid fever. We had a doctor who came every other day. I had to be a nurse. I had no experience in such things. But we had a book called Hälsan framför allt [Health above all], published in Sweden, which we had received as a premium with the Svenska Amerikanaren [newspaper] at the time that Onkel Ole [sic] was its editor.[1] *In this book there was much to learn about nursing. So I learned from the book how to take care of him and to protect ourselves from contamination. I must have done well, because I got a compliment from the doctor. He was kind enough to go to a neighbor and tell them that typhoid was not so dangerous or contagious and that I kept it very clean and disinfected so they did not need to be afraid. Nobody was infected. There was typhoid in the city where he had worked, so he had received the germ of the illness from there.*

Our child was born two weeks after my husband took ill.[2] *He had just passed his crisis then. I had not been out of my clothes the whole time. The doctor couldn't come, so there was only a neighbor woman. The doctor came the day after and looked in on us all. I had a young girl in to help for four days, and then I was alone. A neighbor helped me with the cattle for a few days, and then I had to do that, too, but we didn't have so many cattle then. We had a few dollars saved but they were used up while my husband was sick. Luckily I had hatched fifty or so chicks. These came in handy when my husband got better and started to eat. He had to be careful with what he ate and was very hungry.*

It was the worst winter I have lived as a settler's wife. We fed ourselves from the butter of one cow. I churned five or six pounds a week. We got twenty cents a pound, but everything was inexpensive. One dollar for fifty pounds of flour. Coffee was ten cents a pound. The best meat was ten or twelve cents and everything else was cheap. We had enough clothes. We managed. Even if the food was meager, we were not hungry. With time my husband got well and strong, although he was weak for a long time. In

March he was completely well and then his spring season started. He went to town again and started to work. We pawned our gold [wedding] rings so that he would have travel money. We were free of debt but didn't want to mortgage our home for such a small amount. He found work right away and it didn't take long before there was money to get the rings out of pawn and money for the children and I to live.

The land was not plowed then. There was only a little bit of wild hay. I grew some vegetables and potatoes for our own needs. The first years after the fire one could plant potatoes in the ashes between the tree stumps. I have never seen such large and beautiful potatoes since. . . . Acre after acre was laid under the plough. More cows were raised. They [settlers] didn't have enough land to grow much grain, so they raised [dairy] cows instead. First we sold butter in the store in exchange for goods. The storekeeper never wanted to give us cash. I remember one time when I asked for ten cents for postage and the storekeeper answered that I couldn't have it, since it was against their principles to give cash. I got angry and said that they always took my money when I had cash. That storekeeper lost a customer. I never shopped there again.

Most of the time my husband was out on jobs, so I usually shopped with cash and never went in debt. . . . I have worked hard as a pioneer, but have had the satisfaction that I worked for myself. . . . It was the love for the land you owned, the hope for a better future that drove the first pioneers to persevere.[3]

MARRIAGE, LEAVING THE PAID WORKFORCE, AND RAISING A FAMILY were common aspirations for most single Swedish immigrant women, just as they were for most young women in late nineteenth- and early twentieth-century America.[4] Minnie Anderson began to meet these goals within only three years of her immigration, leaving her domestic employment and accepting the role of wife with her marriage in 1892 and becoming a mother with the birth of her first child in 1893. With the family's move from St. Paul to a small piece of land in Mille Lacs County in 1894, Minnie also took on the role of farmwife. Her marriage brought with it new demands and duties. Swedish immigrant wives bore primary responsibility for the tasks of social reproduction—the activities necessary to ensure the maintenance and perpetuation of the family and household, such as pregnancy and childbirth, child rearing, attending to the family's needs for food, clothing, and shelter, and caring for the sick and elderly.[5] Married Swedish immigrant women, especially those who became rural farmwives, often found their lives more physically and emotionally demanding than they had as single wage earners. Yet Minnie's experiences as wife and mother suggest the ways in which many Swedish immigrant women continued to have things better in America, though their definition of having things better changed as they moved through their life course. Where good wages and working conditions and an active social life had been important for women like Minnie as single wageworkers, having things better as a Swedish American wife, mother, and farmer was viewed in terms of the ability to maintain "a nice little nest" by supporting a growing family, owning land, and, as Minnie stated so succinctly, having the "satisfaction that I worked for myself."

Courtship and Marriage: "An Orderly and Kind Man"

Minnie Anderson and Jacob P. Halgren were married on March 2, 1892. Minnie had recently turned twenty-five, and Jacob would turn twenty-nine a few days after the wedding. Since they did not meet until after Minnie's arrival in St. Paul in early 1891, their courtship lasted at most fourteen months. Although Minnie's move to the Twin Cities may have been motivated in part by a desire to increase her marriage prospects, her memoir suggests the decision was based mostly on economic rather than matrimonial prospects. If marriage patterns in the homeland provided any kind of standard for Minnie, she probably felt no great urgency to marry. The average age at marriage in Sweden in the 1890s was 26.8 for women and 28.8 for men, and Minnie was just turning twenty-four when she moved to St. Paul.[6] The mean age at marriage in Minnie's home province in Sweden was even higher, especially in the 1890s. A study of several Dalsland parishes in 1892 revealed the average age at marriage as 30.2 for women and 35.8 for men.[7]

The financial and personal freedom Minnie enjoyed as a domestic might also have dampened her eagerness to marry, though she did not, like some Swedish immigrant women, delay her marriage with other goals in mind. Hilda Linder refused a marriage proposal because, as she wrote, she "could not think of myself as getting married and renting an apartment and staying in the city [Worcester, Massachusetts] without having seen something of America."[8] Linder sought new experiences before settling down, but other Swedish immigrant women delayed marriage out of concerns for maintaining economic security and social status. E. H. Thörnberg studied Swedish immigrants in

Minnie and Jacob Halgren's wedding photo, 1892.

Chicago and found that males generally preferred to marry within their own ethnic group, but that finding a Swedish wife might be a challenge because Swedish American servant girls were known to delay (or even decline) marriage if they did not feel they could maintain the same standard of living after marriage that they had become accustomed to as domestics.[9] The comments of Hädda Carlson, writing from Pennsylvania in 1883, illustrate this attitude: "You asked me if I had a fiancé. I can't say I don't have one, but I haven't decided on one yet, because I believe that if I get married I won't have things as good as I have them now."[10]

Such experiences offer a stark contrast to those of young women in Sweden. Research on women and marriage in Stockholm in the late nineteenth century revealed that women like Minnie who came from poor families—lacking property or dowry—were not considered desirable in the marriage market and had limited chances of marrying up. A rural girl from a landless family who moved to Stockholm had to work for several years to save money in order to increase her attractiveness as a marriage partner.[11] Although Swedish immigrant women did not generally mention increased prospects for marriage when they wrote about their reasons for immigration in letters and memoirs, the Swedish American marriage market favoring females played a role in some young women's decisions to emigrate. Olga Johnsson emigrated from Sweden in the 1890s in part because she hoped to marry a young man from her region who was also emigrating. She ultimately ended up having to choose between two potential fiancés—the one she had known back home and another Swedish American who sought her hand. She ultimately chose the hometown boy.[12] Similarly, Anna Israelsdotter wrote home from Minnesota in the 1890s that she was having difficulty deciding between two suitors.[13]

Perhaps Jacob was the more eager to marry. After all, he was only one male in a pool of eligible males in St. Paul from which young women like Minnie could choose. In the 1895 Minnesota state census for Ramsey County (of which St. Paul residents made up the largest number) there were 102 Swedish-born females ages twenty-one to thirty for every 100 Swedish-born males in the same age range (figures include married and unmarried men and women).[14] This ratio approximates the overall figures for single Swedish emigration to the United States in the 1890s, with 98 single women emigrating for every 100 single men.[15] Swedish immigrant women were drawn to urban areas because of higher domestic wages and better working conditions, but young Swedish immigrant men may have been drawn to urban areas not only for employment opportunities but also to participate more successfully in the marriage market.[16]

Some Swedish immigrant men resorted to more unique strategies to find potential spouses, such as the man who advertised in the Swedish women's magazine *Qvinnan och hemmet* (Women and the Home) for a "respectable and competent girl or childless widow from a good family" between the ages of twenty-seven and forty to marry.[17]

Minnie was likely pursued by a number of suitors. She was an attractive young woman whose occupation as a domestic also contributed to her popularity. Johan Person argued in a 1912 study that among Swedish immigrant women it was Swedish American domestics who found the best marriage partners because the women's newly acquired habits, their upper-class appearance and manners, and their skills in managing a home made them more attractive to men.[18] And though Minnie had facility with English and familiarity with American households, it is not surprising that she married a fellow Swede. Endogamy—marrying within the ethnic group—was a common pattern for Swedish immigrants in the late nineteenth and early twentieth centuries.[19]

The man Minnie ultimately chose to marry, Jacob Peter Halgren, was born in 1863 in Tidersum, Östergötland, a province on the opposite coast from Minnie's home province of Dalsland. Jacob's surname in Sweden had been Petersson (son of Peter Johansson, who lived on a farm named Halltorp), but he took the name Halgren after arriving in the United States in 1887. Trained in Sweden as a tailor, Jacob had first worked in Chicago, but by 1890 he was listed in a St. Paul city directory as working for merchant tailor Herman Gall, where he sewed coats.[20]

Minnie did not tell us in her personal documents exactly how she and Jacob met, but, considering the enjoyment she had found dancing in Sweden, it is possible that they met at one of the dances sponsored by local Swedish groups such as the Swedish Brothers fraternal organization.[21] Yet Minnie was careful to describe Jacob as an "orderly and kind man," and perhaps by that she meant that he did not approve of dancing and preferred church-sponsored social activities (concerts, picnics, and the like). That P. J. Swärd, pastor of the First Swedish Evangelical Lutheran Church in St. Paul, performed the couple's wedding suggests that Minnie and Jacob had some connection to religious activities, although neither of them was listed as a member of Swärd's congregation.[22] Whether dancing or not, they likely based their social life, both while courting and after marriage, on St. Paul's East Side, where newly arrived Swedish immigrants concentrated and where Swedish businesses and institutions developed.[23]

Minnie's reference to Jacob's good conduct may also have reflected how his behavior compared to that of the other men she had encountered. Minnie's

Minnie and Jacob Halgren married at St. Paul's First Swedish Evangelical Lutheran Church. While neither Minnie nor Jacob was an enrolled member, they may have attended church services or social events.

daughter related two incidents her mother had told her about potential suitors whose manners she had found distasteful. In the first instance, Minnie was walking down a street with a male friend who was accompanied by another male acquaintance. When her friend departed for work, the acquaintance asked Minnie if she would care to join him for a cup of coffee. She agreed, but when they walked up the street and the man opened the door of his residence, all Minnie could see was a bedroom. Her reaction was to hit the man over the head and depart immediately. In the second instance, she was walking to her employer's home one evening, carrying a jar of honey, when a man "acted fresh" toward her, so she emptied the sticky contents of her jar over the man's head.[24]

Though some women who worked as domestics (both native-born and immigrant) made complaints about the occupation placing limits upon social life, Minnie's experiences indicate that she found ample opportunities to meet the opposite sex and develop relationships. Contrary to popular belief,

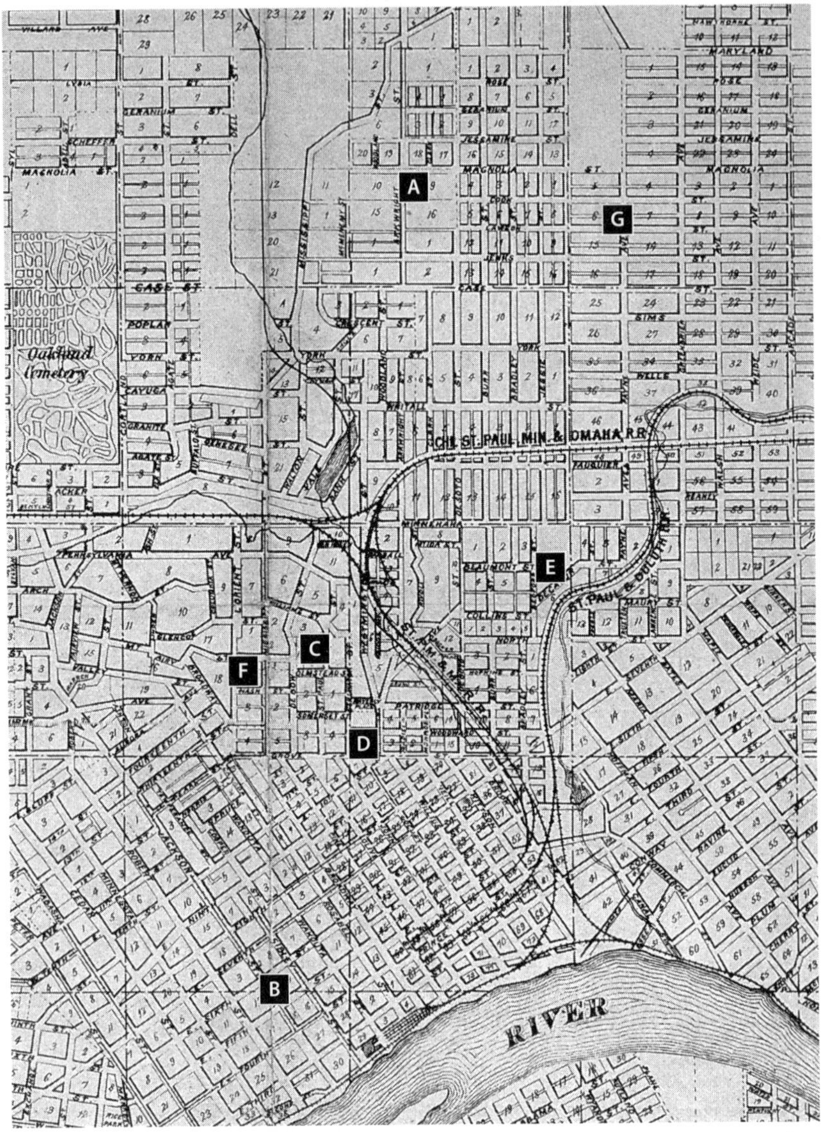

Central Saint Paul, 1880s.

The places where Jacob and Minnie lived and worked as they courted and, later, lived as a married couple are all within or near downtown St. Paul. Businesses owned by Swedish immigrants along Payne Avenue provided opportunities for the couple to enjoy Swedish American products as well as occasions for Swedish American-style leisure and entertainment.

Map key on opposite page.

a domestic's occasions for social interaction were not always limited to the maid's day off. Jacob may have courted Minnie in the same manner that Einar Pearson courted Lina Olsen in 1905. After Einar, a mill worker, met Lina, a domestic, the two met nearly every evening after Einar finished work, usually on her employer's front porch, in addition to Lina's regular time off.[25]

Minnie's marriage to an "orderly and kind" man may also have reflected her desire for economic security once she was no longer working for wages. Living in the Twin Cities in the late nineteenth century, Minnie had ample opportunity to observe the economic struggles of Swedish immigrant wives around her and how those troubles could be tied to the personal habits of husbands. In a study of relief cases concerning Swedish immigrant women from a Minneapolis welfare agency in the early twentieth century, 85 percent of the cases of married women involved husbands who were unable to support them. Explanations for nonsupport included unavoidable causes such as illness and death but also reasons tied to behavior, including alcoholism, desertion, unemployment, and low wages. Karl B.'s wife, Emma, sought economic relief after the family had been evicted from two different dwellings for nonpayment of rent. Karl drank heavily, leaving little of his earnings for support of the family. When Emma went directly to Karl's employer to collect his wages, Karl reacted so angrily that she was afraid to attempt the strategy again. Karl was eventually sentenced to a term in the county workhouse, probably for drunkenness. Unfortunately, his punishment left Emma with the entire burden of supporting the family.[26] Karl's behavior was not unusual. Of the 360 Swedes sentenced to the Minneapolis city workhouse in 1907, 87 percent (313) were charged with drunkenness.[27] Similarly, Thörnberg noted how Swedish men in early twentieth-century Chicago were prone to excessive drinking.[28]

Minnie likely chose for her spouse an "orderly and kind man" with specialized job skills and a profession in order to ensure that she would continue

---

A 347 E. Magnolia Street, one of the homes where Minnie was employed as a domestic servant

B 390 Jackson Street, the tailor shop where Jacob was working when he and Minnie were courting

C 181 Williams Street, Jacob's rooming house when he and Minnie were courting

D First Swedish Evangelical Church, where Minnie and Jacob were married in 1892

E 603 Fred Street, Minnie and Jacob's first home as newlyweds

F 219 Nash Street, the home of Minnie and Jacob and their son Henry

G Payne Avenue, an area with many Swedish businesses

to have things better in America. This is suggested by Minnie's own words. After telling of her marriage in part by noting some of Jacob's personal character traits, Minnie continued by describing him as a man "whom I learned to love." In late nineteenth- and early twentieth-century Swedish America, marriages were based on rationality, practicality, and convenience as often as romantic love. Hilda Linder's experience offers additional evidence of this trend. Recalling her marriage decision, she described dating a "very polite poetic man" who wrote verse and worked at a furniture factory for five dollars a day (in 1919). According to Hilda, marrying this poet who made barely enough money to live on would have meant having "to go out and clean like many Swedish housewifes did. I could not see that." She instead chose to marry a farmer, or as she put it, "I married 'wheat' and a man to plant it."[29] Though Linder's comment may appear coldhearted, it is also true that romance, practicality, and convenience are not necessarily mutually exclusive. This is suggested by the way in which Minnie completed her statement introducing her marriage, when she noted that Jacob had given her "a home and his love."

Swedish Immigrant Women as Urban Housewives: "A Home in Which to Receive Her"

Minnie had saved enough money in about three years in American domestic service to pay back her uncle, contribute to marrying her husband and establishing a household, and purchase a ship's ticket allowing her sister Christine to immigrate—accomplishments attesting to her skill in managing money. That Minnie had saved enough money to travel home herself but instead chose to spend her earnings to help her sister, and eventually her brother and mother, leave the homeland suggests the degree to which she felt things were indeed better in America. When Minnie wrote about Christine's arrival, her pride in having "a home in which to receive her" was evident. She did not go on in the memoir to describe her life as a St. Paul housewife, but other sources provide evidence of how young wives like Minnie carried out the responsibilities that came with having a home and family in an urban setting.

Marriage signaled the end of employment in household service. A married woman rarely worked as a live-in domestic unless her husband was also employed in the household, perhaps as a butler, gardener, or chauffeur. Although day labor jobs, as a cleaning woman or laundress perhaps, were available to Minnie (the kind of day labor Hilda Linder disdained), cultural norms in both Sweden and America dictated that married women not take wage work outside the home unless forced to do so by economic pressures.[30] Becoming a Swedish American urban housewife marked an improvement from Swedish rural married life. In rural Sweden, although marriage signaled an end to employment in domestic service, it also meant taking on tasks assisting husbands in farm and field or managing the farm when the husband was away logging or fishing.[31] As housewives in large urban areas in the United States, Swedish immigrant women's energies were focused primarily on attending to household and family.

City directories indicate that Minnie and Jacob lived at two different St. Paul addresses from 1892 to 1894. Their choice of residence was likely influenced by concerns for affordable rent, pleasant surroundings, and proximity to Jacob's place of work. After the birth of their first child, the amount of living space probably also played a role. Minnie and Jacob started their family very soon after their marriage, as did many other Swedish American (and other immigrant) families in Minnesota. The U.S. Immigration Commission examined fecundity of immigrant women in Minneapolis and twenty-one rural Minnesota counties in 1900. The study indicated that immigrant women had a childbearing rate one and a half times that of native-born women. The average number of years a Minneapolis Swedish immigrant mother was married per child born was 3.2; the average number of years a native-born Minneapolis mother was married per child was 5.2.[32] Minnie and Jacob's first child, born January 19, 1893, about ten months after their wedding date, was a son, Henry.

Births in immigrant families in the late nineteenth and early twentieth centuries were often attended by midwives rather than doctors and usually took place at home. A 1921 study estimated that midwives attended nearly 40 percent of all births, and the majority of these births were to immigrant mothers, who chose midwives for a variety of reasons: to be attended by a female and to carry on traditions from the homeland and because the fees were usually lower than those of physicians.[33] Minnie likely gave birth to Henry in their home and with a midwife, though she writes little about this event. Her experience probably mirrored that of Ada Andersson, who, after giving birth in 1895, wrote a letter relating her own American childbirth and infant care experience in Chicago to her sister in Sweden:

> Here a woman is not allowed up for nine days [after childbirth], however healthy she is, and if she is tired and weak she can stay in bed eleven days or more. Midwives come two times a day the first three days and then no more than once after, if the woman is well, and they charge from five up to fifteen and twenty dollars. Here they

> never swaddle the child but put diapers on them . . . and connect the diapers with safety pins; their arms are free and they are dressed in a warm sweater and long skirt fastened together and dressed in long skirts and dresses for five months, then short skirts and dresses for boys and girls alike.[34]

Andersson's comments suggest that some aspects of American childbirth were similar to practices she and Minnie would have been familiar with from the homeland: births took place at home and mothers were attended by midwives.[35] In other ways, however, childbirth for Minnie was probably quite different from what she might have encountered giving birth in her Swedish home province. Childbirth in nineteenth-century Dalsland was, according to one scholar, "surrounded by many superstitions and rules." Fearing attacks from evil supernatural creatures, mothers in Dalsland were kept indoors for six weeks postpartum and then brought to the parish church for a cleansing ceremony. Children were "wrapped in swaddling clothes from head to toe—a protection against the evil eye" and were restrained in that way until they began to crawl.[36]

Minnie's comment about having a "good life" in St. Paul suggests that her transition from domestic servant to urban housewife and mother was relatively smooth. Certainly some of the skills Minnie had learned in her years of domestic service, especially in American homes, were helpful in setting up her own household. She was familiar with the kinds of foods available in the Twin Cities and how to prepare them, and she had experience with American standards and methods of housekeeping and laundry. Yet employment in an American household, especially if the position was a specialized one such as cook, nurse, or laundress, was rather different from establishing and managing a household on one's own. Not only was the immigrant family's living space probably much smaller than the employer's had been; more significantly, so was the immigrant household's budget. And managing that budget—trying to make the male breadwinner's earnings stretch as far as possible—was usually the task of the Swedish American housewife.

Margareta Matovic has described the life of married Swedish immigrant women in a late nineteenth- and early twentieth-century Chicago neighborhood as "a constant struggle to make ends meet."[37] This phrase could just as easily be used to portray the experience of Swedish housewives in St. Paul while Minnie lived there, particularly after the economic depression of the 1890s had developed. In addition to rising costs for rent, food, clothing, and transportation, urban areas like Chicago and St. Paul offered Swedish American men numerous temptations to spend hard-earned wages in drinking establishments. Since married women's employment outside the home was usually a last resort, when economic pressures mounted the primary methods urban Swedish immigrant wives might use to bring additional money into the family economy were taking in laundry or letting rooms (or beds) to boarders.[38] Minnie does not indicate having had to resort to such strategies, and the fact that she and Jacob had money saved when they decided to move to Mille Lacs County is evidence that Jacob had well-paying employment and did not carouse and that Minnie carefully managed the family's finances. Minnie's "good life" in St. Paul included marrying a "good man" who provided a degree of economic security, establishing her own household, and starting a family. Immigrant women's letters suggest other ways that Swedish immigrant women like Minnie might feel that they had things better as a result of their immigration to the United States, even though marriage brought with it many changes. A married Swedish immigrant woman might also feel she had things better in terms of the size, quality, and furnishings of her home. For example, Swedish immigrant wife Erika Nyqvist wrote boastfully to friends in the homeland about her house in Brainerd, Minnesota:

> We have things very nice here; we have two rooms and a kitchen and fine furniture, a sofa that is upholstered with brown silk plush, fine Turkish wool rug over the whole floor, a table in front of the sofa, and an album that cost 6 dollars, and a bureau with a high mirror, rocking chair, flower stand full of flowers, desk and chair it is what we have in the parlor all American style. In the bedroom we have a bed; it is the one thing I don't like [because] it is so big that four can sleep in it; it cannot be folded up, such beds you don't find in America, a little table, night table and chairs.[39]

Similarly, Elisabet Lindström Franker wrote to her mother shortly after her marriage: "I have steam heat up here so I need not have any fire at all. We don't need to go out of *the house* at all because we have a bathroom. We have two [bathrooms] here where I live, so what do you think, mamma? You think it is too comfortable, or what?"[40] Nyqvist's letter suggests pride in the ability to purchase fine household furnishings, as well as the pleasure in using these furnishings. Franker's comments suggest ways in which life as a Swedish American urban housewife required less physical labor and often had more comforts than households back home.

Part of household management was providing nourishing food. Because there was limited opportunity in St. Paul to grow or produce one's own food, Minnie needed to be a good steward of the family's budget while still providing the family with a healthful diet, and Minnie probably used recipes and menus more common from her homeland years than from the wealthier households in which she had been employed. Since she lived in a heavily Swedish-settled area of St. Paul in the 1890s, she could purchase Swedish products from Swedish immigrant businesses—produce from a Swedish green grocer, meats from a Swedish butcher, sweets from a Swedish confectionary, and even medicine from a Swedish pharmacy.[41] Perhaps Swedish immigrant wives who had worked as domestics enjoyed the freedom to plan their own menus rather than preparing meals according to what an employer demanded. Former domestic Elisabet Franker, who had a fondness for herring, stated with pride in a letter to her mother: "Now I am my own boss so I can cook and eat what I want."[42] Herring and knäckebröd (similar to hardtack) had probably not been regular items on her employers' menus.

Though the time Minnie spent as a housewife in St. Paul was relatively brief, her experiences suggest the opportunities and challenges Swedish urban housewives encountered. Prior employment in the city gave wives like Minnie familiarity with goods and services available there. In good economic times, a variety of employment opportunities were available for Swedish husbands to support the family. Children could have access to public education. Living within an ethnic enclave, as Minnie and Jacob did, ensured availability of Swedish products for the household, the comfort of hearing Swedish and observing Swedish habits on a regular basis, and access to culturally familiar leisure and recreational activities. Challenges faced by women like Minnie in urban areas included potentially crowded and unhealthy living conditions, limited opportunities to contribute to the family economy, especially in times of economic stress, and numerous temptations that might draw husbands away from family responsibilities. Families weighed these and other factors as they made decisions as to whether or not to remain urban residents. Geographic location, time of settlement, and primary versus secondary migration could also shape Swedish immigrant women's urban experience. The ethnic, social, and economic environment that Swedish immigrant women found in Seattle, Washington, in the 1890s was quite different from that of the Twin Cities.

Janice Reiff Webster found that Scandinavian women in Seattle were eager to acculturate and did not seek out ethnic enclaves. Most had initially settled and worked in other American communities where they had "learned the basics of American life" and found Seattle a city with economic and social opportunities that facilitated incorporation into American neighborhoods and social circles rather than ethnic ones.[43]

Urban to Rural Migration: "We Would Never See People Anymore"

Minnie and Jacob moved from St. Paul to Mille Lacs County in part out of concern for the health of their young son, Henry. Nineteenth-century child mortality rates were higher in urban than rural areas, and most Swedish immigrants had, like Minnie, come from healthier rural origins as young adults.[44] The couple had started their family, and Minnie felt that a rural environment was a better place for raising children than the city. As she noted in her memoir, rural living provided children "freedom" and "a natural life," as well as less contact with "bad company."[45]

Raising the family in the country was a goal important enough to Minnie and Jacob that they were willing to tolerate Jacob's prolonged absences from the farm in order to accomplish it. Other factors likely also contributed to the couple's move to the country. Minnie might have come to share the views that Hilda Linder expressed about life as an urban housewife, which she described as "a monotonous life [where] the wife never came out."[46] The couple may also have realized that Jacob's tailoring income might not be adequate to support a growing family in difficult economic times, that purchasing a farm could provide a legacy of land to one or more of their children, and that the increasing popularity of ready-made clothing might eventually limit Jacob's trade.

Though apparently not the case for Jacob and Minnie, immediate economic pressures drove some Swedish immigrants from urban to rural areas, settling where they could make a small down payment on land near an area where employment opportunities were available in such industries as lumber or agricultural production. Describing the economic crisis of the 1890s, Minnie noted: "Many lost their homes in the cities. They became unemployed and could not pay their mortgages."[47] During an economic depression that made it difficult for laborers to find work in urban areas, a farm at least offered the possibility of a garden and a little livestock to produce some of the food necessary to support a family while the male family wage earner or wage earners sought work.

Thus, Minnie and Jacob left St. Paul for Mille Lacs County in July 1894. They had purchased 160 acres of land in Bogus Brook Township for 240 dollars.[48] According to an 1852 surveyor's report on the township, it contained "2nd rate" or "3rd rate" soil and was covered with forests of white pine, white oak, black ash, sugar maple, and elm.[49] By the time Minnie and Jacob came to Mille Lacs County, most of the white pine had been harvested, leaving cutover areas on large segments of the county with stumps two to three feet in diameter and several feet high. Minnie's description of the family's first journey out to their land makes clear that she found the move to a small log cabin five miles from the nearest town arduous. Her usually good spirits plummeted as she and Jacob walked the miles from the train station in Milaca through the forest with clothing and supplies and a child and a cat in tow: "I complained and said that we'd come so far from civilization that we would never see people anymore. . . . I was almost ready to cry."[50] She was pregnant with her second child. Her spirits were lifted by the discovery of abundant berries and wildflowers in the forest. A deep love of nature had continued through Minnie's immigration and years as an urban domestic.

Swedes in Mille Lacs County: "Pure Water and Beautiful Woodlands"

Just as patterns of Swedish chain migration drew Swedish immigrant women to urban locations such as Chicago and the Twin Cities, so too did chain migration draw Swedish Americans to rural settlements. Jacob and Minnie probably heard about the availability of land in Mille Lacs County from other Swedes who had settled there.[51] A few Swedes were attracted to Mille Lacs County in the 1880s by opportunities for employment in the forests and sawmills that emerged with the harvesting of the rich timber resources in the area. Of 1,897 residents in Mille Lacs County in 1885, only about 2 percent were Swedish-born.[52] Word of the area's potential for settlement spread, and by 1900 Swedes made up 16 percent (of a total population of 8,066).[53] Settlement was also encouraged by newspaper advertisements about the region, some of which directly targeted potential Swedish settlers. The June 7, 1894, issue of the *Mille Lacs County Times* included a Swedish-language advertisement proclaiming "Land! Land! Land!," which went on to describe 20,000 acres of "fertile and productive" land for sale in the county, with easy purchasing terms.

According to the records of the Swedish Lutheran church in Milaca, most of the early Swedes had initially emigrated from Sweden to other locations,

Land! Land! Land!

20,000 acres till salu

på vilkor som bäst lämpar sig för köparen.

Detta land är belåget i Mille Lacs Co., Minnesota, och genomskäres af Minnesota Eastern och Great Northern-jernvägarne. Dessa vägar förskaffa en ständig afsättning af Ties och ved och vid många tillfällen kan timmer huggas å landet som härigenom betalar det.

Detta land är äfven skattskyldigt till Milaca, en stad på 1,000 innevånare, belägen nästan i centrum af detta county, och der Eastern Minnesota och Great Northern-jernvägarne förenas. Denna stad växer ständigt och det är antagligt att den inom få år kommer att blifva countyets hufvudsäte. Under sista 2 åren hafva följande bygnader blifvit uppförda: en qvarn med en kapacitet af 50 tunnor dagligen, en Feedqvarn med en kapacitet af 1 ton dagligen, ett hospital, stort nog att rymma 40 patienter, ett ståtligt operahus, handelsbutiker och boningshus förmånga att här uppräkna. Ett Heading Factory Co., är under inkorporation och kommer att bygga en fabrik för 8,000 dollars, som kommer att gifva sysselsättning åt ett stort antal personer, jemte en torgplats för timmer. Här i staden är äfven Mill Lacs Lumber Co's. sågverk beläget och gifver sysselsättning åt 150 män.

Detta land är beläget endast 60 mil från de stora syskonstäder-

Swedish-language ads enticed settlers with the promise "Land! Land! Land! 20,000 acres for sale on conditions best suited for the buyer." (*Mille Lacs County Times*, June 7, 1894)

although their arrival in Milaca represented at least a secondary migration within the United States. A few individuals and families had migrated from as far away as Pennsylvania and New York, but most were from Minnesota or other midwestern locations. For example, four families came to Milaca from Anoka, Minnesota, between 1887 and 1892.[54] New Scandinavian settlers were welcomed to the community. In the same issue of the local newspaper that had the Swedish land advertisement was a news note: "Milaca may well congratulate herself upon the class of settlers who are settling in the vicinity. They are for the most part Scandinavians—industrious, sober, honest, hardworking men. They are the class who will transform the wilderness into productive farms, adding wealth and beauty to the county. They are peaceable, law-abiding citizens. We want more such."[55]

Railroad mogul James J. Hill and his associate J. S. Kennedy had established the town of Milaca in 1886 through a corporation they developed called the Mille Lacs Lumber Company. It was located on Hill's St. Paul, Minneapolis, and Manitoba railroad line, which ran from St. Cloud through Hinckley and to Duluth. Milaca's initial attractions for settlers included employment opportunities in the lumber industry and in railroad construction, a lumber mill and company store for building materials and supplies, and a land company to sell cutover timber land and railroad land. Because many Swedes worked as laborers for Hill's railroad, it is not surprising that Swedes settled heavily in the railroad towns of Milaca and Bock in Mille Lacs County. Some of these workers purchased cutover timber land at reasonable prices and worked toward developing farms, in the hope that by the time the timber supply was depleted and the railroad lines completed, they would have developed a farm that could support them.[56]

The experience of Swedish immigrant Mary Norlander (who eventually became a friend of Minnie's) illustrates this pattern. Norlander moved with her

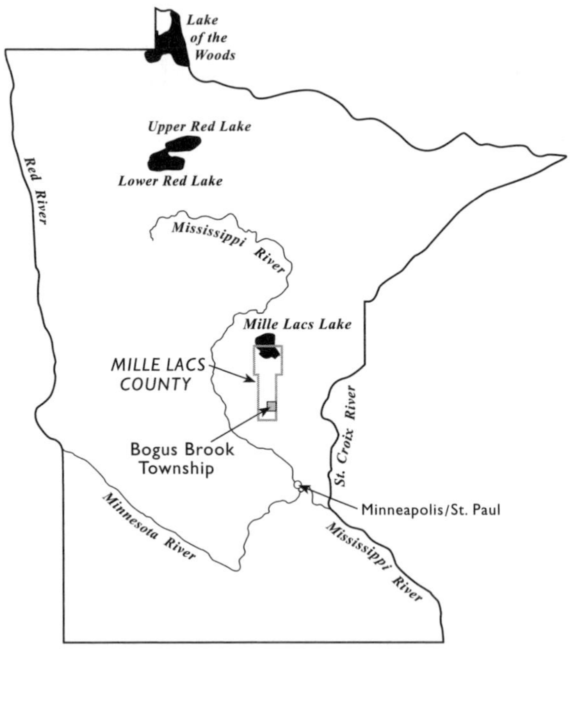

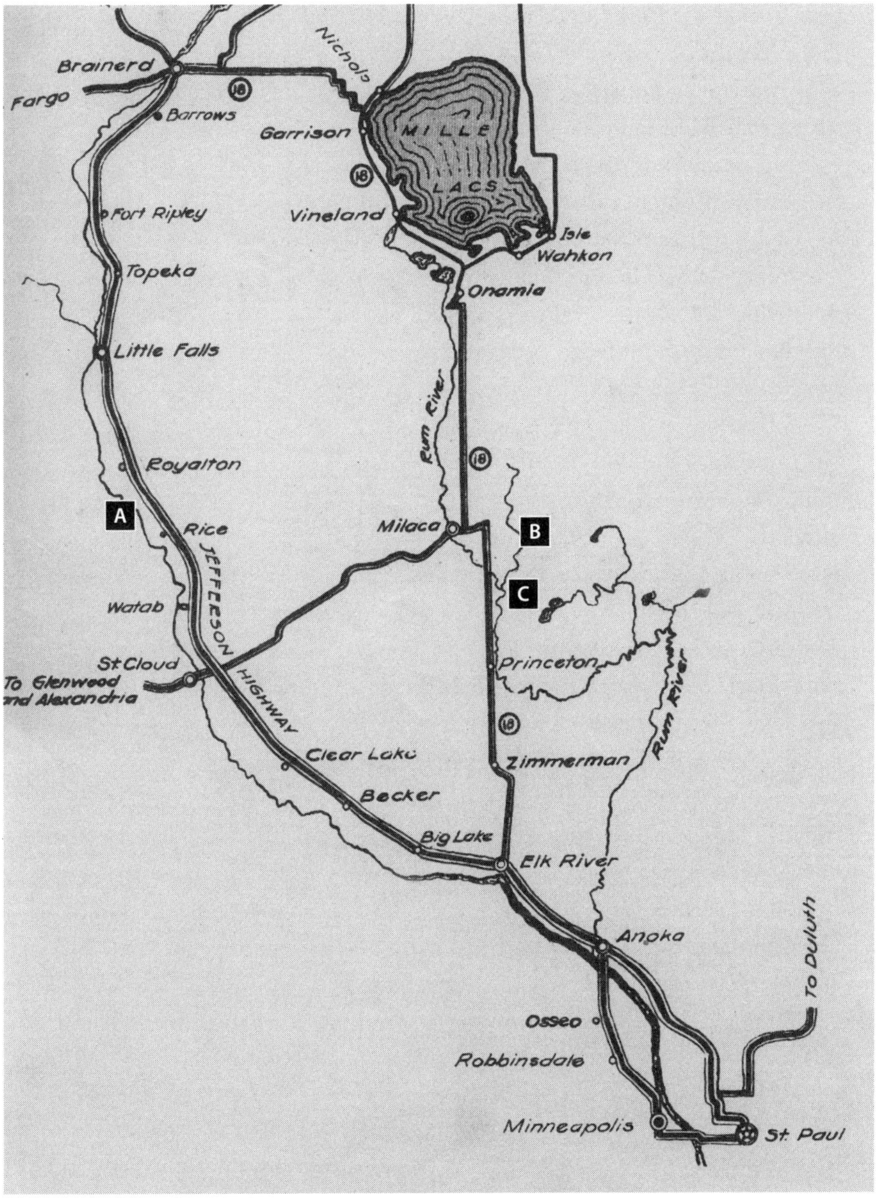

East central Minnesota.

A Mississippi River

B Vondell (Wondell) Brook

C Halgren farm

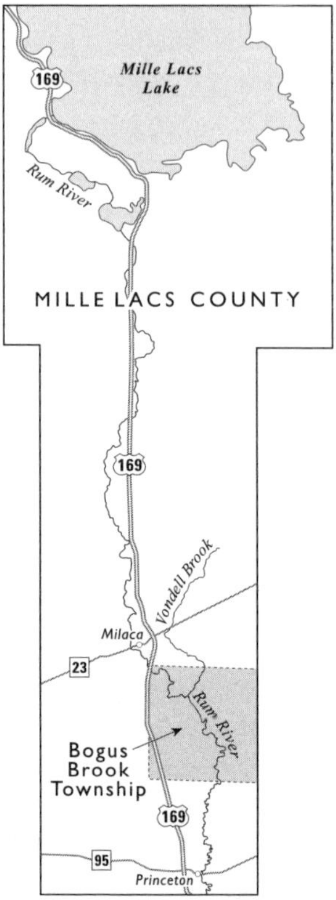

family from St. Paul to Mille Lacs County in 1891 at the age of fifteen. The family lived next to a sawmill where her father worked, about four miles from Milaca, initially accessible only by walking on the railroad tracks. Norlander's father early on purchased some cutover land for five dollars per acre and built a "quite comfortable home" on it. He continued to work for the mill while beginning the slow process of clearing the land. According to Norlander, as word spread to Swedish workers in the nearby Twin Cities that jobs and land were available, a number of Swedish families decided to move away from the city to try their hand at farming.[57] Similarly, when Einar Pearson immigrated in 1901, he already had three sisters married and living in the county, and, after a few years of work at the Milaca sawmill and at a lumber camp in the northern part of the county, he was also able to bring over from Sweden his parents and five remaining siblings.[58] Geographer Helge Nelson's 1943 study of Swedish settlements in America found that Swedes settled in the parts of Mille Lacs County where other Swedes already lived. Nelson noted that the Mille Lacs County town of Bock was made up mostly of individuals of Swedish heritage, as was Borgholm Township and the northern part of Bogus Brook Township, the latter being exactly the area where Jacob and Minnie settled.[59]

Although the Milaca sawmill was closed down for a time in the 1890s, it was reopened when more timber was made available for harvest on the Mille Lacs Lake Indian Reservation. This also contributed to Swedish settlement in the county. Swedish settlers continued the pattern of finding employment in the sawmill and purchasing plots of land with the expectation that they would eventually become full-time farmers. The mill closed permanently in 1906, and in 1907 the Farmer's Cooperative Creamery was organized. This marked a shift from the once-timber-based economy to one more diversified but centered on the dairy industry.[60]

As the lumber industry dwindled, Mille Lacs County communities sought other ways to encourage continued settlement. A Mille Lacs County promotional

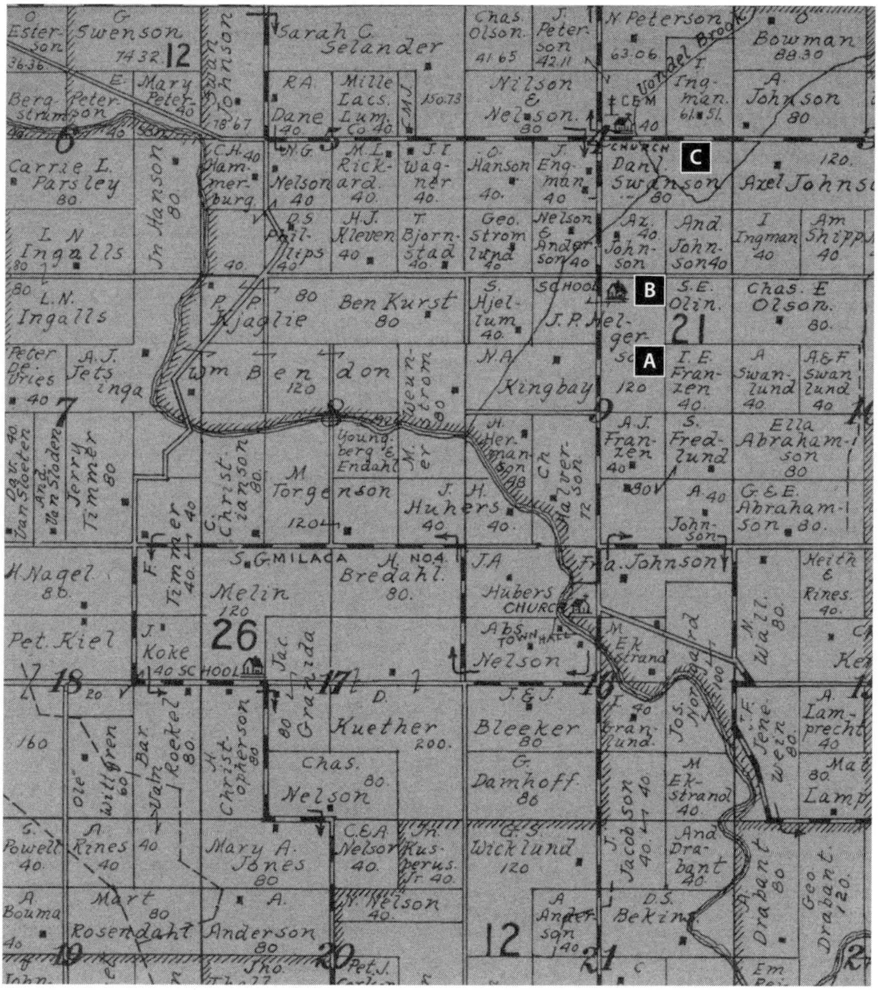

Bogus Brook Township (portion), Mille Lacs County.

A Halgren farm (identified incorrectly on map as "J. P. Helgerson")

B School (located on one acre of land that Minnie and Jacob donated)

C Vondell Brook Chapel

Milaca, shown here in 1905, sprang up along the St. Paul, Minneapolis, and Manitoba railroad line, which employed many Swedes.

booklet published in 1909 to encourage further migration to the area especially encouraged people to settle on area farmland, where, according to the title page, "Homeseekers Find Productive Fields, Pure Water and Beautiful Woodlands." The soil was described as appropriate especially for clover and grasses as well as root crops, and the booklet included separate sections entitled "Dairy Industry," "Grain and Vegetables," and "Potato Raising." Among the many other features extolled were good transportation access to markets and shipping in Duluth/Superior and Minneapolis/St. Paul, a healthy climate, and excellent schools. Church denominations listed for the county included Swedish and Norwegian Lutheran.[61]

The booklet also contained vignettes about Mille Lacs County settlers, including some Swedish immigrants. Though these accounts surely represent the most successful rather than the most typical settlers' experiences, they are useful for illustrating the pattern of stepped Swedish migration from urban to rural areas and for representing the potential for economic security and success that could result from such moves. For example, John F. Kallstrom arrived in the United States from Sweden in 1887 and worked as a day laborer in Minneapolis. He moved with his family (four young children) to Mille Lacs County in April 1898. Putting five dollars down on a forty-acre plot of cutover

Milaca's businesses, including the Eberhardt general store, welcomed Swedish immigrants.

land in Milo Township — just west of Bogus Brook Township — Kallstrom built a log cabin and cleared about ten acres that year. With so few acres under tillage, he had to seek other means to earn cash and found seasonal winter work in a sawmill during the family's first three years on the farm. By 1909 he owned eighty acres and had built an eight-room home and a barn. Quoted in the booklet, he noted: "I have twelve head of cattle, the milk from which I sell to the creamery. I also have four horses and also pigs and chickens. My land is very productive in hay, potatoes, and small grain and the crops together with our dairy give us a good living."[62]

Swedish immigrant Alick Bostrom had also worked in an urban area (laying sidewalks) before settling in Mille Lacs County with his wife and two children in 1894, purchasing eighty acres of land at seven dollars per acre. Bostrom lost virtually all his personal property in a fire on September 1, 1894, one of many on that date, including the infamous Hinckley fire (which completely destroyed that small Minnesota town). Though he had to borrow money in order to purchase basic supplies such as clothes for his family, he remained on his land. In 1909 his farmstead included, in addition to a residence, two barns, a machine shed, a granary, and a chicken house, and he had cleared forty-three acres of land, had twelve dairy cows, and raised farm produce to sell as well.[63]

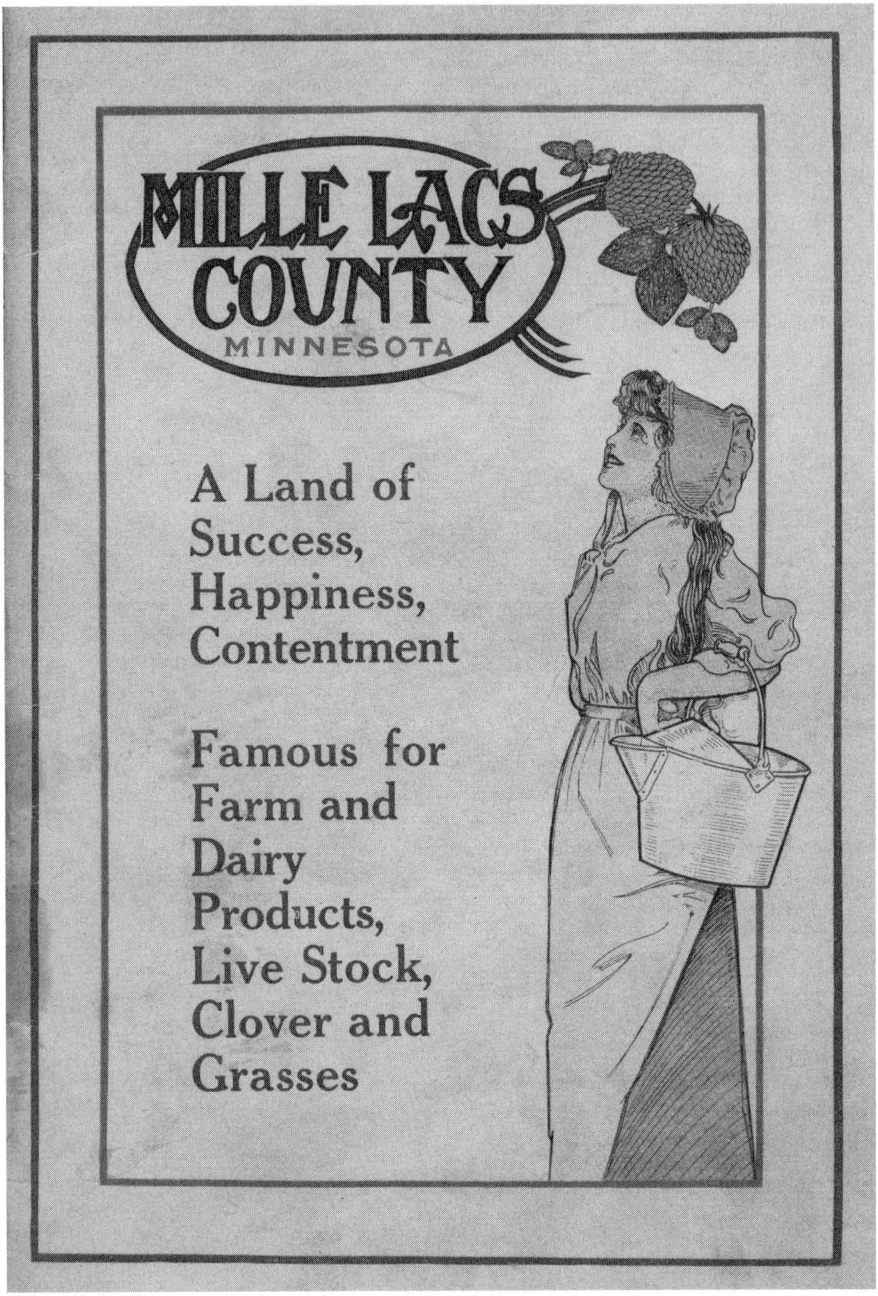

Cities and counties encouraged immigrants to settle outside the Twin Cities through widely distributed materials such as this 1909 booklet touting "fertile and productive" land. (*Mille Lacs County, Minnesota* [Princeton, 1909])

Minnie and her family fared much better than Alick Bostrom in the 1894 fire, which could have been fatal to them, during the family's first months in Mille Lacs County. The fire that threatened Minnie and Jacob's new log cabin was one of many fires throughout the Upper Midwest that day. The result of a very dry season and methods of lumbering that left quantities of combustible deadwood, such fires were especially devastating when firestorms developed that created huge flames as well as toxic gases.[64] Luckily, and perhaps because she had grown up in a forested region of Sweden, Minnie had the presence of mind and know-how to build a backfire, which ultimately saved the lives of her family and her newly constructed home. Minnie's building a backfire in spite of the protests of a male lodger attests to her self-confidence and determination. The matter-of-fact way in which she described the fire in her memoir belies the terror she must have felt when it was taking place, though its impact on her is suggested by her recollection of the fate of friends and acquaintances less fortunate:

> We knew a family who had moved out into the country at the same time as we—the husband, the wife, two small children and her [the wife's] brother and sister who had just walked out there for a visit. They were a part of what was called the "unlucky thirteen." That was thirteen families, mostly Norwegians, who all knew each other, and had moved out into the forest that summer to form a colony and live near each other. All perished. The Molander family, whom we knew, were all found dead in a small clearing, suffocated by smoke.[65]

Minnie had lived in her log cabin less than two months when she saved it from the fire. The cabin still stands (in 2008), though with a wood-frame house—the "better and bigger house" Minnie mentioned—built around it. It was considerably smaller than the accommodations the family had occupied in St. Paul, and Minnie noted that they had to keep most of their furniture in the cabin's attic. She did not describe in detail the cabin's furnishings, but one can imagine what this two-room cabin might have looked like filled with the furniture and tools that the state of Minnesota supplied for a typical family of five who were Hinckley fire survivors in 1895:

The young family's stylish clothing and their purchase of a studio portrait suggest that the "good life" Minnie experienced in St. Paul included a measure of economic stability; photo about 1893.

Furniture—Three bedsteads; 3 w. w. springs; 3 excelsior mattresses; 3 pairs pillows; 12 wood chairs; 1 rocker; 1 drop-leaf table.

Hardware—One No. 9 stove; 1 heating stove; 5 joints pipe; 1 elbow; 1 iron kettle; 1 fry pan; 1 tea kettle; 1 coffee pot; 1 dishpan; 2 milk pans; 1 sauce pan; 1 boiler; 1 washboard; 1 dipper; 1 water pail; 6 knives and forks; 12 spoons; 6 teaspoons; 1 basting spoon; 1 wash basin; 1 butcher knife; 1 drip pan; 1 dust pan; 1 broom; 2 flat irons; 1 one-gallon can; 1 axe; 1 buck saw; 1 shovel; 1 hammer.

Crockery—Twelve plates; 6 pint bowls; 12 cups and saucers; 6 tumblers; 1 ten-inch platter; 2 seven-inch vegetable dishes; 1 glass water pitcher; 1 salt and pepper; 1 glass lamp; 2 chambers.

Bedding—Four blankets; 2 comforters; 52 yards sheeting; 15 yards toweling.[66]

Minnie might have been able to use more of her St. Paul furniture had she been less welcoming to others, but hospitality and a sense of community were values Minnie held from her Swedish childhood and youth at Hamnevattnet—and necessary qualities for the survival of early rural communities. She wrote of receiving many travelers and homeseekers into her cabin as the county became more settled. The first winter the family spent in the two-room, sixteen- by twenty-eight-foot cabin, it was shared with four and sometimes six grown men.[67] Minnie's comment that the cabin "looked like a forest camp" suggests that the cramped quarters frustrated her attempts to keep her household in order. Similarly, Swedish immigrant Kajsa Erickson in the early years of settlement (in Wright County, Minnesota) housed so many new settlers on her log cabin floor that "the ones by the door had to get up first and go out so the rest could get up and move around."[68]

Visitors and lodgers were probably also welcomed as a way to ease loneliness. Because Milaca was too small a town to support a shop to employ a tailor with Jacob's specialized skills, he traveled to different urban locations seasonally to practice his trade. Jacob often worked in St. Paul, but also in Minneapolis, St. Cloud, and Tracy, Minnesota, typically spending the months of March through June and September through December living and working away from home.[69]

Married Life: "We Had Built It with the Labor of Our Own Hands"

Several times in her memoir Minnie mentioned having to spend time alone, even though it is clear that she opened her home to many temporary lodgers. These references suggest a particular kind of isolation, a loneliness for Jacob. This loneliness suggests Minnie's strong feelings for her spouse, but it is impossible to determine fully the nature and quality of their relationship as husband and wife. Minnie's comments about their courtship and marriage indicate that their relationship was initially based upon practical and economic considerations, though it also came to include love and affection. Neither the couple's younger daughter, Jennie, nor their grandchildren (two were raised by Minnie and Jacob and others often visited in the summer for weeks at a time) recalled significant conflicts in the household.[70] Other Swedish couples in Mille Lacs County were not so fortunate. The local newspaper, the *Mille Lacs County Times*, included the following item in its issue for February 25, 1897:

Milaca, Feb. 23, 1897

I hereby let the publik know that I am leaving my husband Albin Petterson on the ground that he will not let me have 5 cent for clothes[.] he has not furnished any flour or potatoes sense we was married.

Amelia M. Petterson

Her husband responded on March 4, 1897, with the following:

A False Impression

I wish to correct the false impression given by the notice about me in your last issue. I refer to Mr. A. Flink [a local storekeeper] as authority that my wife has been amply provided with the necessary things of life while living with me. I wish further to state that as my wife, Amelia Peterson, has left my bed and board I will no longer be responsible for any debts she may contract, nor will I claim any of her earnings.

Albin Peterson[71]

Amelia Petterson's newspaper notice implies that she occupied a subordinate position within her household, with her husband making decisions regarding the purchasing of food and clothing and controlling the family finances, including money or store credit she may have earned from selling goods she had produced at home. The notice also makes clear that he was obligated to provide her with material support. The couple apparently managed to reconcile their differences, as they are listed together on the 1900 census for Milaca, with Albin employed at the sawmill. Whether the experience of Minnie or of Amelia was the more common for Swedish immigrant wives is unclear. Determining the degree of autonomy, cooperation, power, and contentment Swedish immigrant women found in their marriages is a difficult task. Primary sources are sparse, because, with few exceptions, married Swedish immigrant women seemed to have little time, energy, or inclination to write about their married lives, whether in the form of letters, diaries, or memoirs.

Existing scholarship on the lives of Swedish immigrant wives is also limited and somewhat ambiguous. Jane Telleen, in a study of Swedish American women (mostly urban and middle-class) in the Augustana Synod of the Lutheran Church, wrote that upon marriage women became "dependent and powerless," felt dissatisfaction with their positions, and sought autonomy and meaning in their lives through participation in groups such as the Woman's Missionary Society.[72] H. Arnold Barton, relying primarily on Swedish immigrant letters, found that married women who came to America were satisfied with their lot (though like Moberg's Kristina they were "long-suffering" and "courageous") and did not rebel against the traditional roles and expectations as wife, mother, and homemaker they found in America. Barton also noted that by the time single Swedish immigrant women chose to marry they "embrace[d] enthusiastically the restrictive conventions of American middle-class gentility."[73]

In her investigation of immigrant literature, Dorothy Burton Skårdal found Swedish American wives in subordinate roles, only rarely daring to question decisions made by their husbands.[74] Cynthia Meyer's research on Swedish Mission Covenant women indicated that immigrant wives were usually devoted to family and home and took pride in fulfilling what they saw as their roles as Christian women. Although they might be frustrated with the effort and tedium of managing a household and raising children, they found meaning and fulfillment in providing children with a moral upbringing and thus influencing the world beyond their homes.[75] These studies generally agree that most married Swedish immigrant women focused their time and energies upon the domestic sphere of child rearing and housekeeping, but they indicate that women carried out these duties with varying degrees of enthusiasm or fulfillment. Minnie's writing suggests satisfaction with her life as a married woman and a relationship with Jacob as a cooperative partner. Both she and Jacob fulfilled roles and carried out tasks necessary to the survival and advancement of the family (and of the farm, which represented security for the family's future).[76]

Swedish Immigrant Farmwives and Farmers: "Soon I Could Drive Any Horse at All"

The 1900 Federal Census for Bogus Brook Township lists Minnie as head of household with an occupation of farmer.[77] When the census was taken on June 2, 1900, Minnie was on the farm with four young sons (ages one, three, five, and seven), while Jacob was away doing his seasonal tailoring work.[78]

Jacob's employment meant that for the greater part of each year, for at least the first two decades of their marriage, Minnie was left to fill the role of farmer as well as farmwife and to carry out not only the tasks of managing the log cabin and the growing family it housed but also the entire farm operation.[79] Although this was a significant shift from the role of urban housewife, Minnie's ability to take on such responsibilities is not surprising given her experiences prior to marriage. She had been independent and self-supporting from a young age and had also observed the roles played by rural Swedish wives in the homeland, especially those whose husbands worked in forestry or fishing occupations requiring their absence from farm and household for portions of the year.[80] The gradual establishment of a working farm, with husbands seeking supplemental off-farm employment in railroad, mining, or other industries and wives and children remaining on the homestead, was a common pattern of rural life in the late nineteenth-century midwestern United States.[81]

Minnie's role as farmwife and farmer entailed feeding, clothing, and raising a growing family as well as the daily and seasonal work to maintain cabin, farmyard, garden, and fields. Some of these duties were familiar, such as providing her family with adequate clothing. Minnie purchased some of the family's clothing in Milaca stores, but she also produced some of it herself. She had a Swedish spinning wheel and spun yarn and knitted, supplying the family with socks, mittens, scarves, and sweaters.[82] She clearly also had to learn new skills—such as how to harness and drive a horse and wagon—but her positive attitude and diligent work ethic stood her well: "Soon I could drive any horse at all."[83] Since Jacob was away tailoring in the spring, Minnie probably also learned to plow and plant crops as she and Jacob slowly brought more of their land under cultivation.[84] She likely also cut and split wood for the family's fuel supply in Jacob's absence, suggested by her comment that "nobody who could chop wood needed to freeze, even if the house was not so warm."[85] Though Minnie did not assist in the actual construction of the family's log cabin, she worked to maintain its comfort and integrity with efforts such as applying mud between the logs to help provide insulation against the cold winter weather.[86]

Minnie and Jacob's first livestock purchase was a cow rather than a horse. Their savings exhausted after paying for their land and cabin (and a log barn), Jacob borrowed money from a coworker to buy the animal. Their willingness to take a loan for this purchase indicates a cow's importance to the family's well-being. It not only provided milk for the family but also allowed for the

MILACA, MILLE LACS COUNTY, MINNESOTA, THURSDAY, OCTOBER 21st, 1897.

Good butter wanted at McClure & Wilkes store. Will pay good prices.

Have you seen the new line of cloaks at the Foley Bean Lumber Co.'s?

Mrs. Steven Mitchell and two little daughters, of Big Lake, are visiting relatives in Milaca this week.

Chas. Revoir, the wellknown stock dealer, was in town yesterday looking after the interests of E. Mark.

George Searle, of Augusta, Wis., is visiting relatives in Milaca this week.

FINE LINE OF STATIONERY, BOOKS and SCHOOL SUPPLIES,

Our Stock of Drugs is the Largest in the County.

JOHN PETERSON & CO.

......SVENSKA APOTHEKE.

Though the Halgrens produced most of the things they needed for daily living, Minnie could trade butter for additional household goods, including medicines from a countryman. The local newspaper reported that a store would pay top prices for good butter, while a nearby advertisement noted the existence of a Svenska apotheke, or pharmacy. (*Mille Lacs County Times*, October 21, 1897)

production of butter—a tradable commodity in the cash-short economy. This is illustrated by newspaper ads such as one in an 1897 *Mille Lacs County Times*: "Good butter wanted at McClure and Wilkes store. Will pay good prices."[87] A cow represented labor for the farmwife. In most early farm households, the care of cows and chickens was a chore for the wife; care of the larger animals that performed field work was in the husband's purview.[88] Dairy cows required twice-a-day milking much of the year. They needed food and water—from pasture and brook in the summer and hay and drawn water in the winter. Barns that provided winter shelter needed cleaning. In an ironic twist of fate, a young Swedish woman who had been happy to avoid dairying when employed as a Swedish American rural domestic might find herself doing the milking and caring for dairy cows once she became a farmwife.

When the husband was absent, the farmwife's responsibilities expanded. Minnie not only tended cows and chickens but eventually goats, sheep, and horses as well.[89] In her memoir, she recalled the family's first horse with particular fondness, probably reflecting both her appreciation of the labor the horse provided as well as her love of animals. She was so fond of the horse that she later wrote a poem about him. It provides some vivid images of Minnie as a farmwife: driving on muddy dirt "roads" into Milaca, probably with children and butter in the wagon behind, leading the horse from pasture with three or four small children on its back, and quiet moments of affection. (The poem is included here in unrhymed and rough English translation.)

Our first horse,
That horse was nothing to brag about.
It was just a pinto from the Dakota
prairies.
It wasn't a steel horse, you must not
think that.
He looked more like a crooked cow.

The poor one, he certainly had to work
for his food.
There were no state roads made then.
They looked more like a narrow chute
that curved among the trees,
And the horse had to wade in mud up
to his knees.

It never happened that the horse was
lazy.
I petted him and gave him sugar and
food
Because he was friendly, safe, and secure
And the children rode in a row on his
back.

Now he is gone, still my thoughts go
To the time when at Rum River banks
I drove him to town in the shade of the
trees
And listened to children's laughter and
the song of the birds.

And now we have a big road and other
things up to par,
And we drive into town in a car,
But the happiest days I've had in this
world
Were when I drove with the pinto in
the shade of the trees.[90]

Minnie Anderson Halgren

Minnie's field work gradually increased over time, as more of the farm was cleared for cultivation. Mille Lacs County farmers commonly cleared one to two acres a year—though with Jacob's absence the Halgrens' clearing might have proceeded more slowly.[91] On the forested or cutover land that made up most of the county, the process of removing tree stumps and roots from the soil was painstaking. Some farmers relied on their horses to pull out stumps. Other farmers resorted to blasting out stumps with dynamite (the *Mille Lacs County Times* in the 1890s includes numerous tales of accidents related to dynamite use). Land could be used to some extent even without removing stumps—Minnie was able to plant potatoes between the tree stumps in the years following the fire, and she may also have planted oats or clover between the stumps, providing pasture in the summer for livestock and hay and grass for winter feed.[92] The farm eventually focused mainly on corn and dairy products, but the family also grew some oats, alfalfa, and wheat.[93]

Minnie's labor in farmyard and field was in addition to her care for the family. After her marriage, she entered a stage of life that found her pregnant or breast-feeding for approximately the next fifteen years, giving birth to five sons and two daughters between January 1893 and May 1907. The longest period of

Like this family of Isanti County farmers, photographed in 1900, Minnie and Jacob Halgren raised potatoes on logged cutover land.

time between any of the children was the approximately three years between her sixth and seventh children. Though Minnie and Jacob's continually growing family might seem surprising given the economic downturns of the 1890s and 1900s, their large family may be explained by limited access to birth control, a desire to have children to help with the farmwork, a vision of America as a land full of opportunities for the next generation, and their regular reunions on Jacob's returns home.[94]

Minnie's ability to spend a significant part of her childbearing years as head of the farm household attests to her physical and mental endurance. A letter from another Minnesota woman in the 1890s provides another glimpse of what a Swedish farmwife's role might encompass. Annie Johnson apologized for having little time to write and described her reasons why: "I have so much to do. I have been in such a hurry this week. Gustav [her husband] is often away so I have to take care of the livestock. And then we butchered a pig. And this week I have washed and ironed and scrubbed a good deal. And yesterday

Five of Minnie's seven children; photo early 1900s.

I baked. And now I have the kitchen to scrub. And then I will bake the pastry that I wrote home about one time."[95]

Similarly, Mathilda Arthur managed her farm household and growing family on a homestead in Minnesota while her husband spent winters working in northern Minnesota forests. Even when her husband was present, establishing a farm required significant labor. Her son recalled: "As soon as winter was over, Mother spent her spare time clearing land; cutting, piling, and burning brush while Father cut timbers, hauled stones, and plowed the ground."[96]

Childbirth and raising young children added to the burdens of managing the small farm. Minnie noted that she "never dared leave the children alone when they were small. I used to have them with me in a cart wherever I went."[97] Minnie made work into play at times, as suggested in the poem about her horse and when she described fetching the horse from its pasture and allowing as many of her "little riders" as would fit on the horse to have some fun. When the tasks of managing household and farm made it difficult to keep a watchful eye on her young children, Minnie employed fear as a way to help keep them safe. Concerned that her children might drown in the brook near their house, which periodically flooded, with an accompanying strong current, she told them that "Näcken," a magical water creature who lived there, might steal them away. Her use of a figure from the Swedish magical landscape indicates her adoption of child-rearing strategies from her own Dalsland upbringing, where children were told tales of fairy creatures and trolls to frighten them into following rules.[98]

In Sickness and in Health: "The Worst Winter I Have Lived as a Settler's Wife"

Limited access to medical care was a reality in the lives of nineteenth- and early twentieth-century midwestern farm families, and, like most rural women, Swedish immigrant women played important roles in maintaining their family's health and caring for the sick. The challenges of fulfilling these roles are evident from Minnie's experiences in the winter of 1896–97. Jacob had come home early from his tailoring work because the couple was anticipating the birth of their third child (their older two sons were then three and a half and twenty-two months), but he became ill with typhoid. Although a doctor checked in on the family every other day, it was Minnie who nursed Jacob back to health, relying on the physician's advice as well as a book entitled *Hälsan framför allt* (Health above all) that she had received as a premium for subscribing to the Chicago Swedish American newspaper *Svenska Amerikanaren.*[99] She felt pride in her abilities as she recalled the event, noting that she "got a compliment from the doctor," but her memoir reveals the challenges Jacob's illness presented as well. When Minnie gave birth to her third son, Theodore, on November 5, 1896, she had not even had time to change clothes for the two weeks since Jacob had become ill. The local doctor was unable to attend her childbirth, so she had only the assistance of a neighbor woman for the delivery. Following the birth, a young girl helped in the household for four days and a neighbor briefly helped to care for the cattle. After that it was up to Minnie to care for her convalescing husband, her newborn, two toddlers, and the farm.

Minnie described how the chickens she had hatched were an important food resource for Jacob's recovery, highlighting the importance of women's farm production in a farm family's survival by providing food for the family as well as tradable commodities. Minnie exchanged the butter she churned from the milk of her cow for coffee, flour, and meat. Numerous documents about Swedish farmwives report their selling butter and milk, eggs, and sometimes garden vegetables or wild foods gathered in the countryside (such as maple

Minnie feeding her chickens, photo late 1910s. Chickens and eggs were important elements of rural women's farm production.

syrup, blueberries, raspberries, and cranberries) in exchange for needed store-bought goods.[100] One Swedish immigrant wife in Nebraska wrote to her parents that she had 225 hens and collected 115 eggs every day. She had raised 400 chickens the year before. She acknowledged that raising this many chickens was a lot of work but added that "it is good to be able to work and at the same time have a sense of supporting [the family]."[101] Kajsa Erickson paid for her first cookstove with profits she had made from trapping muskrats and selling their pelts.[102] In a rural Swedish settlement in Maine, Kjersti Carlson obtained food for her children and ailing husband by making cedar shakes and carrying them five miles to the nearest town to trade for provisions. To produce the shakes, she cut down cedar trees, sawed and split the wood, and shaved the wood into shingles.[103]

Jacob's recovery was probably also aided by produce Minnie had stored in her root cellar—carrots, potatoes, and onions she had harvested the previous summer.[104] The "large and beautiful potatoes" she mentioned growing were due to the forest fire, which left behind ashes high in potassium, a nutrient upon which potatoes thrive (similar to "slash and burn" methods of land clearing). Though "the food was meager," Minnie and her family did not go hungry.[105] This might not have been the case had the family still lived in St. Paul, where raising much of one's own livestock or produce was difficult to impossible. One can get some idea of other elements of rural Swedish families' diets from the relief records for the Hinckley fire. The state of Minnesota issued the following rations to a family of five as a thirty-day supply in 1895:

> Two hundred lbs. flour; 3 lbs. coffee; 15 lbs. sugar; 1 lb tea; 1 lb baking powder; 1 lb soda; ½ bu beans; 10 lbs. rice; 8 pounds fish; 10 bars soap; 2 pkgs. yeast; 2 sacks salt; 1 pkg. Matches, 6 lbs. lard; 1 bottle bluing [for laundry]; 45 lbs. pork; 2 pails jelly; 1 gal. syrup; 8 lbs. crackers; 1 box pepper; 3 lbs. breakfast food.[106]

Jacob's bout with typhoid also illustrates the degree to which, especially in the early settlement years, the farm operated with little margin to spare, also suggested by Jacob's habit of working right up to the Christmas holiday—arriving in Milaca late on Christmas Eve. The farm itself did not yet produce enough to support the family—Jacob's earnings were an essential element of the family economy. Writing her memoir some fifty years later, Minnie still recalled 1897 as the "worst winter I have lived as a settler's wife." Finances were so tight that year that the couple pawned their wedding rings so Jacob could get to the city to seek tailoring employment. He soon found work, and, as Minnie wrote, "it didn't take long before there was money to get the rings out of pawn and money for the children and I to live."[107] It may have been during this time that Minnie had her frustrating encounter with a local storekeeper who refused her ten cents cash for postage in exchange for her goods. Exhibiting her usual strong spirit and independence, Minnie never conducted business there again.[108]

Periodic economic challenges such as Jacob's illness had caused were common for Swedish immigrants as they worked to develop their farms. When Einar and Lina Pearson began farming in rural Mille Lacs County in the spring of 1907, they had sixty-seven acres of land, with one acre cleared to plant potatoes, a tarpaper shack (a cellar was dug and lumber collected to build a wood home in the fall), and a little livestock (one horse, one cow, one pig, and a hen with twelve chicks). They were able to harvest hay over the summer to feed the livestock. Yet even with this good start, once the couple had a growing family to support, it was at times difficult to keep up with mortgage payments. More than once Einar had to negotiate with bankers or mortgage companies regarding late payments.[109]

The Halgrens were lucky that Jacob's illness was only temporary, not the case for Swedish immigrant Ellen Johnson, who immigrated to the United States in 1872. After working as a domestic at various locations on the East

Coast, she married Andrew Anderson in 1877 and the couple settled in rural Illinois. Soon after they started their family, Andrew contracted tuberculosis. He was able to perform only limited chores on the farm, leaving Ellen to provide the bulk of the family's support while the family size grew to include eight children. Only when the children were old enough to help out did her burdens ease. She performed heavy field work until her late forties.[110] Her experience—and Minnie's—illustrates how family demographics helped shape the nature and quantity of farm labor Swedish immigrant women performed. Having children old enough to assist with chores in farm and field, especially when illness or economic downturns occurred, eased the burdens resting on the farmwife. Jacob's illness would not have been as hard on Minnie had it struck when the family's children were older.

Minnie recalled in her memoir a time when she and Jacob looked out on the "nest" they had built together: "How beautiful we thought it was and how happy we were. It was ours; we had built it with the labor of our own hands. We felt proud and happy." Minnie clearly took pride in her role as a Swedish immigrant wife, whether as an urban housewife or a farmwife/farmer. Her "good life" in St. Paul suggests how Swedish immigrant women in urban areas might "have things better" in terms of living conditions and household management than did married women in Sweden—at least when the economy was good and the family was healthy. When personal or family circumstances encouraged families to move from urban to rural areas, the roles of Swedish immigrant wives could change. In Mille Lacs County, Minnesota, and in other areas of the Midwest where settlement took place after the best and most easily cultivated land was taken up, establishing a successful farm required the farmwife to manage the farm as well as the household and child rearing for significant portions of the year while the husband was out earning cash wages. Such was the case for many Swedish farm families who, like Minnie and Jacob, accepted that establishing a prosperous farm was a slow process that might take many years of labor and struggle. As Minnie's recollections have made clear, the role of Swedish immigrant wife at home could be difficult at times, but with a positive attitude and a strong work ethic one could survive the hardships. And even if the benefits of hard work and sacrifice were not bountiful, a Swedish immigrant wife could still, as Minnie noted, take satisfaction in the work she had completed and maintain her "hope for a better future."

CHAPTER 6

"I Was Happy When I Heard Them Hammering"

In 1895, the year after we arrived, many settlers came here. I was happy when I heard them hammering and pounding in the vicinity because then I knew that I would have neighbors. I used to walk across the forest in the direction where I heard they were building and introduce myself. I said I was happy we would be neighbors and bid them welcome.

Almost all who came here were either Swedes or Norwegians. They were all good neighbors. There was never any feuding and they helped each other all they could. All were poor; some had only a few dollars for a down payment on their land. They built their own log houses and bought a cow. . . . Eventually a school was built on our land. One of the first teachers we had was a young Swedish [seminary] student. He preached in the Lutheran church in town, and in another place and was a teacher in our school. In the evenings he used to drive around the neighborhood for many miles and hold prayer meetings. . . .

I have today been at the funeral of one of my female friends, an old pioneer woman. We were neighbors for over forty years. I often drove to town in all kinds of weather. If it was cold and dreadful when I drove home she always came out and invited me in. [Here Minnie includes a poem she has written about her friend.]

I remember so well when I came from town
My hands and nose had almost frozen.
She waved so kindly with a coffee cup
And asked me into her house
And the coffee pot was put on
And I was warm and full when I was allowed to go.

After we had lived here for a time and things had improved, we always used to have a Christmas party. There was always Swedish food and Swedish customs. We slaughtered. We made sylta [jellied pork or veal] and sausage and everything else that we were used to from Sweden. At our Christmas table there was always julsylta, sausage, cheese, sirapslimpa [a sweet brown bread made with rye flour and molasses], and Swedish pastries of all kinds. We brewed a Christmas drink made from syrup and hops, and didn't forget lutfisk and rice pudding. The only thing we didn't have was glögg [a traditional Christmas drink of mulled wine, vodka or aquavit, sugar, and spices], but sometimes in honor of Christmas we had a bottle of aquavit [liquor made from distilled potatoes or grains] or wine. It was not often that such things occurred in our circle of friends.

Midsommar we used to cut branches and set them up and dress the house with leaves. I remember my husband and I used to sit outside in the evenings around Midsommar and talk about the beautiful Nordic summer night. We also used to put up a julkärve for the sparrows, an old Swedish custom [sheaves of grain were placed outside the home for the birds]. Many birds coming to eat the grain would signal a successful year for the household.

We used to have the adults for dinner (at midday), and in the evening we had the young people over and then there were games and dancing afterwards. . . . We used to let them dance in the kitchen, and later when we built a large barn, with a hayloft and a floor of smooth boards, they danced there. The girls brought cake and sandwiches. I made coffee and I was along as a chaperone. All the young people who were with us then are now old. But when I meet any of them they always talk about how much fun they had when they were young and came to our home. They never brought any alcohol to drink and everything was orderly. Young people of course must have a good time, but if they meet in the homes one knows where they are. . . . Our own children grew up and came out into the world and thus it was with the children of our neighbors. So the happy group that used to gather either at our house or at the house of one of our neighbors was soon scattered.

I had a son who was always with us then, and who was the most cheerful among the cheerful, the happiest among the happy. He died through an accident. Then I could not see the youth gathered, it reminded me too much of him. . . .

When I first came here [to the United States] I tried to get employment where I would have been allowed to go to night school and learn English, but since I always worked in a family, I could never finish in time to get to school at eight o'clock in the evening. I soon learned to read English, but I had never written a letter in English until one of my sons, who never took enough interest in the Swedish language to learn to read it, left home. I wanted so much to reply to his letters, so I decided to learn to write English. I was then over fifty years old, but I managed to learn, and soon I could write so that anybody could understand it. There are certainly mistakes in spelling and grammar sometimes, but even those who have gone to school here make mistakes sometimes. Now I write English most of the time, so both my Swedish and my English are equally bad, since I have never gone to an English school and only four years of school in Sweden. . . .

My younger children have attended high school. The older ones had to be satisfied with the eighth grade. There were no opportunities for high school in those first years. The pioneers were too poor to send their children where there were better schools. Our first school here was in a farmhouse; there were only five children the first term. The next year a little one-room schoolhouse was built—which was later replaced by another. The high school is in town, and now all the children go there by school bus. It is a modern school in the town, nearly everyone goes through high school, many go to university or college.

Children of the first settlers had no such opportunity. They stayed home to have food and clothing, helped their parents and sometimes they left home and earned a little bit for themselves. Often they came home with what they had earned, and bought machinery or made improvements on the farm. Times were hard for many years, and they were happy to have a home when there was no work available. At harvest time they used to go out to the prairie and work, they had to sleep in the haystacks, but they were used to hardship so it didn't matter. . . .

As it is now, a good education is the best inheritance parents can give their children. The pioneers' children, however, had to learn to work and most of them turned out to be competent and decent citizens in whatever community they settled and whatever profession they chose. . . . A pioneer has neither time nor money to travel when one is young. I have no family in Sweden to visit. Now I am too old to make such a journey. Still I sometimes long to see the dear places where I lived the years of my childhood and youth. The only contact I have with Sweden is the Swedish newspapers which I prefer above the English because of their better content.

I have never regretted leaving Sweden. I got a better life here from the beginning. I was paid more, and didn't need to work as hard, either. I have had a better life here than I could have had in Sweden, poor as I was. . . . Now they have a good life in Sweden, in many cases perhaps better than here. It pleases me to hear it. The memory that I have of Sweden is of something entirely different.

I am always at Svenskarnas Dag in the Twin Cities and sometimes I go to the meetings of the Dalsland Society, hoping that I will meet somebody from my own home area. Sometimes I have succeeded, but nobody that I ever knew personally. The older you get, the better you remember your childhood and youth. We will never forget the friends from our childhood and youth. The house where we were born, the paths we tramped as children, school and our teachers—those are things we never forget. We are a part of the country where we were born. Perhaps that is because these memories were the first that our brain was imprinted by. There is so much else that happens later in life that we forget, but never our childhood and youth. . . .

Perhaps, if I had had the opportunity to learn other than hard labor in my youth, I would never have chosen the hard settler life. I have, however, always felt happy, and I have loved nature. To walk around in the forest picking berries and flowers. Nothing tunes my mind more to solemn worship than walking in the forest alone on a beautiful Sunday. I get more out of that, than out of the most beautiful sermon in a church. . . . One of the greatest pleasures anyone can have is on some beautiful summer or autumn day, to travel around in an automobile on the wide asphalted roads in Minnesota with its thousand lakes, green forests, and well-built farms with fields and cattle herds.

Minnesota is our second Sweden. We Swedes have participated in creating what it is today. . . . Now most of the old pioneers are gone, but they have left an inheritance for their descendants in the tilled fields and houses, good roads, schools, and improvements. They have not lived in vain. Their lot has been toil and work.

They broke stone, and tree stumps, and ground until they were gray,
When the farm was in order, their strength was also gone.
Some have gone to their rest, in the quiet nest of the grave,

And others have moved away, to enjoy the peace of old age.
But all have put down here their best effort and labor
And they were all young when they came here.[1]

CONSIDERING THE "TOIL AND WORK" NECESSARY FOR MINNIE HALGREN to raise a family and create a productive farm, it might seem surprising that she had no regrets about her immigration. The demands made upon Minnie as a Swedish American farmer and wife were heavy and are well documented in her memoir. Her writing also reveals other elements of her experience beyond work and toil, especially the social worlds in which she participated beyond house and home. Besides her roles as wife, mother, and farmer, Minnie was neighbor, friend, informal midwife, wet nurse, organization member, Swedish American, and published writer. While she was raising her children and working the farm, as well as later in her life, Minnie participated, like many other rural Swedish immigrant women, in a variety of informal and formal communities and relationships beyond the farmstead.[2] Some involved ethnic connections; others did not. Immigrant women's social worlds provided them with support and friendship that enriched their lives. Their networks of association eased the burdens of making ends meet, facilitated their adjustment to life in the American Midwest, countered the sense of loneliness and isolation that might accompany rural life, and helped them to maintain and celebrate their Swedish heritage. Examining Minnie's participation in various communities through the course of her life illustrates ways in which rural Swedish immigrant women engaged in social worlds outside their homestead and family and the important roles such communities played in their lives.

Communities of Neighbors: "There Was Never Any Feuding"

Minnie felt joy when she heard the sound of neighbors building nearby. Sparsely settled Bogus Brook Township brought quite a change from the densely occupied neighborhoods where she and Jacob had lived in St. Paul. After the family's move in the summer of 1894, Minnie felt isolated, but she did not have to wait long to hear the sound of hammering. By June 1895, when a Minnesota census was taken, Bogus Brook Township included 143 residents in 36 households. Minnie recalled that "almost all who came here were either Swedes or Norwegians," but the census data indicate a slightly broader mix of settlers.

Eighty-eight of those Bogus Brook residents had been born in the United States (most in Minnesota), twenty-four in Sweden, twenty in Germany, two in Norway, and the remaining nine in other European nations or Canada.[3] (See Appendix, Table 5, which shows that in 1905 Swedes and Germans were still the two largest immigrant groups in the township.)[4]

Although Bogus Brook Township had a definite Scandinavian flavor in the decade following Minnie and Jacob's arrival, Swedish residency never reached the density of some other Swedish-settled rural regions of Minnesota. For example, Robert Ostergren studied a Swedish settlement in Isanti County, just east of Mille Lacs County. In 1880 Swedes owned nearly 80 percent of the farms in his study area of several townships.[5] Differing from the Swedish settlement pattern around Milaca, Swedes first came to Isanti County in the 1860s. The land-taking process there was earlier and more gradual than in Bogus Brook Township, allowing more intentional family and community transplantation over time. Unlike the case in Mille Lacs County, most of the Isanti settlements were of Swedes who came directly from Sweden to rural Minnesota.[6]

Minnie felt the strongest sense of community with her neighbors from Sweden and Norway rather than with those from Germany or with her nonimmigrant neighbors. Although geographic distances between households in rural Minnesota exceeded what they had been in the urban ethnic community in St. Paul, shared language and culture still drew people together. Minnie had learned to read and speak English during her first years in the United States, but her strong Swedish accent may have made her feel awkward or shy among native English speakers or immigrants from non-Scandinavian countries. For example, Minnie said "pay tree you tic" rather than "patriotic" and "an yell" rather than "angel." And she would find the location of places by looking at the "mop" rather than at the map.[7] Many Swedish immigrants retained a strong accent in their spoken English. Like Minnie, Emma Dahl retained elements of her Swedish pronunciation even decades after immigration, especially for words beginning with "j" or "y" (for example, pronouncing both "Jell-o" and "yellow" incorrectly).[8]

Minnie wrote that the Swedes and Norwegians in Bogus Brook Township were "good neighbors" and that "there was never any feuding."[9] She may have mentioned the lack of feuding, because the years of the late nineteenth and early twentieth centuries, when the area where she lived was being settled, were also the years leading up to and following Norway's 1905 independence from Sweden. Norway's push for independence nearly resulted in war with Sweden, and ill will existed between some Norwegians and Swedes, both in Scandinavia and in immigrant communities in the United States.[10]

"Picknic on the banks af the Rum River," a family photo with Minnie's handwritten caption blending Swedish and English; photo mid-1930s.

Minnie's neighbors "helped each other all they could."[11] Basic survival in newly settled rural areas required cooperation and mutual aid among neighbors, especially among farm women like Minnie whose husbands worked away from the homestead for parts of the year. The *Mille Lacs County Times* recorded an instance of Minnie receiving typical neighborly assistance in 1908 when Jacob was working away and illness struck the family. The "local news" item read: "Mrs. J. P. Helgren [*sic*] is very sick with the measles. She is having quite a hard siege as all of the children had had a run of them and were just recovering. Mrs. J. Vager is attending her."[12] (Mrs. Vager, or Wager, was a Norwegian neighbor in Bogus Brook Township.) Helen Bengston, who with her husband homesteaded in Minnesota's Red River Valley in the 1880s, summed up the caring relationships that social networks with neighbors provided:

> When illness or other misfortune overtook any pioneer family the rest of the folks in the neighborhood chipped in with food and whatever was needed in the way of helping to keep things going. . . . We were all "newcomers" and we lived together in friendly cooperation. It was a privilege to work together in the new homeland in the building of our homes—the hardships and sacrifices we encountered only brought us to a deeper appreciation of what a good home really meant.[13]

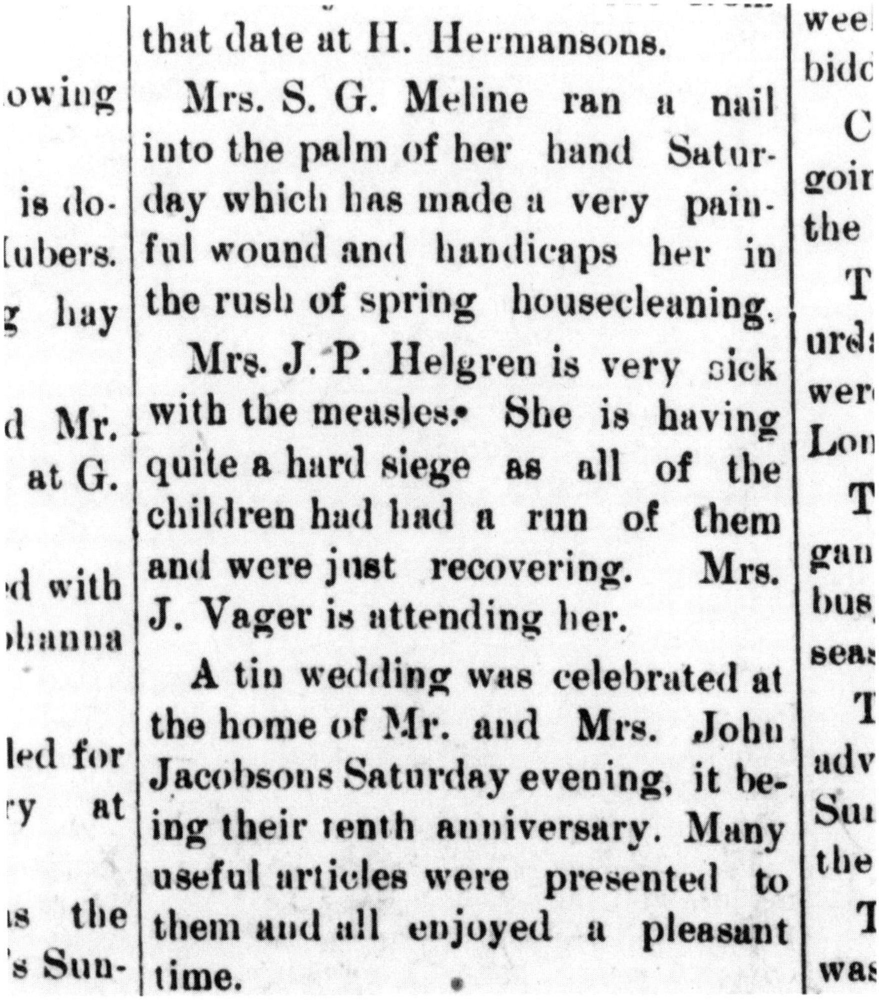

that date at H. Hermansons.

Mrs. S. G. Meline ran a nail into the palm of her hand Saturday which has made a very painful wound and handicaps her in the rush of spring housecleaning.

Mrs. J. P. Helgren is very sick with the measles. She is having quite a hard siege as all of the children had had a run of them and were just recovering. Mrs. J. Vager is attending her.

A tin wedding was celebrated at the home of Mr. and Mrs. John Jacobsons Saturday evening, it being their tenth anniversary. Many useful articles were presented to them and all enjoyed a pleasant time.

Survival in newly settled rural areas required mutual aid and assistance. (*Mille Lacs County Times*, April 21, 1909)

Neighborhood social networks were important for women, especially during childbirth. When Minnie's third child was born, in 1897, during Jacob's bout with typhoid, only a neighbor woman assisted her. One of Minnie's grandsons also recalled Minnie serving as a "halfway midwife" for neighbor women and remembered her leaving the household to help them give birth.[14] At such times she probably joined other neighborhood women in assisting with deliveries, gathering at the laboring woman's home as the birthing process progressed. Minnie had no formal training as a midwife but could offer advice and support based on her own childbirth experiences. For at least one neighbor's labor, Minnie was either the only person in attendance or the most experienced informal midwife present—she is listed in the Bogus Brook Township birth records as having delivered a Norwegian neighbor's child on April 15, 1912.[15] Minnie assisted another of her neighbors, a Norwegian woman who had emigrated and settled with her husband across the road from the Halgrens in 1903, in a very personal way. When the woman was unable to provide enough breast milk for her son, Minnie served as a wet nurse for the child.[16]

Networks of neighborhood families, and women in particular, also gathered to accomplish work tasks (a practice many were accustomed to from their experiences in the homeland). The Swedish immigrant women in Minnie's rural neighborhood met together to make the traditional *julost* (Christmas cheese). Mary Norlander, one of Minnie's acquaintances, who lived on a farm outside of Milaca (in Borgholm Township, just north of Bogus Brook Township), recalled with pleasure the cheese making in her neighborhood, in a description that illustrates how rural Swedish immigrant women's work and social activities often overlapped. She wrote:

> We got together and made cheese. Scandinavians, all, we called it julost as we'd save it till Christmas. None of us had milk enough to make one by herself and with no refrigeration it couldn't be kept till we got enough of it. So several women got together on it. Each would come with her pail of milk and while the cheese was being made drank coffee and partook of all the good coffee bread and other goodies the Swedish housewife is so adapt [*sic*] at making. Then in a few days all would go to another and so on till we all had our cheese.

Neighbors also enjoyed similar get-togethers for building construction or for farm production, such as making lye soap, butchering livestock, shearing sheep, weaving, or quilting.[17] On one Friday in 1914, after the Halgrens had built a new wood board barn to replace their old log barn, they held a shingling bee, followed by a dance in the new barn the next day.[18]

Other interactions of Swedish immigrants with neighbors were less work oriented and more purely social in nature. The poem about a neighbor woman that Minnie included in her memoir offers a wonderful image of a common feature of rural Swedish immigrant social interaction: an apron-clad woman with a coffee cup. Coffee was a popular beverage in Swedish American households, consumed not only at mealtimes but also in between, at midmorning and midafternoon. One of Minnie's children recalled how Minnie's mother, Maja, would "sit and spin and drink coffee all day long."[19] Offering coffee (which would have been accompanied by the ubiquitous Swedish cardamom-flavored coffee bread or perhaps some sweet cookies) to visitors represented an important expression of hospitality in Swedish immigrant communities. Even when household economies were tight and would not stretch enough to allow inviting friends over for a meal, coffee and bread could almost always be offered. A Swedish immigrant woman in northern Minnesota recalled attending "get-togethers in homes, often on Sunday afternoons. . . . We'd play [music] and sing, play games, and have lunch and coffee. Lots of coffee."[20] When groups of women gathered in friends' homes for coffee, bread, and conversation, they were often referred to as coffee klatches (from the German term *kaffeeklatsch,* meaning informal gatherings to drink coffee and chat).[21] Sometimes Minnie and her mother even traveled to Minneapolis to attend coffee klatches.[22]

Friends and neighbors might gather in homes to share more than coffee, especially during the holiday season. Minnie described the "Swedish style Christmas celebration" she shared with friends and neighbors, which included traditional Swedish foods: "We had headcheese and pickled pigs' feet, and roast meat, rice pudding, red pudding, cheese, a drink that we made of syrup and hops, rolls and cookies and we made everything ourselves in the Swedish way."[23] These holiday meals were not necessarily expensive if farm production had been good. As Minnie pointed out: "I think we didn't buy more than flour, coffee, sugar, and rice, and the rest we made ourselves from what we had produced ourselves. I think the only thing we were missing was Swedish glögg."[24] With neighbors and friends reciprocating, the Yule season could be a very busy, and festive, social time. A woman who grew up on a farm in a heavily Swedish area in Pine County, Minnesota, remembered the Christmas holidays lasting about a month. She recalled the *julakalas* (Christmas parties): "Father and mother would tuck us little children in the sleigh, with quilts over us to keep us warm and we drove off to these parties. Father always put the old Swedish bells on the horses and they would ring merrily as we drove along, sometimes two or three miles away."[25]

When Minnie hosted Christmas parties, she invited the adults to a noon meal, with the younger generation arriving for food in the evening with "games and dancing afterwards." Even after giving birth to seven children, Minnie still loved dancing.[26] The Halgrens hosted neighborhood dances not only at Christmas but at other times of the year as well. Minnie's youngest

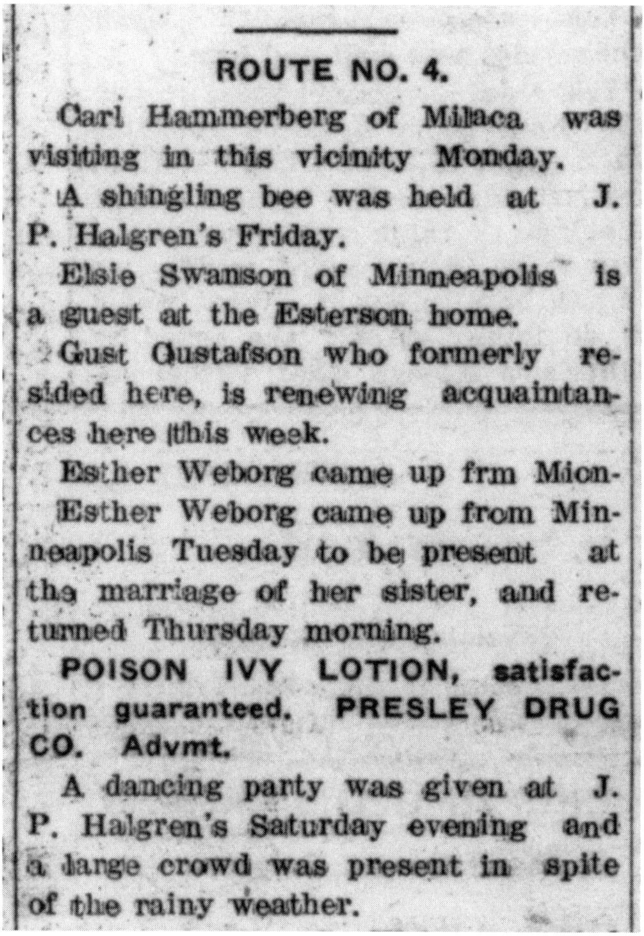

ROUTE NO. 4.

Carl Hammerberg of Milaca was visiting in this vicinity Monday.

A shingling bee was held at J. P. Halgren's Friday.

Elsie Swanson of Minneapolis is a guest at the Esterson home.

Gust Gustafson who formerly resided here, is renewing acquaintances here this week.

Esther Weborg came up frm Mion-

Esther Weborg came up from Minneapolis Tuesday to be present at the marriage of her sister, and returned Thursday morning.

POISON IVY LOTION, satisfaction guaranteed. PRESLEY DRUG CO. Advmt.

A dancing party was given at J. P. Halgren's Saturday evening and a large crowd was present in spite of the rainy weather.

Minnie's social worlds included a mix of work and pleasure, including hosting a shingling bee on Friday followed by a dance on Saturday evening. (*Mille Lacs County Times*, July 2, 1914)

child, Jennie, recalled the family holding barn dances about twice a year, often including one at Midsommar. The haymow would be swept and cleaned. Everyone would bring food, but Minnie would also make "gallons of coffee" and maybe ice cream and sandwiches. Usually there was live music, with two neighbors playing dance tunes on accordion and violin. When these musicians became tired, or if they were not available, the Halgrens' big Victrola was carried up to the haymow. These dances helped socialize children in Swedish American families. They were opportunities for young people to become acquainted and enjoy themselves in a safe and supervised atmosphere. Minnie served as a chaperone, and no alcohol was consumed. Dancing was a popular social activity, but the Halgrens also held other events in their rural neighborhood. Summertime included swimming in the brook that ran by the

Halgren home, and the family hosted bonfires with hot dogs and skating in the winter months.[27]

Children, Schooling, and Community: "Everybody Is Invited, and the Girls Are Asked to Bring Baskets"

Mille Lacs County School District 21 was established in 1896, encompassing several sections of land in Bogus Brook Township, including and surrounding section 9, where the Halgrens lived. The first District 21 classes were held in a settler's home. It was probably Minnie's convictions about the importance of education (and regrets about how abbreviated her own had been) that motivated her and Jacob to donate an acre of their land to the school district in 1897. A wooden schoolhouse was erected the same year. Families with children attending rural schools represented another important network of association for Swedish immigrant women like Minnie, one that included Scandinavian as well as non-Scandinavian members.

The Halgren children all graduated from District 21 rural school. Of the seven children, all but the first, Henry, were born on the farm in Bogus Brook Township. The *Mille Lacs County Times* noted the arrival of the couple's second child, William, on January 29, 1895.[28] Oscar was the third child in the family, born November 5, 1896, in the midst of Jacob's illness. The couple's fourth child was another boy, born April 5, 1899, whom they named Theodore. A fifth son, Albert, was born November 12, 1901. Minnie and Jacob's last two children were girls. Agnes was born on April 4, 1904; Jennie was born on May 2, 1907.

When asked on a survey whether her children's names were Swedish or American, Minnie responded that they were Swedish.[29] The names that she and Jacob picked, however, were not difficult to pronounce in English and were relatively common among native-born Americans, and they may have been chosen to honor the family's Swedish heritage as well as to provide the children with names that would not cause them to be singled out or teased by their nonimmigrant peers.

Though Minnie's younger children were able to continue their schooling into high school, the older siblings did not have that opportunity.[30] Accessibility and finances help explain why Minnie's sons did not pursue education beyond the rural school. Milaca had completed construction of its first high school by 1902, but public bus transportation for rural students was not available when the Halgren children were growing up. When the Halgren daughters, Jennie and Agnes, attended high school, they had to board in Milaca during

Minnie and Jacob worked hard to feed and care for their seven children; portrait about 1918.

the week, coming back to the farm only on the weekends. Boarding would mean additional expenses for the family. Minnie's reference to pioneer children helping their parents suggests another reason the Halgren boys did not attend high school—their labor was needed on the farm. A grandson recalled hearing how his uncles "Hank and Okkie" (Henry and Oscar) helped to clear the land.[31] And as the amount of land under cultivation increased, so did the family's livestock. In 1897 the Halgrens had one horse and four dairy cows. By 1910 the family still owned only one horse, but the dairy herd had grown to eleven head.[32] And even as late as 1913, Jacob was still working away from the farm a good part of the year. A news item in the January 16, 1913, *Mille Lacs County Times* reads: "J. P. Helgren has gone to Tracy, where he is working at the tailoring business."[33] The Halgren children's school attendance also provides evidence of the boys' labor on the farm as they grew into young men. At age sixteen, Henry Halgren attended classes for only about half of the 1909 school year (80.5 of 160 days), while Oscar, Theodore, and Albert (eleven, nine, and seven) all attended over 100 days. Similarly, in 1915 when Theodore was fifteen years old, he attended only 73 school days. That same year Agnes, then age ten, was present for 141.[34]

Some regret is evident in Minnie's words as she describes her children's education: "The older [children] . . . had to be satisfied with the eighth grade."[35] Still, looking back to her own limited education in Sweden, she must have felt some satisfaction that all had completed eight years of public school. And although it was assumed in Minnie's childhood that she would leave home and seek full-time employment shortly after her confirmation, her daughters Agnes and Jennie encountered no such expectations. Minnie also believed that working on the family farm was a type of education, where young people "learned to work." By work, she meant physical labor, which she viewed as an honorable and essential means of livelihood, even if the broader society did not. She wrote:

> It is only recently that labor has become honored, though even today the one who does not do physical labor is considered superior. Still it is primarily those who labor who have produced our prosperity. A house can be built without an architect's drawing, but it cannot be built without the laborer who cuts the lumber, saws it to boards, lays the foundation and builds the house.
>
> Only after common labor has taken place, can intellectual labor come and make improvements. But the labor of both body and brain are necessary. They must go hand in hand, the one is as necessary as the other and should be equally honored.[36]

Minnie was proud that although the children of many of the early settlers were, like her own sons, unable to obtain secondary or higher education, they had still become "competent and decent citizens in whatever community they settled and whatever profession they chose."[37]

When Henry Halgren began attending District 21 school, probably in 1899 at age six, he spoke only Swedish.[38] His transition to the English language may have been eased through the work of a Swedish immigrant seminary student, O. E. Elmquist, the schoolteacher in 1899 and 1900, who held the job while also serving as pastor of the Swedish Lutheran congregation in Milaca.[39] Younger brother William also spoke only Swedish when he began school a year or two later. But by the time Oscar began his public education, about 1902, he had learned some English at home. Minnie's youngest child, Jennie, recalled that English was the language of the household as she grew up (she was born in 1907). She probably meant that English was the language the children spoke with each other and with their friends. When Minnie was asked in a survey, "Do you speak mostly Swedish with your children?," she responded, "Yes, but they answer in English."[40] Swedish was the language of choice between Minnie and Jacob and between Minnie and her mother, who spoke very little English and who lived with the Halgrens periodically between her arrival in 1900 and her death in the 1930s. But like many children of immigrants, the Halgren sons and daughters chose not to use Swedish for their everyday conversations. In a township that included children of Swedish, German, Norwegian, and other immigrant parents, English was the common language of the schoolroom and of the friendships made there.

Though the younger Halgrens did not learn to speak Swedish in their home, they had at least one opportunity for formal education in the language. In the summer of 1913, the *Mille Lacs County Times* included a notice that a Swedish-language class was being taught for a few weeks at the District 21 school.[41] Whether this "Swedish school" was a regular offering (as it was in a number of other rural and urban Swedish communities) is unknown.[42] Only Minnie and Jacob's oldest child, Henry, having been taught Swedish as his first language, retained Swedish-language facility as an adult. (William may have been able to speak and write Swedish, but he lived only to age nineteen and little evidence of his language ability exists.)

None of Minnie's writings suggest frustration or concern about her children's limited Swedish. She accepted it as a necessary step in the family's becoming American, even if it meant that she had to continue to develop her own English-language skills. When the family's third child, Ted (Theodore), who, Minnie noted, "never took enough interest in the Swedish language to learn to read it," left home as a young man, Minnie taught herself to write in English so she could respond to his letters. As she stated in her memoir, she "managed to learn" and could soon "write so that anybody could understand it."[43] Some of Minnie's letters to her children survive, and they provide interesting glimpses of immigrant language acquisition and the way that Swedish immigrants, when they learned to write English (especially if self-taught), might do so with a Swedish accent.

The District 21 school, like most rural schools, was a place not only for classes but also for social activities. Because Minnie lived close to the school building and had children attending classes there for about two decades, she participated in school activities and in the social network of families nearby. Minnie assisted with school events. Her daughter Jennie recalled in particular

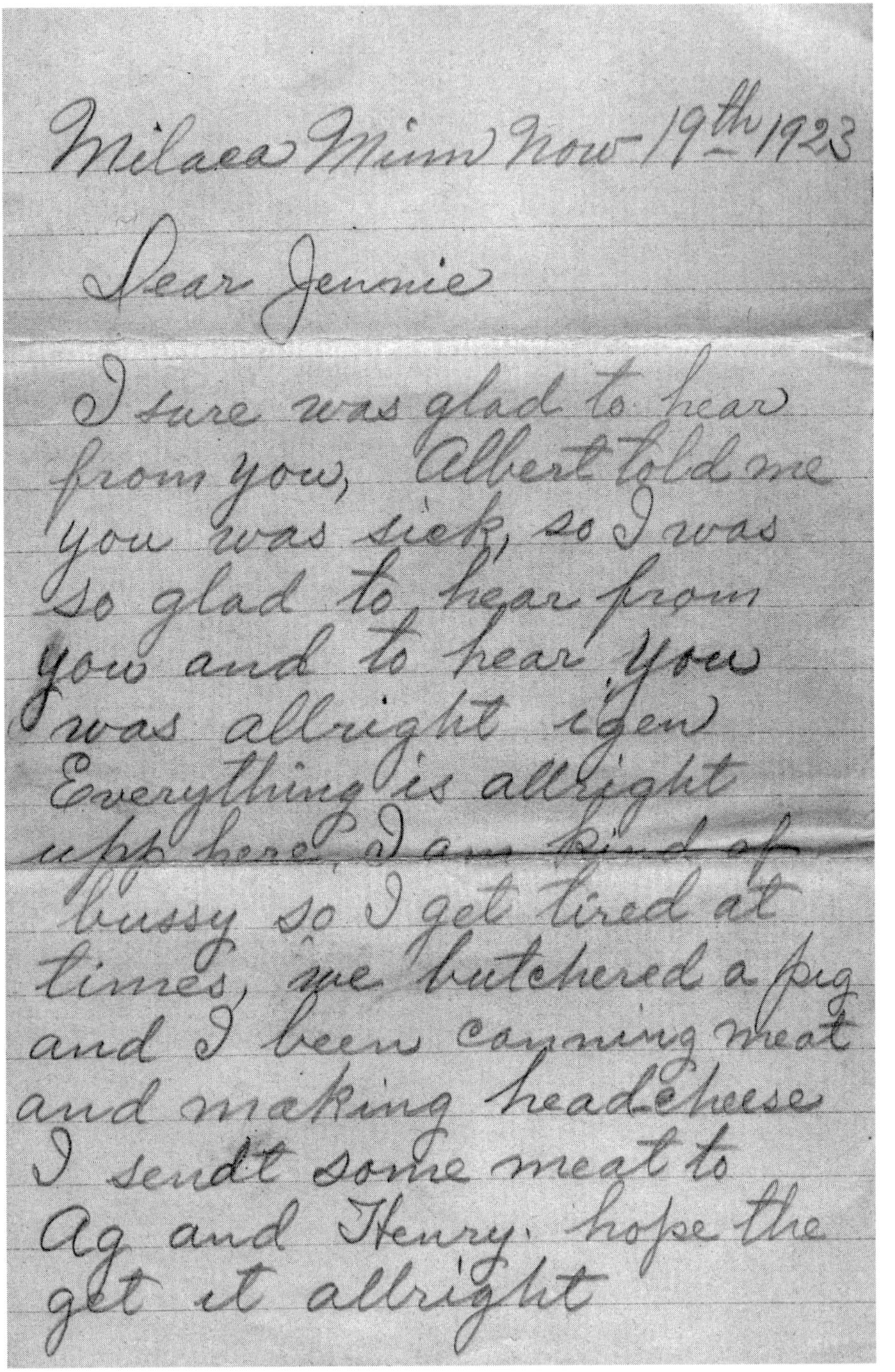

Milaca Minn Nov 19th 1923

Dear Jennie

I sure was glad to hear
from you, Albert told me
you was sick, so I was
so glad to hear from
you and to hear you
was allright igen
Everything is allright
upp here, I am kind of
bussy so I get tired at
times, we butchered a pig
and I been canning meat
and making headcheese
I sendt some meat to
Ag and Henry. hope the
get it allright

Minnie's letter to her daughter, written in English with a few words in Swedish, refers to butchering, canning meat, and making headcheese, perhaps in preparation for holiday celebrations.

her mother's important role at school class picnics, when she provided the ice cream.[44] Rural schools also held programs where schoolchildren performed, reciting lessons they had learned and singing or playing on musical instruments. These programs also provided opportunities for parents to become acquainted and extended the Swedish immigrant woman's social networks beyond that of her Scandinavian neighbors. Parents of schoolchildren, immigrant and nonimmigrant alike, shared concern for their children's education and socialization and pride in their accomplishments.

Both parents and children in rural Swedish immigrant communities attended social activities at country schools. These included events such as basket socials held at the school to raise funds for the purchase of schoolbooks, furniture, and supplies. At these socials a school program was performed, and young women were expected to decorate baskets (or boxes), which, filled with food, would be auctioned off to the highest bidder. The person bidding the most for a basket was expected to eat the contents in the company of the girl who had prepared it. In theory it was an anonymous process, but a young woman might express her interest in a young man by revealing to him, prior to bidding, which box was hers. Attendees who did not participate in the basket making or bidding brought their own food and enjoyed observing the activities. That the immigrant child's school class was also a potential marriage pool was additional incentive for Swedish immigrant women to get to know the parents of their children's friends. According to the *Mille Lacs County Times*, the Halgrens' school (District 21) in 1913 planned a basket social for Valentine's Day, noting, "Everybody is invited, and the girls are asked to bring baskets." The event netted school funds of $15.25.[45] Though social networks built around the children's school community did not provide the same kind of physical and emotional support that the network of neighbors did, they still played important roles in Swedish immigrant women's lives as they sought to raise their children to become honest and respectable adults.

Church, Religion, and Community: "We Say a Hearty Welcome to You"

Churches and organized religion have only a limited presence in Minnie's writings. Her memoir contains a reference to her confirmation in Sweden, a comment about Scandinavian churches writing their histories, a statement that the first District 21 schoolteacher was a student pastor, a remark that most pioneers sent their children to church and Sunday school, and a declaration that she found more meaning "walking in the forest alone on a beautiful Sunday . . . than out of the most beautiful sermon in a church."[46] Although her words convey minimal involvement with organized religion, Minnie in fact participated in various ways in church communities. Her membership in religiously based communities appears to be more socially than religiously motivated, however, even though her writings indicate she was a spiritual and perhaps even deeply religious person.

One might expect that Minnie and Jacob would join a church once they had settled in Milaca. After all, they had both been baptized and confirmed in the Lutheran state church in Sweden, and they chose to be married by a Swedish Lutheran pastor in St. Paul. And Milaca's Swedish Lutheran congregation had been established just prior to the Halgrens' move to Mille Lacs County. The Zion Lutheran Church began with meetings in the homes of Milaca residents in October 1893. By December of 1894 (six months after Minnie and Jacob's arrival in Bogus Brook Township), Zion Lutheran had constructed a church building on Milaca's south side. A Christmas service (*julotta*) was held there in that year.[47] But Minnie and Jacob do not appear on the membership rolls for Zion Lutheran Church.

Minnie and Jacob's absence has several possible explanations. They might have been among the growing number of immigrating Swedes who were frustrated with the religious conflicts in Sweden (opposition to the state church and the rise of free churches) and chose not to participate in formal congregational life in America. There are also less ideological explanations for the Halgrens' nonmembership. Regular church attendance in Milaca would have involved a long journey over difficult roads with a growing family of young children (and a periodically absent father). Attesting to the relative infrequency of trips from Bogus Brook Township to Milaca is that even in 1907 a trip to town was uncommon enough to merit mention in the "Bogus Brook" local news section of the *Mille Lacs County Times*.[48]

In addition to the challenges of travel, given the shortage of cash in the family's first years on the farm, financial contributions to a church congregation would have been difficult. As more Swedish families settled in Bogus Brook Township, Zion Lutheran started organizing services in family homes nearer to the Halgren farm. Attendance was large enough to justify the building of Vondell Brook Chapel, constructed in 1914 and located a mile south of the Halgren farm.[49] That the Halgrens did not join the Zion Lutheran congregation even after the chapel was built nearby may indicate that Jacob and Minnie harbored some ill will against the Lutheran church as an institution that had symbolized state power and authority back home. Still, Minnie's daughter and grandson both recalled Minnie and Jacob periodically attending services there, and the couple's children were all confirmed in the Lutheran faith. The Halgren family's experience suggests that Swedish American church membership records may not accurately reflect those who participated in church communities. At least in some Swedish Lutheran churches, formal church membership was not a requirement for participating in church organizations.

Besides periodically attending church services, Minnie eventually joined in the Swedish Lutheran church community by becoming a member of the Vondell Brook Ladies Aid. This group had been established by Zion Lutheran by 1899, though the organization was then called Women's Society of Bogus Brook. Minnie was not among the early participants. In 1913 the group was opened to both men and women and the name was changed to Swedish Evangelical Lutheran Church Mission Society in Vondell Brook. Jacob never joined the organization, but Minnie became a member of this society (along with her mother, Maja) in February 1921, five years before the group became the Vondell Brook Ladies Aid.

Minnie's decision not to join the Vondell Brook group in its earlier years was likely due to the many demands on her time. The first two decades of the twentieth century were busy ones in the Halgren household and on the Halgren farm, which made regular participation in a formal organization difficult. Jacob's employment continued to leave Minnie to manage the homestead for most of these years, though her work with livestock and land decreased as her sons increasingly contributed their labor. In 1908 the *Mille Lacs County Times* news for Rural Route 2 noted, "J. P. Helgren is working for Thunell, the tailor these days, and his boys are running the Vondell dairy farm."[50] (At that time most of the labor probably came from Henry, William, and Oscar, then ages fifteen, thirteen, and eleven. The other children were at that time nine, six, four, and one.) In spite of the older boys' help, feeding, clothing, and raising the household of children kept Minnie occupied. She would knit, spin, and weave, and make the children's clothing, as well as braid large rugs for the home from strips of carpet rags. She kept both a vegetable and a flower garden and regularly canned meat as well as vegetables.[51] Minnie performed all of these tasks in a home with a woodstove and no indoor plumbing, electricity, or running water (the water was brought to the kitchen from a pump in the barn).[52]

Minnie probably also, like many rural Swedish immigrant women, helped out with the seasonal farmwork, such as haying in July, threshing in September, and potato digging in October, in addition to managing the household. And if, as the acreage under tillage increased, the family traded labor with friends and neighbors for the haying and threshing, time not spent in the field would be taken up by the extra work of feeding additional workers. Minnie's physical ability to manage the farm likely began to decrease in the 1910s as she entered midlife. She had a hysterectomy around 1918, suggesting that in the months and years prior to the operation she had been suffering physical maladies associated with menopause.[53] The children's ability to contribute their labor to the farm also decreased as they sought employment on their own. By 1910 Henry was working off the farm periodically, in the harvest fields of western Minnesota and the Dakotas.[54] In May of 1913 Henry was back in Milaca, working at the cooperative creamery that had been established there. In August that same year Oscar and William left home to work in the harvest fields, returning in November.[55] Henry joined the Minnesota National Guard in 1915, serving in Texas with Minnesota Company G in 1916 during the Mexican border dispute.[56] Oscar and William both fought in World War I. Sometimes the boys substituted financial contributions for their physical labor. Until they married and established their own families, the Halgren children often moved back to the family home between jobs and contributed some of their earnings to the household. Minnie recalled: "Sometimes they left home and earned a little bit for themselves. Often they came home with what they had earned, and bought machinery or made improvements on the farm."[57]

In 1921, a decreased workload and improved finances finally allowed Minnie the time and financial resources (members paid monthly dues ranging from ten to seventy cents) for regular participation in the church group. By the 1920s, Minnie's children were nearly all grown and living outside the household. In joining the Vondell Brook society Minnie might have been seeking to replace the school-related community in which she had participated with her children or the events she had hosted for neighborhood youth. She recollected: "The happy group that used to gather either at our house or at the house of one of our neighbors was soon scattered."[58] For some Swedish immigrant women, associational activity was possible (or desired) only once children were raised and had left home. Swedish immigrant Mathilda Arthur joined women's organizations only after she became "lonesome and melancholy" when she had only one of her fourteen children remaining at home.[59]

After July 1919 Minnie probably also found gatherings with her neighbors and their children painful, as she grieved over the death of her son William. She wrote: "I could not see the youth gathered, it reminded me too much of him."[60] Minnie took the death of William very hard. She had been concerned

Beautiful bouquets mark the grave of Minnie's son William, who died tragically in 1919.

for his safety when he was drafted to fight in World War I. Though he saw military action in France, he was never wounded and was back home safely by February 1919. In July of that year William took a train west seeking agricultural employment. He was standing on the rear platform of the train when his hat blew off. He decided to hop off the slow-moving locomotive to retrieve the hat, planning to jump back up on the rear car. But his foot caught when he hopped off, and he landed headfirst on a concrete sidewalk. He never regained consciousness.[61]

By 1921, two years after William's death, Minnie was probably ready for more social outlets, and the Vondell Brook group seemed a logical choice. She now had more time for such activity, as well as an emotional need for companionship. In August 1921, Minnie hosted the society's meeting in her home. The program consisted of the following: an opening prayer, reading of the meeting minutes, devotions by the pastor, and refreshments followed by prayer and song.[62] Some scholars have found that Ladies Aid societies played a significant role in helping women develop leadership skills, and that in their funding of immigrant churches Ladies Aid members obtained a degree of power and influence within the church structure.[63] The Vondell Brook group's activities show little evidence of these trends. Their small funds (from dues and from events like the ice cream socials they sponsored in 1921 and 1926) were used primarily to support a summer school at the Vondell Brook Chapel that offered confirmation instruction for rural Lutheran youth in the area. Such summer schools were common in the Augustana Synod churches. The public school did not provide religious education, and especially in small and economically struggling rural Swedish Lutheran communities like that in and around Milaca, establishing a regular parochial school was not feasible.

Given Minnie's stated preference for forests over sermons, her interest in joining the Mission Society/Ladies Aid probably displays her desire more for social interaction than for piety. The monthly meetings provided an opportunity for sharing conversation and food. The pleasure such gatherings brought is suggested in the meeting minutes for April 15, 1926: "[Following the regular program,] Mrs. Helgren [*sic*] then served coffee and accompaniments after which we all had a pleasant little time together."[64] Minnie and her mother found community, friendship, and support in the Vondell Brook group. This is apparent in the way in which Minnie's mother, Maria, is referred to in the meeting minutes. From 1929 through 1934 the organization's January meetings included birthday celebrations for "grandma Johnson" (Mrs. Maria Johnson, or Maja Jansson, Minnie's mother). In the meeting following Maria's death in 1936, the minutes note: "We shall miss her. Our dear old grandma."[65] At the next meeting, the group decided to plant flowers around Maria Johnson's grave.

The Vondell Brook group most likely also provided support and consolation for Minnie in the mid-1920s when she lost another son and gained two new members in her household. Minnie's fourth son, Theodore, married Ruth Nelson sometime in the late 1910s. The couple had two children, Florence, probably born in 1915, and Merrill, born in 1921. The couple separated when the marriage failed, and the children remained with their mother, but she found it difficult to care for them. In 1924, when Merrill was three and Florence was eight or nine, they came to live with Minnie and Jacob. Minnie was fifty-seven years old; Jacob was sixty-one. The children's father, Theodore, was too ill at that time to help with their care and support. He died of tuberculosis in 1925.

Minnie and Maria were members of the Vondell Brook group from 1921 through 1934. Why they stopped attending in 1934 is not known. Maria was ninety-six when she died in 1936, and she may have become too ill or feeble to attend regularly. Minnie might not have wanted to go to the meetings without her and then grown out of the habit of attending. The 1930s were also Depression years. In the dues listings in the organization's minute books for the 1920s, it is clear that Minnie and Maria were not always able to contribute their monthly dues, and when they did, their contributions were among the lowest in the group. Family finances became even tighter in the 1930s. Merrill recalled that cash was always in short supply in those times but that the family never went hungry. As was the case for many rural Swedish immigrant families during this era, they learned to make do. Merrill remembered Jacob picking a special vine for him to use as shoestrings, as they could not afford to buy any.[66] After Maria's death, with the economic struggles of the Depression persisting, Minnie most likely chose not to attend meetings for both personal and financial reasons.[67]

Minnie reappeared on the Vondell Brook Ladies Aid membership rolls in 1950, when she attended meetings with her daughter-in-law Arvilla, Albert's wife. She was received back into the group with open arms. The minutes for September 21, 1950, read: "Mrs. Minnie Halgren, a former member joined our society in September. We say a hearty welcome to you." In November, the minutes included the following: "Motion was made and carried that Mrs. Minnie Halgren be written in as an honor member in our society." The honor member designation probably meant she would be exempt from normal membership duties such as paying dues and hosting meetings.[68]

The Vondell Brook Ladies Aid represented a social world with both similarities to and differences from her social networks of neighbors and school families. Unlike the other groups, the Ladies Aid was religious in nature, including Bible reading, devotions, and pastoral participation. It was more formal and structured than other gatherings, with regularly scheduled meetings, a set program, and monthly dues. Its membership was strictly adults rather than families and children. Like Minnie's network of neighbors, however, the Vondell Brook Ladies Aid included primarily first- and second-generation Scandinavian immigrants and was a place where ethnic heritage could be shared and celebrated. And because the society was based around the Vondell Brook Chapel near the Halgren farm, the communities based on neighborhood and on the church shared some of the same participants.

Zion Lutheran Church records indicate that the church provided the primary social network for some Swedish immigrant women in and around Milaca, who remained active in the church and its various organizations throughout their lives. Minnie's periodic rather than long-standing participation in the Vondell Brook Ladies Aid indicates that the group was only one of several communities upon which she relied for support and companionship. Churches were not always at the core of immigrant women's social worlds.

Newspapers, Reading, Writing, and Community: "A Good Newspaper Is a Valuable Companion"

Minnie was part of another kind of community through nearly all her life in the United States, one that, although it usually did not involve face-to-face interaction, was still an important source of support and friendship—the readers and writers in the Swedish American press.[69] Minnie took part in this ethnic community in a variety of ways over the years, most consistently as a reader but also at various times as an active and vocal contributor. She subscribed to Swedish American newspapers for most of her life and found in this community of readers and writers a place where she could, through publication in its pages, tell of her pioneer experiences, convey her opinions on contemporary or philosophical issues, participate in debates and conversations with other Swedish immigrants, and express her creative muse through fiction and poetry.

Minnie wrote in at least two Swedish American newspapers (*Svenska Amerikanska Posten* and *Svenska Amerikanaren Tribunen*) over the years, but her work most often appeared in *Posten*. In a 1929 reader letter she described her first contact with *Posten*, noting that the newspaper had arrived in Bogus Brook Township even before she and Jacob did. She went on to relate how when she was waiting for the family's log cabin to be constructed and staying for a time in a nearby logging camp, one of the men there had a subscription to *Posten*. As Minnie anxiously watched the slow progress toward completion of her new home, the newspaper became her "favorite way to make the time pass quickly." *Posten* was also a welcome companion for Minnie during the rather lonely first year of her residence on the homestead, substituting for personal conversations and relationships before many other settlers had arrived in the area.[70]

Other Swedish immigrants echoed Minnie's appreciation of *Posten*. P. R. Nelson wrote in a 1930 reader letter that he had "read *Svenska Amerikanska Posten* for many years." It had become a "friend which it is difficult to do without. . . . A good newspaper is a valuable companion."[71]

The Minneapolis-based *Posten* began publication as a pro-temperance newspaper in 1885. The paper struggled for survival in the 1880s, but by the time Minnie began reading the paper, in 1894, the editorship of the paper had changed, as had the paper's focus. From the 1890s on, the paper sought to provide information and enjoyment for a broad Swedish American readership, and, by 1894 the paper had adopted a format that included features designed to appeal to many different Swedish immigrant interest groups. In addition to editorials and assorted news coverage, ranging from local items from Swedish American communities, to general U.S. news, to news from Sweden and Scandinavia, *Posten* boasted pages focusing on farming, women and the home, labor issues, temperance, and reform. The paper also contained serialized novels and a readers' letters section.[72]

Though Minnie most likely perused the entire weekly *Posten*, her favorite reading was clearly the letter section, entitled "Folkets Röst" (Voice of the people).[73] She was not alone in this choice. The comment of farmwife Mrs. A. Nilsson of Hayes, North Dakota, that "it is interesting to read your newspaper, and especially 'Folkets Röst,'" expressed a frequent opinion in *Posten*'s reader's letters page.[74] Journalism scholar Jonas Björk, who has published several studies of *Posten*, has also found that "Folkets Röst" was "one of the most popular features" of *Posten*, "the one to which readers [often] turned to first when they received their paper."[75] It was through "Folkets Röst" that Minnie actively participated in the community created by the Swedish American press.[76]

The content of "Folkets Röst" shifted over time. When the section first began in the early 1890s, *Posten*'s editors provided no specific guidelines for reader submissions. In 1896, however, the paper stated that the page was a place for "a civil exchange of views," where writers could focus on any topic, as long as their submissions were moral and decent.[77] In 1902, *Posten* noted that readers could also submit "descriptions and accounts from various localities that may be of considerable interest to countrymen," but by 1907, overwhelmed by these types of letters, the editors stated such submissions would be included only when space allowed. The readers' page would now focus on specific topics chosen by the editors.[78] In 1910, the editors asked readers to refrain entirely from submitting autobiographical pieces or place descriptions and to focus on contemporary political and social issues instead. By the 1920s, in addition to discussion of political and social issues, fiction and tales set in Sweden were increasingly common contributions. From the late 1920s and until the paper's final issue in 1940, "Folkets Röst" also included regular and rather lengthy contributions from a number of readers—resembling regular columns more than the earlier reader letters.[79]

Personal papers shared by Minnie's family members and examination of numerous issues of *Posten* suggest that Minnie published at least forty-one pieces in the newspaper. These include twenty-six reader letters and fifteen contributions of poetry or short fiction.[80] These convey aspects of her identity and experience not evident in her memoir or in other sources. In her poetry, fiction, and prose, aspects of her life—values, interests, concerns, and abilities—that would otherwise lie hidden are revealed.

Minnie's writing also leaves lingering questions. For example, the bulk of Minnie's work was published in the late 1920s and early 1930s. Given the course of her life and responsibilities, this timing makes sense. By the late 1920s, her children were grown and the grandchildren in the household were of school age. Jacob no longer worked away from home, and Merrill could provide some farm labor. With the easing of her daily duties for home and farm, Minnie would have had time to write. But complicating this scenario is the timing of the earliest examples of Minnie's newspaper writing: four poems published in 1907 and 1908. Minnie's last child, Jennie, was born in 1907. When the poems were printed, Minnie was tending to the farm as well as seven children, ages one to fourteen. Jacob was still absent for over half of each year. As she stated so aptly near the end of her memoir, her life was "filled with work and care for a large family."[81] Given these circumstances, how did Minnie find time to write poetry? Did she sit up by lamplight and write late into the night, in a finally quiet and peaceful household? Or were the poems written long before and she only decided to submit them in 1907 and 1908? Aside from an opinion letter published in *Posten* in 1910, no more submissions appear until the 1920s. Perhaps after 1910 the demands on her time finally became too great to allow her to write. Or her participation in the communities created by the District 21 school or her neighbors and friends may have provided her with a satisfying outlet for her creative energies. She offered her writing as a gift on special occasions, composing poems for birthdays and anniversaries.[82] Minnie may also have chosen to submit her writing to another Swedish American newspaper in the 1910s and much of the 1920s. Definitive answers to these questions remain unknown.

It is also a mystery why Minnie nearly always wrote under a pen name (Cecilia and the spelling variants Cicelia, Cicilia, and Cecelia), both in her newspaper writing and in the memoir. Perhaps she did not want friends and neighbors who read the newspapers to know about her writing. She may have felt concerned that others would view her writing as silly or irresponsible—scribbling rather than performing more practical and productive work on the farm. Using a pseudonym might also have made her feel more like a professional writer. Minnie was relatively well read, making references in her *Posten* letters to literary figures such as Tolstoy and the Swedish poet and hymn-writer Johan Wallin.[83] Also, most of the other regular "columnists" in "Folkets Röst" used pen names (proper names like "Joan," or "Ragnar," as well as more descriptive ones such as "en gammal farmaregumma" [an old farm woman]). Minnie may have used the pseudonym because it appeared to be the general practice of the other "Folkets Röst" writers, although she had already used the name Cicelia in 1907, long before "Folkets Röst" developed the practice of regular contributors.

Minnie's submissions to "Folkets Röst" address a variety of topics and issues. In seventeen of her twenty-six reader letters she expresses her opinions on contemporary issues or philosophical questions, in seven she recalls various times past (in both Sweden and the United States), and in two she offers brief greetings and comments about *Posten.* Her opinion letters indicate her awareness of contemporary social and political issues and her desire to express her views on them in the forum that *Posten* provided. She was not afraid of public criticism and had confidence in her abilities, in spite of her limited education.

Minnie's writing illustrates her concern for women's issues. Her 1910 opinion letter addressed woman suffrage, a frequently discussed topic in "Folkets Röst" at that time.[84] She posed the following question: "Why is it that so many men do not wish for women to have the right to vote?"[85] In making her case in defense of woman suffrage, she used arguments that mirror many of those put forth in broader society. She pointed out that girls and boys performed equally well in the schoolroom, and that a visitor to a prison would find more men than women behind bars. She asked why, if ignorance and dishonesty were legitimate reasons for denying a person the right to vote, did a "convicted criminal or an ignorant Negro" vote but not the "most intelligent white woman?" Here her arguments reveal a degree of the racism also found among many suffragists and probably one shared by other Swedish Americans as well. She continued by noting that contemporary society had a good deal of corruption with only men as voters and public officials and contended that if women were given the right to vote "all intelligent and just men and women could help to do a thorough housecleaning." She closed by noting that if that were the case, the one who used the softest brush "would not be Cicelia."[86]

Minnie's concern for contemporary political and social issues is still evident in her writing nearly two decades later. In an October 1928 letter about the difficulties farmers faced in the 1920s, Minnie posed the following questions for debate: "What is the reason for the regularly occurring economic crises? Are they a necessary evil in our financial system, or are they chess moves of big capitalists, that allow the country's resources to land in the hands of only a few?"[87] Reflecting on both the 1890s economic crisis that she had survived, as well as the one she was experiencing farming in the 1920s, she declared that speculation was part of the problem. Minnie viewed speculation as attempting to make money that had not been earned by honest labor. She observed that when people speculated and were then caught by an economic crisis, they usually met financial ruin. Minnie averred that labor produces all prosperity, but when the fruits of that labor were used for speculation, it was the wealthy, not the laborer, that benefited.

Minnie's interest in women's issues continued across two decades as well. In July 1930 she responded to a question posed by another reader: "Was the new emancipated woman really emancipated, or was she now enslaved by the need to work outside the home to help support her family?" Minnie stated clearly her view that women with children under age twelve should not work outside the home "unless absolutely necessary." A married woman who was "handy and thrifty" at home could, by being a good steward of her husband's earnings, ultimately contribute more to the family than if she worked outside the home. She could manage the household finances carefully and produce herself, rather than purchase, much of what a family needed. More importantly, she would be at home to raise her children. Minnie acknowledged that some women of the "younger generation" were not skilled as housewives, and for those women, if they had no children, employment outside the home might be a good choice. Even one of her own daughters, she wrote, was "newly married and childless" at the time and was employed outside the home. But women with young children who chose to work outside the home, she stated, were "to be pitied," as were their children.[88]

Minnie commented upon political issues surrounding the Great Depression. In 1935 she began a letter by referring to the Townsend Plan, one remedy that had been proposed for the country's economic ills. A California physician, Francis Townsend, wanted the government to provide two hundred dollars a month to every person over age sixty, with the stipulation that they spend the money by the end of each month. Townsend argued that his plan would drive cash into the economy and would create jobs because people would eagerly retire and the younger generation would take their places. Minnie did not support Townsend. She suggested instead a smaller pension (thirty dollars a month), that did not have to be immediately spent. She also critiqued other readers' proposed solutions for ending the Depression. One reader had suggested that more Americans move to rural areas, just as Minnie and Jacob had done during the 1890s crisis. Minnie provided reasons why she thought moving to the country was a poor solution: Unlike in the 1890s, there was in the 1930s little good land available and taxes and prices were much higher than when she and Jacob had purchased their farm. She closed her letter with a criticism of government policies: "As long as there is money to be made by importing and foreign countries can pay their war debts with commodities, then the American working class will remain sitting in the middle."[89]

When Minnie submitted letters addressing philosophical rather than political issues to *Posten*, she usually contributed to ongoing debates among the circle of regular contributors to "Folkets Röst." One contributor would pose a question, such as "What is love?" or "Is life meaningless?" and in the following weeks various readers would offer their opinions on the matter.[90] Sometimes the editor of *Posten* would step into the conversation, as in December 1928, when readers were asked to stop discussing the question of immortality, but for the most part relatively open discussions were allowed to play out in "Folkets Röst."[91]

Minnie's opinions focused on those issues about which she held a strong opinion or cared deeply. One such topic was the question, "Why do we hate?" Minnie offered her views on this question in a lengthy letter published in 1930 entitled "Justified and Unjustified Hate." She first pointed out that "we hate those persons who do us an injustice or harm their fellow beings" and went on to offer several examples of this "justified hate." She described how when her sons were called to war (Oscar and William), she hated the war as well as the people who were responsible for it (though she did not specify who she thought that was). She also recalled how she and other coworkers had hated an employer who treated them poorly. Regarding "justified hate," Minnie asserted, "Most people who are hated are themselves the cause [of that hate]. There are not many who hate a good person." She then shifted to a discussion of "unjustified hate," referring to another reader's assertion that "we should hate ignorance." Minnie disagreed, arguing that people who possessed more than others, whether knowledge or material wealth, ought to share with those who had less. Here Minnie's socialist leanings are evident. Though Minnie never directly declared she was a socialist in *Posten*, she did respond to a survey question, "What political views do you hold," with the answer "Socialist."[92] She went on to suggest that in order for hate to end, the reasons for hate must be cleared away. Minnie argued that just as Jesus cleared the temple, so must the usury in society be cleared away. Then the poor might not have to "dig in garbage cans for a bit of food," as she had seen them doing on a recent trip to Chicago. She ended the letter noting that her views regarding hate were probably in opposition to those held by most other letter writers and identified a writer named Myran in particular. But she also observed that "there is no discussion without opposition" and, in a closing that illustrated the spirit of friendly debate prevalent in "Folkets Röst," offered greetings to "Myran, Joan, Mrs. Lindblad and all the others who write in *Posten*."[93] Her letter did elicit

Minnie, writing under her pseudonym, "Cecelia," won a prize for her poem "Graduation." (*Svenska Amerikanska Posten*, June 27, 1928)

På grund af det stora antal bref, som hvarje vecka inflyter till Folkets Röst-afdelningen, kunna vi icke förbinda oss att vare sig publicera eller returnera dem till skribenterna. Vi komma att lägga oss vinn om att utvälja och publicera, delvis eller helt sådana bidrag, som i vår tanke erbjuda intresse för majoriteten af den stora läsekretsen. Bref, som äro klart och sakligt skrifna ha de bästa utsikterna att bli införda. Vi förbehålla oss rätten att afsluta påbörjade debatter, närhelst vi så finna önskvärdt. Hvarje insändt bidrag måste vara försedt med vederbörande skribents fulla namn och adress, ehuru om så önskas endast en signatur införes i tidningen. Skrif tydligt och endast på ena sidan af papperet.

PRISTAGARE UNDER JUNI.

Följande insändare till Folkets Röst-avdelningen hava tillerkänts vårt månatliga pris á $2 vardera: Ellen Morton, Johan W. Hertzberg, "Svensk Arbetarhustru", "Erna" och "Cecelia". Den förstå juli sändas dessä pris i check till prisvinnarne.

Samtidigt tillkännagives att ingen prisutdelning kommer att ske under sommarmånaderna. Detta får icke fattas som en vink till våra skribenter att under tiden låta pennan vila. Meningen med vår prisutdelning var ju icke, som vi förut framhållit, att betrakta som en ersättning för insända bidrag, utan tjänade endast som

one friendly but critical response, from Bokvän (Bibliophile). Bokvän praised Minnie's letter overall but found fault with her point about not many people hating a good person. Bokvän noted that history is full of examples of good people who were hated (Jesus and other Christian martyrs, among others).[94] Minnie responded a few weeks later, acknowledging Bokvän's criticism and clarifying her own position, and then shifted to another of the topics under discussion in "Folkets Röst"—assistance for the sick and unemployed in the midst of the Great Depression.[95]

Also among Minnie's contributions to "Folkets Röst" were recollections about her youth in Sweden and her early days as a settler in rural Minnesota. In 1929 she published a letter entitled "Nybyggareliv" (Settler life) describing her arrival in the Milaca area. She related several settler vignettes that were also part of her memoir (which she wrote nearly two decades later): the journey from Milaca to the homestead, saving her home from the Hinckley fire, and her affection for the family's first horse, including the poem she wrote in honor of him.[96] Another of her "Folkets Röst" submissions," "En saga från Dalsland" (A tale from Dalsland) described a plateau near her birthplace where, in spite of the rich surrounding farmland, nothing but scrub grass would grow. She told the story behind the barren plateau through the words of a song her mother used to sing to her—about a wealthy, arrogant, and stingy woman who had owned a productive farm there, but who had been punished by God for her conceit and disregard for others. Her forest, farm, and home had burned to the ground, and since that time the land was no longer productive.[97]

She also published a letter entitled "Fosterlandet" (Fatherland). In this letter she wrote about the fascination that people hold for the time and place where they grow up. She described her own fondness for her home area, for the flowers that grew there and even for the stones that she had used to build a playhouse. She went on to refer to a performance of the Swedish comedic group Olle Skratthult & Company she had attended. She recalled that when the group sang the lines "The little red cottage by the gate, that once was my childhood home," from the immigrant song "Barndomshemmet" (Childhood home), there was hardly a dry eye in the house.[98] Minnie's own nostalgia for the homeland is evident in this letter. She wrote: "Immigrants are of course transplanted here, and perhaps like a transplanted tree flourish and prosper, but the thoughts still wander back to the land where we were born. I myself never forget the place where I went to school and played as a child." She concluded with a poem she had written about her childhood home, entitled "Det gamla smedsbruket" (The old ironworks).[99]

Thoughts of the homeland were not the only inspiration for Minnie's poetry and prose. She also wrote poems and short stories in conjunction with holidays and celebrations. In the 1920s and 1930s, issues of *Posten* in the weeks before Christmas were filled with short stories and poetry by most of the paper's regular "Folkets Röst" contributors. Minnie published six Christmas contributions from 1931 through 1936. In one of these essays, she told of Christmas in her own childhood in Sweden.[100] The other five were short stories, typically highly moralistic and didactic, illustrating the damage to family and society from behaviors such as immorality, selfishness, and drunkenness and the benefits resulting from morality, commitment, and sobriety. Some of her stories were set in Sweden and others in Swedish immigrant communities in the United States.

Minnie's story entitled "När Axel kom hem" (When Axel came home) is representative of the style of fiction written by Minnie and many of the other *Posten* writers. In this story Minnie examines a young immigrant's commitment to his mother and the home he left behind. She tells of a woman named Karna preparing her humble home for Christmas. Karna's husband had emigrated to the United States but, after a brief period of sending his wife letters and money, was never heard from again. Karna had struggled to raise their son, Axel, on her own, sometimes just barely making ends meet. Through her efforts, however, Axel grew up a strong young man and found employment as a farmhand on a large farm near his mother's home. To his mother's dismay, after some years Axel decided to journey to America to explore his father's fate. At first he sent letters and money back to Karna as his father had, but as the story opens, Karna has not heard from Axel for nearly a year. She fears the worst. On Christmas Eve, just when she is ready to go to the forest to fetch a Christmas tree, Axel returns. He has found success in America and brings home food and gifts for a wonderful Christmas together. After Christmas Axel asks his former employer for his daughter's hand in marriage. Though the landowner would never have considered allowing his daughter to marry a farmhand when Axel had been in his employ, Axel's success in America has made him acceptable in the farmer's eyes. The couple marry and raise a family, and everyone lives happily ever after. Axel's hard work and commitment to his mother are rewarded.[101]

Like her other writing, Minnie's poems addressed philosophical topics as well as nostalgia for the homeland. These themes are evident in the titles of her first four published poems: "Midsommar Memory," "Happiness," "A Long Time Ago," and "The Hope."[102] Her poetry for special occasions included poems entitled "Memorial Day," "Mother" (for Mother's Day), and "Graduation."[103] That Minnie found an admiring and appreciative audience for her writing was made apparent in 1928. In January of that year *Posten* announced that the newspaper would offer three cash prizes every month for the best writing (first prize, five dollars; second prize, three dollars; and third prize, two dollars). Editors would serve as judges, and awards would be based on four criteria: content, style, size of submission, and clarity and organization with which the manuscript was prepared.[104] In June 1928 "Cecelia" was one of five "Folkets Röst" contributors to receive a two-dollar prize.[105] Minnie's prize was based on her poem "Graduation."

Some of Minnie's poems, such as "Midsommar Memories," clearly expressed nostalgia for her homeland. Yet poems such as one she wrote entitled "Minnesota" suggest that her longing for Sweden did not prevent her from also developing a deep fondness and appreciation for her adopted homeland.

The community surrounding *Posten* to which Minnie belonged usually came together through ideas, opinions, and experiences communicated through

"Minnesota"

I know a state,
for Swedes the best of all,
and Minnesota is what we call it.
Here Lake Superior's
wild waves swell. . .

Here many clear brooks run,
between trunks of elm and pine,
and here you can still
find in the forest,
a bit of undisturbed nature,
where you can find wild berries on a
grassy hill
as shy deer watch between the trees.

On the hilltops
you find beautiful farms
here cultivators have received payment
for all their toil,
and through valleys
beautiful streams run
and fat cows pasture there.
Now the grain fields billow,
where in times past pines grew,
and the scent of honey rises,
from red clover pastures.

Here are found big
cities, beautiful parks
and homes in town, in country, by the
thousands
where not so long ago
were unoccupied lands
and dark forests
over hill and valley.
And here have many sons
from Norden's lands
built homes and cultivated land,
with work-worn hands. . . .

O Minnesota,
wonderfully beautiful.
In summer sun, in winter garb,
when your meadows
shine emerald green,
when you in winter are dressed like a
bride,
what can give our youth more joy
than to swim in your lakes and dive in
your waves.[106]

Minnie Anderson Halgren

words on a page. At times, though, some of the regular *Posten* writers actually met face-to-face, for social gatherings, and Minnie participated in some of these events. For example, the June 11, 1930, issue of *Posten* included an invitation to "our writers" from "Joan" for an outing to her home outside Milaca. Her invitation suggests that these gatherings were fairly common occurrences: "I would like you to come here for lunch rather than for 'supper,' as has been common during our meetings." Joan welcomed all writers but mentioned some in particular whom she hoped would attend. Among those named was Cicilia (Minnie).[107] A report of the outing by "Ragnar" was included in the July 9, 1930, "Folkets Röst." As Ragnar described the attendees, he noted the arrival of " 'Cicilia,' one of the old writers." He continued: "Soon enough . . . [we] . . . became acquainted, and the conversation began." The group ate lunch outdoors and was treated to "plentiful and good-tasting food." The writers sang songs, gathered for photographs, and, according to Ragnar, had a "real party out there on the farm."[108]

In his study of the Swedish immigrant press, Ulf Jonas Björk found that "immigrant newspapers were, in essence, community papers, although they served communities defined by ethnicity rather than physical territory."[109] Minnie's participation in the Swedish immigrant newspaper community as both reader and writer allowed her a life of the mind quite different from her everyday existence. She could express her longing for Sweden and her fondness for Minnesota to an audience that understood her ideas and emotions. She could share her experiences as a pioneer immigrant woman. Minnie offered her opinions on issues that were important to her and engaged in debate about them with others who respected her views and ideas. In this community Minnie was not only a Swedish immigrant farmwife who wrote and spoke with an accent that her children and grandchildren found funny. She was also a published poet and writer, accomplishments she was unlikely to have achieved had she not emigrated.

Most rural Swedish immigrant women were not regular contributors to the Swedish American press. Many were, however, regular readers.[110] Mrs. Ida Johnson wrote in 1935 that she had subscribed to *Posten* since 1897. She noted that while it had not always been easy to scrape together the money for a subscription, she "could not be without the newspaper."[111] Regular readers were also members of the community created by the Swedish American press. And while they might not offer their own ideas and opinions in the public forum that "Folkets Röst" offered, they benefited from the writing of others included there. Swedish immigrant women found many of their own experiences and

A gathering of Swedish writers who contributed to the *Svenska Amerikanska Posten*, including Minnie Halgren ("Cecilia"), far right; photo about 1930.

emotions mirrored in "Folkets Röst" autobiographical letters. When Minnie and others narrated their experiences as early settlers, readers could feel pride in the contributions that Swedish immigrant women had made to develop America. Letters discussing contemporary social and political issues, such as woman suffrage or national economic policy, helped inform Swedish immigrant women, especially those in rural areas, about the broader American society in which they lived and modeled participation in American society and culture. The poetry and prose contributions provided enjoyable and informative reading for immigrant women whose budgets might not allow for the purchase of books.

Communities and Swedish Heritage: "Our Native Province . . . We Will Not Forget You"

Minnie became an American citizen on April 30, 1894, when Jacob swore allegiance to the United States Constitution and signed his final naturalization papers.[112] An 1855 naturalization law established that a female immigrant like Minnie would obtain citizenship at the same time as her spouse. Though just the husband received a citizenship certificate, the wife was also then considered a citizen. Only with the passage of the Cable Act in 1922 were female immigrants able to apply for naturalization on their own.[113] Minnie was an American citizen, sought the right to vote, and kept herself informed about current issues in the United States, yet she also felt a strong connection with her homeland. As she reflected in her memoir, "We are a part of the country where we were born."[114]

In fact, Swedish heritage figured as a common element in many of the communities in which Minnie chose to participate. Most of her friends and neighbors were Swedish or Norwegian, and she shared traditional Swedish foods and customs with them. The Vondell Brook Ladies Aid she joined was also a group made up primarily of first- and second-generation Swedish immigrants. During the time Minnie was a member, meetings were mostly conducted in the Swedish language, and the group's religious practices were based upon the Swedish Lutheran church. And Minnie's reading and writing in *Posten* took place in the Swedish language, frequently addressing Swedish or Swedish American topics.

In addition to her participation in these communities, opportunities for Minnie to practice and celebrate her Swedish heritage were provided in Milaca. The church provided some of these opportunities. For the first several decades of its existence, Milaca's Zion Lutheran celebrated religious holidays as they had been celebrated in the homeland, with *julotta* (early Christmas morning services), as well as other social events. In August 1900, Zion Lutheran, along with a sister church in the village of Bock, sponsored a "grand picnic" that included free lemonade and singing in both Swedish and English.[115] The local newspaper, the *Mille Lacs County Times*, published in Milaca, also helped Swedish immigrants maintain connections with the homeland. Through at least 1909 the newspaper carried sections of news about Sweden and the other Scandinavian nations, variously entitled "Tidbits of News for Scandinavians" or "In the Scandinavian North." Local settlers clearly followed this news in the early twentieth century: after reading about famine conditions in the Nordic countries in 1902–03, Milaca Scandinavians raised over 150 dollars for "starving people in Norway and Sweden."[116]

Other opportunities for practicing and celebrating Swedish heritage are evident in the pages of the newspaper. Advertisements in the 1890s and 1900s (some of which were in the Swedish language) boasted Swedish products for sale. Notices were included about the availability of lutfisk for holiday meals.[117] In 1899 Presley's Drug Store ran numerous notices announcing a "full line of novels and religious books printed in the Swedish language," and in 1907 it

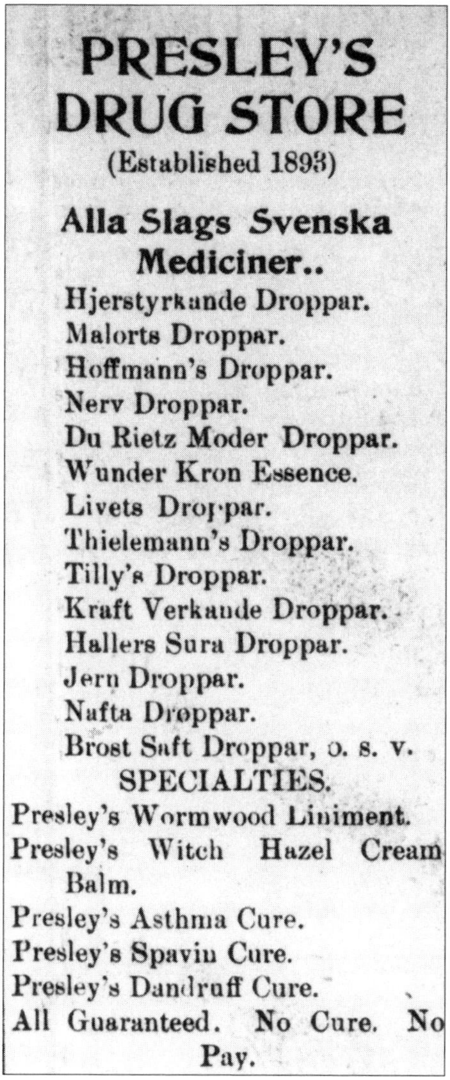

PRESLEY'S DRUG STORE
(Established 1893)

Alla Slags Svenska Mediciner..
Hjerstyrkande Droppar.
Malorts Droppar.
Hoffmann's Droppar.
Nerv Droppar.
Du Rietz Moder Droppar.
Wunder Kron Essence.
Livets Droppar.
Thielemann's Droppar.
Tilly's Droppar.
Kraft Verkande Droppar.
Hallers Sura Droppar.
Jern Droppar.
Nafta Droppar.
Brost Saft Droppar, o. s. v.

SPECIALTIES.
Presley's Wormwood Liniment.
Presley's Witch Hazel Cream Balm.
Presley's Asthma Cure.
Presley's Spavin Cure.
Presley's Dandruff Cure.
All Guaranteed. No Cure. No Pay.

Presley's Drug Store stocked "Svenska" medicines for the surrounding community. (*Mille Lacs County Times*, June 26, 1907)

listed a whole line of *svenska mediciner* (Swedish medicines) for sale.[118] Various Swedish American vaudeville and theatrical groups performed in Milaca in the early twentieth century, providing opportunities for Swedish Americans to meet and enjoy shared musical and comedic performances connected to their ethnic heritage. Minnie and some of her neighbors might have attended a performance of "Ole Swanson Just from Sweden" in 1908. The famed Swedish comedian "Olle i Skratthult" performed in Milaca numerous times in the years 1919 through 1922.[119]

Ole I
Scratthult
The foremost Swedish Comedian and his popular company will be at the
Casino Theatre
Mon. June 9
8:30 P. M.
Olga Lindgren Peterson
Soprano
Maria Dejenson, Alto
Otto Benson
Tenor
Werner Noreen, Bass, Pianist
Erickson & Johnson
Accordianists
Swedish National Dancers from Chicago
Solos, Songs, Duets, Quartettes, Stories and Comical Songs, Swedish National Dances, Accordian Music, etc.
ADMISSION 50c
and 5c War Tax

Swedish ethnic entertainers, including comedians, actors, and singers, regularly performed in the Milaca area. (*Mille Lacs County Times*, May 29, 1919)

Minnie's memoir indicates that her interest in celebrating her heritage increased as she grew older, in part because she watched the practice and celebration of Swedish ethnicity shift and diminish during her lifetime, and in part because she found more time to engage in Swedish American activities as she aged. As the twentieth century progressed, the number of merchants in Milaca carrying Swedish goods decreased, and entertainments focused on Swedish American audiences became less frequent. In the Vondell Brook church group, fewer and fewer members were able to speak and write Swedish. *Posten* stopped publication in 1940, unable to remain viable given ever-decreasing subscriptions (although the Chicago-based *Svenska Amerikanaren Tribunen* continued, and Minnie read, and periodically wrote letters to, this newspaper from 1940 until her death in 1955). As ethnicity became less a part of her existing networks of association, Minnie sought out new opportunities to maintain her connections to her homeland. She wrote: "I am always at Svenskarnas Dag [Swedish Day] in the Twin Cities." Svenskarnas Dag in Minnehaha Park in Minneapolis is a celebration of Swedish heritage that began in 1934 and continues to the present day.[120] Held on the fourth Sunday in June, at Midsommar, Svenskarnas Dag typically includes Swedish foods, a church service (in Swedish), a music and cultural program featuring Swedish and Swedish American performers, and sometimes speeches or lectures about Sweden or Swedish heritage.[121] Minnie's faithful attendance attests to the value she saw in the celebration. As other scholars of Swedish immigration have noted, increased attention to more formal and institutionalized honoring of ethnic heritage in the 1930s may have been, for Minnie and other Swedish immigrants, "a reaction against the assimilation that had been taking place."[122]

Other organizations focusing on regional rather than national history and culture also developed as the twentieth century progressed.[123] One such group was the Dalslandsföreningen (Dalsland Society), whose meetings Minnie sometimes attended. The society began in November 1945 when a meeting was held at the American Swedish Institute in Minneapolis to establish a society for Swedish Americans from the province of Dalsland. Those in attendance determined to meet on the second Saturday of every month and were careful to note that not only Dalbon, but "a person from Småland, Värmland, or any other 'land' who is married to a person from Dalsland, is warmly welcomed."[124] Many local Dalbon seized this opportunity to celebrate their heritage, and within six months of its creation, the organization had reached a membership of 125 persons. The group participated in Svenskarnas Dag that year, and when the Dalsland Society hosted a Swedish Christmas party in 1947, the membership had reached 160.

Minnie's participation in the Dalsland Society was in part motivated by her desire to meet someone she had known in her childhood (a goal she never accomplished). But she also saw the Dalsland Society as serving the important functions of retaining and honoring language and heritage, expressed in the first stanza of a poem she wrote for the group:

> Our native province Dalsland we will not forget you
> we who wander in other lands
> and thus seek comfort from each other.
> We do not hide our beautiful Swedish language
> it is for us an honor!
> And we preserve Dalsland's old customs
> that is the goal that we work for.[125]

Minnie participated in many networks of association throughout her life, and these often allowed her opportunities to practice and preserve elements of her Swedish heritage. With increasing age and decreasing demands upon her time she reflected more often upon the "dear places" where she had "lived the years of . . . childhood and youth." Yet a sentence later she wrote: "I have never regretted leaving Sweden. I got a better life here from the beginning."[126] It might seem odd that Minnie expresses sadness and longing for Sweden but then proclaims having no regrets about emigration in the next. However, such statements are not, as Orm Øverland has noted, the result of a tortured psyche or a "divided heart" torn between two conflicting identities. They are rather examples of what he terms "situational nostalgia"—occasions when circumstances encourage an immigrant to reflect upon the homeland, such as writing a letter to relatives in Sweden or composing works of poetry. Moberg's request that Minnie reflect upon her life as pioneer housewife triggered a similar situation. As Øverland states, while immigrants might look back to the homeland with longing, they were generally "a forward-looking rather than a backward-looking group" who were "more preoccupied with finding a place in their new society than with pondering the one they had left."[127] That Swedish immigrant women like Minnie could be concerned with practicing and preserving their Swedish heritage while also exhibiting a fondness and appreciation for their adopted homeland also provides evidence of what Jon Gjerde has referred to as "complementary identity," the notion that immigrants could rely upon, celebrate, and enjoy both their ethnic and their American identities throughout their lives.[128] Thus, while Minnie would never forget the forests and flowers of

Dalsland, she could still write: "Minnesota is our second Sweden. We Swedes have participated in creating what it is today."[129]

After interviewing several hundred first- and second-generation Swedish Americans in the 1960s, Swedish linguist Folke Hedblom reported finding "now and then among old immigrants, most often women," a kind of homesickness that "steadily ground at their inner being." He told of one such woman who had lived on a farm in western Wisconsin in the late nineteenth century, about fifty miles east of Minnie. The woman's daughter, Anna Fink, described to Hedblom how her mother had "cried every day when she came here."[130] She had lived by a major roadway in Sweden and longed to return to the life and community she had known there. Her experience echoes that of Vilhelm Moberg's fictional Kristina Nilsson, who regretted coming to America and knew isolation and persistent unhappiness, with a circle of association that included few people outside her family and small church community. This was the experience of some Swedish immigrant women, especially if they came in family groups and had little say in the decision to emigrate. More common were experiences like Minnie's. As a Swedish American woman in rural Minnesota, Minnie engaged in a wide variety of social networks during the course of her life. Minnie consistently chose to participate in social worlds outside her home and family, social worlds surrounding neighbors, school, church, Swedish American newspapers, and Swedish American ethnic organizations. Communities such as these provided Minnie and many other Swedish immigrant women like her with physical, emotional, and financial support in times of need; companionship to counter feelings of isolation, loneliness, or homesickness; and a sense of pride and respect in being a Swedish American woman who had no regrets about her emigration.

Epilogue

The evening of my life has so far been light. I have not been alone for such a long time! My husband died after a brief illness three years ago. It feels empty without him, but my children and grandchildren are all good to me, and I have a good life.

Now that I have time to think, my thoughts often fly to the dear fatherland where I lived the days of my childhood and youth, and to friends who I never was allowed to see again. But such is life.

I have never regretted that I left Sweden; I have it better here. Perhaps because I was not spoiled in Sweden, and I've always had it better here. Many times I think it would be fun to exchange letters with someone from the areas where I used to live, but I have not kept up contact with anybody for many years. My life has been filled with work and care for a large family. Now, in the days of my old age, I'm sitting here at the same place where my husband and I settled down fifty-four years ago. I am eighty-one years old as I write these lines. I sit here in stillness and peace and look out over the beautiful area. The fields that we have tilled bear rich harvests, the grain is cut, and the fields shine gray-brown; the grass is still green. The autumn flowers are still standing in their full beauty; no frost has touched them yet. The leaves have started to change and are shimmering in all shades of red, brown, and yellow, between the ones that are still in part green. The air is clean and the sky is clear and blue. Nothing can be more beautiful than a clear fall day in Minnesota.

I sit here and I think of my life. That, too, has changed! I have faded like the autumn leaves and soon I am ready, like them, to become mold again. I thank God for the days that have passed, both the joyful and the sad. I thank God for the gift of life, and for the fact that I have been able to see so much of his beautiful creation. I have health and can travel. I have been to the south last winter and shall go there again this winter. Minnesota is so beautiful in the summer, but the winter is cold, when you get old and cannot stay active. I have a daughter there and I am welcome everywhere.

I have been allowed to live a long life, and now in my old age I have had time to think over my life and see much with other eyes than I did in my younger days.

I hope for God's forgiving love for what I have failed, and I have the hope to see again the friends of my childhood and youth, and my dear ones here, who have gone before me, in the land where life and love are eternal.

The life of most who settled here resembles quite closely what I have written about my own life here, and my story is in most ways like the others. It varies for different settlers, but basically what we had to go through was about the same.

Cicelia

JACOB HALGREN DIED OF A HEART ATTACK ON THE BOGUS BROOK farm on May 6, 1945, at the age of eighty-two. Minnie was then seventy-eight. Though she found things somewhat "empty without him," she continued to lead a full and active life. Minnie maintained close contact with her children, often exchanging letters and visits. Albert and his family lived on the Halgren farmstead alongside Minnie. Henry, Oscar, Agnes, and Jennie spent most of their working lives in St. Paul, making it easy for grandchildren to spend happy summer days at the old home place. When her daughters and their husbands retired and moved to Arizona, Minnie spent her winters there, too. As she wrote: "Minnesota is so beautiful in the summer, but the winter is cold, when you get old and cannot stay active."[1] She enjoyed traveling around the western United States in these years as well.

The more leisurely days of her old age also provided Minnie ample time to write. It was during these years that she agreed to write about her life for Vilhelm Moberg, a decision that, according to her daughter, she came to regret. Minnie read the first half of Moberg's immigrant series, the two novels *Utvandrarna* (*The Emigrants*) and *Invandrarna* (*Unto a Good Land*) that were published prior to her death. Like many of Moberg's readers at the time, Minnie was particularly offended by the rough language and ribald stories that were part of his portrayal. She was also disappointed that she received no financial compensation for her contribution to Moberg's work.[2]

Had Minnie been able to read the final volumes of Moberg's emigrant saga, her dissatisfaction might have been even greater. Though Moberg's depiction of the arduous work required of Swedish American pioneer women

Jacob and Minnie Halgren at their fiftieth wedding anniversary celebration, 1942.

through his character Kristina would have resonated with Minnie's own life of "work and care for a large family," Kristina's long-standing isolation, her lack of facility in English, and her inability to ever feel at home in America belied Minnie's experience. Moberg was selective in his use of Minnie's memoir and his other documentary sources and chose only those words and experiences that fit his own conceptions of Swedish immigrant women and his desire to tell a compelling story.[3] No doubt reflecting in part the patriarchal society in which he lived, Moberg gave to Kristina a life constrained by the physical and emotional demands of frontier childbirth and motherhood, subordination to her husband, and geographic and linguistic seclusion.

Fiction should not be allowed to overpower history. Women who migrated as wives and mothers from rural Sweden to the rural midwestern frontier in the 1860s and 1870s certainly shared some of the constraints that shaped Kristina Nilsson's life, but the experiences of Minnie Halgren and thousands of other women like her show how the reality of most Swedish immigrant women's lives

Minnie Anderson Halgren on her Bogus Brook farm, with the schoolhouse visible in the background.

was more complex and rich. Unlike Kristina, who only hesitantly agreed with her husband's decision to emigrate, many young Swedish women like Minnie spent several years working independently in Sweden before making their own choices to leave the homeland, in hopes of "having things better." Although their wages in Sweden made it difficult to purchase ship's tickets on their own, young Swedish women found a variety of ways to finance their journeys, whether, like Minnie, through a relative already in America or by piecing together their own meager savings with loans from family and friends. Drawn to urban areas by the opportunities for wage earning and the established ethnic communities there, many found things better soon after their arrival, in the form of ready employment, especially in domestic service. As young female wage earners in urban America, Minnie and other single Swedish immigrant women continued to exercise autonomy and self-determination. They changed employers and geographic locations frequently as they sought the best combination of wages, working conditions, and personal freedom. Their earnings provided them with opportunities to fulfill a range of personal goals, from financing other family members' immigration or supporting aging parents back home, to accumulating personal savings or purchasing a fashionable wardrobe.

As had Minnie, most single Swedish immigrant women gained a rudimentary knowledge of English within months of their arrival. If they were employed as domestic servants, their jobs not only helped them learn the language of their new homeland but also introduced them to American middle-class society and culture. Single Swedish immigrant women chose to live and work where they could have active social lives and prospects for developing relationships with the opposite sex. Some even felt enough economic security and self-assurance to turn down marriage proposals and remain single; others found in America meaningful improvements in their opportunities to find suitable mates. Those who chose to marry often began their married lives on a more stable economic footing than would have been possible in the homeland.

Marriage resulted in changes in Swedish immigrant women's lives. Their concerns shifted from wages, working conditions, and recreation to the tasks of social reproduction: giving birth to and raising children, caring for the sick and elderly, and maintaining the household and feeding the family. For some Swedish immigrant women, like Minnie, marriage entailed moving away from urban areas. Born and raised in a homeland where land acquisition represented economic security, some Swedish immigrants saw in farming a means to create an economically stable and self-sufficient life and provide a healthy setting in which to raise a family. Rural settlement added to the responsibilities of hearth and home many of the tasks of establishing and operating a farm, especially when husbands were away earning money to finance the agricultural enterprise.

Still, marriage and rural settlement did not sentence Swedish immigrant women to the kind of lonely, isolated life emblemized by Moberg's Kristina. Rural Swedish immigrant women in fact created and participated in strong communities and networks of sociability and support. From cheese making to childbirth, rural Swedish immigrant women shared friendships, leisure activities, and work tasks with neighbors, which provided them with sustenance, strength, and support. Swedish immigrant women's social worlds included the educational and recreational activities created by rural schools. They attended religious services and church-sponsored gatherings, often finding there celebrations of ethnic heritage as well as spiritual and emotional support.

Rural Swedish immigrant women also remained well connected to mainstream society. Subscriptions to Swedish American newspapers allowed them, in spite of the demands of family and farm, to keep informed about contemporary political and social issues. Ethnic newspapers also provided opportunities, of which Minnie and other Swedish immigrant women (in both farm and city) took advantage, to express and exchange opinions on current events and national social and political agendas, to write and publish poetry and prose, and to maintain contacts with other like-minded Swedish Americans who, though separated by significant geographical distances, shared a community within the pages of Swedish American newspapers. Though only some Swedish immigrant women chose to write to ethnic newspapers, many more Swedish immigrant women read them. And although the act of writing in the press was unusual for rural Swedish immigrant women, the opinions, experiences, and outlooks their words expressed were not. As Minnie stated, "The life of most who settled here resembles quite closely what I have written about my own life here, and my story is in most ways like the others."[4]

The lives and experiences of the many "Minnies" examined in this study require a recasting of our understanding of Swedish immigrant women. Like Minnie Halgren (but not Kristina Nilsson), a majority of Swedish female immigrants arrived in the United States as single, wage-earning women. Framed by their experiences in Sweden and entering a favorable American labor market, these women made independent choices about their lives and work. And this autonomy did not disappear with matrimony. The same self-reliance and independence that Minnie exhibited in her employment choices in the homeland, in her decision to emigrate, in her departure from her uncle's rural home, and in her frequent changes in employers were evident throughout her life. Whether fighting a forest fire that threatened her home, boycotting a local storekeeper who refused her cash, or calling for woman suffrage in the pages of *Svenska Amerikanska Posten*, Minnie made her own well-reasoned decisions within the social, economic, political, and geographic constructs within which she lived. It is likely that the stories of other Swedish immigrant women's lives, had they been shared as Minnie's has, would be similar chronicles of autonomy and agency.

Minnie Halgren died on April 5, 1955, in the Milaca Community Hospital. She was suffering from an enlarged heart and breast cancer. She was eighty-eight years old. In the course of my investigation of Minnie's life, I met with two of her granddaughters. From their visits to the Bogus Brook farm in their childhoods, the Minnie they remembered was "the lady that made the wonderful sponge cake and the wonderful raspberry sauce, and fed us."[5] After hearing the story of Minnie's life told through her memoir and her other writing, they felt surprise at her achievements and great pride in their heritage. She and the many other single Swedish female immigrants who settled in the Midwest in the late nineteenth and early twentieth centuries have left a rich legacy of children grown, farms and homes tended, and words written. Their accomplishments provide ample reason to appreciate and celebrate the hard work, creativity, and sacrifices, as well as the joys and accomplishments, of our Swedish foremothers.

Appendix

Table 1. Land Use and Population Growth in Vedbo Härad, Sweden, 1805–1880

PARISH	TOTAL AREA*	ARABLE LAND (%)	MEADOW (%)	FOREST (%)	OTHER (%)	1805 POPULATION	1865 POPULATION	1880 POPULATION
Rölanda	89	22.0	3.6	62.2	12.2	1,061	2,049	2,044
Töftedal	146	7.2	1.2	72.0	19.6	586	1,092	1,118
Dals Ed	259	8.0	1.9	75.2	14.9	1,341	2,773	2,843
Gesäter	29	26.4	5.2	64.1	4.3	387	809	758
Nösemark	206	6.1	1.3	86.1	6.5	1,043	2,085	2,234
Torrskog	128	7.1	1.9	85.4	5.6	929	1,784	1,798
Värvik	118	9.2	1.4	83.8	5.6	837	1,560	1,509
Tisselskog	104	7.0	1.1	86.4	5.5	580	1,313	1,286
Hålbol	143	7.8	1.2	85.1	5.9	939	1,721	1,745
Ärtemark	172	12.6	1.9	80.8	4.7	1,423	2,863	2,998
Laxarby	212	8.4	1.6	84.8	5.2	1,543	2,848	2,867
Steneby	131	16.2	1.2	79.9	2.7	1,435	2,631	2,529
Bäcke	45	11.3	1.6	74.6	12.5	356	883	770
Ödsköld	94	11.5	1.0	78.8	8.7	703	1,513	1,244
Vedbo *härad*	1,876	10.1	1.7	79.7	8.5	13,163	25,924	25,743

Source: Adapted from Ernst Lundholm, "Vedbo och nordmarks härader," in *EU,* 5.

Note: Mina grew up in Bäcke and Ödsköld parishes. The lower figures in 1880 reflect emigration from Dalsland.

* In square kilometers.

Table 2. Average Annual Wages of Farm Servants, in Swedish Kronor, 1861–1913

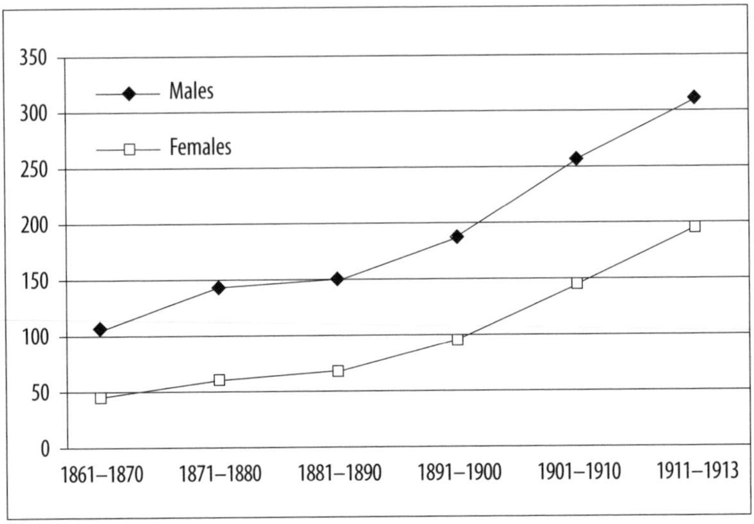

Source: Adapted from table 19, in Dorothy Swaine Thomas, *Social and Economic Aspects of Swedish Population Movements, 1750–1933* (New York: Macmillan, 1941), 97.

Table 3. Emigration from Sweden to Non-European Nations, by Marital Status and Sex, 1861–1930

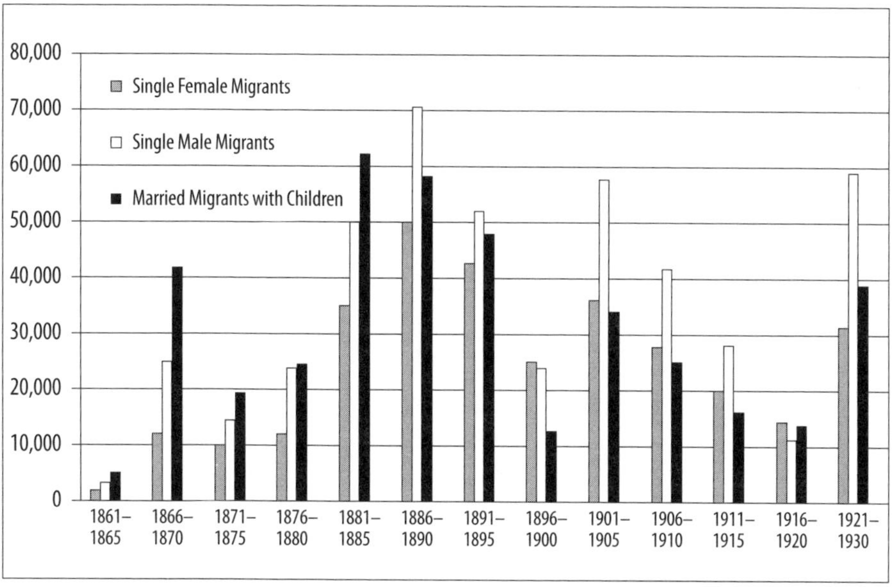

Source: Data drawn from tables 49 and 50 in *Historisk statistik för Sverige,* vol. 1, *Befolkning* (Stockholm: Statistiska Centralbyån, 1969), 129–30.

The proportion of single adult women emigrating to non-European lands (primarily the United States) in the years covering Swedish emigration phases two through five. In the Swedish migration statistics from which these data are drawn, the designation of single women includes women who were single, widowed, and divorced, and, until 1868, married women who traveled to America separately from their husbands. Although these figures are consequently imprecise, they nevertheless provide a good idea of single women's migration trends over time.

Table 4. Largest Occupational Groups for First-Generation Swedish Immigrant Women in the United States, 1900

OCCUPATION	NUMBER	PERCENT
Servants/waitresses	35,075	61.5
Needle trades*	6,042	10.6
Laundresses	3,501	6.1
Agriculture†	2,272	4.0
Housekeepers/stewardesses	2,124	3.7
Trade and transportation‡	1,684	3.0
Textile mill operatives	1,316	2.3
Nurses and midwives	1,106	1.9
Professional service§	906	1.6
All others, all classes	3,019	5.3
Total	57,045	100.0

Source: Adapted from table 48, *Reports of the Immigration Commission, 1907–1910,* 61st Congress, 2nd sess., Senate document no. 282, vol. 28, *Occupations of First and Second Generations of Immigrants in the United States: Fecundity of Immigrant Women* (Washington, DC: GPO, 1911), 71.

*Includes dressmakers, milliners, seamstresses, and tailoresses.
†Includes agricultural laborers, farmers, planters, and overseers.
‡Includes bookkeepers, accountants, clerks, copyists, saleswomen, stenographers, and typists.
§Includes musicians and music teachers, teachers and professors in colleges.

Table 5. Birthplace of Foreign-Born Residents of Bogus Brook Township, 1905

BIRTHPLACE	NUMBER OF RESIDENTS
Sweden	100
Germany	84
Norway	63
Denmark	19
Finland	21
All other nations	27

Source: Minnesota State Population Census Schedules, 1905, Minnesota Historical Society, St. Paul.

Notes

Abbreviations

EI	Emigrant Institute, Växjö, Sweden
EU	*Emigrationsutredningen* (Emigration investigation), 21 vols. (Stockholm: P. A. Norstedt, 1908–13)
LCC	Landelius Clipping Collection, EI
LS	*Livets skola* (The school of life), Vilhelm Moberg Collection, EI
MCT	*Mille Lacs County Times*
MHS	Minnesota Historical Society, St. Paul
MJ	*Minneapolis Journal*
NM	Folkminnessamling, Nordiska Museet, Stockholm
SAHQ	*Swedish-American Historical Quarterly*
SAP	*Svenska Amerikanska Posten*
SSIRC	Swenson Swedish Immigration Research Center, Augustana College, Rock Island, IL

Introduction (pages 3–11)

1. Minnie Halgren (maiden name, Mina Anderson) survey response, Albin Widén, Swedish-American Sociological Surveys Collection, EI. Minnie Halgren was responding to the survey question, "What did your relatives say about your emigrating, when you first talked about it?" The survey was written and distributed by Albin Widén, a scholar and writer who collected immigrant reminiscences and sociological data in the 1930s and 1940s.

2. Approximately 244,000 young women left Sweden. *Bidrag till befolkningsstatistiken för 1890*, vol. 41; *Bidrag till Sveriges Officiella Statistik*, vol. A, *Befolkningsstatistik*, table 31; *Befolkningsrörelsen: Översikt för Åren 1901–1910*, table 53; *Befolkningsrörelsen: Översikt för Åren 1911–1920*, table 66.

3. Mina Anderson (Minnie Halgren), 7:3:1:1–75, *LS*, handwritten in Swedish in two tablets, 27. Unless otherwise indicated, quotations from the memoir are based on an unpublished English translation prepared by Anne-Charlotte Hanes Harvey and Joy K. Lintelman.

4. Draft page of "Livets skola," obtained from Beverly Siedow, in author's possession.

5. *LS*, 13.

6. Kristina's death occurs in the fourth book of Moberg's immigrant novels, *Last Letter Home*, 146. On Moberg's depiction of Kristina, see Rochelle Ann Wright, "Vilhelm Moberg's Image of America" (Ph.D. diss., University of Washington, 1975), 146.

7. The Karl Oskar and Kristina statue image is also found on Minnesota highway signs marking the "Moberg Trail," a twenty-two-mile stretch of U.S. Highway 8. On Kristina's destiny as an immigrant archetype, see Gunnar Eidevall, *Vilhelm Mobergs emigrantepos: Studier i verkets tillkomsthistoria, dokumentära bakgrund, och konstnärliga gestaltning* (Stockholm: P. A. Norstedt, 1974), 254. On Kristina's decision to emigrate, see Moberg, *The Emigrants*, 91–108; and Moberg, *The Settlers*, 395.

8. Moberg, *The Emigrants, Unto a Good Land, The Settlers*, and *The Last Letter Home*.

9. On the musical, see http://www.duvemala.com.

10. Eidevall, *Vilhelm Mobergs emigrantepos*, 34.

11. *Svenska Dagbladet*, May 22, 1960, quoted in Erland Lagerroth and Ulla-Britta Lagerroth, *Perspektiv på utvandrarromanen* (Stockholm: Rabén & Sjögren, 1971), 67.

12. Mrs. Minnie Halgren, Milaca, MN, to Vilhelm Moberg, August 16, 1949, L144:1A:10, Moberg Papers 219, Royal Library, Stockholm, author's translation. This letter was somehow separated from the memoir and is found here rather than with the emigrant novel materials in Växjö.

13. *LS*, 31.

14. Eidevall, *Vilhelm Mobergs emigrantepos*, 30. "Kristina kommer ensam till Amerika = Cecilia [Kristina comes alone to America = Cecilia]."

15. Moberg's materials on Minnie Halgren at EI include the two handwritten notebooks, a typewritten copy of the notebooks, and a seven-page summary of Mina's writing, which he titled "A Pioneer Housewife's Memories: Material Compiled for Kristina's Experiences."

16. Moberg, *The Settlers*, 397. See also Gunnar Eidevall, "Emigranteposets tillkomst och tillväxt," in Lagerroth and Lagerroth, *Perspektiv på utvandrarromanen*, 30.

17. *LS*, 47.

18. *LS*, 32.

19. Moberg, *The Settlers*, chap. 1, "New Axes Ringing in the Forest," 6–11.

20. *LS*, 62.

21. Moberg's views about history and historical fiction are summarized in Eidevall, *Vilhelm Mobergs emigrantepos*, especially pp. 20–60. Moberg's comment is quoted in Eidevall but originally appeared in Vilhelm Moberg, "Om historiska romaner," *Vintergatan* (1943): 124–25.

22. Joseph A. Amato, *Rethinking Home: A Case for Writing Local History* (Berkeley: University of California Press, 2002), 131.

23. Minnie Halgren to Albin Widén, January 5, 1947, Albin Widén Collection, 15:7:10, EI.

Chapter 1 (pages 12–38)

1. Mina's reasons for choosing the pseudonym "Cecilia" (and its variants "Cicilia," "Cicelia," and "Cecelia") are unclear, but since she used it throughout the several decades during which she wrote for a public audience, it clearly held significance for her.

2. As a testament to both the depth and accuracy of Minnie's memory (at age eighty-one), parish records indicate that Anders Jonasson Glader and his wife, Kajsa Johansdotter, lived in the "castle." See Bäckefors Hembygdsförening, *De grå stugornas folk i bäcke socken* (Munkedal, Sweden: Munk-Reklam AB, 1994), 127.

3. Literally *skaren* (snow crust)—the top surface of the snow that has melted and frozen again so it is sharp enough to cut skin.

4. *LS*, 1–8. Unless noted otherwise, the words in brackets are the author's.

5. Margareta Matovic, "Maids in Motion: Swedish Women in Dalsland," in *Peasant Maids—City Women: From the European Countryside to Urban America*, ed. Christiane Harzig (Ithaca, NY: Cornell University Press, 1997), 136; *Historisk statistik för Sverige, 1720–1967*, 2d ed. (Stockholm: Statistiska Centralbyrån, 1969), 127.

6. Sten Carlsson, "Chronology and Composition of Swedish Emigration to America," in *From Sweden to America: A History of the Migration*, ed. Harald Runblom and Hans Norman (Minneapolis: University of Minnesota Press, 1976), 147.

7. Ernst Lundholm, "Vedbo och nordmarks härader," in *Emigrationsutredningen* [hereafter *EU*], vol. 8, *Bygdeundersökningar* (Stockholm: P. A. Norstedt, 1908), 5.

8. In Swedish, the flowers are *snödroppe*, *krokus*, *gullvivor*, and *blåslippa*.

9. Minnie Halgren, "Amerikabrevet," *Dalsländsk hembygd* 4, no. 2 (1953): 22–23.

10. On the Lancashire method of iron forging, see Barbro Bursell, *Träskoadel: En etnologisk undersökning av lancashiresmedernas arbets- och levnadsförhållanden på Ramnäs bruk vid tiden kring sekelskiftet 1900* (Lund, Sweden: Berlinksa, 1974); and Göran Rydén, "Skill and Technical Change in the Swedish Iron Industry, 1750–1860," *Technology and Culture* 39, no. 3 (1998): 383–407.

11. Olof Ljung, "Smeder och bruksfolk vid Bäckefors," in Bäckefors Hembygdsförening, *Bäcke-boken: Historik från en socken på Dal* (Uddevalla, Sweden: Risbergs Tryckeri, 1977), 83.

12. Arvid Keterlin, "Bäckefors Bruk," in *Hembygden 1991*, ed. Per Hultqvist et al. (Uddevalla, Sweden: Risbergs Tryckeri AB, 1990), 126–29; Sven Axel Hallbäck, *Dalsland* (Stockholm: Awe/Gebers, 1982), 8–11, 31–70, 146–49.

13. Björn Trägårdh, *Fri eller ställd: Om friställda industriarbetare i periferin—exemplet Lear i Bengtsfors* (Göteborg, Sweden: Gothenburg Research Institute, Göteborg University, 2002), 6–10, http://cent.hgus.gu.se/epc/data/html/pages/PDF/2002-1 (accessed March 21, 2005); Bursell, *Träskoadel*, 22–42.

14. Bäckefors Hembygdsföreningen, *De grå stugornas folk*, 85–86. For a good, brief summary of rural Swedish industrial communities, see Åsa Lundqvist, "Conceptualizing Gender in a Swedish Context," *Gender and History* 11, no. 3 (November 1999): 584.

15. Robert Ostergren, *A Community Transplanted: The Trans-Atlantic Experience of a Swedish Immigrant Settlement in the Upper Middle West, 1835–1915* (Madison: University of Wisconsin Press, 1988), 34–36; Hans Norman and Harald Runblom, *Transatlantic Connections: Nordic Migration to the New World after 1800* (Oslo: Norwegian University Press, 1988), 38–42; Ovind Osterud, *Agrarian Structure and Peasant Politics in Scandinavia* (Oslo: Scandinavian University Books, 1978), 170–95.

16. Bäckefors Hembygdsförening, *Bäcke-boken*, 139–42.

17. Bäckefors Hembygdsförening, *De grå stugornas folk*, 85, 127–28; Bäckefors Hembygdsförening, *Bäcke-boken*, 140. *Bäcke-boken* also indicates that Mina's mother, Maja, was known as Hamne-Maja, even after the family moved to Bäckefors bruk, because of her earlier residence at Hamnevattnet.

18. Ann-Sofie Ohlander, *Kvinnor, barn och arbete i Sverige, 1850–1993* (Report for the UN Conference on Population and Development in Cairo; Stockholm: Utrikesdepartementet, 1994), 14–18.

19. Barbro Holmdahl, *Tusen år i det svenska barnets historia* (Lund, Sweden: Studentlitteratur, 2000), 41–54; Matovic, "Maids in Motion," 110–11.

20. Bäckefors Hembygdsförening, *De grå stugornas folk*, 133–34.

21. Neil Kent, *The Soul of the North: A Social, Architectural, and Cultural History of the Nordic Countries, 1700–1940* (London: Reaktion Books, 2000), 195.

22. Bäckefors Hembygdsförening, *De grå stugornas folk*, 134.

23. *Historisk statistik för Sverige, 1720–1967*, 46–47.

24. P. Gösta Dalgård, "Befolkningsförändringar på Dal under 1800- och 1900-talen," in *Hembygden 1983* (Åmal, Sweden: Dalslands Fornminnes- och Hembygdsförbund, 1983), 181–89; Britt Liljevall, *Självskrivna liv: Studier i äldre folkliga levnadsminnen* (Stockholm: Nordiska Museets Förlag, 2001), 131–32.

25. For a thorough discussion of these population changes, see Tommy Bengtsson and Rolf Ohlsson, "The Demographic Transition Revised," in *Population, Economy, and Welfare in Sweden*, ed. Tommy Bengtsson (New York: Springer-Verlag, 1994), 13–36.

26. Ernst Lundholm, "Vedbo och nordmarks härader," vol. 8, in *EU*. The study is also useful for examining the causes for and patterns of emigration from Dalsland.

27. Olof Ljung, "Vi vill minnas: Om utvandringen och emigrant forskning," in *Hembygden 1983* (Åmal, Sweden: Dalslands Fornminnes- och Hembygdsförbund, 1983), 148; Matovic, "Maids in Motion," 101. On the baking of such bread, see Kilens Hembygdsgård (Sideby, Finland), "Barkbröd," Kilens barkbrödsprojekt, http://sydaby.eget.net/swe/bark.htm (accessed March 29, 2005).

28. Ernst Lundholm, "Vedbo och nordmarks härader," vol. 8, in *EU* (author's translation).

29. Ibid., 6–9.

30. Ibid., 7.

31. *LS*, 2.

32. Matovic, "Maids in Motion," 100–128.

33. See Holmdahl, *Tusen år i det svenska barnets historia*, 71.

34. *Handbok Ther uti är författat huruledes gudztiensten med Christelige Ceremonier och Kyrkioseder uti våra Swenska Församlingar skal blifwa hållen och förhandlad* (Stockholm, 1693), 107 ff., quoted in Ann-Sofie Kälvemark, "Kommer familjen att överleva? Historiska aspekter på äktenskap och familj i det svenska samhället," in *Den utsatta familjen*, ed. Hans Norman (Stockholm: LTs Förlag, 1983), 21–22.

35. Regarding the degree to which the *Hustavla* influenced everyday life, see Hilding Pleijel, *Hustavlans värld: Kyrkligt folkliv i äldre tiders Sverige* (Stockholm: Verbum, 1970); Carin Bergström, *Lantprästen: Prästens funktion i det agrara samhället 1720–1800: Oland-Frösåkers kontrakt av ärkestiftet* (Stockholm: Nordiska Museet, 1991); Peter Aronsson, *Hustavlans värld—Folklig mentalitet eller överhetens utopi,"* in *Västsvensk fromhet: jämförande studier i västsvensk religiositet under fyra sekler,* ed. Christer Ahlberger et al. (Göteborg Humanistiska fakulteten, 1993), 5–12; and Eva Österberg, "Folklig mentalitet och statlig makt: Perspektiv på 1500- och 1600-talens Sverige," *Scandia* 1 (1992): 81–102.

36. Bäckefors Hembygdsförening, *Bäcke-boken*, 139–43; author's conversations with Mina's descendants, 1993–2007. On family size, see Bengtsson and Ohlsson, "The Demographic Transition Revised," 30.

37. *LS*, 4.

38. Minnie Halgren, "Reflektioner," *SAP*, July 30, 1930, 15. Although Mina may have consciously tried to cast her experiences in an overly positive light, the fact that she was accustomed to writing for a public audience likely worked to counter that tendency. She wrote letters to Swedish American newspapers for years, often including recollections from her past, and knew that her fellow letter contributors and readers would not hesitate to call her to task for presenting misinformation. For more on "Folkets Röst" (Voice of the people), the letters section in *Svenska Amerikanska Posten* to which Mina contributed, see the work of Ulf Jonas Björk, " 'Folkets Röst,' " the Pulse of the Public: *Svenska Amerikanska Posten* and Reader Letters, 1907–1911," *SAHQ* 50 (1999): 1, 4–17.

39. Mats Sjöberg, "Working Rural Children: Herding, Child Labour, and Childhood in the Swedish Rural Environment, 1850–1950," in *Industrious Children: Work and Childhood in the Nordic Countries, 1850–1990*, ed. Ning DeConinck-Smith, Bengt Sandin, and Ellen Schrumpf (Odense, Denmark: Odense University Press, 1997), 106–28; Liljevall, *Självskrivna liv*, 242.

40. Hilda Linder, handwritten autobiography (January 1971), 22:1:12:E, EI.

41. Inez Stridh, biography of Emma Persson, NM.

42. On dairy production as women's work, see Lena Sommestad and Sally McMurry, "Farm Daughters and Industrialization: A Comparative Analysis of Dairying in New York and Sweden, 1860–1920," *Journal of Women's History* 10, no. 2 (Summer 1998): 139–40.

43. Matovic, "Maids in Motion," 122.

44. Some scholars refer to these tasks and roles often performed by women as "social reproduction." For a more detailed discussion of social reproduction in relation to immigrant women, see Suzanne M. Sinke, *Dutch Immigrant Women in the United States, 1880–1920* (Urbana: University of Illinois Press, 2002), 1–13.

45. Cicelia [Minnie Halgren], "Moder," *SAP*, May 25, 1932, 15. Author's translation, with thanks to Marita Karlisch for her assistance in translating several lines of the poem.

46. Matovic, "Maids in Motion," 121–22.

47. On nineteenth-century Swedish women's employment outside the home, see Tom Ericsson, "Women, Family, and Small Business in Late Nineteenth-Century Sweden," *History of the Family* 6, no. 2 (2001): 233–34. Ericsson found increasing numbers of women operating small shops, often selling handicrafts or food.

48. *LS*, 2.

49. Ohlander and Strömberg, *Tusen svenska kvinnoår*, 159.

50. *LS*, 8; Holmdahl, *Tusen år i det svenska barnets historia*, 62–68.

51. *LS*, 8.

52. Inez Stridh, biography of Emma Persson, NM.

53. Liljevall, *Självskrivna liv*, 143.

54. Ingeborg Frankmar, autobiography and letters, NM.

55. Hilda later emigrated to the United States. Hilda Hammar, "Till landet i väster" (autobiographical essay), Hilda Hammar Collection, NM; Holmdahl, *Tusen år i det svenska barnets historia*, 95–102. For more information on this system of foster care, see Elisabeth Engberg, "Boarded Out by Auction: Poor Children and Their Families in Nineteenth-Century Northern Sweden," *Continuity and Change* 19 (2004): 431–57.

56. Olga Pettersson, with Monica Andrae, *Olga berätter* (Stockholm: Sveriges Radio, 1979), 3–22.

57. Ibid., 12–13.

58. Nils-Arvid Bringéus, *Livets högtider* (Stockholm: LTs Förlag, 1987), 54; Matovic, "Maids in Motion," 113.

59. Thea Persson, Nellie Baskette biography, 1897–1960, Thea Persson Collection, NM. Nellie eventually emigrated to the United States.

60. As of January 1, 2000, Sweden no longer has a state church.

61. Bringéus, *Livets högtider*, 53.

62. *Husförhörslängd* (household examination record) for Bäcke parish, AI:14 (1881–1885), EI. Changes in the format of household examination records began in 1895 when the records were renamed *församlingsböcker* (congregational books).

63. Ibid., AI:16 (1891–95), EI.

64. *LS*, 5.

Chapter 2 (pages 39–66)

1. Swedish parish records indicate that Mina was actually sixteen years old when she took this position (in November 1883).

2. Erik Axel Karlfeldt (1864–1931) was a well-known Swedish poet, famous especially for his depictions of the cultural and natural landscapes of rural Sweden. He was awarded a Nobel Prize in 1931.

3. *LS*, 8–12. Omitted from the original memoir in this excerpt are a chapter heading and chapter title (12).

4. *Woman in Sweden: In Light of the Statistics* (Stockholm: Arbetsmarknadens Kvinnoämnd, 1971), 2; Tom Ericsson, "Women, Family, and Small Business in Late Nineteenth-Century Sweden," *History of the Family* 6, no. 2 (2001): 225–39.

5. Ann-Sofie Ohlander, *Kvinnor, barn och arbete i Sverige, 1850–1993* (Report for the UN Conference on Population and Development in Cairo; Stockholm; Utrikesdepartementet, 1994), 142–82; Florian Waldow, "Measuring Human Capital Formation in Sweden in the Nineteenth and Early Twentieth Centuries," *Historical Social Research* 27, no. 4 (2002): 145.

6. See Gunhild Kyle, *Svensk flickskola under 1800-talet* (Göteborg, Sweden: Kvinnohistorisk Arkiv, 1972).

7. Gunnar Qvist, *Kvinnofrågen i Sverige, 1809–1846* (Göteborg, Sweden: Elanders Boktryckeri, 1960). Fictionalized accounts of Swedish women in this time period are also useful in understanding the difficulties they faced. See, in English, Moa Martinson, *Women and Appletrees*, trans. and afterword by Margaret S. Lacy (Old Westbury, NY: Feminist Press, 1985); and Marianne Fredriksson, *Hanna's Daughters: A Novel of Three Generations* (New York: Ballantine Books, 1998).

8. Martin Dribe, "Dealing with Economic Stress through Migration: Lessons from Nineteenth Century Rural Sweden," *European Review of Economic History* 7 (2003): 281; Martin Dribe and Christer Lundh, "People on the Move: Determinants of Servant Migration in Nineteenth Century Sweden," *Continuity and Change* 20, no. 1 (2005): 60.

9. On dairying as another employment option for women in some rural areas of Sweden, see Lena Sommestad and Sally McMurry, "Farm Daughters and Industrialization: A Comparative Analysis of Dairying in New York and Sweden, 1860–1920," *Journal of Women's History* 10, no. 2 (Summer 1998): 137–64.

10. *Historisk statistik för Sverige, 1720–1967*, 2d ed. (Stockholm: Statistiska Centralbyrån, 1969), 46–47.

11. *LS*, 8.

12. Ann-Sofie Kälvemark, "Utvandring och självständighet: Några synpunkter på den kvinnliga emigrationen från Sverige," *Historisk Tidskrift* 2 (1983): 156.

13. Kerstin Moberg, *Från tjänstehjon till hembiträde* (Uppsala, Sweden: Acta

Universitatis Upsaliensis, 1978), 14–17. The Household Servant Law was not repealed until 1926.

14. Hilda Linder, handwritten autobiography (January 1971), 22:1:12:E, EI.

15. Transcription of domestic contract for Kattrine Andersdotter, Einar Johansson Collection, NM. My thanks to Marita Karlisch and Cheri Register for assistance in translating archaic Swedish words.

16. *EU*, vol. 7, *Utvandrarnas egna uppgifter* (1908), 105.

17. Ritwa Herjulfsdotter, *Kvinnominnen från Dalsland: Att vara piga* (Bengtfors, Sweden: Affärs & Industritryck and Bengtfors Kommuns Interntryckeri, 1992), 5. Thanks to Marita Karlisch for translation assistance.

18. Gertrud Adelborg, "Svenska tjänsteflickors utvandring till Danmark," *Dagny* 1 (1890): 2–3.

19. Dribe and Lundh, "People on the Move," 69.

20. *EU*, vol. 7, *Utvandrarnas egna uppgifter*, 106.

21. Ibid., 110.

22. Hilda Linder, handwritten autobiography, EI.

23. Ester Blenda Nordström, *En piga bland pigor* (Stockholm: Wahlström & Widstrand, 1914), 6. Nordström was among the first generation of Swedish female journalists. She gained national fame when her account of her servant experience was published in the Swedish newspaper *Svenska Dagbladet* as "En månad som tjänsteflicka på en bondgård i Södermanland."

24. Dribe and Lundh, "People on the Move," 62.

25. Paul Noreen, *Emigrationen från Sundals härad i Dalsland, 1860–1895* (Mellerud, Sweden: Vasa Ordern av Amerika, 1967), 115–18.

26. Dribe and Lundh, "People on the Move," 18–19.

27. *EU*, vol. 7, *Utvandrarnas egna uppgifter*, 121.

28. David Gaunt, *Familjeliv i Norden* (Malmö, Sweden: Gidlunds, 1983), 115; Uno Gustafson, "Kvinnornas arbetsmarknad i Stockholm, 1870–1910," in *Arbeids- lønns- og rettsforhold for yrkesaktiv kvinner i de nordiske land ca. 1850–1914*, ed. Grete Authen Blom (Trondheim, Norway: Tapir, 1978), 5–6. On the domestic servants in Stockholm, see Fred Nilsson, *Emigrationen från Stockholm till Nordamerika, 1880–1893: En studie i urban utvandring* (Stockholm: Läromedalsförlaget, 1970), 134–50.

29. Margareta R. Matovic, *Stockholmsäktenskap: Familjebildning och partnerval i Stockholm, 1850–1890* (Stockholm: Margareta Matovic and Committee for Stockholm Research, 1984), 68. See also *Hembiträdet berätter om liv och arbete i borgerliga familjer i början av 1900-talet* (Stockholm: Civiltryck AB, 1975).

30. For a brief overview of women's efforts for equality, see Byron Nordstrom, *Scandinavia since 1500* (Minneapolis: University of Minnesota Press, 2000), 248–53.

31. *Tjännarinebladet* (Stockholm), May 1905, 1.

32. Kerstin Moberg, *Från tjänstehjon till hembiträde*, 236–38.

33. For examples of these differing goals, see the Swedish journals *Idun* (a

Swedish middle-class women's journal) and *Morgonbris* (a Social Democratic women's publication).

34. Walborg Ulrich, "Ur verkligheten. Stockholms bild," *Tjänarinnebladet*, serialized, 1906–7.

35. *Tjänarinnebladet*, no. 2, 1906, 2–3.

36. *Tjänarinnebladet*, no. 1, 1907, 5.

37. Iréne Artæus suggests in her published dissertation, *Kvinnorna som blev över: Ensamstående stadskvinnor under 1800-talets första hälft—fallet Västerås*, that such exploitation has perhaps been underrated by historians (Stockholm: Almqvist & Wiksell, 1992), 116–33, 189.

38. Jonas Frykman, *Horan i bondesamhället* (Lund, Sweden: Jonas Frykman and LiberLäromedal, 1977), 221–26. On the increasing numbers of landless women with illegitimate children in the nineteenth century, see Marie Lindstedt Cronberg, *Synd och skam: Ogifta mödrar på svensk landsbygd 1680–1880* (Lund, Sweden: Lund University, 1997).

39. Ulf Ebbeson, *Emigration från en bruksbygd i Östergötland* (Sweden: N.p., 1970), 79. See also Ylva Karlsson, "Utomäktenskapliga barn i Klövedal under 1800-talet," B-uppsats, Tjörns Släktforskare, http://www.tjsf.org/bera/ua.asp (accessed June 15, 2005). On illegitimacy trends in Sweden and explanations for regional variations, see Sigrid Håkanson, "Då skall han taga henne till äkta," *Oäkta födslar, äktenskapsmarknad och giftermålssystem i Östsverige och Västsverige 1750–1850* (Stockholm: Stads och Kommunhistoriska Institutet, 1999).

40. Oscar Nissen, *Om våra tjänsteflickors ställning* (Stockholm: Walfrid Wilhelmsson, 1892), 3, 5–6; Gustav Henriksson Holmberg, *Tjänarinnorna i städerna* (Stockholm: Björck & Björesson, 1907), 35–36.

41. Lyn Karlsson, *Women Workers in Figures: A Picture of Swedish Industry, 1863–1912* (Uppsala, Sweden: Uppsala University, Department of Economic History, 1996), 8–9.

42. Joseph Linck, *Det qvinliga arbetat* (Stockholm: Isaac Marcus, 1884), 87–89.

43. Fred Nilsson, *Emigrationen från Stockholm till Nordamerika, 1880–1893*, 104.

44. Gerda Meyerson, *Svenska hemarbetsförhållanden: En undersökning utförd som grund för Centralförbundets för Socialt Arbete Hemarbetsutställning i Stockholm* (Stockholm: Ekmans Förlag, 1907); Gerda Meyerson, *Arbeterskornas värld: Studier och erfarenheter* (Stockholm: Hugo Gebers Förlag, 1917).

45. Meyerson, *Arbeterskornas värld*, 35, 102–3.

46. *De kvinnliga kontors- och butikbiträdenas ställning* (Stockholm: Aftonbladet, 1903). For more information about individual Swedish women workers at the turn of the century, including women in both industrial and domestic labor, see the personal stories related in *Det hände i vår tid—om det gamla som var och det ny som kom* (Stockholm: Sveriges Radios Förlag, 1967).

47. *LS*, 9.

48. Ibid. For a brief discussion of late nineteenth-century Swedish youth dance culture, see Gunnar Ermedahl, "Spelmannen stryker på violen up: Om spelmannen och

hans musik," in *Folkmusikboken*, ed. Jan Ling et al. (Stockholm: Prisma, 1980), 258–59. On dances popular in Dalsland, see Ernst Klein, *Om folkdans* (Södertälje, Sweden: Olga Klein and LTs Förlag, 1978), 50.

49. For information about the experiences of Swedish immigrant women from pietistic origins, see Cynthia Nelson Meyer, "Creating a Swedish-American Woman: The Views of Women in the Swedish Evangelical Mission Covenant Church, 1915–1920" (Ph.D. diss., Indiana University, 1998). On pietistic attitudes toward Swedish folk dancing, see Ermedahl, "Spelmannen stryker på violen up: Om spelmannen och hans musik," 246–47.

50. *LS*, 11.

51. *LS*, 12.

52. *LS*, 10–11. On class separation of servants, including physical arrangements (eating and sleeping) as well as recreational activities, see Orvar Löfgren, "Family and Household: Images and Realities, Cultural Change in Swedish Society," in *Households: Comparative and Historical Studies of the Domestic Group*, ed. Robert M. Netting et al. (Berkeley: University of California Press, 1984), 456.

53. Sten Carlsson, *Fröknar, mamseller, jungfrur och pigor: Ogifta kvinnor i det svenska ståndssamhället* (Uppsala, Sweden: Acta Universitatis Upsaliensis, 1977), 123. See also Christer Lundh, "Swedish Marriages: Customs, Legislation, and Demography in the Eighteenth and Nineteenth Centuries," *Lund Papers in Economic History* 88 (2003): 40–41.

54. *LS*, 12.

55. Ingeborg Frankmar, "Amerikabrevet," autobiography and letters, Ingeborg Frankmar Collection, NM.

56. Nils Runeby, *Den nya världen och den gamla: Amerikabild och emigrationsuppfattning i Sverige, 1820–1860* (Uppsala, Sweden: Acta Universitatis Upsaliensis, 1969).

57. From *Uppsala Nya Tidning*, quoted in "De svenska fruntimmerna i Amerika," *Social Demokraten*, October 26, 1893, 2.

58. Isidor Kjellberg, *Amerika-bok* (Linköping, Sweden: Isidor Kjellbergs Boktryckeri, 1892), 39.

59. Oscar Nilsson, *Skildring af min vistelse i Minnesota i Amerika, 1881* (Venersborg, Sweden: Bagge och Pettersson, 1881), n.p.

60. Axel E. Lindvall, *Minnen från en färd genom Amerika* (Karlskrona, Sweden: Författarens Förlag, 1890), 28.

61. Ernst Beckman, *Amerikanska studier* (Stockholm: Haeggstroms, 1883), 103. Kjellberg, Beckman, and Lindvall were among several authors who visited the United States and then returned to Sweden to publish their findings. H. Arnold Barton offers critical analysis of these authors and others who depicted America in positive terms, noting their high regard for America as well as their desire to provide a critique of Sweden. See H. Arnold Barton, *A Folk Divided: Homeland Swedes and Swedish America, 1840–1940* (Carbondale: University of Illinois Press, 1994), 44–52.

62. Inge Lund, *Guld med täljknivar: Roman om svenskamerikaner* (Stockholm: Åhlen & Åkerlunds, 1918).

63. For more information on the National Society against Emigration and its activities, see Anna Lindkvist, *Jorden åt folket: Nationalföreningen mot emigrationen, 1907–1925* (Umeå, Sweden: Institutionen för Historiska Studier, Umeå University, 2007); and Ann-Sofie Kälvemark, "Swedish Emigration Policy in an International Perspective, 1840–1925," in *From Sweden to America: A History of the Migration*, ed. Harald Runblom and Hans Norman (Minneapolis and Uppsala: Acta Universitatis Upsaliensis and University of Minnesota Press, 1976), 94–113.

64. Welma Swanston Howard, *När Maja-Lisa kom hem från Amerika* (Stockholm: Folkskrifter Utgifven af Nationalföreningen mot Emigrationen, 1908), 6.

65. Ibid., 11.

66. Cecilia Milow, "Älskar du ditt fosterlandet?" (Stockholm: P. A. Norstedt, 1904).

67. Maria Janson of Lafayette, IN, to family, January 12, 1855, and August 27, 1855, Collection 22:16:5:E, EI. I have read hundreds of Swedish immigrant women's letters during twenty years of research. Janson's letter and the other excerpts included in this chapter are representative of these letters in both tone and content.

68. A Swedish pastor writing to his colleague in Chicago summarized the contents of this woman's letter. The woman writer was making twenty riksdaler in the United States, compared to twelve riksdaler back in Sweden. S. W. Olson, trans. and ed., "Early Letters to Erland Carlson," *Augustana Historical Society Publications* 5 (1935): 115.

69. Josefina Larsson of Altoona, IA, to Augusta Nilson, December 4, 1898, Collection 10:5:4:D, EI.

70. Anna Nygren of Flatbush, NY, to family, November 12, 1908, Collection 22:13, EI.

71. Elisabet Olson in Portland, OR, to family in Dala Järna, January 17, 1913, Collection 22:13:2/3/4, EI.

72. Olga Johnsson in Cambridgeport, MA, to her father, May 17, 1896, Collection 22:17:16:I, EI.

73. Doris Svensson, "Anna Israelsdotters gripande levnadssaga" (biography and letters), March 1966, Collection 10:3:8:G, EI, pp. 8–9.

74. Alma Persson in Milleville (no state listed) to brother Nils, November 29, 1907, Collection 22:16:6, EI.

75. Alma Persson to cousin Alma Anderson, June 28, 1909, Collection 22:16:6, EI.

76. *EU*, vol. 7, *Utvandrarnas egna uppgifter*, 114.

77. Ibid., 121.

78. Nan Enstad, *Ladies of Labor, Girls of Adventure: Working Women, Popular Culture, and Labor Politics at the Turn of the Twentieth Century* (New York: Columbia University Press, 1999), 62.

79. Birger Johnson, "Hisults pastorat: Hallands län," *EU*, vol. 17, *Utdrag ur inkomna utlåtanden*, 160. The role of letters and photographs in encouraging immigration to

America was also underscored by Ernst Lundholm, "Vedbo och nordmarks härader," in *EU*, vol. 8, 44–50.

80. Hilda Hammar, "Till landet i väster," Hilda Hammar Collection, NM.

81. Irma Wibling, *Eva Wallström berätter—Minnen från ett långt liv* (Härnosänd, Sweden: Alex och Eva Wallströms Stiftelse för Vetenskaplig Forskning och Utbildning, 1982), 20–21.

82. May Vontver, *Utvandrare till Nebraska* (Stockholm: Harriers Förlag, 1961), 7–8.

83. Adina Eriksson, *Flicka med tur reste till U.S.A.* (Stockholm: Författares Bokmaskin, 1976), 5–6.

84. Hulda Neslund, "Amerikabrev" binder, American History Library, Uppsala University, Uppsala, Sweden.

85. *EU*, vol. 7, *Utvandrarnas egna uppgifter*, 121–22.

86. Ellen Svanström, "Description of Emigration from Hällaryds skärgård, Bräkne härad, Blekinge," Ellen Svanström Collection, NM.

87. Hilda Linder, handwritten autobiography, EI.

88. Wibling, *Eva Wallström berätter*, 25.

89. C. W. Olson, "Varför jag reste till Amerika," February 17, 1960, Anna Andersson Collection, NM.

90. *EU*, vol. 7, *Utvandrarnas egna uppgifter*, 107, 115–16, 118, 121–22, 119, 115.

91. Moli Nilsson in Omaha, NE, to Maria Nilsson in Sweden, March 18, 1890, Asta Fridstrom Collection, NM. On immigration as a means to gain independence, see Kälvemark, "Utvandring och självständighet."

92. *EU*, vol. 7, *Utvandrarnas egna uppgifter*, 110, 123, 113; see also 103, 122.

93. Oscar Nilsson, *Skildring af min vistelse i Minnesota i Amerika, 1881*, n.p.

94. See *Befolkningsrörelsen: Översikt för Åren 1901–1910* (Stockholm: P. A. Norstedt, 1917), table 53; *Befolkningsrörelsen: Översikt för Åren 1911–1920* (Stockholm: P. A. Norstedt, 1929), table 66; *Bidrag till Befolkningsstatistken för 1890*, vol. 41 (Stockholm: P. A. Norstedt, 1897), xli; *Bidrag till Befolkningsstatistken för 1890*, vol. A, *Befolkningsstatistik* (Stockholm: P. A. Norstedt, 1908), table 31.

95. C. A. Arfvidson, "Ur ett gammalt album," C. A. Arfvidson Collection, NM.

96. Kerstin Johansson, Report on Emma, Anna Svanberg Collection, NM (surname removed to maintain confidentiality).

97. Margareta Strömberg, Report on Alida, Margareta Strömberg Collection, NM (surname removed to maintain confidentiality).

98. Personal communication with Kevin J. Olson, Minneapolis, October 1989.

99. Ulf Beijbom, *Utvandrarkvinnor: Svenska kvinnöden i Amerika* (Stockholm: P. A. Norstedt, 2006), 38; Olov Isaksson, *Bishop Hill, Illinois: A Utopia on the Prairie* (Stockholm: LTs Förlag, 1969).

100. *EU*, vol. 7, *Utvandrarnas egna uppgifter*, 105.

101. "Utdrag ur Provinsialläkares uttalanden," in *EU*, vol. 17, *Utdrag ur inkomna utlåtanden*, 202.

Chapter 3 (pages 67–91)

1. Omitted from this paragraph are several sentences in which Minnie reflects upon having no regrets about immigrating and upon the need to work hard in America to get ahead. An excerpt and discussion of similar reflections are included in a later chapter.

2. Omitted in this paragraph are a few sentences about Minnie's sleigh overturning on her final departure from her Norwegian employer.

3. "Frithiof's Saga" was a famous Swedish national romantic epic poem written in 1825. It was one of the most popular pieces of Swedish literature in the nineteenth century.

4. Castle Garden closed in April 1890. Mina probably entered the United States at the Barge Office in Manhattan, the immigrant processing station that preceded Ellis Island, which opened in 1892.

5. *LS*, 12–23.

6. *Från folkbrist till en åldrande befolkning: Glimtar ur en unik befolkiningsstatistik under 250 år, Fakta inför 2000-talet* (Stockholm: Statistiska Centralbyrån, 1999), 21–24.

7. Sten Carlsson, "Chronology and Composition of Swedish Emigration to America," in *From Sweden to America: A History of the Migration*, ed. Harald Runblom and Hans Norman (Minneapolis: University of Minnesota Press, 1976), 114–48; Robert Ostergren, *A Community Transplanted: The Trans-Atlantic Experience of a Swedish Immigrant Settlement in the Upper Middle West, 1835–1915* (Madison: University of Wisconsin Press, 1988), 111–13.

8. For more information about the Bishop Hill colony, see Paul Elmen, *Wheat Flour Messiah: Eric Jansson of Bishop Hill* (Carbondale: Southern Illinois University Press, 1976); *Western Illinois Regional Studies* 12 (Fall 1989): 5–108 (a special issue on Bishop Hill); Jon Wagner, "Eric Jansson and the Bishop Hill Colony," in *America's Communal Utopias*, ed. Donald L. Pitzer (Chapel Hill: University of North Carolina Press, 1997), 297–318; and Mark L. Johnson, John E. Norton, and Inez Tornblom, trans., "Accounts of Conditions at Bishop Hill, 1847–1850," *Journal of Illinois History* 5, no. 3 (2002): 213–36. Other early group migrations included a settlement in New Sweden, IA, led by Peter Cassel in the mid-1840s and a settlement of Swedes from a mining region who established the community of Stockholm, WI. On the New Sweden settlement, see Ardith K. Melloh, "Life in Early New Sweden, Iowa," *Swedish Pioneer Historical Quarterly* 32, no. 2 (April 1981): 124–46; Eric Corey, "Eric Corey's New Sweden, Iowa," ed. and trans. Kevin Proescholdt, *SAHQ* 43, no. 2 (1992): 73–91; and H. Arnold Barton, *The Search for Ancestors: A Swedish-American Family Saga* (Carbondale: Southern Illinois University Press, 1979), 29–63. Swedish Mormons were another group of religiously motivated migrants. Between 1850 and 1905, over 16,000 Swedish Mormons emigrated to America, which followed the more general pattern of shifting from family to individual migration. Women made up an increasing portion of this emigrant group as the years progressed. See William Mulder,

Homeward to Zion: The Mormon Migration from Scandinavia (Minneapolis: University of Minnesota Press, 1957, 2000).

9. John S. Lindberg, *The Background of Swedish Emigration to the United States* (Minneapolis: University of Minnesota Press, 1930), 192.

10. Albin Widén, *Vår sista folkvandring* (Stockholm: Almqvist & Wiksell, 1962), 35. On America widows, see Olof Ljung, " 'America Widows Had to Get by Alone!" in *De for åt Amerika* (Mellerud, Sweden: Niklassasons Tryckeri AB, 1988), 59–62.

11. Margareta Matovic, "Maids in Motion: Swedish Women in Dalsland," in *Peasant Maids—City Women: From the European Countryside to Urban America*, ed. Christiane Harzig (Ithaca, NY: Cornell University Press, 1997), 137.

12. Distinctions between family and single migration become more difficult to discern in the later phases of migration. Some individuals were migrating with the goal of reconstituting the family in America or were migrating to get married and form families upon arrival—subtleties that would not be reflected in emigration statistics.

13. Ann-Sofie Ohlander, *Kvinnor, barn och arbete i Sverige, 1850–1993* (Report for the UN Conference on Population and Development in Cairo; Stockholm: Utrikesdepartementet, 1994), 157.

14. Hans Norman and Harald Runblom, *Transatlantic Connections: Nordic Migration to the New World after 1800* (Oslo: Norwegian University Press, 1988), 79.

15. Ibid., 88.

16. Ann-Sofie Kälvemark, "Utvandring och självständighet: Några synpunkter på den kvinnliga emigrationen från Sverige," *Historisk Tidskrift* 2 (1983): 164–65.

17. According to one of the documents in this collection, Widén's goal was "to collect material for an exhaustive study of Swedish-America from an historical as well as a sociological point of view. Questions in general are not sufficient; it is necessary to ask specific questions in order that detailed answers will be given. In this way, it will be possible to make clear what Swedish-America really is and what the Swedish immigrants have given to America, not only of human material but also of cultural traditions. For this reason it is necessary to receive cooperation from as many Swedish-Americans as possible." Albin Widén, "Swedish-American Sociological Research," Albin Widén Sociological Surveys Collection, 15:7:10:A, EI. My findings from an initial analysis of Widén's questionnaires, entitled "Gender, Memory, and Meaning: An Analysis of Albin Widén's Immigrant Sociological Survey," were presented at the Nordic Association for American Studies Conference, May 26–29, 2005, Växjö and Karlskrona, Sweden.

18. Nils Johansson, "An Immigrant Story," Nils Johansson Collection, NM.

19. Albin Widén, Swedish-American Sociological Surveys.

20. Joachim Prahl, *Vägledning för svenska utvandrare till Amerika* (Helsingborg, Sweden: Skånes Allehandas Boktryckeri, 1890).

21. Ibid., 36.

22. Christer Lundh, "Life Cycle Servants in Nineteenth Century Sweden—Norms

and Practice," *Lund Papers in Economic History* 84 (2003): 6, http://www.ekh.lu.se/publ/lup/84 (accessed June 14, 2007).

23. Anna J. Olson, autobiography, Anna J. Olson Collection, NM, n.p.

24. Ohlander and Strömberg, *Tusen svenska kvinnoår*, 145.

25. Albin Widén, Swedish-American Sociological Surveys. Regarding familial influence on marriage in propertied classes, see Marie Lindstedt Cronberg, *Synd och skam: Ogifta mödrar på svensk landsbygd 1680–1880* (Lund, Sweden: Lund University, 1997).

26. Ivar Andersson Collection, NM. See also Kälvemark, "Utvandring och självständighet," 173.

27. Gertrud Adelborg, "Kan något göras för att minska den kvinnliga emigrationen och dess faror?" *Dagny* 9 (1903): 218.

28. Kälvemark, "Utvandring och självständighet," 155.

29. Merrill Halgren, personal conversations with author, June 1995.

30. Nina Svärd, "My Memory of My Trip as an Emigrant to North America," Nina Svärd Collection, NM, n.p.

31. *LS*, 17.

32. Maria Elfström in Chicago to her brother, January 1, 1895, Elsa Palm-Elfström Collection, NM.

33. Klara Jakobsson, biographical essay about Tilda Northen and sisters, Klara Jakobsson Collection, NM.

34. Ostergren, *A Community Transplanted.*

35. Elisabet Olson in Portland, OR, to her family, February 17, 1913, Collection 22:13:2/3/4, EI.

36. Ida Petersson, biographical statement, Ida Petersson Collection, NM.

37. On chain migration, see also June Granatir Alexander, "Moving into and out of Pittsburgh: Ongoing Chain Migration," in *A Century of European Migrations, 1830–1930*, ed. Rudolph J. Vecoli and Suzanne M. Sinke (Chicago: University of Illinois Press, 1991), 200–220; and Charles Tilley, "Transplanted Networks," in *Immigration Reconsidered: History, Sociology, and Politics*, ed. Virginia Yans-McLaughlin (New York: Oxford University Press, 1990), 79–95. Chain migration can also be considered one result of ongoing transnational networks. On transnational theory, see Peter Kivisto, "Theorizing Transnational Immigration: A Critical Review of Current Efforts," *Ethnic and Racial Studies* 24, no. 4 (July 2001): 549–77; and Elliott R. Barkan, "America in the Hand, Homeland in the Heart: Transnational and Translocal Immigrant Experience in the American West," *Western Historical Quarterly* 35, no. 3 (Autumn 2004), http://www.historycooperative.org/journals/whq/35.3/barkan.html (accessed June 13, 2007).

38. Maja Johansson, autobiographical essay, Maja Johansson Collection, NM; Hilma Svenson, "Daybook Written by Hilma Svenson during her Jönlöping/Chicago Trip, August 14 to September 1901," Collection 9:9:18:J, EI, n.p.

39. Klara Jakobsson, biographical essay about Tilda Northen, NM.

40. *LS*, 18.

41. Robert L. Wright, *Swedish Emigrant Ballads* (Lincoln: University of Nebraska Press, 1965).

42. May Vontver, *Utvandrare till Nebraska* (Stockholm: Harriers Förlag, 1961), 56.

43. Nina Svärd, "My Memory of My Trip as an Emigrant to North America," Nina Svärd Collection, NM.

44. Norman and Runblom, *Transatlantic Connections*, 115.

45. On the climatic conditions on the North Sea, see "North Sea Geography, Hydrography and Climate," in *OSPAR Commission 2000, Quality Status Report 2000, Region II—Greater North Sea* (London: OSPAR Commission, 2000), http://www.ospar.org (accessed July 19, 2005).

46. See, for example, Elisabet Olson, ship *Eldorado* to her family, June 27, 1912, Collection 22:13:2/3/4, EI; Elizabeth Lindström to sister and brother-in-law, November 15, 1916, Collection 10:3:1:G, EI; and letter between sisters (names missing), July 4, 1870, Gunnarson Family Papers, MSS P:122, SSIRC.

47. Passenger lines between Gothenburg and Hull ended with the outbreak of World War I. When the numbers of Swedish immigrants increased again following the war, steamship companies used routes traveling directly from Sweden to America. See Nils William Olsson, "Emigrant Traffic on the North Sea," *Swedish American Genealogist* 4, no. 4 (December 1984): 158–63.

48. B. J. Hovde, "Notes on the Effects of Emigration upon Scandinavia," *Journal of Modern History* 6, no. 3 (September 1934): 263.

49. Most of the Swedes emigrating from 1869 to 1930 were registered in passenger lists at the police station in their departure city. These records have been compiled in a database (a compact disk entitled *Emigranten*) and include information such as a passenger's age, his or her last parish of residence, final destination, and a contract number that can be linked to a departure ship. On the database, Mina's name appears on a passenger list for the steamer *Ariosto*, another Wilson Line ship. This is probably an error, since in her memoir she refers to the ship name *Romeo*. I have found very few inaccuracies in the factual data Mina included in her memoir. The fact that the *Ariosto* was built in 1890, the year Mina emigrated, also supports the hypothesis that *Romeo* is probably the correct ship. Ship passenger lists, vol. 216604, 1890, 42:171:5520, EI.

50. *LS*, 18.

51. *Historisk statistik för Sverige*, 128. These figures do not distinguish between single and married females.

52. Anna J. Olson, autobiography, Anna J. Olson Collection, NM; Nina Svärd, "My Memory of My Trip as an Emigrant to North America," Nina Svärd Collection, NM.

53. Nina Svärd, "My Memory of My Trip as an Emigrant to North America," Nina Svärd Collection, NM.

54. Hilma Svenson, "Daybook," EI.

55. Thea Persson, Nellie Baskette biography, 1897–1960, Thea Persson Collection, NM; see also Linnea Cederholm, "Utdrag ur dagbok från Amerikaresa 1916," Linnea Cederholm Collection, NM.

56. Nina Svärd, "My Memory of My Trip as an Emigrant to North America," Nina Svärd Collection, NM.

57. Deirdre M. Moloney, "Women, Sexual Morality, and Economic Dependency in Early U.S. Deportation Policy," *Journal of Women's History* 18, no. 2 (2006): 95–122; Amy L. Fairchild, *Science at the Borders: Immigrant Medical Inspection and the Shaping of the Modern Industrial Labor Force* (Baltimore: Johns Hopkins University Press, 2003).

58. Selma in Denver, CO, to her family, in *Emigration från Dalarna* (Falun, Sweden: Dalarnas Hembygdsbok, 1966), 34–35.

59. Albin Widén, Swedish-American Sociological Surveys.

60. Linnea Cederholm, "Utdrag ur dagbok från Amerikaresa 1916."

61. Elisabet Olson in LaCenter, WA, to her parents and siblings, July 20, 1912, Collection 22:13:2/3/4, EI.

62. Adina Ericksson, *Flicka med tur reste till U.S.A.* (Stockholm: Författares Bokmaskin, 1976), 6–15.

63. E. H. Mullan, "Mental Examination of Immigrants, Administration and Line Inspection at Ellis Island," *U.S. Public Health Reports* (May 18, 1917): 733–39.

64. Donna Gabaccia, *From the Other Side: Women, Gender, and Immigrant Life in the U.S., 1820–1990* (Bloomington: Indiana University Press, 1994), 40.

65. Gertrud Adelborg, "Kan något göras för att minska den kvinnliga emigrationen och dess faror?" *Dagny* 9 (1903): 220–21. The U.S. government was concerned enough about immigration and white slavery that it was included in the forty-one-volume study of immigration under the Dillingham Commission. See Senate Immigration Commission, *Importation and Harboring of Women for Immoral Purposes*, Reports of the Immigration Commission, vol. 37, 61st Cong., 3d sess., 1911.

66. Britta Ek, "Ett kvinnoöde i det nya landet," in *Emigranternas spar: Om utflyttningen från Dalarna till Amerika*, ed. Margaretha Hedblom and Gunnar Ternhag (Falun, Sweden: Dalarnas Museum, 1983), 7–10; Ellen Seagren, interview by author, December 1985, February 1986.

67. Mrs. A. Palmer, autobiography, Albin Widén Collection, February 1943, 15:7:12, EI.

68. Dag Blanck and Harald Runblom, eds., *Swedish Life in American Cities* (Uppsala, Sweden: Center for Multiethnic Research, 1991).

69. U.S. Bureau of the Census, *Thirteenth Census of the United States Taken in the Year 1910*, vol. 1, *Population: General Report and Analysis*, tables 30 and 41 (Washington, DC: GPO, 1913), 829, 871–73.

70. For males, 53,157; for females, 55,229. Niles Carpenter, *Immigrants and Their Children*, 1920 Census Monographs 7 (Washington, DC: GPO, 1927), 330–32.

71. Rural areas selected were Arizona, North Dakota, and Wisconsin outside of Milwaukee. For males, 20,178, versus 13,037 for females. Ibid., 334–36.

72. *LS*, 12–13.

Chapter 4 (pages 92–134)

1. When Minnie says "two girls" she means two servants in the household—the German American nursemaid and herself.

2. *LS*, 22–26. Segments of the memoir omitted here are two short paragraphs. In the first Minnie referred to her marriage and to sending a ticket for her sister to emigrate. The second described briefly what she was going to write about in the following paragraphs.

3. *Svensk Engelskt Lexikon* (Stockholm: Natur och Kultur, 1983), 137.

4. Albin Widén, Swedish-American Sociological Surveys. The total number of respondents in the survey was eighty-six. Although this is a small sample size, it is reflective of the qualitative evidence regarding immigrants' first years as revealed in Swedish immigrant letters and literature.

5. *LS*, 25.

6. Lina Eriksson in Moline, IL, to her family in Bräkne-Hoby, Blekinge, Sweden, December 5, 1883, Collection 10:3:19, EI. The material in this chapter draws heavily upon research included in the author's dissertation and in several published articles: Joy K. Lintelman, "'More Freedom, Better Pay': Single Swedish Immigrant Women in the United States, 1880–1920" (Ph.D. diss., University of Minnesota, 1991); Joy K. Lintelman, "'America Is the Woman's Promised Land': Swedish Immigrant Women and American Domestic Service," *Journal of American Ethnic History* 8, no. 2 (Spring 1989): 9–23; and Joy K. Lintelman, "'Our Serving Sisters': Swedish-American Domestic Servants and Their Ethnic Community," *Social Science History* 15, no. 3 (Fall 1991): 381–95.

7. Hilma Andreen in Chicago, IL, to her niece Hilma in Sweden, December 2, 1902, Collection 22:6:16:M, EI.

8. Maja Johansson, autobiographical essay, Maja Johansson Collection, NM.

9. Klara Jakobsson, biographical essay of Tilda Northen, NM.

10. Carl Erik Karlgren from Sioux City, IA, to mother and sisters, May 5, 1889, Adolph Larsson Collection, NM.

11. Anna J. Olson, autobiography, Anna J. Olson Collection, NM.

12. Swedish Home of Peace [Fridhem], Records, Swedish Congregational Church, Boston, microfilm SC-47, SSIRC. The home was active into the 1930s, by which time it had expanded its mission to accepting girls of all nationalities.

13. "Chicago Immanuel Woman's Home Forty-fifth Anniversary Booklet," Immanuel Woman's Home Association, Chicago, 1907–52, SSIRC; Swedish Home of Peace [Fridhem], Corporation Paper, Swedish Congregational Church, Boston, SA-

111:2, SSIRC; "Esther Scherling drager sig tillbaka som matrona vid Kvinnohemmet," *W.[?] Nyheter*, Denver, CO, July 1, 1937, LCC. A notice of Lutheran Homes for Women in New York, Chicago, and Vancouver was included in *Almanack för året*, 1941, ed. Birger Swenson (Rock Island, IL: Augustana Book Concern, 1941), 62.

14. According to the 1900 federal census, Hanna [Johanna] Stromquist lived at 617 Eighth Avenue South, Minneapolis, with the occupation of "employment agent." U.S. Census of Population, 1900, Manuscript Census, City of Minneapolis, Hennepin County, MN, available from Heritage Quest, http://www.heritagequestonline.com/ (accessed May 4, 2006). She emigrated from Sweden in 1864 and was fifty-eight years old when the 1900 census was taken. See also "A Cooperative Kitchen: And More Maids Coming," *MJ*, August 9, 1902, p. 7. On Myhrman, see "Mrs. Othelia Myhrman har gått ur tiden," *Skandia*, June 4, 1936, LCC; and E. W. Olson and M. J. Engberg, *History of the Swedes of Illinois*, part 2 (New York: Engberg-Holmberg Publishing Co., 1908). On Annie Anderson, see Thure Hanson, "Mrs. Annie C. Anderson," in *Swedish-American Souvenir* (Worcester, MA: n.p., 1910), 23.

15. Hilda Linder, handwritten autobiography, January 1971, 22:1:12:E, EI.

16. Alexandra Johnson, autobiography, Alexandra Johnson Collection, NM.

17. Elisabet Olson in Portland, OR, to her family in Sweden, August 17, 1915, Collection 22:13:2/3/4, EI.

18. Hilda Linder, handwritten autobiography, EI.

19. Hilda Hammar, "Till landet i väster," Hilda Hammar Collection, NM.

20. Carol Ann Bales, *Tales of the Elders: A Memory Book of Men and Women Who Came to America as Immigrants, 1900–1930* (Chicago: Follett, 1977), 122.

21. Quoted in Frithiof Bengtsson et al., eds., *Halländska emigrantöden 1860–1930* (Halmstad, Sweden: Spektra, 1976), 89.

22. The article was described in *Svenska Journalen Tribunen* (Omaha, NE), September 15, 1892, p. 1.

23. *First Biennial Report of the Bureau of Labor Statistics of the State of Minnesota for the Two Years Ending December 31, 1887–8* (St. Paul: Thos. A. Clark, 1888), 157, 154, 165, 160.

24. "A Cooperative Kitchen: And More Maids Coming," *MJ*, August 9, 1902, 7. Christiania is now the city of Oslo, Norway.

25. Hilda Christina Pärson in Woodhull, IL, to her brother in Sweden, November 14, 1879, Collection 22:1:14:A, EI.

26. *LS*, 25.

27. "A Cooperative Kitchen: And More Maids Coming," *MJ*, August 9, 1902.

28. Mrs. Ingeborg [Johansson] Carlson, interview by Carolyn Wilson and Betsy Doermann, July 19, 1984, p. 7, transcription, James H. Hill House, Minnesota Historical Society, St. Paul, MN. Johansson instead took a kitchen maid position in a household with an Irish cook.

29. Unknown in Minneapolis to sister, April 10, 1888, quoted in Eric H. Andersson, "Emigrationen från Pjätteryds socken," in *Hylten Cavallius-Föreningen* (1941 årsbok) (Växjö, Sweden: Nya Växjöbladets boktryckeri), 188.

30. Else Larsson, interview by author, December 8, 1987.

31. Olga Johnsson in River Du Loup, Canada, to her father, July 2, 1895, Collection 22:17:16:I, EI.

32. "A Swedish Scandal," *Brooklyn Daily Eagle*, August 1, 1880, 4, http://www.brooklynpubliclibrary.org/eagle (accessed June 6, 2008).

33. "A Swedish Girl Disappears," *Brooklyn Daily Eagle*, October 8, 1888, 1, http://www.brooklynpubliclibrary.org/eagle (accessed June 6, 2008).

34. Carl Grimsköld, *Svensk-amerikansk kokbok samt rådgifvare för svenskt tjenstefolk* [Swedish-American Book of Cookery and Adviser for Swedish Servants in America] (Stockholm: A. B. Norman, 1882); later editions were published in the United States by various publishers. For more discussion of cookbooks and what they can reveal about the experiences of Swedish American women, see chapter 12, "Vad kokböckerna berätta," in Ulf Beijbom, *Utvandrarkvinnor: Svenska kvinnöden i Amerika* (Stockholm: P. A. Norstedt, 2006), 278–87.

35. Charlotta Andersson in New Britain, CT, to her brother, October 1901, Collection 10:5:4:F, EI.

36. *LS*, 26.

37. Minnie Halgren survey, Albin Widén, Swedish-American Sociological Surveys.

38. Ellen Seagren, interview by author, December 1985, February 1986.

39. I. M. Rubinow, "The Problem of Domestic Service," *Journal of Political Economy* 14, no. 8 (October 1906): 508.

40. For a detailed discussion of differences between the experiences of immigrant versus nonimmigrant domestic servants, see Lintelman, "America Is the Woman's Promised Land." Inga Holmberg, in her study of Swedes in Jamestown, MA, has suggested that Swedish immigrant women's choice of domestic service was strongly influenced by the fact that they immigrated alone, and such employment met their immediate needs for food and shelter. See Inga Holmberg, "Taboos and Morals or Economy and Family Status? Occupational Choice among Immigrant Women in the United States," in *Swedish Life in American Cities*, ed. Dag Blanck and Harald Runblom (Uppsala, Sweden: Center for Multiethnic Research, 1991), 25–43.

41. Elisabet Olson in Portland, OR, to her family, September 13, 1912, Collection 22:13:2/3/4, EI. Work tasks and work schedules with only minor variations from Elisabet's were described by a number of other Swedish immigrant women as well: Hilda Christina Pärson, Woodhull, IL, to her family, Sweden, December 10, 1879; Josefina Larsson in Altoona, IA, to Augusta Nilsson, September 20, 1898, Collection 10:5:4:D, EI; and Olga Johnsson in Cambridgeport, MA, to her father, November 11, 1895, Collection 22:17:16:I, EI.

42. Thilda Janson in Red Wing, MN, to her mother in Sweden, July 7, 1882, Collection 22:16:5:E, EI.

43. Elisabet Olson in Portland, OR, to her family in Sweden, September 13, 1912, Collection 22:13:2/3/4, EI.

44. On accommodations for servants in Sweden, see chapter 2, as well as Hilda Linder, handwritten autobiography, EI.

45. Hilda Christina Pärson in Oneida, IL, to her brother in Sweden, August 30, 1882, Letters, Collection 22:1:14:A, EI.

46. Moli Nilsson in Omaha, NE, to Maria Nilsson in Sweden, March 18, 1890, Asta Fridstrom Collection, NM.

47. Anna Nygren in Flatbush, NY, to family, March 12, 1908, Collection 22:13, EI.

48. Carl in Sioux City, IA, to his sister Stina in Sweden, April 12, 1910, Svea Jönsson Collection, NM.

49. The figures for average servant wages are drawn from table 19, in Dorothy Swaine Thomas, *Social and Economic Aspects of Swedish Population Movements, 1750–1933* (New York: Macmillan, 1941), 97. The exchange rate figure of 3.73 kronor to one U.S. dollar is drawn from Douglas Fisher and Walter N. Thurman, "Sweden's Financial Sophistication in the Nineteenth Century: An Appraisal," *Journal of Economic History* 49, no. 3 (September 1989): 625–26.

50. Kristina Eriksson in Pennock, MN, to her family in Sweden, May 21, 1906, Kristina Eriksson Collection, NM.

51. Quoted in "Amerika, Möjligheternas Landet," *Svenska Journalen* (Omaha, NE), August 18, 1902. On gendered attitudes toward dairying, see Lena Sommestad, "Farm Daughters and Industrialization: A Comparative Analysis of Dairying in New York and Sweden, 1860–1920," *Journal of Women's History* 10, no. 2 (Summer 1998): 137–66.

52. Lars-Göran Tedebrand, "Remigration from America to Sweden," in *From Sweden to America*, ed. Harald Runblom and Hans Norman (Minneapolis: University of Minnesota Press, 1976), 201–27. For another example of a trip to Sweden changing a woman's desire to remigrate, see Inge Lund (Ingeborg Lundström), *En piga i USA* (Stockholm: Åhlen & Åkerlund, 1917), 203.

53. Hilma Andreen in Chicago, to Hilma Ohlson, December 13, 1904, Collection 22:6:16:M, EI. Swedish immigrant women generally had better marriage prospects in the United States than in Sweden.

54. "Many Went Abroad," *MJ*, August 6, 1900, 3.

55. While early 1890s city directories for Minneapolis and St. Paul listed a number of domestic servants named "Minnie Anderson," this Minnie most likely worked in St. Paul. Her future husband, Jacob, resided and worked at that time in St. Paul, and for the two young Swedish immigrants to meet and develop a relationship, they probably lived near each other. That Minnie and Jacob were eventually married and lived in St. Paul until their move to Mille Lacs County in 1894 also supports the idea that Minnie worked as a St. Paul domestic. *Dual City Blue Book, 1891–92* (St. Paul: R. Polk, 1892), 176.

56. A payment of $15.00 is listed for July 9, 1891; then, on July 13, 1891, a notation

listed "Minnie Anderson in full" with a payment of $4.20. Frank Wright Noyes Family Papers, AN954, vol. 7, MHS. Noyes was a bookkeeper for a St. Paul firm.

57. Albert L. Noyes, "Chronicles of the Noyes Family," Frank Wright Noyes Family Papers, AN954, MHS, 53.

58. "The Kitchen Queen," *MJ*, April 17, 1900, 6. Swedish immigrant women arriving in Duluth by 1869 were similarly met by potential employers seeking their services, as noted in Albin Widén, *Vår sista folkvandring* (Stockholm: Almqvist & Wiksell, 1962), 58.

59. Signe Nygren in Monclair, NY, to parents, ca. 1915, Collection 22:13, EI. Other examples of descriptions of changes in employment in immigrant letters and biographies include the following: "Viola got a place as a cook with a doctor for 20 dollars. But she had to move soon so that she could get better wages" (Kristina Vestberg, biography of her aunt, Kristina Vestberg Collection, 1960, NM); and "I have now quit as a waitress. I was not there more than three weeks. I now have another place and it is much better. I have very little to do here. I have nearly every afternoon free, and my employer is very nice and friendly toward me" (Charlotte Bergström, Rockford, IL, to her parents, 1890s, Elisabet Jönsson Collection, NM).

60. Thilda Janson, Des Moines, IA, to her friend Lina, Sweden, January 14, 1887, Collection 22:16:5:E, EI.

61. Elisabet Olson in Portland, OR, to family, February 4, 1918, Collection 22:13:2/3/4, EI.

62. *SAP*, January 3, 1900, 8.

63. On Swedish women's independence and their decisions to emigrate, see Kälvemark, "Utvandring och självständighet," 166. On immigrant letters as sources, see H. Arnold Barton, "As They Tell It Themselves: The Testimony of Immigrant Letters," in *The Future of Their Past*, ed. Odd S. Lovoll (Northfield, MN: Norwegian American Historical Association, 1993), 138–45.

64. *LS*, 26.

65. Elisabet Olson in Portland, OR, to family, May 3, 1916, Collection 22:13:2/3/4, EI.

66. Hilda Pärsson in Woodhull, IL, to family, December 6, 1880, Collection 22:1:14:A, EI.

67. Hilma Frideborg, unknown address, to mother, 1897, Collection 22:17:14:I, EI.

68. Hilda Linder, handwritten autobiography, EI.

69. "Servant Girls' Reasons," *MJ*, November 15, 1902, 6.

70. Anna Nilsson in Flatbush, NY, to her parents, November 12, 1908, Collection 22:13, EI.

71. Elisabet Olson in Portland, OR, to her family in Sweden, December 31, 1912, Collection 22:13:2/3/4, EI.

72. Elisabet Lindström in Arkville, NY, to her mother in Sweden, June 2, 1917, Collection 10:1:3:G, EI.

73. Charlotta Andersson in New Britain, CT, to her brother in Sweden, June 29, 1900, Collection 10:5:4:E, EI.

74. Olga Johnsson in Cambridgeport, MA, to her father, December 16, 1895, Collection 22:17:16:I, EI.

75. Olga Johnsson in Cambridgeport, MA, to her father in Sweden, May 17, 1896, Collection 22:17:16:I, EI.

76. Elisabet Olson in Portland, OR, to her family, September 27, 1913, Collection 22:13:2/3/4, EI.

77. Ibid., December 17, 1915.

78. Ellen Seagren, interviews by author, December 1985, February 1986.

79. E. H. Thörnberg, *Lefnadsstandard och sparkraft: Med särskild hänsyn till den svenska befolkningen i Chicago* (Stockholm: Hugo Geber Förlag, 1915), 37–38.

80. John Rice, "The Swedes," in *They Chose Minnesota: A Survey of the State's Ethnic Groups*, ed. June Drenning Holmquist (St. Paul: Minnesota Historical Society Press, 1981), 263; Anne Gillespie Lewis, *Swedes in Minnesota* (St. Paul: Minnesota Historical Society Press, 2004), 26–27.

81. Charles Larson, "Else's Story," typewritten biography distributed at Else [Olsson] Larson's funeral in February 2002, copy courtesy of David Sandgren, in author's possession. The schottische is a couple's dance that was popular in the late nineteenth and early twentieth centuries in Europe as well as the United States.

82. Stina Johansson in Portland, OR, to Per Erik Larsson, November 28, 1913, Per Erik Larsson in Noret Dala Järna Collection, EI. On recreational and social activities for young single women in the Twin Cities, see also Joan M. Jensen, "Out of Wisconsin: Country Daughters in the City, 1910–1925," *Minnesota History* 59, no. 2 (Summer 2004): 48–61.

83. Charlotta Andersson in Meriden, CT, to her brother Oskar, June 19, 1901, Collection 10:5:4:E, EI.

84. Irma Wibling, *Eva Wallström berätter—Minnen från ett långt liv* (Härnosänd, Sweden: Alex och Eva Wallströms Stiftelse för Vetenskaplig Forskning och Utbildning, 1982), 41.

85. Olga Johnsson in Cambridgeport, MA, to her father, November 11, 1895, Collection 22:17:16:I, EI.

86. Olga Johnsson in Cambridgeport, MA, to her father, October 7, 1895, Collection 22:17:16:I, EI.

87. Olga Johnsson in Brighton, MA, to her father, July 22, 1906, Collection 22:17:16:I, EI.

88. Selma Carlson in LaPorte, IN, to family, January 21, 1886, Collection 10:3:15:C, EI.

89. *LS*, 27.

90. Maja Johansson, autobiographical essay, Maja Johansson Collection, NM.

91. See the numerous letters by Lina Eriksson to her family during the period 1882

to 1890, Collection 10:3:19, EI; and the letters of Signe Nygren in New York, NY, to her family, EI.

92. Thörnberg, *Lefnadsstandard och sparkraft*, 82.

93. "Servant Girls' Reasons," *MJ*, November 15, 1902, 6.

94. Josefina Larsson in Altoona, IA, to Augusta Nilsson, December 4, 1898, Collection 10:5:4:D, EI.

95. *EU*, vol. 7, *Utvandrarnas egna uppgifter*, 256.

96. Margareta Matovic, "Migration, Family Formation, and Choice of Marriage Partners in Stockholm, 1860–1890," in *Urbanization in History*, ed. M. van der Woude et al. (Oxford: Clarendon Press, 1990), 229.

97. On the experiences of Swedish domestics working in upper-class households, see Margareta Matovic, "Embracing a Middle-Class Life: Swedish-American Women in Lake View," in *Peasant Maids—City Women: From the European Countryside to Urban America*, ed. Christiane Harzig (Ithaca, NY: Cornell University Press, 1997), 289–93; and Anne Gillespie Lewis, *So Far Away in the World* (Minneapolis: Nodin Press, 2002), 59–66.

98. Johan Person, *Svensk-amerikanska studier* (Rock Island, IL: Augustana Book Concern, 1912), 98, 106.

99. "Our Sisters Who Serve," *Svenska Nyheter*, March 21, 1905, in Chicago Foreign Language Press Survey (Chicago: Works Progress Administration, 1942). On the attitude of the Swedish ethnic community toward domestic service, see also Joy K. Lintelman, "'Our Serving Sisters': Swedish-American Domestic Servants and Their Ethnic Community," *Social Science History* 14, no. 5 (Fall 1991): 381–95.

100. Alma E. Swanson, interview by Terry Kirker, 1977, 58.

101. Isidor Kjellberg, *Amerika-bok* (Linköping, Sweden: Isidor Kjellbergs Boktryckeri, 1892), 36.

102. Matovic, "Embracing a Middle-Class Life," 280.

103. Nan Enstad, "Fashioning Political Identities: Cultural Studies and the Historical Construction of Political Subjects," *American Quarterly* 50, no. 4 (1998): 760–61.

104. "Amerika, Möjligheternas Landet," *Svenska Journalen* (Omaha, NE), August 18, 1902.

105. Lund, *En piga i USA*, 217.

106. Anna Pettersson, Chicago, to her mother, September 30, 1888, Collection 9:9:18:O, EI.

107. Matovic, "Embracing a Middle-Class Life," 297.

108. Angel Kwolek-Folland, "Cows in Their Yards: Women, the Economy, and Urban Space, 1870–1885," May 2001, 22, available at http://www.sscnet.uclaa.edu (accessed July 14, 2005).

109. Fannie Hurst, *Lummox* (New York: Harper, 1923).

110. Ellen Seagren, interview by author, December 1985, February 1986; Else Larsson, interview by author, December 8, 1987.

111. David Katzman, *Seven Days a Week: Women and Domestic Service in Industrializing America* (New York: Oxford University Press, 1978), 8–9, 268, 278–79.

112. "Thirty-one Years Service," *MJ*, September 8, 1902, 5.

113. Elisabet Olson in Portland, OR, to her family, May 27, 1920, Collection 22:13:2/3/4, EI. Recall that her wage in 1916 was approximately thirty-five dollars per month.

114. Wibling, *Eva Wallström berättar*, 26.

115. Thörnberg, *Lefnadsstandard och sparkraft*, 30.

116. Ida Rasmusson, Waltham, MA, to her mother and sister, August 17, 1902, November 17, 1902, March 19, 1903, May 21, 1903, February 17, 1907, December 6, 1907, Collection 10:15:6, EI. It is difficult to find detailed evidence, even in the qualitative sources. For example, with regard to letters, only an extended chronological run with relatively frequent correspondence can reveal frequent job changes.

117. Maria Elfström, Chicago, to her brother Theodor, January 1, 1895, Elsa Palm-Elfström Collection, NM.

118. Olga Johnsson, Cambridgeport, MA, to her father, Sweden, May 17, 1896, Collection 22:17:16:I, EI.

119. "Female Doctor in America," *Idun*, September 18, 1891, LCC. A Swedish barber-surgeon was trained not only to cut hair but also to perform some medical procedures such as bloodletting, pulling teeth, and some types of surgery.

120. [Advertisement], *Medborgaren* (Chisago County, MN), March 16, 1905; similar advertisement in *Chisago County Press*, November 21, 1907, LCC.

121. See advertisements in *Vestkusten*, January 9, 1896, November 8, 1906, and July 21, 1910, LCC. The collection also includes clippings about a Swedish sculptress, a masseuse, a handicraft teacher, and an industrial inspector.

122. This information was obtained from a clipping taped into the front cover of Evelina Månsson, *Amerika-Minnen: Upplevelser och iaktagelser från en 6-årig vistelse I U.S.A.* (Hvetlanda, Sweden: Svenska Allmogeförlaget, 1930), EI.

123. For other analyses of this book, see Byron Nordstrom, "Evelina Månsson and the Memoir of an Urban Labor Migrant," *Swedish Pioneer Historical Quarterly* 31 (July 1980): 182–89; Lars Olsson, "Evelina Johansdotter, Textile Workers, and the Munsingwear Family: Class, Gender, and Ethnicity in the Political Economy of Minnesota at the End of World War I," in *Swedes in the Twin Cities,* ed. Philip J. Anderson and Dag Blanck (St. Paul: Minnesota Historical Society Press, 2001), 77–90. A translated excerpt of the book is included in Anne Gillespie Lewis, *Swedes in Minnesota* (St. Paul: Minnesota Historical Society Press, 2004), 73–77.

124. Here and five paragraphs below, Månsson, *Amerika-minnen,* 16–21, 27, 30, 33, 34, 35, 49.

125. Here and three paragraphs below, Månsson, *Amerika-minnen,* 36, 37, 39, 32, 48, 51.

126. Månsson, *Amerika-minnen,* 54.

127. Nordstrom, "Evelina," 195n15.

128. Here and below, Månsson, *Amerika-minnen,* 88, 89, 90, 94–95.

129. Here and below, Månsson, *Amerika-minnen,* 83–84, 102–9. Månsson does not explain why she and her husband decided to move back to Sweden at that particular time. Perhaps with their combined savings they had enough capital to start their business venture in Sweden. On the one hand, her remigration is not surprising—she originally planned to settle permanently in Sweden. On the other hand, many Swedish immigrant women came to America with a similar goal that, for a variety of reasons—marriage to a non-Swede, hopes for a better future for one's children, difficult economic circumstances—they were never able to fulfill. That Månsson eventually fulfilled her goal is a testament both to her abilities and to her determination.

130. Here and below, Maria Elfström in Chicago to her brother, January 1, 1895, Elsa Palm-Elfström Collection, NM.

131. Olga Johnsson in Brighton, MA, to her father, September 18, 1896, Collection 22:17:16:I, EI.

132. Månsson, *Amerika-minnen,* 104.

133. Here and below, Adina Eriksson, *Flicka med tur reste till U.S.A.* (Stockholm: Författares Bokmaskin, 1976), 41, 42; U.S. Bureau of Labor, *Report on Conditions of Women and Child Wage-Earners in the United States,* vol. 5, *Wage-Earning Women in Stores and Factories* (Washington, DC, 1910), 42, 44, 57–60.

134. For a brief overview of Irish immigrant women in the U.S. labor movement, see Hasia R. Diner, *Erin's Daughters in America: Irish Immigrant Women in the Nineteenth Century* (Baltimore: Johns Hopkins University Press, 1985), 100–102.

135. *SAP,* May 8, 1900, 12.

136. Katzman, *Seven Days a Week,* 234–35.

137. Hilda Linder in Sacramento, CA, to author, May 21, 1988, in author's possession.

138. Domestic Workers Union No. 15836, Central Labor Council, King County, Box 19, University of Washington Libraries, Seattle.

139. Mary Anderson, *Woman at Work: The Autobiography of Mary Anderson as Told to Mary N. Winslow* (Minneapolis: University of Minnesota Press, 1951), 3–31; Mary V. Robinson, "Mary Anderson," *American Swedish Monthly* (August 1935): 9.

140. Anderson, *Woman at Work,* 3–31; Robinson, "Mary Anderson," 9.

141. Inez Stridh, biography of Emma Persson, NM.

142. "Amerikaarv i rätta händer," *Svenska Amerikanaren Tribunen,* January 24, 1952, LCC.

143. "Swedish Nurses Graduate," May 25, 1909; "Nurses Graduate," June 22, 1909, *Svenska Tribunen Nyheter,* Chicago Foreign Language Press Survey, Immigration History Research Center, Minneapolis.

144. Alfred E. Strand, *A History of the Swedish-Americans of Minnesota,* vol. 1 (Chicago: Lewish Publishing Co., 1910), 194–95; Pat Gaarder and Tracey Baker, *From*

Stripes to Whites: A History of the Swedish Hospital School of Nursing, 1899–1973 (Minneapolis: Swedish Hospital Alumnae Association, 1980), 65.

145. Swedish American women made significant contributions to churches and other religious associations, especially with regard to financial contributions, leadership, and time. Because much of the activity was voluntary, it is not addressed in this chapter on occupational experiences. Although single Swedish American women's participation in religious activities is touched upon briefly elsewhere in this book, the topic clearly needs further study.

146. "Mrs. Sigrid Hansen går till vila," *Vestkusten,* April 1, 1954, LCC.

147. "Esther Scherling drager sig tillbaka som matrona vid Kvinnohemmet," *W.[?] Nyheter* (Denver, CO), July 1, 1937, LCC.

148. Obituary notice for Maria Rabenius, *Svenska Dagbladet,* July 25, 1953, LCC.

Chapter 5 (pages 135–76)

1. "Onkel Ola" was the pseudonym for Swedish American F. A. Lindstrand. He wrote weekly letters in the Chicago newspaper *Svenska Amerikanaren* from 1889 through 1908. Emory Lindquist, "'Onkel Ola' and His Letters in 'Svenska Amerikanaren': One Aspect of the Career of Frank Albin Lindstrand," *Swedish Pioneer Historical Quarterly* 19, no. 4 (1968): 245–55.

2. Theodore Halgren was born on November 5, 1896.

3. *LS,* 26–70. About one-third of the way through her memoir, Minnie's writing shifts away from a straightforward chronological narrative to one that is more random. She writes almost as if she is speaking and periodically includes comments about the younger generation or about society. Because of the shift in her writing, in order to maintain the sense of her experience over time, I have excerpted materials from throughout the remainder of the memoir. To indicate what topics were addressed between the excerpted selections, as I have done in the previous chapters, would prove too cumbersome.

4. On Swedish expectations about marrying, see Robert Ostergren, *A Community Transplanted: The Trans-Atlantic Experience of a Swedish Immigrant Settlement in the Upper Middle West, 1835–1915* (Madison: University of Wisconsin Press, 1988), 63; and Margareta Matovic, "Maids in Motion: Swedish Women in Dalsland," in *Peasant Maids— City Women: From the European Countryside to Urban America,* ed. Christiane Harzig (Ithaca, NY: Cornell University Press, 1997), 105–7, 117–20. For a discussion of attitudes of Swedish immigrant women in Chicago toward marriage, see Margareta Matovic, "Embracing a Middle-Class Life: Swedish-American Women in Lake View," in *Peasant Maids— City Women: From the European Countryside to Urban America,* ed. Christiane Harzig (Ithaca, NY: Cornell University Press, 1997), 270–72.

5. "Social reproduction" is a term that developed within the field of sociology but which has also been used in social history and in the study of immigration. See

Barbara Laslett and Johanna Brenner, "Gender and Social Reproduction: Historical Perspectives," *Annual Reviews in Sociology* 15 (1989): 381–404; and Suzanne M. Sinke, *Dutch Immigrant Women in the United States, 1880–1920* (Urbana: University of Illinois Press, 2002).

6. *Historisk statistik för Sverige, 1720–1967*, 2d ed. (Stockholm: Statistiska Centralbyrån, 1969), 103.

7. Matovic, "Maids in Motion," 106.

8. Hilda Linder, handwritten autobiography (January 1971), 22:1:12:E, EI.

9. E. H. Thörnberg, *Lefnadsstandard och sparkraft: Med särskild hänsyn till den svenska befolkningen i Chicago* (Stockholm: Hugo Geber Förlag, 1915), 40.

10. Hädda Carlson in Bradford, PA, to her brother[?], September 10, 1883, Hulda Maria Hellberg Collection, NM.

11. Margareta R. Matovic, *Stockholmsäktenskap: Familjebildning och partnerval i Stockholm, 1850–1890* (Stockholm: Margareta Matovic and Committee for Stockholm Research, 1984), 371–76.

12. Olga Johnsson in Brighton, MA, to her father, September 18, 1896, Collection 22:17:16:I, EI.

13. Anna Israelsdotter in Lundby, MN, to her sister Hilda, August 2, 1892, Collection 10:3:8:G, EI.

14. Hamp Smith, MHS, email message to author, June 9, 2006. About 20 percent of Swedes age fifteen and over immigrating from 1891 through 1900 were married (*Historisk statistik för Sverige*, 129).

15. *EU*, vol. 4, *Utvandringsstatistik* (1908), 50, 166.

16. *Historisk statistik för Sverige*, 129–30. Margareta Matovic found, however, that some Swedish immigrant men in Chicago were not eager to marry, primarily because they wanted to begin marriage having achieved a sense of economic stability, a goal not always easy to achieve for an immigrant laborer. Matovic, "Embracing a Middle-Class Life," 272.

17. "Är de damer!" *Qvinnan och Hemmet* 13, no. 11 (November 1900): 353.

18. Johan Person, *Svensk-amerikanska studier* (Rock Island, IL: Augustana Book Concern, 1912), 102.

19. See, for example, Matovic, "Embracing a Middle-Class Life," 271; Gunnar Thorvaldsen, "Marriage and Names among Immigrants to Minnesota," *Journal of the Association for History and Computing* 1, no. 2 (1998), http://mcel.pacificu.edu (accessed July 20, 2006); Dag Blanck, "Intermarriage and the Melting Pot in Moline, 1910," in *Swedes in America: Intercultural and Interethnic Perspectives on Contemporary Research: A Report of the Symposium Swedes in America: New Perspectives*, ed. Ulf Beijbom (Växjö, Sweden: Swedish Emigrant Institute, 1993), 59–66; Ulf Beijbom, *Utvandrarkvinnor: Svenska kvinnöden i Amerika* (Stockholm: P. A. Norstedt, 2006), 162–63.

20. Minnie Halgren survey, Albin Widén, Swedish-American Sociological Surveys; *St. Paul City Directory* (St. Paul: R. L. Polk & Co., 1890).

21. On Twin Cities Swedish immigrants and dancing, see David Markle, "Dania Hall: At the Center of a Scandinavian American Community," in *Swedes in the Twin Cities*, ed. Philip J. Anderson and Dag Blanck (St. Paul: Minnesota Historical Society Press, 2002), 173–97.

22. Emil Lund, *Minnesota-Konferensens av Augustana-Synoden och dess församlingars historia* (Rock Island, IL: Augustana Book Concern, 1926), 444–45. Swärd served as pastor from 1886 through the spring of 1894. In 2005 I viewed a copy of Minnie and Jacob's marriage certificate at the Ramsey County Department of Public Health in St. Paul.

23. See David A. Lanegran, "Swedish Neighborhoods of the Twin Cities: From Swede Hollow to Arlington Hills, From Snoose Boulevard to Minnehaha Parkway," in Anderson and Blanck, *Swedes in the Twin Cities*, 39–56; and Mollie Price, "Swede Hollow: Sheltered Society for Immigrants to St. Paul," *Ramsey County History* 17, no. 2 (1981): 12–22.

24. Jennie Halgren Lonsdale, telephone conversation with author.

25. Bernard Pearson, *Einar and Lina* (Foreston, MN: B. Pearson, 1980), 54.

26. Case 4372 on reel 131 of Associated Charities/Family Welfare Association Case Records, Social Welfare History Archives, Minneapolis. See also Joy K. Lintelman, "'She Did Not Whimper or Complain': Swedish-American Female Charity Cases in Minneapolis, 1910–1930," *SAHQ* 45, no. 1 (January 1994): 5–23.

27. Joy K. Lintelman, "'Unfortunates' and 'City Guests': Swedish American Inmates and the Minneapolis City Workhouse, 1907," in Anderson and Blanck, *Swedes in the Twin Cities*, 57–76.

28. Thörnberg, *Lefnadsstandard och sparkraft*, 43–44.

29. Hilda Linder in Sacramento, CA, to author, February 18, 1989. While five dollars a day may seem like a good wage for this time, 1919 was an inflationary year. In Chicago, the prices of basic foodstuffs such as milk, butter, cheese, bread, rice, potatoes, and most meats had more than doubled between 1913 and 1919. "Cause of High Prices," *Chicago Daily News Almanac and Yearbook for 1920* (Chicago: Chicago Daily News, 1920), 148–49.

30. Anita Nyberg, "The Social Construction of Married Women's Labour-Force Participation: The Case of Sweden in the Twentieth Century," *Continuity and Change* 9, no. 1 (1994): 146; Anita Nyberg, "From Foster Mothers to Child Care Centers: A History of Working Mothers and Child Care in Sweden," *Feminist Economics* 6, no. 1 (2000): 7. See also Murray Gendell, *Swedish Working Wives* (Totowa, NJ: Bedminster Press, 1963), 45–60. On Swedish women in the late nineteenth and early twentieth centuries, see Gunnar Qvist, "Policy towards Women and the Women's Struggle in Sweden," *Scandinavian Journal of History* 5 (1980): 51–74; Gunnar Qvist, *Konsten att blifva en god flicka: Kvinnohistoriska uppsatser* (Stockholm: Liber, 1978); and Kerstin Moberg, *Från tjänstehjon till hembiträde* (Uppsala, 1978).

31. Orvar Löfgren, "Family and Household among Scandinavian Peasants: An Exploratory Essay," *Ethnologica Scandinavica* (1974): 28–30.

32. U.S. Senate, Immigration Commission, *Occupations of the First and Second Generations of Immigrants in the United States: Fecundity of Immigrant Women*, Reports of the Immigration Commission, vol. 28, 61st Cong., 2d sess. (1909, 1910), 795, 799–800. The study also showed higher childbearing rates for both immigrant and native-born women in rural versus urban populations.

33. Michael M. Davis Jr., *Immigrant Health and the Community* (New York: Harper, 1921), 196–201. See, for example, the records of one St. Paul midwife, although she did not attend Minnie: "Ramsey County Births: A Midwife's Record Book, 1891–1906," *Minnesota Genealogical Journal* 25 (March 2001): 2489–94.

34. Ada Andersson, Chicago, to her sister, April 1, 1895, Collection 10:8:5:H, EI.

35. On locations of birth, see Signild Vallgårda, "Hospitalization of Deliveries: The Change of Place of Birth in Denmark and Sweden from the Late Nineteenth Century to 1970," *Medical History* 40 (1996): 173–96. On midwifery in Sweden, see Pia Höjeberg, *Jordemor: Barnmorskor och barnföderskor i Sverige* (Stockholm: Carlssons, 1991), 166; and Stephan Curtis, "Midwives and Their Role in the Reduction of Direct Obstetric Deaths during the Late Nineteenth Century: The Sundsvall Region of Sweden (1869–1890)," *Medical History* 49 (2005): 321–50.

36. Matovic, "Maids in Motion," 110–11.

37. Matovic, "Embracing a Middle-Class Life," 277.

38. For descriptions of Swedish American households with boarders, see ibid., 279.

39. Erika Nyqvist, Brainerd, MN, to friends, December 28, 1891, Collection 9:8:8:B, EI.

40. Elisabet [Lindström] Franker in Allenhurst, NJ, to her mother, February 7, 1922 (emphasis in original), EI.

41. Lanegran, "Swedish Neighborhoods of the Twin Cities: From Swede Hollow to Arlington Hills, From Snoose Boulevard to Minnehaha Parkway," in Anderson and Blanck, *Swedes in the Twin Cities*, 39–56.

42. Elisabet Lindström Franker in Allenhurst, NJ, to her mother, February 7, 1922, EI.

43. Janice Reiff Webster, "Domestication and Americanization: Scandinavian Women in Seattle, 1888–1900," *Journal of Urban History* 4, no. 3 (May 1978): 287.

44. See Samuel H. Preston and Michael R. Haines, *Fatal Years: Child Mortality in Late Nineteenth-Century America* (Princeton, NJ: Princeton University Press, 1991), especially chapter 3.

45. *LS*, 56.

46. Hilda Linder, handwritten autobiography, EI.

47. *LS*, 28.

48. According to records in the Mille Lacs County Recorder's Office, the land, the NE ¼ of NW ¼ of Section 9, Township 37, Range 26W, 4th Meridian, was purchased on January 17, 1894, for $240. In 1900, Jacob obtained an additional 39 acres under the

Homestead Act. By 1909, Jacob had also purchased the W ½ of the NE ¼ of Section 9, minus 1 acre for school land. The land and home were mortgaged on May 7, 1909, and paid off in 1914. Additional money was borrowed on the land but was paid off in 1919. In 1897 Jacob deeded 20 rods N of SW corner of NW ¼ of NE ¼ of Section 9 for school purposes (1 acre).

49. U.S. Surveyor General Field Notes, 4th Meridian, T37N, R26W, 111.E.6.2(F), MHS.

50. *LS*, 30–31.

51. Many Swedes had already begun settling in neighboring Isanti County in the 1860s. See Ostergren, *A Community Transplanted*, 161–76.

52. Swedes numbered 42 in a total population of 1,897 in 1885, and 1,286 in a total population of 8,066 in 1900. "1885 Minnesota Census Birthplaces Mille Lacs County," KinSource, http://www.kinsource.com/MinnesotaCensus/Census1885/Birthplaces/Birth1885MilleLacs.htm (accessed December 6, 2004). "Population of Counties by Decennial Census: 1900 to 1990," compiled and edited by Richard L. Forstall, http://www.census.gov/population/cencounts/mn190090.txt.

53. *Inventory of the County Archives of Minnesota, Mille Lacs County*, Minnesota Historical Records Survey Project, Division of Community Service Program, WPA, No. 48, Mille Lacs County (St. Paul: MHS, 1940), 23.

54. From Church Register and Record of Ministerial Acts, Zion Evangelical Lutheran Church, Milaca, MN.

55. "Local News," *MCT*, June 7, 1894, 1.

56. Norma Hervey, "A Company Town Becomes a Community: Milaca, Minnesota, 1880–1915" (Ph.D. diss., University of Minnesota, 1991).

57. Mary Olson Norlander, typescript autobiography, 1969, Materials Relating to Swedish American History, ca. 1854/1950, microfilm collection, MHS.

58. Pearson, *Einar and Lina*, 16, 24, 40.

59. Helge Nelson, *The Swedes and the Swedish Settlements in North America* (New York: Arno Press, 1979; Lund, Sweden: Royal Society of Letters, 1943), 201–2.

60. "Mill Ceases Forever," MCT, June 28, 1906, 5; Karen Schlenker, "Creamery Cooperative Established 100 Years Ago," *Mille Lacs County Times,* accessed July 27, 2011, http://millelacscountytimes.com/2007/may/30creamery.html.

61. *Mille Lacs County Minnesota: A Land of Success, Happiness, Contentment* (Princeton, MN: Princeton Commercial Club, 1909), title page.

62. Ibid., 41–42.

63. Ibid., 40; Daniel James Brown, *Under a Flaming Sky* (Guilford, CT: Lyons Press, 2006), 193–95; and Grace Stageberg Swenson, *From the Ashes* (Stillwater, MN: Croixside Press, 1979), 20.

64. On firestorms, see Brown, *Under a Flaming Sky,* 64.65. *LS*, 34.

66. *Report of the Minnesota State Commission for the Relief of Fire Sufferers to the Governor* (St. Paul: Pioneer Press Co., State Printers, 1895), 14.

67. The cabin's dimensions are included in a letter from Minnie Halgren to Albin Widén, February 2, 1947, Collection 15:7:12, EI.

68. Mrs. Clara Nelson, February 28, 1949, Folder N, Farmer Collection of Reminiscences, P2081, MHS.

69. Merrill Halgren (grandson of Minnie), telephone conversation with author, June 1995. In Minnesota State Population Census Schedules, 1895, MHS, Jacob is listed as working in St. Paul as a tailor, living at 272 E. 7th Street. Jacob is listed in the *St. Cloud City Directory, 1898–99*, as a tailor in the employ of Walter S. Elliot and boarding at Grant Union Hotel, and in *Davison's Minneapolis City Directory* for 1900 and 1905–6 as working for Iver Peterson, tailor.

70. Jennie Halgren Lonsdale, telephone conversation with author; periodic conversations with Beverly Halgren Siedow and Merrill Halgren in the late 1990s and early 2000s.

71. *MCT*, February 25, 1897, 1; *MCT*, March 4, 1897, 1.

72. Jane Telleen, "'Yours in the Master's Service': Emmy Evald and the Woman's Missionary Society of the Augustana Lutheran Church, 1892–1942," *Swedish Pioneer Historical Quarterly* 30, no. 3 (July 1979): 187.

73. H. Arnold Barton, "Scandinavian Women's Encounter with America," *Swedish Pioneer Historical Quarterly* 25 (January 1974): 37–42.

74. Dorothy Burton Skårdal, *The Divided Heart: Scandinavian Immigrant Experience through Literary Sources* (Oslo: Universitetsförlaget, 1974), 187, 236–38.

75. Cynthia Nelson Meyer, "Creating a Swedish-American Woman: The Views of Women in the Swedish Evangelical Mission Covenant Church, 1915–1920" (Ph.D. diss., Indiana University, 1998), 132–34, 177–94.

76. This is also in keeping with the views held by the Swedish peasant classes of marriage as primarily a productive and reproductive unit. See Jonas Frykman and Orvar Löfgren, *Culture Builders: A Historical Anthropology of Middle-Class Life*, trans. Alan Crozier (New Brunswick, NJ: Rutgers University Press, 1987), 91–93.

77. She is listed as Minnie Hengren on this census. Minnie and Jacob's surname, Halgren, was spelled in a variety of ways on official documents relating to the family: Halgren, Hallgren, Hellgren, Helgren, Helgerson, and Hengren are among the variations I have encountered.

78. U.S. Census of Population, 1900, *Twelfth Census of the United States*, Manuscript Census, Bogus Brook Township, Mille Lacs County, available from Heritage Quest, http://www.heritagequestonline.com/.

79. The 1910 census was taken in April, listing Jacob as a farmer and Minnie as having no occupation. Ibid.

80. Beata Losman, "Kvinnoliv på landet," in *Handbok i svensk kvinnohistoria*, ed. Gunhild Kyle (Stockholm: Carlsson Bokförlag, 1987), 64–65.

81. For an example of these patterns in another region in Minnesota, see Harold H.

Johnson, *The Swedes at West Rock* (New Hope, MN: Review Corporation, 1989), 14–15, 49–56.

82. Jennie Halgren Lonsdale, telephone conversation with author.

83. *LS*, 38.

84. Barbara Handy-Marchello found that North Dakota farm women often assisted with field work in the early years of settlement. Barbara Handy-Marchello, *Women of the Northern Plains* (St. Paul: Minnesota Historical Society Press, 2005), 55–58.

85. *LS*, 50.

86. *LS*, 49.

87. *MCT*, October 21, 1897, 1.

88. Handy-Marchello, *Women of the Northern Plains*, 116.

89. Chickens and horses are mentioned in the memoir. Minnie's youngest daughter, Jennie, recalled the yearly butchering of a steer and a pig. Jennie Halgren Lonsdale, telephone conversation with author.

90. *LS*, 39.

91. Tom Dell, "Jobs Were Limited," *MCT—Milaca Centennial Edition*, July 2, 1986, 5.

92. Such was the case for the Norlander family. See Wallace C. Norlander, "Mary Olson Norlander's Father Found Work at Sawmill," *MCT—Milaca Centennial Edition*, July 2, 1986, 6.

93. Merrill Halgren, interview by author, November 12, 1993.

94. Urban Swedes were more likely to limit family size. See Matovic, "Embracing a Middle-Class Life," 274.

95. Doris Svensson, "Anna Israelsdotters gripande levnadssaga [biography and letters]," March 1966, Collection 10:3:8:G, EI, 17. Annie was pregnant at the time she wrote this letter, and she died during childbirth. Her husband placed the child in a neighbor's care.

96. Port Arthur, "'Giants in the Earth' . . . : A Mother's Mission," *Lutheran Companion* (October 8, 1947): 13.

97. *LS*, 42.

98. Matovic, "Maids in Motion," 111.

99. *LS*, 50. Kathleen Stokker writes about similar health manuals among Norwegian immigrants ("doctor books") in *Remedies and Rituals: Folk Medicine in Norway and the New Land* (St. Paul: Minnesota Historical Society Press, 2007), 105–22.

100. See, for example, Mrs. A. L. Enger Reminiscence, Box 1, Letter E, Farmer Collection of Reminiscences, P2081, MHS; and Shirley Anderson Heath, "From Skåne to Kansas," in *Stories of Swedish Pioneers in North America*, vol. 2 (N.p.: n. p., 1948).

101. Annie in Genoa, NE, to her family, March 15, 1926, Collection 10:2:15:C, EI.

102. Mrs. Clara Nelson, February 28, 1949, Folder N, Farmer Collection of Reminiscences, P2081, MHS.

103. Nancy Holt, "The Promised Land," in *Stories of Swedish Pioneers in North America*, vol. 3 (1948).

104. Minnie's daughter also recalled her butchering and canning beef and pork each fall. Jennie Halgren Lonsdale, telephone conversation with author.

105. *LS*, 52.

106. *Report of the Minnesota State Commission for the Relief of Fire Sufferers to the Governor*, 14.

107. *LS*, 52.

108. It is likely that the episode in Moberg's novel *Unto a Good Land* (chapter 23) in which Karl Oskar was unable to obtain a long-awaited letter because he lacked cash was inspired by Minnie's experience.

109. Pearson, *Einar and Lina*, 120–21, 129–30, 166–67.

110. Heath, "From Skåne to Kansas."

Chapter 6 (pages 177–217)

1. *LS*, 32–61 (selected passages).

2. I use "community" in the same sense as historian Thomas Bender, who defined it as "a network of social relations marked by mutuality and emotional bonds." Thomas Bender, *Community and Social Change in America* (New Brunswick, NJ: Rutgers University Press, 1978), 7.

3. Minnesota State Population Census Schedules, 1895, MHS.

4. In the county as a whole there were only 254 Swedish-born residents in 1889. It was in the decade of the 1890s that the Swedes became a dominant ethnic group. By 1900 there were 1,286 Swedish-born residents, increasing to 1,517 in 1920. *Inventory of the County Archives of Minnesota, Mille Lacs County*, Minnesota Historical Records Survey Project, Division of Community Service Programs, WPA, No. 48, Mille Lacs County (February 1942), 23.

5. Robert Ostergren, *A Community Transplanted: The Trans-Atlantic Experience of a Swedish Immigrant Settlement in the Upper Middle West, 1835–1915* (Madison: University of Wisconsin Press, 1988), 196.

6. Ibid., 155–89.

7. Beverly Siedow and Alice Tobler, interview by author.

8. Richard M. Chisholm, with transcriptions of interviews with Ruth Dahl Chisholm, "Vignettes of a Prairie Childhood: Anecdotes of Swedish-American Immigrant Life in North Dakota," *SAHQ* 55, no. 2 (April 2004): 97–98.

9. *LS*, 33.

10. In an examination of Swedish and Norwegian immigrant newspapers from around the time of dissolution, Norwegian historian Olav Tysdal found strong feelings of enmity between immigrants from the two groups, expressed in newspaper reporting as well as in letters to the editor. See Olav Tysdal, "The Dissolution of the Union

between Norway and Sweden and the Scandinavian Americans," *Scandinavian Studies* 79, no. 2 (Summer 2007): 167–96.

11. *LS*, 33.

12. *MCT*, April 21, 1909, 8.

13. Mrs. Helen Bengtson, 1949, Box 1, Folder B, Farmer Collection of Reminiscences, P208, MHS.

14. Merrill Halgren, interview by author, June 1995.

15. Birth Records for Bogus Brook Township, 1908–14, MHS. On April 15, 1912, Minnie served as midwife for Milfred (Gurine) Ranem, wife of Oliver Ranem. The Ranem family had moved to Bogus Brook Township in 1910.

16. Merrill Halgren, interview by author, June 1995.

17. Mary Norlander, typewritten autobiography, MHS.

18. *MCT*, July 2, 1914, 8.

19. Jennie Halgren Lonsdale, telephone conversation with author.

20. Mrs. Helen Bengtson, Farmer Collection of Reminiscences, MHS.

21. On coffee drinking among Swedish Americans, see Albin Widén, *Vår sista folkvandring* (Stockholm: Almqvist & Wiksell, 1962), 114; on coffee-drinking traditions in Minnie's native Dalsland, see Margareta Matovic, "Maids in Motion: Swedish Women in Dalsland," in *Peasant Maids—City Women: From the European Countryside to Urban America*, ed. Christiane Harzig (Ithaca, NY: Cornell University Press, 1997), 131.

22. Jennie Halgren Lonsdale, telephone conversation with author.

23. Red pudding is made with berries, traditionally with lingonberries, but immigrants also used currants or blackberries.

24. These descriptions of the meal are quoted from a handwritten draft version of Minnie's memoir, in author's possession.

25. Mrs. Dick Rye, February 8, 1949, Box 3, Folder R, Farmer Collection of Reminiscences, P2081, MHS.

26. *LS*, 45. Minnie's descendants recall that she was over eighty years old when she taught one of her granddaughters to dance. Beverly Siedow and Alice Tobler, interview by author.

27. Jennie Halgren Lonsdale, telephone conversation with author.

28. "Local News: The arrival of a baby boy on January 29th at the home of Mr. and Mrs. Jacob Helgren [*sic*], Soule's Siding, was reported this week." Soule's Siding was an early name for the small community of Pease, about three miles from the Halgren farm. *MCT*, February 7, 1895, 1.

29. Minnie Halgren survey, Albin Widén, Swedish-American Sociological Surveys, EI.

30. *LS*, 67.

31. Merrill Halgren, interview by author, November 12, 1993.

32. Mille Lacs County, Mille Lacs County Assessment Rolls, MHS.

33. "Wondell Brook" [news], *MCT*, January 16, 1913, 8. It is unclear why Jacob left for his tailoring work in January rather than in March of this year.

34. Minnesota Common School District No. 1153 (Bogus Brook Township), School records, Mille Lacs County, School District #21, MHS.

35. *LS*, 67.

36. *LS*, 58.

37. *LS*, 56.

38. Jennie Halgren Lonsdale, interview by author.

39. *Zion Lutheran Church: Its History, 1893–1993* (Milaca, MN: Zion Evangelical Lutheran Church, 1992), 20; Jennie Halgren Lonsdale, telephone conversation with author.

40. Minnie Halgren survey, Albin Widén, Swedish-American Sociological Surveys, EI.

41. "Wondell Brook," *MCT*, August 21, 1913, 8.

42. For an example of a regularly offered Swedish school, see Ostergren, *A Community Transplanted*, 229.

43. *LS*, 66.

44. Jennie Halgren Lonsdale, telephone conversation with author.

45. *MCT*, February 6, 1913, 8; *MCT*, February 20, 1913, 8.

46. *LS*, 8, 13, 44, 58, 69. On churches and immigrant history, Minnie wrote: "Churches and associations have written about their activities and they have done much to hold Scandinavians, like other nations, together. But few of them have sampled what it is to clear a home in the wilderness or live in a dugout on the great prairies."

47. *Zion Lutheran Church: Its History, 1893–1993*, 19.

48. For example, the "Bogus Brook" local news section for June 12, 1907, includes: "S. C. Moline and daughter, Ester, drove to Milaca Saturday" and "Andrew Anderson drove to Milaca Tuesday."

49. *Zion Lutheran Church: Its History, 1893–1993*, 38.

50. *MCT*, September 16, 1908, 8.

51. Beverly Siedow and Alice Tobler, interview by author.

52. Minnie was finally able to enjoy some modern household conveniences in the last decade of her life. After World War II, the Halgren home was outfitted with electricity and indoor plumbing.

53. Jennie Halgren Lonsdale, telephone conversation with author.

54. *MCT*, October 5, 1910, 5.

55. *MCT*, May 1, 1913, 8; *MCT*, August 7, 1913, 8; *MCT*, November 13, 1913, 8.

56. *MCT*, December 21, 1916, 1.

57. *LS*, 67.

58. *LS*, 46.

59. Port Arthur, "'Giants in the Earth' . . . : A Mother's Mission," *Lutheran Companion* (October 8, 1947): 14.

60. *LS*, 46.

61. "Drafted Men Will Leave for Training Camps on Monday February 25th," *MCT*, February 21, 1918, 1; "A Milaca Soldier Boy Meets Tragic Death," *MCT*, July 10, 1919, 1.

62. Minute book of the Swedish Evangelical Lutheran Church, Mission Society at Wondell Brook, Zion Lutheran Church, Milaca, MN, name list and minutes for August 10, 1921.

63. Erik Luther Williamson, "'Doing What Had to Be Done': Norwegian Lutheran Ladies Aid Societies of North Dakota," *North Dakota History* 27, no. 2 (1990): 2–13; Handy-Marchello, *Women of the Northern Plains*, 99–109.

64. Minute book of the Swedish Evangelical Lutheran Church, minutes for April 15, 1926.

65. Ibid., minutes for September 4, 1936.

66. Merrill Halgren, telephone conversation with author, June 1995.

67. If Maria Johnson had lived a few more years, she might have chosen to withdraw from the Vondell Brook group for reasons relating to language rather than to age or ill health. Minnie's mother spoke very little English, and the organization's minutes attest to a gradual shift in membership from Swedish speakers to English speakers. As early as 1931, meeting minutes periodically noted the pastor speaking both Swedish and English. In 1940, the minutes read: "Pastor gave short service first in Swedish and then in English. We do appreciate this very much as we have several old members that do not fully understand the English and several new members that don't understand the Swedish." By 1944, all of the meeting minutes, and most likely the meetings as well, were entirely in English.

68. Minute book of the Swedish Evangelical Lutheran Church, minutes for September 21, 1950, and November 16, 1950.

69. For further discussion of the communities created by the immigrant press, see Ulf Jonas Björk, "'Folkets Röst,' the Pulse of the Public: *Svenska Amerikanska Posten* and Reader Letters, 1907–1911," *SAHQ* 50, no. 2 (April 1999): 4–18; and Ulf Jonas Björk, "The Swedish-American Press: Three Newspapers and Their Communities," Ph.D. diss., University of Washington, 1987.

70. Cicelia [Minnie Halgren], "Nybyggarliv," *SAP*, January 23, 1929, 9. (Hereafter, unless otherwise noted, the *SAP* articles cited are written by Minnie.)

71. P. R. Nelson, "Ett Värdefullt Sällskap," *Svenska Amerikanska Posten*, June 25, 1903, 15.

72. Jonas Björk, "*Svenska Amerikanska Posten:* An Immigrant Newspaper with American Accents," in *Swedes in the Twin Cities*, ed. Philip J. Anderson and Dag Blanck (St. Paul: Minnesota Historical Society Press, 2001), 210–14.

73. The page was first titled "Bref från folket" (Letters from the people).

74. *SAP*, May 23, 1899, 10.

75. Björk, "Folkets Röst," 4. For a discussion of "reader letters," as opposed to "letters to the editor," see Ulf Jonas Björk, "Perhaps There Is Someone Who Wants to Know How We Live: 'Public' Immigrant Letters in Swedish-American Newspapers," *SAHQ* 56, nos. 2–3 (April–July 2005): 184–85.

76. For an examination of a different type of Swedish immigrant women's newspaper writing, see Cynthia Meyer's study of letters to a women's section, "Kvinnan och hemmet" (Women and the home), in the Swedish American Covenant newspaper *Förbundets Veckotidning*. Cynthia Nelson Meyer, "Creating a Swedish-American Woman: The Views of Women in the Swedish Evangelical Mission Covenant Church, 1915–1920" (Ph.D. diss., Indiana University, 1998).

77. "Om oss sjelfva," *SAP*, December 29, 1896, 4; "En högtidsdag," *SAP*, March 9, 1897, 4; as quoted in Björk, "Folkets Röst," 6.

78. "Svenska Amerikanska Posten 1903," *SAP*, December 23, 1902, 1; "Till våra skribenter," *SAP*, February 12, 1907, 8; as quoted in Björk, "Folkets Röst," 6.

79. Björk, "Folkets Röst," 12; Björk, "Perhaps There Is," 187–88.

80. Siedow clipping collection. Minnie's descendants provided clippings and transcriptions of some of her writings (often with no date or newspaper title included). I have also examined nearly every issue of *SAP* for the 1890s and most issues from the latter part of the decade 1900 to 1910, as well as most issues from the 1920s and 1930s. Minnie also contributed to the *Svenska Amerikanaren Tribunen*, published in Chicago, and may have contributed to other Swedish American newspapers as well.

81. *LS*, 73.

82. Merrill Halgren, telephone conversation with author; copy of a poem written for a neighbor's twenty-fifth wedding anniversary and reference in eulogy and funeral guest book for Minnie Halgren, in author's possession.

83. "Det förlorade paradiset," *SAP*, date unknown; "Blandgods," *SAP*, December 11, 1929, 9.

84. Björk, "Folkets Röst," 10.

85. Cicelia, untitled, *SAP*, n.d., 1910.

86. Cicelia, untitled, *SAP*, n.d., 1910.

87. Cicelia, "En fråga," *SAP*, October 31, 1928, 10.

88. Cicelia, "Reflektioner," *SAP*, July 30, 1930, 15.

89. Cicelia, "Småprat," *SAP*, March 20, 1935, 9.

90. Cicilia, "Blandgods," *SAP*, December 22, 1929, 9.

91. "Till skribenterna i Folkets Röst," *SAP*, December 19, 1928, 7.

92. Minnie Halgren survey, Albin Widén Collection, 15:7:10, EI.

93. Cecelia, "Berättigat och oberättigat hat," *SAP*, November 12, 1930, 14.

94. Bokvän, "Ett svar till Cecilia," *SAP*, January 7, 1931, 15.

95. Cecilia, "Svar till Bokvän," *SAP*, February 25, 1931, 14.

96. Cicelia, "Nybyggareliv," *SAP*, January 25, 1929, 9.

97. Cicelia, "En saga från Dalsland," *SAP*, December 31, 1930, 14.

98. This was an immigrant song introduced by the Olle Skratthult group that became popular among Swedish Americans beginning in the 1920s. See Timmerhus Productions, "Paul and Mary Sing Nikolina and Other Scandinavian Favorites," http://www.brainerd.net/~pwilson/timmerhus/nikolina.html (accessed July 25, 2007); and James Porter, review of "Memories of Snoose Boulevard," by Anne Charlotte Harvey, *Ethnomusicology* 20, no. 1 (January 1976): 153–54.

99. Cicilia, "Fosterlandet," *SAP*, September 18, 1929, 8.

100. Cicelia, "Min barndoms jul," *SAP*, December 16, 1936, 8.

101. Cicilia,"När Axel kom hem," *SAP*, December 18, 1935, 3.

102. Cicelia, "Lyckan," *SAP*, November 1907; "Midsommarminnen," *SAP*, n.d., 1907; "Langes'n," *SAP*, January 1, 1908; "Hoppet," *SAP*, April 1, 1908 (all cited from clippings obtained from Beverly Siedow and Merrill Halgren).

103. Cicelia, "Gravsmyckningsdagen," *SAP*, June 3, 1931, 14; Cecilia, "Moder," *SAP*, May 25, 1932, 15; "Graduation," *SAP*, June 27, 1928, 14.

104. "Ett storartadt tillfälle för meddelarne till denna afdelning," *SAP*, January 11, 1928, 10.

105. "Pristagare under juni," *SAP*, June 27, 1928, 16.

106. Cecilia, "Minnesota," *SAP*, April 18, 1928, 12, translation by author.

107. "'Joan' bjuder 'Folkets Röst' till utflykt," *SAP*, June 11, 1930, 14.

108. Ragnar, "Kvarnstadskrönika," *SAP*, July 9, 1930, 14.

109. Björk, "Perhaps There Is," 184.

110. In the years just before World War I, when *SAP* had more than 50,000 subscribers, the number of Swedish American papers in the United States was about fifty, with a circulation of approximately 1.5 million (Ulf Jonas Björk, *Svenska Amerikanska Posten*, 217).

111. Ida Johnson, "Tack för tidningen," *Svenska Amerikanska Posten*, December 4, 1935, 9.

112. Ramsey County District Court, Naturalization Records, 1849–1931, roll 45, MHS.

113. Nancy F. Cott, "Marriage and Women's Citizenship in the United States, 1830–1934," *American Historical Review* 103, no. 5 (December 1998): 1456–74. Women who were considered immoral, such as prostitutes, would not be granted citizenship under this legislation.

114. *LS*, 63.

115. *MCT*, August 16, 1900, 1.

116. *MCT*, February 19, 1903, 1.

117. *MCT*, November 5, 1900, 1.

118. *MCT*, 1899; *MCT*, June 26, 1907, 5.

119. *MCT*, October 14, 1908, 5; for Skratthult, May 29, 1919, 4; and October 14, 1920, 4.

120. Similar Swedish heritage days were established, and some continue, in other areas of the United States where Swedes settled. Swedes in Illinois had already begun a Svenskarnas Dag in 1911 (see "Swedish Day," at http://www.swedishday.net, accessed July 29, 2007).

121. The program for the 1935 Svenskarnas Dag was printed in *SAP* on August 14, 1935, along with pictures of the festivities. The Minnehaha Park festivities remain quite similar today (see "Svenskarnas Dag" at http://www.svenskarnasdag.com, accessed July 29, 2007).

122. John Rice, "The Swedes," in *They Chose Minnesota: A Survey of the State's Ethnic Groups*, ed. June Drenning Holmquist (St. Paul: Minnesota Historical Society Press, 1981), 269.

123. See Ulf Beijbom, "Swedish American Organizational Life," in *Scandinavia Overseas*, ed. Harald Runblom and Dag Blanck (Uppsala, Sweden: Center for Multiethnic Research, 1976), 66.

124. Untitled, *Svenska Amerikanaren Tribunen*, November 15, 1945, clipping in Dalslands-Föreningen Collection, American Swedish Institute, Minneapolis.

125. Minnie Halgren, "För Dahlslands Föreningen," copy obtained from Merrill Halgren, in author's possession.

126. *LS*, 62.

127. Orm Øverland, *Immigrant Minds, American Identities: Making the United States Home, 1870–1930* (Chicago: University of Illinois Press, 2000), 26–27.

128. Jon Gjerde, *The Minds of the West: Ethnocultural Evolution in the Rural Middle West, 1830–1917* (Chapel Hill: University of North Carolina Press, 1997), 8.

129. *LS*, 69.

130. Folke Hedblom, *Svensk-Amerika berättar* (Malmö, Sweden: Gidlunds, 1982), 99.

Epilogue (pages 219–24)

1. *LS*, 72, 74.

2. Jennie Halgren Lonsdale, telephone conversation with author.

3. On the controversies surrounding the novels, see Arthur Landfors, "Sedlighetsfejden," in *Perspektiv på utvandrarromanen: Dokument och studier*, ed. Erland Lagerroth and Ulla-Britta Lagerroth (Stockholm: Rabén & Sjögren, 1971), 147–60.

4. *LS*, 75.

5. Beverly Siedow and Alice Tobler, interview by author.

Selected Bibliography

Abbreviations

EI	Emigrant Institute, Växjö, Sweden
EU	*Emigrationsutredningen* (Emigration investigation), 21 vols. (Stockholm: P. A. Norstedt, 1908–13)
LCC	Landelius Clipping Collection, EI
LS	*Livets skola* (The school of life), Vilhelm Moberg Collection, EI
MCT	*Mille Lacs County Times*
MJ	*Minneapolis Journal*
MHS	Minnesota Historical Society, St. Paul
NM	Folkminnessamling, Nordiska Museet, Stockholm
SAHQ	*Swedish-American Historical Quarterly*
SAP	*Svenska Amerikanska Posten*
SSIRC	Swenson Swedish Immigration Research Center, Augustana College, Rock Island, IL

Books

Amato, Joseph A. *Rethinking Home: A Case for Writing Local History.* Berkeley: University of California Press, 2002.

Anderson, Mary. *Woman at Work: The Autobiography of Mary Anderson as Told to Mary N. Winslow.* Minneapolis: University of Minnesota Press, 1951.

Anderson, Philip J., and Dag Blanck, eds. *Swedes in the Twin Cities.* St. Paul: Minnesota Historical Society Press, 2002.

Andersson, Eric H. "Emigrationen från Pjätteryds socken." In *Hylten Cavallius-Föreningen,* 167–91. 1941 årsbok. Växjö, Sweden: Nya Växjöbladets boktryckeri.

Artæus, Iréne. *Kvinnorna som blev över: Ensamstående stadskvinnor under 1800-talets första hälft—fallet Västerås.* Stockholm: Almqvist & Wiksell, 1992.

Bäckefors Hembygdsförening. *Bäcke-boken: Historik från en socken på Dal.* Uddevalla, Sweden: Risbergs Tryckeri AB, 1977.

———. *De grå stugornas folk i Bäcke socken.* Munkedal, Sweden: Munk-Reklam AB, 1994.

Bales, Carol Ann. *Tales of the Elders: A Memory Book of Men and Women Who Came to America as Immigrants, 1900–1930.* Chicago: Follett, 1977.

Beckman, Ernst. *Amerikanska studier.* Stockholm: Haeggstroms, 1881.

Beijbom, Ulf. "Swedish American Organizational Life." In *Scandinavia Overseas*, edited by Harald Runblom and Dag Blanck, 47–67. Uppsala, Sweden: Center for Multiethnic Research, 1976.

———. *Utvandrarkvinnor: Svenska Kvinnöden i Amerika.* Stockholm: P. A. Norstedt, 2006.

Bender, Thomas. *Community and Social Change in America.* New Brunswick, NJ: Rutgers University Press, 1978.

Bengtsson, Frithiof, et al., eds. *Halländska emigrantöden 1860–1930.* Halmstad, Sweden: Spektra, 1976.

Bengtsson, Tommy, and Rolf Ohlsson. "The Demographic Transition Revised." In *Population, Economy, and Welfare in Sweden*, edited by Tommy Bengtsson, 13–35. Berlin: Springer Verlag, 1994.

Blanck, Dag, and Harald Runblom, eds. *Swedish Life in American Cities.* Uppsala, Sweden: Center for Multiethnic Research, 1991.

Bringéus, Nils-Arvid. *Livets högtider.* Stockholm: LTs Förlag, 1987.

Bursell, Barbro. *Träskoadel: En etnologisk undersökning av lancashiresmedernas arbets- och levnadsförhållanden på Ramnäs bruk vid tiden kring sekelskiftet 1900.* Lund, Sweden: Berlinksa, 1974.

Carlsson, Sten. *Fröknar, mamseller, jungfrur och pigor: ogifta kvinnor i det svenska ståndssamhället.* Uppsala, Sweden: Acta Universitatis Upsaliensis, 1977.

Carpenter, Niles. *Immigrants and Their Children.* 1920 Census Monographs 7. Washington, DC: GPO, 1927.

Cronberg, Marie Lindstedt. *Synd och skam: Ogifta mödrar på svensk landsbygd 1680–1880.* Lund, Sweden: Lund University, 1997.

Dalgård, P. Gösta. "Befolkningsförändringar på Dal under 1800- och 1900-talen." In *Hembygden 1983.* Åmal, Sweden: Dalslands Fornminnes- och Hembygdsförbund, 1983.

Davis, Michael M., Jr. *Immigrant Health and the Community.* New York: Harper, 1921.

Davison's Minneapolis City Directory, 1900. Minneapolis: C. R. Davison, 1900.

Davison's Minneapolis City Directory, 1905–6. Minneapolis: C. R. Davison, 1906.

De kvinnliga kontors- och butikbiträdenas ställning. Stockholm: Aftonbladet, 1903.

Det hände i vår tid—om det gamla som var och det ny som kom. Stockholm: Sveriges Radios Förlag, 1967.

Dual City Blue Book, 1891–92. St. Paul: R. Polk, 1892.

Ebbeson, Ulf. *Emigration från en bruksbygd i Östergötland.* Sweden: N.p., 1970.

Eidevall, Gunnar. *Vilhelm Mobergs emigrantepos: Studier i verkets tillkomsthistoria, dokumentära bakgrund och konstnärliga gestaltning.* Stockholm: P. A. Norstedt, 1974.

Enstad, Nan. *Ladies of Labor, Girls of Adventure: Working Women, Popular Culture, and Labor Politics at the Turn of the Twentieth Century.* New York: Columbia University Press, 1999.

Eriksson, Adina. *Flicka med tur reste till U.S.A.* Stockholm: Författares Bokmaskin, 1976.

Fairchild, Amy L. *Science at the Borders: Immigrant Medical Inspection and the Shaping of the Modern Industrial Labor Force.* Baltimore: Johns Hopkins University Press, 2003.

First Biennial Report of the Bureau of Labor Statistics of the State of Minnesota for the Two Years Ending December 31, 1887–88. St. Paul: Thos. A. Clark, 1888.

Från folkbrist till en åldrande befolkning: Glimtar ur en unik befolkningsstatistik under 250 år, Fakta inför 2000-talet. Stockholm: Statistiska Centralbyrån, 1999.

Frykman, Jonas. *Horan i bondesamhället.* Lund, Sweden: Jonas Frykman and Liber-Läromedal, 1977.

Gaarder, Pat, and Tracey Baker. *From Stripes to Whites: A History of the Swedish Hospital School of Nursing, 1899–1973.* Minneapolis: Swedish Hospital Alumnae Association, 1980.

Gabaccia, Donna. *From the Other Side: Women, Gender, and Immigrant Life in the U.S., 1820–1990.* Bloomington: Indiana University Press, 1994.

Gaunt, David. *Familjeliv i Norden.* Malmö, Sweden: Gidlunds, 1983.

Gjerde, Jon. *The Minds of the West: Ethnocultural Evolution in the Rural Middle West, 1830–1917.* Chapel Hill: University of North Carolina Press, 1997.

Grimsköld, Carl. *Swedish-American Book of Cookery and Adviser for Swedish Servants in America.* New York: Otto Chils' Print, 1890.

Gustafson, Uno. "Kvinnornas arbetsmarknad i Stockholm, 1870–1910." In *Arbeidslønns- og rettsforhold for yrkesaktiv kvinner i de nordiske land ca. 1850–1914*, edited by Grethe Authen Blom, 1–14. Trondheim, Norway: Tapir, 1978.

Hallbäck, Sven Axel. *Dalsland.* Stockholm: Awe/Gebers, 1982.

Handy-Marchello, Barbara. *Women of the Northern Plains.* St. Paul: Minnesota Historical Society Press, 2005.

Hanson, Thure. *Swedish-American Souvenir.* Worcester, MA: N.p., 1910.

Harzig, Christiane, ed. *Peasant Maids—City Women: From the European Countryside to Urban America.* Ithaca, NY: Cornell University Press, 1997.

Heath, Shirley Anderson. "From Skåne to Kansas." In *Stories of Swedish Pioneers in North America*, vol. 2. N.p.: n.p., 1948.

Hedblom, Folke. *Svensk-Amerika berättar.* Malmö, Sweden: Gidlunds, 1982.

Hedblom, Margaretha, and Gunnar Ternhag, eds. *Emigranternas spår: Om utflyttningen från Dalarna till Amerika.* Falun, Sweden: Dalarnas Museum, 1983.

Hembiträdet berätter om liv och arbete i borgerliga familjer i början av 1900-talet. Stockholm: Civiltryck AB, 1975.

Hembygden 1991, edited by Per Hultqvist et al. Uddevalla, Sweden: Risbergs Tryckeri AB, 1990.

Herjulfsdotter, Ritwa. *Kvinnominnen från Dalsland: Att vara piga.* Bengtfors, Sweden: Affärs & Industritryck and Bengtfors Kommuns Interntryckeri, 1992.

Historisk statistik för Sverige, 1720–1967. 2d ed. Stockholm: Statistiska Centralbyrån, 1969.

Holmberg, Gustav Henriksson. *Tjänarinnorna i städerna.* Stockholm: Björck & Börjesson, 1907.

Holmdahl, Barbro. *Tusen år i det svenska barnets historia.* Lund, Sweden: Studentlitteratur, 2000.

Holt, Nancy. "The Promised Land." In *Stories of Swedish Pioneers in North America,* vol. 3. N.p.: n.p., 1948.

Howard, Welma Swanston. *När Maja-Lisa kom hem från Amerika.* Stockholm: Folkskrifter Utgifven af Nationalföreningen mot Emigrationen, 1908.

Hurst, Fannie. *Lummox.* New York: Harper, 1923.

Isaksson, Olov. *Bishop Hill, Illinois: A Utopia on the Prairie.* Stockholm: LTs Förlag, 1969.

Johnson, Harold H. *The Swedes at West Rock.* New Hope, MN: Review Corporation, 1989.

Karlsson, Lyn. *Women Workers in Figures: A Picture of Swedish Industry, 1863–1912.* Uppsala, Sweden: Uppsala University, Department of Economic History, 1996.

Katzman, David. *Seven Days a Week: Women and Domestic Service in Industrializing America.* New York: Oxford University Press, 1978.

Kent, Neil. *The Soul of the North: A Social, Architectural, and Cultural History of the Nordic Countries, 1700–1940.* London: Reaktion Books, 2000.

Kjellberg, Isidor. *Amerika-bok.* Linköping, Sweden: Isidor Kjellbergs Boktryckeri, 1892.

Kyle, Gunhild. *Svensk flickskola under 1800-talet.* Göteborg, Sweden: Kvinnohistorisk Arkiv, 1972.

Kyle, Gunhild, ed. *Handbok i svensk kvinnohistoria.* Stockholm: Carlsson Bokförlag, 1987.

Lagerroth, Erland, and Ulla-Britta Lagerroth. *Perspektiv på utvandrarromanen: Dokument och studier.* Stockholm: Rabén & Sjögren, 1971.

Lewis, Anne Gillespie. *So Far Away in the World.* Minneapolis: Nodin Press, 2002.

———. *Swedes in Minnesota.* St. Paul: Minnesota Historical Society Press, 2004.

Liljevall, Britt. *Självskrivna liv: Studier i äldre folkliga levnadsminnen.* Stockholm: Nordiska Museets Förlag, 2001.

Linck, Joseph. *Det qvinliga arbetet.* Stockholm: Isaac Marcus, 1884.

Lindberg, John S. *The Background of Swedish Emigration to the United States.* Minneapolis: University of Minnesota Press, 1930.

Lindkvist, Anna. *Jorden åt folket: Nationalföreningen mot emigrationen, 1907–1925.* Umeå, Sweden: Institutionen för Historiska Studier, Umeå University, 2007.

Lindvall, Axel E. *Minnen från en färd genom Amerika.* Karlskrona, Sweden: Författerens Förlag, 1890.

Ljung, Olof. *De for åt Amerika.* Mellerud, Sweden: Niklassasons Tryckeri AB, 1988.

———. "Vi vill minnas: Om utvandringen och emigrant forskning." In *Hembygden 1983*, 141–80. Åmal, Sweden: Dalslands Forminnes- och Hembygdsförbund, 1983.

Lund, Inge [Anna Ingeborg Aurora Lundström]. *Guld med täljknivar: Roman om svenskamerikaner.* Stockholm: Åhlen & Åkerlund, 1918.

———. *En piga i USA.* Stockholm: Åhlen & Åkerlund, 1917.

Månsson, Evelina. *Amerika-minnen: Upplevelser och iaktagelser från en 6-årig vistelse i U.S.A.* Hvetlanda, Sweden: Svenska Allmogeförlaget, 1930.

Matovic, Margareta. "Embracing a Middle-Class Life: Swedish-American Women in Lake View." In *Peasant Maids—City Women: From the European Countryside to Urban America*, edited by Christiane Harzig, 289–93. Ithaca, NY: Cornell University Press, 1997.

———. "Maids in Motion: Swedish Women in Dalsland." In *Peasant Maids—City Women: From the European Countryside to Urban America*, edited by Christiane Harzig, 100–137. Ithaca, NY: Cornell University Press, 1997.

———. "Migration, Family Formation, and Choice of Marriage Partners in Stockholm, 1860–1890." In *Urbanization in History*, edited by M. van der Woude et al., 220–42. Oxford: Clarendon Press, 1990.

———. *Stockholmsäktenskap: Familjebildning och partnerval i Stockholm, 1850–1890.* Stockholm: Margareta Matovic and Committee for Stockholm Research, 1989.

Meyerson, Gerda. *Arbeterskornas värld: Studier och erfarenheter.* Stockholm: Hugo Gebers Förlag, 1917.

———. *Kvinnorna i industrin.* Stockholm: Bokförlags-Aktiebolaget EOS, 1909.

———. *Svenska hemarbetsförhållanden: En undersökning utförd som grund för Centralförbundets för Socialt Arbete Hemarbetsutställning i Stockholm.* Stockholm: Ekmans Förlag, 1907.

Mille Lacs County Minnesota: A Land of Success, Happiness, Contentment. Princeton, MN: Princeton Commercial Club, 1909.

Moberg, Kerstin. *Från tjänstehjon till hembiträde.* Uppsala, Sweden: Acta Universitatis Upsaliensis, 1978.

Moberg, Vilhelm. *The Emigrants.* St. Paul: Minnesota Historical Society Press, 1995.

———. *The Last Letter Home.* St. Paul: Minnesota Historical Society Press, 1995.

———. *The Settlers.* St. Paul: Minnesota Historical Society Press, 1995.

———. *Unto a Good Land.* St. Paul: Minnesota Historical Society Press, 1995.

Nelson, Helge. *The Swedes and the Swedish Settlements in North America.* New York: Arno Press, 1979; Lund, Sweden: Royal Society of Letters, 1943.

Nilsson, Fred. *Emigrationen från Stockholm till Nordamerika 1880–1893: En studie i urban utvandring.* Stockholm: Läromedalsförlaget, 1970.

Nilsson, Oscar. *Skildring af min vistelse i Minnesota i Amerika, 1881.* Venersborg, Sweden: Bagge och Pettersson, 1881.

Nissen, Oscar. *Om våra tjänsteflickors ställning.* Stockholm: Walfrid Wilhelmsson, 1892.

Nordström, Ester Blenda. *En piga bland pigor.* Stockholm: Wahlström & Widstrand, 1914.

Noreen, Paul. *Emigrationen från Sundals härad i Dalsland, 1860–1895.* Mellerud, Sweden: Vasa Ordern av Amerika, 1967.

Norman, Hans, and Harald Runblom. *Transatlantic Connections: Nordic Migration to the New World after 1800.* Oslo: Norwegian University Press, 1988.

Ohlander, Ann-Sofie. *Kvinnor, barn och arbete i Sverige, 1850–1993.* Report for the UN Conference on Population and Development in Cairo. Stockholm: Utrikesdepartementet, 1994.

Ohlander, Ann-Sofie, and Ulla-Britt Strömberg. *Tusen svenska kvinnoår: Svensk kvinnohistoria från vikingatid till nutid.* Stockholm: Rabén Prisma, 1997.

Olson, E. W., and M. J. Engberg. *History of the Swedes of Illinois.* Part 2. New York: Engberg-Holmberg Publishing Co., 1908.

Ostergren, Robert. *A Community Transplanted: The Trans-Atlantic Experience of a Swedish Immigrant Settlement in the Upper Middle West, 1835–1915.* Madison: University of Wisconsin Press, 1988.

Østerud, Øvind. *Agrarian Structure and Peasant Politics in Scandinavia.* Oslo: Scandinavian University Books, 1978.

Øverland, Orm. *Immigrant Minds, American Identities: Making the United States Home, 1870–1930.* Chicago: University of Illinois Press, 2000.

Pearson, Bernard. *Einar and Lina.* Foreston, MN: B. Pearson, 1980.

Person, Johan. *Svensk-amerikanska studier.* Rock Island, IL: Augustana Book Concern, 1912.

Pettersson, Olga, with Monica Andrae. *Olga berättar.* Stockholm: Sveriges Radio, 1979.

Prahl, Joachim. *Vägledning för svenska utvandrare till Amerika.* Helsingborg, Sweden: Skånes Allehandas Boktryckeri, 1890.

Qvist, Gunnar. *Konsten att blifva en god flicka: Kvinnohistoriska uppsatser.* Stockholm: Liber, 1978.

———. *Kvinnofrågen i Sverige, 1809–1846.* Göteborg, Sweden: Elanders Boktryckeri, 1960.

Report of the Minnesota State Commission for the Relief of Fire Sufferers to the Governor. St. Paul: Pioneer Press Co., State Printers, 1895.

Rice, John. "The Swedes." In *They Chose Minnesota: A Survey of the State's Ethnic Groups,* edited by June Drenning Holmquist, 248–76. St. Paul: Minnesota Historical Society Press, 1981.

Runblom, Harald, and Hans Norman, eds. *From Sweden to America: A History of the Migration.* Minneapolis: University of Minnesota Press, 1976.

Runeby, Nils. *Den ny världen och den gamla: Amerikabild och emigrationsuppfattning i Sverige, 1820–1860.* Uppsala, Sweden: Acta Universitatis Upsaliensis, 1969.

Sinke, Suzanne M. *Dutch Immigrant Women in the United States, 1880–1920.* Urbana: University of Illinois Press, 2002.

Sjöberg, Mats. "Working Rural Children: Herding, Child Labour, and Childhood in the Swedish Rural Environment, 1850–1950." In *Industrious Children: Work and Childhood in the Nordic Countries, 1850–1990*, edited by Ning DeConinck-Smith, Bengt Sandin, and Ellen Schrumpf, 106–28. Odense, Denmark: Odense University Press, 1997.

Skårdal, Dorothy Burton. *The Divided Heart: Scandinavian Immigrant Experience through Literary Sources.* Oslo: Universitetsförlaget, 1974.

St. Cloud City Directory, 1898–99. St. Paul: Pettibone Directory Co., 1899.

St. Paul City Directory. St. Paul: R. L. Polk & Co., 1890.

Thomas, Dorothy Swaine. *Social and Economic Aspects of Swedish Population Movements, 1750–1933.* New York: Macmillan, 1941.

Thörnberg, E. H. *Lefnadsstandard och sparkraft: Med särskild hänsyn till den svenska befolkningen i Chicago.* Stockholm: Hugo Geber Förlag, 1915.

Tilley, Charles. "Transplanted Networks." In *Immigration Reconsidered: History, Sociology, and Politics*, edited by Virginia Yans-McLaughlin, 79–95. New York: Oxford University Press, 1990.

U.S. Bureau of Labor. *Report on Conditions of Women and Child Wage-Earners in the United States.* Vol. 5, *Wage-Earning Women in Stores and Factories.* Washington, DC, 1910.

Vontver, May. *Utvandrare till Nebraska.* Stockholm: Harriers Förlag, 1961.

Wibling, Irma. *Eva Wallström berättar—Minnen från ett långt liv.* Härnosand, Sweden: Alex och Eva Wallströms Stiftelse för Vetenskaplig Forskning och Utbildning, 1982.

Widén, Albin. *Vår sista folkvandring.* Stockholm: Almqvist & Wiksell, 1962.

Woman in Sweden: In Light of the Statistics. Stockholm: Arbetsmarknadens Kvinnoämnd, 1971.

Wright, Robert L. *Swedish Emigrant Ballads.* Lincoln: University of Nebraska Press, 1965.

Zion Lutheran Church: Its History, 1893–1993. Milaca: Zion Evangelical Lutheran Church, Milaca, MN, 1992.

Magazine and Journal Articles

Adelborg, Gertrud. "Kan något göras för att minska den kvinnliga emigrationen och dess faror?" *Dagny* 9 (1903): 217–28.

———. "Svenska tjänstflickors utvandring till Danmark." *Dagny* 1 (1890): 2–4.

"Är de damer!" *Qvinnan och Hemmet* 13, no. 11 (November 1900): 353.

Arthur, Port. " 'Giants in the Earth' . . . : A Mother's Mission." *Lutheran Companion* (October 8, 1947): 13–15.

Barkan, Elliott R. "America in the Hand, Homeland in the Heart: Transnational and Translocal Immigrant Experience in the American West." *Western Historical*

Quarterly 35, no. 3 (Autumn 2004). http://www.historycooperative.org/journals/whq/35.3/barkan.html (accessed June 13, 2007).

Barton, H. Arnold. "Scandinavian Women's Encounter with America." *Swedish Pioneer Historical Quarterly* 25 (January 1974): 37–42.

Björk, Ulf Jonas. " 'Folkets Röst,' " the Pulse of the Public: *Svenska Amerikanska Posten* and Reader Letters, 1907–1911." *SAHQ* 50 (April 1999): 4–17.

———. "Perhaps There Is Someone Who Wants to Know How We Live: 'Public' Immigrant Letters in Swedish-American Newspapers." *SAHQ* 56, nos. 2–3 (April–July 2005): 183–97.

Chisholm, Richard M., with transcriptions of interviews with Ruth Dahl Chisholm. "Vignettes of a Prairie Childhood: Anecdotes of Swedish-American Immigrant Life in North Dakota." *SAHQ* 55, no. 2 (April 2004): 84–106.

Cott, Nancy F. "Marriage and Women's Citizenship in the United States, 1830–1934." *American Historical Review* 103, no. 5 (December 1998): 1456–74.

Dribe, Martin. "Dealing with Economic Stress through Migration: Lessons from Nineteenth Century Rural Sweden." *European Review of Economic History* 7 (2003): 271–99.

Dribe, Martin, and Christer Lundh. "People on the Move: Determinants of Servant Migration in Nineteenth Century Sweden." *Continuity and Change* 20, no. 1 (2005): 53–91.

Engberg, Elisabeth. "Boarded Out by Auction: Poor Children and Their Families in Nineteenth-Century Northern Sweden." *Continuity and Change* 19 (2004): 431–57.

Enstad, Nan. "Fashioning Political Identities: Cultural Studies and the Historical Construction of Political Subjects." *American Quarterly* 50, no. 4 (1998): 745–82.

Ericsson, Tom. "Women, Family, and Small Business in Late Nineteenth-Century Sweden." *History of the Family* 6, no. 2 (2001): 225–39.

Halgren, Minnie. "Amerikabrevet." *Dalsländsk Hembygd* 4, no. 2 (1953): 22–23.

Jensen, Joan M. "Out of Wisconsin: Country Daughters in the City, 1910–1925." *Minnesota History* 59, no. 2 (Summer 2004): 48–61.

Kälvemark, Ann-Sofie. "Utvandring och självständighet: Några synpunkter på den kvinnliga emigrationen från Sverige." *Historisk Tidskrift* 2 (1983): 140–74.

Kivisto, Peter. "Theorizing Transnational Immigration: A Critical Review of Current Efforts." *Ethnic and Racial Studies* 24, no. 4 (July 2001): 549–77.

Laslett, Barbara, and Johanna Brenner. "Gender and Social Reproduction: Historical Perspectives." *Annual Reviews in Sociology* 15 (1989): 381–404.

Lintelman, Joy K. " 'America Is the Woman's Promised Land': Swedish Immigrant Women and American Domestic Service." *Journal of American Ethnic History* 8, no. 2 (Spring 1989): 9–23.

———. " 'Our Serving Sisters': Swedish-American Domestic Servants and Their Ethnic Community." *Social Science History* 15, no. 3 (Fall 1991): 381–95.

———. "'She Did Not Whimper or Complain': Swedish-American Female Charity Cases in Minneapolis, 1910–1930." *SAHQ* 45, no. 1 (January 1994): 5–23.

Löfgren, Orvar. "Family and Household among Scandinavian Peasants: An Exploratory Essay." *Ethnologia Scandinavica* (1974): 17–52.

Lundh, Christer. "Life Cycle Servants in Nineteenth Century Sweden—Norms and Practice." *Lund Papers in Economic History* 84 (2003): 1–18. http://www.ekh.lu.se/publ/lup/84 (accessed June 14, 2007).

———. "Swedish Marriages: Customs, Legislation and Demography in the Eighteenth and Nineteenth Centuries." *Lund Papers in Economic History* 88 (2003): 1–63.

Milow, Cecilia. "Till frågan om det moraliska tillståndet bland svenska tjänstflickor i Amerika." *Dagny* 12 (1904): 293–94.

Moberg, Vilhelm. "Om historiska romaner." *Vintergatan* (1943): 124–25.

Moloney, Deirdre M. "Women, Sexual Morality, and Economic Dependency in Early U.S. Deportation Policy." *Journal of Women's History* 18, no. 2 (2006): 95–122.

Mullan, E. H. "Mental Examination of Immigrants, Administration and Line Inspection at Ellis Island." *U.S. Public Health Reports* (May 18, 1917): 733–39.

Nordstrom, Byron. "Evelina Månsson and the Memoir of an Urban Labor Migrant." *Swedish Pioneer Historical Quarterly* 31 (July 1980): 182–89.

Nyberg, Anita. "From Foster Mothers to Child Care Centers: A History of Working Mothers and Child Care in Sweden." *Feminist Economics* 6, no. 1 (2000): 5–20.

———. "The Social Construction of Married Women's Labour-Force Participation: The Case of Sweden in the Twentieth Century." *Continuity and Change* 9, no. 1 (1994): 145–56.

Olson, S. W., trans. and ed. "Early Letters to Erland Carlson." *Augustana Historical Society Publications* 5 (1935): 107–35.

Olsson, Nils William. "The Exit Permit." *Swedish American Genealogist* 1, no. 2 (June 1981): 71–77.

Price, Mollie. "Swede Hollow: Sheltered Society for Immigrants to St. Paul." *Ramsey County History* 17, no. 2 (1981): 12–22.

Qvist, Gunnar. "Policy towards Women and the Women's Struggle in Sweden." *Scandinavian Journal of History* 5 (1980): 51–74.

"Ramsey County Births: A Midwife's Record Book, 1891–1906." *Minnesota Genealogical Journal* 25 (March 2001): 2489–94.

Robinson, Mary V. "Mary Anderson." *American Swedish Monthly* (August 1935): 9.

Rubinow, I. M. "The Problem of Domestic Service." *Journal of Political Economy* 14, no. 8 (October 1906): 502–24.

Rydén, Göran. "Skill and Technical Change in the Swedish Iron Industry, 1750–1860." *Technology and Culture* 39, no. 3 (1998): 383–407.

Sommestad, Lena, and Sally McMurry. "Farm Daughters and Industrialization: A Comparative Analysis of Dairying in New York and Sweden, 1860–1920." *Journal of Women's History* 10, no. 2 (Summer 1998): 137–64.

Telleen, Jane. "'Yours in the Master's Service': Emmy Evald and the Woman's Missionary Society of the Augustana Lutheran Church, 1892–1942." *Swedish Pioneer Historical Quarterly* 30, no. 3 (July 1979): 183–95.

Thorvaldsen, Gunnar. "Marriage and Names among Immigrants to Minnesota." *Journal of the Association for History and Computing* 1, no. 2 (1998). http://mcel.pacificu.edu (accessed July 20, 2006).

Tysdal, Olav. "The Dissolution of the Union between Norway and Sweden and the Scandinavian Americans." *Scandinavian Studies* 79, no. 2 (Summer 2007): 167–96.

Waldow, Florian. "Measuring Human Capital Formation in Sweden in the Nineteenth and Early Twentieth Centuries." *Historical Social Research* 27, no. 4 (2002): 140–56.

Webster, Janice Reiff. "Domestication and Americanization: Scandinavian Women in Seattle, 1888–1900." *Journal of Urban History* 4, no. 3 (May 1978): 275–90.

Williamson, Erik Luther. "'Doing What Had to Be Done': Norwegian Lutheran Ladies Aid Societies of North Dakota." *North Dakota History* 27, no. 2 (1990): 2–13.

Newspapers

[Advertisement]. *Chisago County Press*, November 21, 1907. Landelius Clipping Collection, EI.

[Advertisement]. *Medborgaren* [Chisago County, MN], March 16, 1905. Landelius Clipping Collection, EI.

[Advertisements]. *Vestkusten*, 1896, 1906, 1910. Landelius Clipping Collection, EI.

"Amerikaarv i rätta hander." *Svenska Amerikanaren Tribunen* [Chicago], January 24, 1952. Landelius Clipping Collection, EI.

Brooklyn [New York] Daily Eagle, 1880, 1888. http://www.brooklynpubliclibrary.org/eagle.

"Cooperative Kitchen: And More Maids Coming," *Minneapolis Journal*, August 9, 1902, 7.

"Esther Scherling drager sig tillbaka som matrona vid Kvinnohemmet." *W.[?] Nyheter* [Denver, CO], July 1, 1937. Landelius Clipping Collection, EI.

"Female Doctor in America." *Idun*, September 18, 1891. Landelius Clipping Collection, EI.

Mille Lacs [MN] *County Times*. 1894, 1895, 1897, 1908, 1909, 1910, 1913, 1914, 1916, 1918, 1919, 1986.

Minneapolis Journal. 1900, 1902.

"Mrs. Othelia Myhrman har gått ur tiden." *Skandia* [Chicago?], June 4, 1936. Landelius Clipping Collection, EI.

"Mrs. Sigrid Hansen går till vila." *Vestkusten* [San Francisco], April 1, 1954. Landelius Clipping Collection, EI.

Obituary notice for Maria Rabenius. *Svenska Dagbladet* [Stockholm, Sweden], July 25, 1953. Landelius Clipping Collection, EI.

Svenska Amerikanaren Tribunen [Chicago]. 1945.

Svenska Amerikanska Posten [Minneapolis]. 1895–1910, 1919, 1920–1930, 1931, 1932, 1935, 1936.

Svenska Journalen [Omaha, NE]. 1902.

Svenska Nyheter [Chicago]. 1905.

Svenska Tribunen Nyheter [Chicago]. 1909. Chicago Foreign Language Press Survey, Immigration History Research Center, Minneapolis.

Tjännarinebladet [Stockholm]. 1905–7.

Ulrich, Walborg. "Ur verkligheten. Stockholms bild." *Tjänarinnebladet*, serialized, 1906–7.

Interviews

Carlson, Mrs. Ingeborg [Johansson]. Interview by Carolyn Wilson and Betsy Doermann, July 19, 1984 (typed transcription), James J. Hill House, St. Paul, MN.

Halgren, Merrill [grandson of Minnie]. Interviews by author, November 12, 1993, June 17, 1995, Milaca, MN.

Larsson, Else. Interview by author, December 8, 1987, Minneapolis, MN.

Lonsdale, Jennie Jean Halgren [daughter of Minnie Halgren]. Telephone conversation with author, July 27, 1995.

Seagren, Ellen. Interview by author, December 1985, February 1986, Minneapolis, MN.

Siedow, Beverly Halgren [granddaughter of Minnie]. Periodic email communications and telephone conversations with author, 1998–2008.

Siedow, Beverly, and Alice Tobler [granddaughters of Minnie]. Interview by author, October 24, 1998, Vining, MN. (Marjorie Bednarek was also present.)

Swanson, Alma E. Interview by Terry Kirker, Swedish-American Project of the Oral History Program at California State University, Fullerton. O.H. 1455. Fullerton: California State University, Fullerton, 1977.

Memoirs, Diaries, Letters, and Other Unpublished Materials

Anderson, Mina [Minnie Halgren]. "Livets skola av Cecilia," Collection 7:3:1:1–75, Vilhelm Moberg Collection, EI.

———. "Livets skola av Cecilia" [typewritten transcript], Collection. 7:3:2:1–35, Vilhelm Moberg Collection, EI.

Andersson, Ada. Letters. Collection 10:8:5:H, EI.

Andersson, Anna. Collection, NM.

Andersson, Charlotta. Letters. Collection 10:5:4:E, EI.

Andersson, Ivar. Biography of mother. Ivar Andersson Collection, NM.

Andreen, Hilma. Letters. Collection 22:6:16:M, EI.

Arfvidson, C. A. Collection, NM.

Bergström, Charlotte. Letters. Elisabet Jönsson Collection, NM.

Birth Records for Bogus Brook Township, 1908–14, MHS.

Carlson, Hädda. Letters. Hulda Maria Hellberg Collection, NM.

Carlson, Selma. Letters. Collection 10:3:15:C, EI.

Cederholm, Linnea. Collection, NM.

"Chicago Immanuel Woman's Home Forty-fifth Anniversary Booklet." Immanuel Woman's Home Association, Chicago, 1907–52, SSIRC.

Church Register and Record of Ministerial Acts. Zion Evangelical Lutheran Church, Milaca, MN.

Dalslands-Föreningen Collection. American Swedish Institute, Minneapolis.

Domestic Workers Union No. 15836 Records. Central Labor Council, King County, Box 19, University of Washington Libraries, Seattle.

Elfström, Maria. Letters. Elsa Palm-Elfström Collection, NM.

Eriksson, Kristina. Letters. Kristina Eriksson Collection, NM.

Eriksson, Lina. Letters. Collection 10:3:19, EI.

Farmer Collection of Reminiscences, P2081, MHS.

Frankmar, Ingeborg. Autobiography and letters, NM.

Frideborg, Hilma. Letters. Collection 22:17:14:I, EI.

Gunnarson Family Papers, MSS P122, SSIRC.

Halgren, Mrs. Minnie, Milaca, MN, to Vilhelm Moberg, August 16, 1949. L144:1A:10, Moberg Papers 219, Royal Library, Stockholm.

Hammar, Hilda. Collection, NM.

Israelsdotter, Anna. Biography. Collection 10:3:8:G, EI.

Jakobsson, Klara. Biographical essay of Tilda Northen and sisters. Klara Jakobsson Collection, NM.

Janson, Maria. Letters. Collection 22:16:5:E, EI.

Janson, Thilda. Letters. Collection 22:16:5:E, EI.

Johansson, Kerstin. "Report on Emma." Anna Svanberg Collection, NM.

Johansson, Maja. Autobiographical essay. Maja Johansson Collection, NM.

Johansson, Nils. "An Immigrant Story." Nils Johansson Collection, NM.

Johansson, Stina. Letters. Per Erik Larsson in Noret Dala Järna Collection, EI.

Johnson, Alexandra. Autobiography. Alexandra Johnson Collection, NM.

Johnsson, Olga. Letters. Collection 22:17:16:I, EI.

Jönsson, Svea. Letters. Svea Jönsson Collection, NM.

Karlgren, Carl Erik. Letters. Adolph Larsson Collection, NM.

Larson, Charles. "Else's Story" (typewritten biography distributed at Else [Olsson] Larson's funeral in February 2002). Copy courtesy of David Sandgren. In author's possession.

Larsson, Josefina. Collection 10:5:4:D, EI.

Linder, Hilda. Handwritten autobiography, January 1971. Collection 22:1:12:E, EI.

Linder, Hilda, to author. May 21, 1988. In author's possession.

Lindström, Elizabeth. Letters. Collection 10:3:1:G, EI.
Mille Lacs County, MN, Mille Lacs County Assssment Rolls, MHS.
Mille Lacs County Recorder's Office, Land Records. Milaca, MN.
Minnesota Common School District No. 1153. Bogus Brook Township. School records, Mille Lacs County, MN, School District #21, MHS.
Minnesota State Population Census Schedules, 1895, microfilm, MHS.
Minute book of the Swedish Evangelical Lutheran Church, Mission Society at Wondell Brook. Zion Lutheran Church, Milaca, MN.
Neslund, Hulda. Autobiographical essay, "Amerikabrev" binder. American History Library, Uppsala University, Uppsala, Sweden.
Nilsson, Anna. Letters. Collection 22:13, EI.
Nilsson, Moli. Letters. Asta Fridstrom Collection, NM.
Norlander, Mary Olson. Typescript autobiography, 1969. Materials Relating to Swedish/American History, ca. 1854/1950, microfilm collection, MHS.
Noyes, Frank Wright. Family Papers, MHS.
Nygren, Anna. Letters. Collection 22:13, EI.
Nygren, Signe. Letters. Collection 22:13, EI.
Nyqvist, Erika. Letters. Collection 9:8:8:B, EI.
Olson, Anna J. Autobiography. Anna J. Olson Collection, NM.
Olson, Elisabet. Letters. Collection 22:13:2/3/4, EI.
Palmer, Mrs. A. Autobiography. Albin Widén Collection, February 1943, 15:7:12, EI.
Pärsson, Hilda. Letters. Collection 22:1:14:A, EI.
Persson, Alma. Letters. Collection 22:16:6, EI.
Persson, Thea. Nellie Baskette biography, 1897–1960. Thea Persson Collection, NM.
Petersson, Ida. Biographical statement. Ida Petersson Collection, NM.
Pettersson, Anna. Letters. Collection 9:9:18:O, EI.
Ramsey County, MN, District Court, Naturalization Records, 1849–1931, roll 45, MHS.
Rasmusson, Ida. Letters. Collection 10:15:6, EI
Stridh, Inez. Biography of Emma Persson, NM.
Strömberg, Margareta. Biographical essay on Alida. Margareta Strömberg Collection, NM.
Svanström, Ellen. Description of emigration from Hällaryds skärgård, Bräkne härad, Blekinge, Sweden. Ellen Svanström Collection, NM.
Svärd, Nina. Collection, NM.
Svenson, Hilma. "Daybook Written by Hilma Svenson during her Jönköping/Chicago Trip, August 14 to September 1901." Collection 9:9:18:J, EI.
Svensson, Doris. "Anna Israelsdotters gripande levnadssaga." Collection 10:3:8:G, EI.
Swedish Home of Peace [Fridhem]. Corporation Paper. Swedish Congregational Church, Boston. Collection SA-111:2, SSIRC.
———. Records. Swedish Congregational Church, Boston. Microfilm SC-47, SSIRC.

Vestberg, Kristina. Biography of aunt. Kristina Vestberg Collection, 1960, NM.

Widén, Albin. Swedish-American Sociological Surveys. Albin Widén Collection 15:7:10, EI.

Government Documents

Befolkningsrörelsen: Översikt för Åren 1901–1910. Stockholm: P. A. Norstedt, 1917.

Befolkningsrörelsen: Översikt för Åren 1911–1920. Stockholm: P. A. Norstedt, 1929.

Bidrag till Befolkningsstatistiken för 1890. Vol. 41. Stockolm: P. A. Norstedt, 1897.

Bidrag till Sveriges Officiella Statistik. Vol. A., *Befolkningsstatistik.* Stockholm: P. A. Norstedt, 1908.

Emigrationsutredningen [Emigration investigation]. Vol. 4, *Utvandringsstatistik* [Emigration statistics]. Stockholm: P. A. Norstedt, 1908.

———. Vol. 7, *Utvandrarnas egna uppgifter* [Immigrants' own testimonies]. Stockholm: P. A. Norstedt, 1908.

———. Vol. 8, *Bygdeundersökningar* [Local case studies]. Stockholm: P. A. Norstedt, 1908.

———. Vol. 17, *Utdrag ur inkomna utlåtanden* [Excerpts from submitted reports]. Stockholm: P. A. Norstedt, 1909.

———. Vol. 20, *Svenskarna i utlandet* [Swedes abroad]. Stockholm: P. A. Norstedt, 1908.

Husförhörslängde [Household examination lists]. Bäcke parish. AI:14 (1881–1885), EI.

———. AI:16 (1891–1895), EI.

Inventory of the County Archives of Minnesota, Mille Lacs County. Minnesota Historical Records Survey Project, Division of Community Service Program, WPA, No. 48. MHS, 1940.

Neill, Charles P. *Wage-Earning Women in Stores and Factories.* Vol. 5, *Report on Conditions of Women and Child Wage-Earners in the United States.* Washington, DC: GPO, 1910.

Ship passenger lists, vol. 216604, 1890, 42:171:5520, EI.

U.S. Census of Population. *Thirteenth Census of the United States.* 1910. Manuscript Census, Bogus Brook Township, Mille Lacs County, MN, available from Heritage Quest, http://www.heritagequestonline.com/ (accessed July 29, 2006).

———. *Twelfth Census of the United States.* 1900. Manuscript Census, Bogus Brook Township, Mille Lacs County, MN, available from Heritage Quest, http://www.heritagequestonline.com/ (accessed July 29, 2006).

———. *Twelfth Census of the United States.* 1900. Manuscript Census, City of Minneapolis, Hennepin County, MN, available from Heritage Quest, http://www.heritagequestonline.com/ (accessed July 29, 2006).

U.S. Department of Commerce, Bureau of the Census. Thirteenth Census of the United States. Vol. 1, *Population.* Washington, DC: GPO, 1910.

U.S. Senate. Immigration Commission. *Importation and Harboring of Women for Immoral Purposes.* Reports of the Immigration Commission, vol. 37, 61st Cong., 3d sess., 1911.

———. *Occupations of the First and Second Generations of Immigrants in the United States: Fecundity of Immigrant Women.* Reports of the Immigration Commission, vol. 28, 61st Cong., 2d sess., 1909, 1910.

Theses and Dissertations

Björk, Ulf Jonas. "The Swedish-American Press: Three Newspapers and Their Communities." Ph.D. diss., University of Washington, 1987.

Hervey, Norma. "A Company Town Becomes a Community: Milaca, Minnesota, 1880–1915." Ph.D. diss., University of Minnesota, 1991.

Lintelman, Joy K. " 'More Freedom, Better Pay': Single Swedish Immigrant Women in the United States, 1880–1920." Ph.D. diss., University of Minnesota, 1991.

Meyer, Cynthia Nelson. "Creating a Swedish-American Woman: The Views of Women in the Swedish Evangelical Mission Covenant Church, 1915–1920." Ph.D. diss., Indiana University, 1998.

Wright, Rochelle Ann. "Vilhelm Moberg's Image of America." Ph.D. diss., University of Washington, 1975.

Electronic Resources

Kwolek-Folland, Angel. "Cows in Their Yards: Women, the Economy, and Urban Space, 1870–1885." May 2001. http://www.sscnet.uclaa.edu (accessed July 14, 2005).

Trägårdh, Björn. *Fri eller ställd: Om friställda industriarbetare i periferin—exemplet Lear i Bengtsfors.* Göteborg, Sweden: Gothenburg Research Institute, Göteborg University, 2002. http://cent.hgus.gu.se/epc/data/html/pages/PDF/2002–1 (accessed March 21, 2005).

Index

Page numbers in italics indicate photographs, illustrations, and maps. The designation "MA" refers to Mina Anderson (Halgren).

Illustration and map credits

Illustrations on the following pages are reproduced with permission: pp. 3, 29, 142, 164, 172, 174, 183, 221, and 222, Beverly Siedow, Vining, Minnesota; p. 6, Wilhelm Moberg Collection, National Library of Sweden, Stockholm; p. 8, Swedish Emigrant Institute, Växjö, Sweden; pp. 12 and 25, Västergötlands Museum, Skara, Sweden; p. 23, Alice Tobler, Sauk Centre, Minnesota; p. 33, Bo Andersson, Dals Rostock, Sweden; pp. 36 and 43, Regional Archives, Gothenburg, Sweden; p. 40, Krafttaget Society, Boxholm, Sweden; p. 46 (photo 2005), and pp. 189, 192, and 197 (courtesy Merrill Halgren), author's collection; p. 62, Amerikaminnen, Fotos I, A-G, Elvira Carlsson, and p. 112, unknown photographer, both Nordiska Museets Archive, Stockholm, Sweden; p. 69, photographic postcard, Wilson Line's Romeo, M. Bernard Hull, photographer, Norway Heritage Project, http://www.norwayheritage.com; p. 77, National Library of Sweden, Stockholm; and p. 211, Mary Norlander Papers, courtesy J. B. Hove, Isanti, Minnesota. All other photographs and visual images, including images reproduced from manuscripts, newspapers, magazines, and books, are in the collections of the Minnesota Historical Society, St. Paul.

The map on p. 20 is based on "Topographical Map of Sweden, 1843" (Översedd 1858), Kartblad Upperud, I.V.34, Swedish Emigrant Institute, Växjö, Sweden. The maps on the following pages are in the collections of the Minnesota Historical Society, St. Paul: p. 146, from D. L. Curtice, "R. L. Polk & Co. City Directory Map of St. Paul, Minn., 1884"; p. 157, from George Joslyn, "The Old Milaca Trail" sheet music (Minneapolis, 1923); and p. 159, detail of "Map of Bogus Brook Township, Mille Lacs County," *Atlas and Farmers' Directory of Mille Lacs County, Minnesota* (St. Paul: The Farmer, 1914). All other maps are by CartoGraphics, Inc.